Ancient Apocryphal Gospels

INTERPRETATION
Resources for the Use of Scripture in the Church

INTERPRETATION

RESOURCES FOR THE USE OF SCRIPTURE IN THE CHURCH

Samuel E. Balentine, *Series Editor*
Ellen F. Davis, *Associate Editor*
Richard B. Hays, *Associate Editor*
Patrick D. Miller, *Consulting Editor*

OTHER AVAILABLE BOOKS IN THE SERIES

Walter Brueggemann, *Money and Possessions*
Ronald P. Byars, *The Sacraments in Biblical Perspective*
Jerome F. D. Creach, *Violence in Scripture*
Ellen F. Davis, *Biblical Prophecy: Perspectives
for Christian Theology, Discipleship, and Ministry*
Robert W. Jenson, *Canon and Creed*
Richard Lischer, *Reading the Parables*
Patrick D. Miller, *The Ten Commandments*

MARKUS BOCKMUEHL

Ancient Apocryphal Gospels

INTERPRETATION *Resources for the Use of Scripture in the Church*

WESTMINSTER
JOHN KNOX PRESS
LOUISVILLE · KENTUCKY

© 2017 Markus Bockmuehl

First edition
Published by Westminster John Knox Press
Louisville, Kentucky

17 18 19 20 21 22 23 24 25 26—10 9 8 7 6 5 4 3 2 1

Scripture quotations are from the New Revised Standard Version of the Bible, copyright © 1989 by the Division of Christian Education of the National Council of the Churches of Christ in the U.S.A. and are used by permission.

Map of Oxyrhynchus is printed with permission by *Biblical Archaeology Review.*

Book design by Drew Stevens
Cover design by designpointinc.com

Library of Congress Cataloging-in-Publication Data

Names: Bockmuehl, Markus N. A., author.
Title: Ancient apocryphal gospels / Markus Bockmuehl.
Description: Louisville, KY : Westminster John Knox Press, 2017. | Series: Interpretation: resources for the use of scripture in the church | Includes bibliographical references and index.
Identifiers: LCCN 2016032962 (print) | LCCN 2016044809 (ebook) | ISBN 9780664235895 (hbk. : alk. paper) | ISBN 9781611646801 (ebook)
Subjects: LCSH: Apocryphal Gospels—Criticism, interpretation, etc. | Apocryphal books (New Testament)—Criticism, interpretation, etc.
Classification: LCC BS2851 .B63 2017 (print) | LCC BS2851 (ebook) | DDC 229/.8—dc23
LC record available at https://lccn.loc.gov/2016032962

♾ The paper used in this publication meets the minimum requirements of the American National Standard for Information Sciences—Permanence of Paper for Printed Library Materials, ANSI Z39.48-1992.

Most Westminster John Knox Press books are available at special quantity discounts when purchased in bulk by corporations, organizations, and special-interest groups. For more information, please e-mail SpecialSales@wjkbooks.com.

CONTENTS

Series Foreword   vii

Acknowledgments   ix

Abbreviations   xii

CHAPTER 1: ANCIENT CHRISTIAN GOSPELS   1
  The Four Gospels—and the Others   8
  Who Read What in the Early Church?   10
  The (Re)Discovery of Noncanonical Gospels   14
  "Gnosticism"?—A Definition   18
  Gospels of the Original Jesus, Suppressed by
    an Authoritarian Church?   21
  The Design and Approach of This Book   28
  How Many Apocryphal Gospels?   31
  What Makes a Gospel "Apocryphal"?   38
  How to Organize the Texts: A Taxonomy   48
  Where to Read the Noncanonical Gospels Today   51

CHAPTER 2: INFANCY GOSPELS   55
  Why Infancy Gospels?   55
  The Infancy Gospel of James   58
  The Infancy Gospel of Thomas   72
  Other Infancy Texts   80
  Conclusion: Infancy Gospels   84

CHAPTER 3: MINISTRY GOSPELS   87
  The Problem of "Fragmentary" Gospels   87
  A Note on Q   89
  "Jewish Christian" Gospels?   92
  Ministry Gospels on Papyrus   104
    Papyrus Egerton 2 (+ Papyrus Köln 255)   106
    "Papyrus" Oxyrhynchus 840   110
    Other Papyrus Fragments   114
  A Secret Gospel of Mark?   120

The Abgar Legend   121
Alternative Whole Narrative Gospels?   123
Conclusion: Ministry Gospels   132

CHAPTER 4: PASSION GOSPELS   137
The Gospel of Peter   137
*The Unknown Berlin Gospel/Gospel
    of the Savior* (P.Berl. 22220)   152
The Strasbourg Coptic Papyrus (P.Argent.
    Copt. 5, 6, 7)   154
The Discourse on the Cross (Nubian Stauros Text)   155
Passion Gospels Associated with Pilate, Nicodemus,
    and Joseph of Arimathea   156
Gospels of Gamaliel?   158
Conclusion: Passion Gospels   159

CHAPTER 5: POST-RESURRECTION
DISCOURSE GOSPELS   161
New Testament Origins?   162
The Gospel of Thomas   163
The Gospel of Philip   183
Other Dialogue "Gospels" or Gospel-Like Texts
    from Nag Hammadi   190
The Gospel of Mary   199
The Gospel of Judas (Codex Tchacos)   204
Gospels of the Egyptians   210
Gospel of Bartholomew   212
The Epistle of the Apostles   215
Conclusion: Post-Resurrection Discourse Gospels   220

CHAPTER 6: HOW TO READ APOCRYPHAL GOSPELS   225

Glossary of Technical Terms   239

Bibliography   243

Index of Scripture and Other Ancient Sources   291

Index of Subjects   302

SERIES FOREWORD

This series of volumes supplements Interpretation: A Bible Commentary for Teaching and Preaching. The commentary series offers an exposition of the books of the Bible written for those who teach, preach, and study the Bible in the community of faith. This new series is addressed to the same audience and serves a similar purpose, providing additional resources for the interpretation of Scripture, but now dealing with features, themes, and issues significant for the whole rather than with individual books.

The Bible is composed of separate books. Its composition naturally has led its interpreters to address particular books. But there are other ways to approach the interpretation of the Bible that respond to other characteristics and features of the Scriptures. These other entries to the task of interpretation provide contexts, overviews, and perspectives that complement the book-by-book approach and discern dimensions of the Scriptures that the commentary design may not adequately explore.

The Bible as used in the Christian community is not only a collection of books but also itself a book that has a unity and coherence important to its meaning. Some volumes in this new series will deal with this canonical wholeness and seek to provide a wider context for the interpretation of individual books as well as a comprehensive theological perspective that reading single books does not provide.

Other volumes in the series will examine particular texts, like the Ten Commandments, the Lord's Prayer, and the Sermon on the Mount, texts that have played such an important role in the faith and life of the Christian community that they constitute orienting foci for the understanding and use of Scripture.

A further concern of the series will be to consider important and often difficult topics, addressed at many different places in the books of the canon, that are of recurrent interest and concern to the church in its dependence on Scripture for faith and life. So the series will include volumes dealing with such topics as eschatology, women, wealth, and violence.

The books of the Bible are constituted from a variety of kinds of literature, such as narrative, laws, hymns and prayers, letters, parables, miracle stories, and the like. To recognize and discern the contribution and importance of all these different kinds of material enriches and enlightens the use of Scripture. Volumes in the series will provide help in the interpretation of Scripture's literary forms and genres.

The liturgy and practices of the gathered church are anchored in Scripture, as with the sacraments observed and the creeds recited. So another entry to the task of discerning the meaning and significance of biblical texts explored in this series is the relation between the liturgy of the church and the Scriptures.

Finally, there is certain ancient literature, such as the Apocrypha and the noncanonical gospels, that constitutes an important context to the interpretation of Scripture itself. Consequently, this series will provide volumes that offer guidance in understanding such writings and explore their significance for the interpretation of the Protestant canon.

The volumes in this second series of Interpretation deal with these important entries into the interpretation of the Bible. Together with the commentaries, they compose a library of resources for those who interpret Scripture as members of the community of faith. Each of them can be used independently for its own significant addition to the resources for the study of Scripture. But all of them intersect the commentaries in various ways and provide an important context for their use. The authors of these volumes are biblical scholars and theologians who are committed to the service of interpreting the Scriptures in and for the church. The editors and authors hope that the addition of this series to the commentaries will provide a major contribution to the vitality and richness of biblical interpretation in the church.

The Editors

ACKNOWLEDGMENTS

Scholarly convention and experience teach us to assume that worthwhile academic projects spring from an original research idea or passion that is then brought to fruition by matching one's relevant expertise with focused hard work.

This book has been a rather different experience. The idea was not my own but that of Richard Hays (and Patrick Miller), who first approached me in 2008 to ask if I would contribute a volume on the extracanonical gospels for their new monograph series promising "Resources for the Use of Scripture in the Church." While this seemed a fine objective in its own right, its intellectual impetus was not mine—nor could I pretend to either passion or expertise in the subject matter. My reply to the invitation therefore weaseled and prevaricated, putting forward the names of other colleagues whom I deemed far more knowledgeable on the subject and more likely to deliver the goods in a timely manner. But still my recruiter persisted. And I relented, rather against what I suspected to be my better judgment. Seven years and a good deal of "focused hard work" later, I do know I have at least learned a good deal more about the subject than I knew before! Rather to my surprise I also seem to have a draft that the current series editors (Richard Hays, Ellen Davis, and Sam Balentine) deem fit for purpose.

For that, and for much persistence and patience, I am most grateful to them (and to Patrick Miller, who retired from the editorship in 2014).

It will perhaps be self-evident, however, that the completion of this book is extensively indebted to many others too. Not all can be mentioned here, but first among them are diverse groups of students, including some who joined me in reading apocryphal gospels over breakfast at my fortnightly graduate colloquium in biblical studies at Oxford (2008), and others who enrolled in courses on these texts both at Oxford (2011) and at the Vacation Term in Biblical Studies (2011). I learned a good deal from audiences who responded actively and graciously to my half-baked early thoughts, especially in material presented at the Clark Lectures at Duke Divinity School (2012), a seminar at Oak Hill Theological College

(2012), lectures for an Open Day and Alumni Weekend in Oxford (2013, 2015), the OCCA Business Programme (2014, 2015), the Logos in Oxford Summer School (2013), and various others.

Anyone who has been in Oxford longer than a tourist will have a hunch that its academics seem to find "focused hard work" on extended writing projects virtually impossible without a period of research leave. The present book too owes much to a sabbatical granted me by the University and Keble College during 2013–2014. An additional Small Research Grant award from Keble College facilitated my recruitment of the exceptional Jeremiah Coogan as a graduate research assistant. His formidable textual and papyrological skills helped improve this book in every part, and he continued to assist with the final draft even after completing a stellar MPhil here and starting his doctorate at Notre Dame.

Several other friends and colleagues were instrumental in the completion of this work. Near the beginning of the project, David Lincicum assisted with preparations for a 2011 course at the Vacation Term in Biblical Studies, while Simon Gathercole repeatedly indulged me with much-needed advice on the *Gospel of Thomas*. My senior colleague Christopher Tuckett, whose learning in these matters outclasses mine in every respect, generously read every page of my draft and provided invaluable comments, saving me from much potential embarrassment in the process. Michael Bird likewise read a draft and provided valuable feedback, as did my graduate student Nabeel Qureshi. Jens Schröter's fruitful and valuable visit to Oxford in May 2015 proved an excellent way to test some of my ideas in most enjoyable conversations. Most moving and encouraging was Richard Hays's characteristically gracious, insightful single-page editorial appraisal sent just after his resignation from the deanship of Duke Divinity School to take extended medical leave.

For extensive assistance with ancient and modern sources, I owe a debt of gratitude to librarians here at Oxford and in several other places, including during repeated research visits to Rome's Pontifical Biblical Institute (along with warm hospitality received at the Pontifical Irish College and from the Sisters at Casa Accoglienza Paolo VI). Yvonne Murphy at Keble College and Hilla Wait at the Philosophy and Theology Faculties Library unstintingly and expeditiously facilitated relevant book purchases. For assistance with papyri I would particularly single out Daniela Colomo of the

x

Oxyrhynchus Papyri project (for P.Oxy. 2949 and 4009 [*Gospel of Peter*], 3525 [*Gospel of Mary*], and the newly published 5072), and Bruce Barker-Benfield for assisting an autopsy of P.Oxy. 1224.

Many others should doubtless be mentioned, whom I thank both for their kind assistance and for their forbearance with my incomplete list. Remaining flaws and errors are of course entirely my own.

To my family as always I owe the greatest debt of all. My wife, Celia, not only read and annotated the entire draft with a conservator's eye but also generously created the space for this unsociable project in our busy family life. Without her unfailing encouragement this book could not have come to be. And I pray that the effort here extended may in time be recognizable to our children, too, as furnishing in its own way a Resource for the Use of the Fourfold Gospel in the Church.

Oxford, September 21, 2015—St. Matthew
the Apostle and Evangelist

ABBREVIATIONS

Biblical Books

Old Testament

Gen.	Genesis
Num.	Numbers
1 Sam.	1 Samuel
Prov.	Proverbs
Isa.	Isaiah
Jer.	Jeremiah
Dan.	Daniel

New Testament

Matt.	Matthew
Rom.	Romans
1 Cor.	1 Corinthians
2 Cor.	2 Corinthians
Gal.	Galatians
Eph.	Ephesians
Col.	Colossians
1 Tim.	1 Timothy
2 Tim.	2 Timothy
Phlm.	Philemon
1 Pet.	1 Peter
2 Pet.	2 Peter
Rev.	Revelation

Papyrus Collection

P.Aberd.	Papyri Aberdeen
P.Argent.	Papyri Argentoratenses (Strasbourg)

P.Berl.	Papyri Berolinenses (Berlin)
P.Cair.	Papyri Cairenses (Cairo)
P.Dura	Papyri Dura (Yale)
P.Eger.	Papyri Egerton (London)
P.Köln	Papyri Köln (Cologne)
P.Merton	Papyri Merton (Oxford)
P.Monts.Roca	Papyri Montserratenses Roca (Montserrat Abbey, Barcelona)
P.Oxy.	Papyri Oxyrhynchus
P.Ryl.	Papyri Rylands (Manchester)
P.Vindob.	Papyri Vindobonenses (Vienna)
PSI	Papiri della Società Italiana (Florence)

Other

BG	Berlin Gnostic Codex
CB	Bruce Codex (or: Codex Brucianus)
CT	Codex Tchacos
CSEL	Corpus scriptorum ecclesiasticorum latinorum
NHC	Nag Hammadi Codex
𝔓	Symbol used to designate New Testament papyri according to the standard Gregory-Aland numbering system

CHAPTER 1

Ancient Christian Gospels

Christians since antiquity have grounded their faith on its authentic attestation in the gospel of Jesus Christ received from his first apostles. This grounding is already explicit in the Bible itself and has remained an uncontroversial aspect of historic Christian praxis and worship since antiquity.

Throughout their history, churches of virtually every stripe have—for all their tacit or fiercely contested differences—shared a core conviction about Jesus of Nazareth as in some sense *both* a human being in history and yet also "God with us." Jesus has always been encountered and experienced in a variety of ways. Most prominent since antiquity have been practices of prayer and common worship that include a liturgical meal celebrating both his memory and his presence, accompanied by the public reading of the four gospels—authoritative writings about his teachings and ministry received in the names of his earliest disciples.

But the early Christian use of gospels also has a fascinating dynamic of its own, operating in theologically powerful and yet surprisingly polyvalent ways in diverse periods and communities.

The term "gospel" surfaces in the earliest tradition as characterizing *Jesus' message.* Matthew and Mark both present "the gospel" (*to euangelion*) as the radical message and praxis of Jesus about the imminent coming of God's kingdom (see esp. Mark 1:14–15; 8:35; 10:29; 13:10; Matt. 4:23; 9:35; 24:14). Luke, who is more aware of

1

the public, imperial context of his writing, does not seem to like this noun, for reasons that will become apparent in a moment. He never uses it in his gospel, and in Acts it appears only once each on the lips of Peter and of Paul (Acts 15:7; 20:24). The verb "to announce good news" (*euangelizomai*), on the other hand, occurs frequently in both Luke and Acts.

Even Matthew and Mark, however, already show a transition in meaning that evidently occurred at a very early stage in the tradition—it is in fact already complete in the Letters of Paul, which predate all four New Testament gospels. Whereas "the gospel" in Matthew and Mark almost invariably reports *what Jesus himself preaches and enacts*, even here there are signs that by the time of these evangelists "the gospel" has become the content of the message he entrusts to his disciples, and indeed the message *about him*. So Matthew's Jesus himself can promise that "*this gospel* of the kingdom" will be proclaimed throughout the world after his death (Matt. 24:14; 26:13). And Mark 1:1 opens with the words, "The beginning of the gospel of Jesus Christ"—a famously ambiguous phrase that leaves unresolved whether the gospel here in view is Jesus' message (as in 1:14), the message *about* Jesus (e.g., 13:10; 14:9), or perhaps even—by a kind of metonymy—Mark's own book that sets forth this message. But it clearly involves the person of Jesus, including his message and ministry as well as his death.

Additionally, and well before Mark writes his account, it is already clear that when in the early 50s Paul preached to the Corinthians the gospel by which they are saved, this entailed at a minimum a narrative passion and resurrection sequence involving "Christ died for our sins, . . . he was buried, . . . he was raised *on the third day*, . . . he appeared to Cephas, *then* to the twelve, *then*" to many others in succession (1 Cor. 15:1–6; cf. 2 Tim. 1:10; 2:8). There seems moreover to be continuity here with the similarly sequential narrative, quoted a few chapters earlier, of words and actions of Jesus "on the night when he was betrayed" (1 Cor. 11:23–25).

A few decades later, in a more retrospective account of Peter's first preaching to the Gentiles during the mid-30s, the narrative of Acts has Peter assuring his audience at the house of Cornelius about "the word" God sent to the children of Israel, "proclaiming the good news [*euangelizomenos*]" of peace through Jesus Christ (Acts 10:36, my translation). That "word" (*logos*), he goes on to say, came to expression through the "message" (*rhēma*) associated with certain particular events that recently transpired in Jewish Palestine,

> beginning in Galilee after the baptism that John announced: how God anointed Jesus of Nazareth with the Holy Spirit and with power; how he went about doing good and healing all who were oppressed by the devil, for God was with him. We are witnesses to all that he did both in Judea and in Jerusalem. They put him to death by hanging him on a tree; but God raised him on the third day and allowed him to appear, not to all the people but to us who were chosen by God as witnesses, and who ate and drank with him after he rose from the dead. (Acts 10:37–41, NRSV)

In other words, even the earliest stages of the tradition, both as attested in Paul and as attributed to the remembered Peter in Acts, envisaged the gospel to include a *narrative* about Jesus' public ministry and message, culminating in his death and resurrection. (Significantly, Luke places a Mark-like apostolic gospel outline on Peter's lips. This is despite its obvious divergences from the structure of Luke's own gospel account with its addition of birth, infancy, and ascension stories.)

Readers familiar with the gospels and with cognate English words like "evangelical" are sometimes surprised to discover the extent of scholarly debate and controversy about the origin and precise meaning of the early Christian use of the term *euangelion*. One school of thought has long stressed the conviction that the term must be understood as originating in connection with the Hellenistic use of *euangelia* (Greek plural) to denote "happy news" or "good news"—as used in the eastern empire most publicly in relation to official Roman imperial announcements about good news like the accession, birthday, or victory in battle of the emperor as "Savior" (*sōtēr*, a word the New Testament uses much more sparingly than later Christian tradition). The most famous pre-Christian example is an inscription in praise of the birthday of Caesar Augustus that was erected at Priene and other cities in Asia Minor in 9 BCE. He is celebrated as "our God" whose birth "signified the beginning of happy news [*euangelia*] for the entire world." Even without using the word "gospel," the Roman poet Virgil's famous *Fourth Eclogue*, composed around 42 BCE, deploys Isaiah-like imagery in anticipation of an age of eschatological peace and salvation associated with the birth of an unnamed child (though

3

not perhaps identifiable as the hoped-for son of Mark Antony and his wife Octavia, as scholars used to think).

The notion of public good news had been common currency for many centuries, being attested ever since Homer (*Odyssey* 14.152, 166: *euangelion*, singular). Indeed the commonplace inflation of such terminology could even become the butt of jokes: the Athenian comic playwright Aristophanes (ca. 446–386 BCE) already had a sausage seller poking fun at bawdy market hyperbole by intoning, "Hey, Senators, I'm the first with tremendous news [*euangelisasthai*]: never since the war began have sardines been so cheap" (*Knights* 642–45; trans. Roche 2005). The familiarity of such terminology can be gauged too by its adoption as a Latin loan word: the Roman writer Cicero repeatedly and somewhat informally does this, as when writing to his friend Atticus in 60 BCE, "First, I have what I think is good news [*euangelia*] . . ." (*Letters to Atticus* 2.3.1).

One might think, therefore, that Christian talk of *to euangelion*, *the* good news, basically just recycled for Jesus a well-known cliché that could evoke little more than a yawning response. That would hardly convey the sort of grandly anti-imperial ambition which the claim of a Christian *euangelion* is sometimes said to advance. To be sure, resistance to the force of empire soon became at least a sporadic occurrence—and sometimes part of the very essence of what it meant to be a Christian, as stories about the trials of martyrs repeatedly affirm. But despite sometimes heated scholarly debate, it remains difficult to document in the New Testament any sense that the use of the term "gospel" serves a clear anti-imperial function.

A related line of argument has sometimes taken such early Christian terminology to imply the church's origin not as a Palestinian Jewish messianic movement but as a Hellenistic divinized hero cult, drawing on culturally commonplace idioms and assumptions about heroes or rulers.

But to acknowledge the existence of such potential Hellenistic resonance is not yet to understand what a (or the) gospel conveys in the early Christian texts. Even for Greek-speaking Jews and Christians, gospel language must have carried a kind of dual significance. On one hand, there will have been at least an awareness of the secular use of "good news," sometimes exploited in the service of ideological ends and propaganda. Jewish writers in Greek like Philo and Josephus repeatedly illustrate the currency of such a

4

meaning of "good news." Secular as well as religious overtones were indeed in the air, even for Jews.

On the other hand, however, we must recognize that the Greek terminology was also already part of a richly textured discourse of prophetic and divine communication in older, pre-Christian Jewish Greek Scriptures. In that respect the Greek words conveyed a Jewish, Old Testament meaning—often associated with the second part of the book of Isaiah, which announces the Servant of the Lord's return to redeem Jerusalem (52:7) and speaks of "good news" to the afflicted and imprisoned (61:1, both times using the verb *euangelisasthai*). While the Greek Old Testament does not deploy the *noun* "gospel" in this fashion in either the singular or the plural, the formative role of widely influential texts like these in the early Christian understanding of the gospel of Jesus is clear. Other Jewish texts in Greek like *Psalms of Solomon* 11:1 clearly highlight such usage, and Paul quite confidently appropriates Isaiah 52:7 in speaking of the activity of the apostles as proclaimers of a message that is *"the gospel"* (see Rom. 10:15–16; cf. 1 Cor. 9:14; also Stanton 2013, 281–92 and passim and Horbury 2005, 2006).

Unlike the Greco-Roman use almost exclusively of the plural *euangelia*, the early Christian writers deploy the *singular* "gospel" (*euangelion*) consistently and uniquely in relation to the message of or about Jesus. That said, even here there is some evidence of semantic ambiguity from the start. As we saw earlier, Jesus' message soon became the message *about* him (Mark 1:1; 14:9; and 16:15; note esp. Matt. 26:13; 24:14, "this gospel," i.e., not only Jesus' words and actions but evidently an *account* of that message and ministry—such as Matthew himself provides; cf. Stanton 2013, 95–98). Already in the corpus of Pauline Letters the term came to be used interchangeably for either the message or its content: the apostle speaks of both "the gospel" and "my gospel" (cf. Phlm. 13 with 2 Tim. 2:8 and Rom. 16:25).

As already noted, Luke never uses the noun "gospel" in his narrative of Jesus (but see Acts 15:7; 20:24), although he does deploy the cognate verb twenty-five times in Luke and Acts. In Acts 13:32–33 he places on Paul's lips a definition of what it means to preach the gospel: "we bring you the good news that what God promised to our ancestors he has fulfilled for us, their children, by raising Jesus." The New Testament's Johannine writings avoid the

Greek *euangel-* word group altogether except at Revelation 10:7 as well as at 14:6, where it denotes a message of judgment.

Matthew's usage in particular evidently had a powerful influence on subsequent understanding of what the gospel might be. Very rapidly, its range of meaning expanded from Jesus' kingdom message or (as in Paul, e.g., 1 Cor. 15) the message *about* Jesus' death and resurrection to include accounts of his life, preaching, innocent death, and resurrection "for us." As we saw earlier, an early narrative form of this is implied in Peter's account in Acts 10:34–42, and in the writings of Ignatius (d. ca. 107) it is already evident that "the gospel" designates for him the crucifixion-resurrection message of Jesus (*Smyrnaeans* 7.2), quite possibly in its Matthean form (cf. *Smyrnaeans* 1.1 with Matt. 3:15; similarly cf. *Didache* 8.2 with Matt. 6:9–13; also *2 Clement* 8.5, more loosely, with Luke 16:10–11; see further Hill 2006; Foster 2005).

Significantly, not later than the middle of the second century the notion of this gospel story "according to" one apostolic figure or another had become attached to gospel *books*—for example, in Justin, *First Apology* 66.3 (see Stanton 2013, 92–97). A little before this, Marcion had already identified his edition of Luke as "the gospel." Similar examples can be found in other early documents: the form of the *Didache*'s reference to its source suggests that "the gospel" was already used to designate "a gospel writing, almost certainly Matthew, some decades before Marcion" (thus Stanton 2013, 77; cf. Kelhoffer 2014, 72).

If this is correct it follows, importantly, that known portions of one or more of the subsequently canonical gospels were known and cited as "the gospel" before *any* of the extant noncanonical gospels were composed. To some extent this is inevitably a judgment about a serendipitous state of affairs at this present time, which the discovery of new sources or compelling reassessments of existing ones might require us to revise. And absence of evidence is not evidence of absence. But in the meantime it matters for our assessment of recent and current claims that while specific literary identifications are sometimes difficult or textually ambiguous (e.g., Luke 16:10–11 in *2 Clement* 8.5, cited above), no ancient author refers to any identifiable version of a noncanonical text like *Thomas* or Q as "the gospel."

Further on this note, it has been repeatedly shown (e.g., Hengel 1984; Gathercole 2013) that while the titles of the existing

New Testament gospels are clearly not from the pen of the original authors, they and the associated authorial attributions are nevertheless both stable and remarkably early, probably from the first half of the second century. Although in theory compatible with simplistic explanations in terms of wholesale deliberate "forgery," as Ehrman (2013) prefers, such a date makes it difficult to rule out the possibility that these apostolic attributions are instead based in some fashion, whether correctly or in error, on an existing chain of collective or individual living memory.

Manuscript evidence suggests that the short forms "according to Matthew" or "according to Luke" are secondary abbreviations from an original longer form, *"the gospel* according to" Matthew or Luke; see, for example, Gathercole 2013. (Gathercole 2012b illustrates this same usage in the flyleaf of Matthew included with manuscript 𝔓⁴, dating from ca. 200. Thus Bovon's assertion that "we have no codices [with inscriptio and subscriptio] of these gospels predating their canonization" [1988, 20–23] turns out to be an argument from increasingly partial silence, which will require fuller facts and rather more nuance. It is hardly the comprehensive refutation of the "extravagant claims of Martin Hengel" that Ehrman [2013, 53 and 53n55] imagines).

Hengel additionally observes that while the title "gospel" is routinely *introduced* in reference to other gospels like *Thomas* or Nag Hammadi's *Gospel of the Egyptians*, it is never *lost* from a text that has once been so designated—even though gospel status itself seems to fade from interest for later compositions at Nag Hammadi, where "dialogues" and "revelations" predominate over narratives of the earthly Jesus. Among other things, this suggests that the relatively rapid successive publication of the Synoptic Gospels between the 60s and the 90s, designated within a few decades as "the gospel according to X," may have established a compelling *precedent* for the choice of titles in later accounts of the teachings of Jesus. This precedent entailed both the term "gospel" and the name of an apostolic guarantor, as evidenced not only in John but also in several noncanonical gospels. (See Hengel 2008b, 110–11, 182–83.)

A related point concerns certain material aspects of conservation and innovation in gospel writing. As we will see, there appears from the start to be greater textual stability in the extant manuscripts of subsequently canonical gospels than in those of *Thomas*, *Peter*, and other apocryphal gospels. In relation to this it has been plausibly suggested that the more widespread copying, liturgical reading, and memorization would have had a stabilizing effect on the textual tradition, certainly allowing for the composition of *new* gospels (like Matthew or Luke) but largely eliminating the scope for successive textual *recensions* of the same text (Evans 2015, 36–37). While Evans's related inferences about the longevity of New Testament autographs look a little problematic in their specificity, a manuscript lifespan of a century and a half was indeed a reasonable expectation (see, e.g., Houston 2014, 175, on Oxyrhynchus)—and might reinforce this stability for texts that circulated widely.

Except for scribal identifications in titles or colophons (i.e., concluding scribal comments), the term "gospel" itself is remarkably rare in the body of ancient gospel-like texts at Nag Hammadi or elsewhere. Leaving aside late works like the *Gospel of Nicodemus* (B 14.1) or the *History of Joseph the Carpenter* (1.2; 30.3), the small handful of examples from antiquity includes the *Gospel of Mary* (9; 18) and the *Gospel of Truth* (17.1–4; 18.11; 34.34–35) for the saving message about Jesus. Nag Hammadi's *Sophia of Jesus Christ*, in a question about why "in the gospel" (evidently a text!) Sophia's Son is called "human" and the "Son of Man" (104.1), also demonstrates this meaning.

The Four Gospels—and the Others

Until the nineteenth century, Western biblical scholars tended to take for granted that the emergence of the early church was based on "one holy catholic and apostolic" faith and that the canon of Scripture was essentially the result of a continuous and intentionally advancing original movement from which others deviated. However challenged that movement may have been by detractors without and heretics within, on this view it proceeded organically from Christ to the apostles, to the fourfold apostolic gospel and the New Testament read in light of the apostolic rule of faith (*regula fidei*). This in turn became crystallized in agreed forms of worship and confession in the Trinitarian creeds of Nicaea and Chalcedon.

I am not myself averse to all aspects of this traditional picture. No doubt it may be said to oversimplify or distort. But this very excess also functions to some extent like a political cartoon, usefully capturing salient features precisely by its clarifying selectivity and

8

exaggeration of a few defining attributes out of the mass of conflicting data.

At the same time, even mainstream accounts of Christian origins are today rightly more nuanced about the ecclesial diversity of the first two centuries. And even among those who (like myself) would wish to retain an account of creedal Christianity's organic connection to the faith of the apostles, most accept the eloquent evidence for a rather more complex picture. In that sense the metaphor of the cartoon may usefully be balanced by that of a pointillist master painting, which is best appreciated from just the right amount of sympathetic distance rather than by overinterpreting its constituent points of detail.

Even a brief encounter with first- and second-century sources shows that the reception and circulation of early Christian writings about Jesus remained remarkably fluid and elusive during that period. This is true even for some of the canonical texts: it is, for example, difficult to know quite how many second- or even third-century Christians could have had regular access to written copies of Paul's Letters, Acts, or indeed the Gospel of Mark: only a few small fragments survive from that period, all of them from Egypt (for environmental reasons, as explained below p. 10; see Hurtado 2013 for statistics).

We do know that the second century was extraordinarily generative and fertile in religious and literary terms; one widely (if perhaps somewhat credulously) cited calculation suggests that our surviving sources from that period represent approximately 15 percent of the known Christian literary output (so, e.g., Markschies 2002, 98; 2015, 21; he likes to refer to the second century as Christianity's "laboratory": Markschies 2003, 120; 2012g, 34 and elsewhere).

And yet it remains the case that by the mid-second century, gospel accounts in the names of Matthew, Mark, Luke, and John were increasingly emerging as the accepted fourfold narrative of the gospel of Jesus Christ. Before the century was out, this had become self-evident to someone like Irenaeus, closely familiar as he was with the practice of the churches both of Asia Minor and of Rome: in the face of multifarious sectarian alternatives, the catholic acceptance of the Four seemed to him as incontrovertible as the four winds of nature (*Against Heresies* 3.11.8). Writing a few decades later on the basis of both Alexandrian and Palestinian experience,

Origen (ca. 185–254) famously quipped that "the Church has four gospels; heretics have many" (*Homilies on Luke* 1.2).

To be sure, few congregations even in urban settings will have owned copies of all four "canonical" gospels. And even in places that affirmed these four as authoritative, they were now often encountered collectively rather than discretely. The extant manuscript tradition and actual evidence of use suggest that Christians at this time may often have physically experienced these texts not so much as four complete individual books, but in more episodic fashion through excerpts, informal or formal harmonies (most influentially Tatian's *Diatessaron*)—or indeed through one particular gospel (most often Matthew or John) understood in light of such a harmony.

Who Read What in the Early Church?

Despite some early attempts to establish definitive lists of all New Testament books, including the gospels, this "canonizing" effort did not achieve an agreed final form until the later fourth century. (Famously this is articulated in the Thirty-Ninth Festal Letter of Athanasius in 367 CE: for the text, see Grosheide 1948; a partial translation is offered in Metzger 1997, 312–13 [and discussion on 210–12]; cf. Brakke 2010b, with a new translation of the surviving letter, 57–66.)

But does this mean, as some scholars continue to assert, that no consensus about authoritative *gospels* existed until fourth-century authoritarian decrees imposed their will upon the previously unlimited flow of early Christian tradition and literature?

A recent inventory of pre-300 Christian literary sources includes a little over thirty gospel texts (Hurtado 2006, 209–21, updated online as Hurtado 2013; cf. Lührmann and Schlarb 2000, 22). It is in the nature of the evidence that statistical statements on this subject are necessarily somewhat tenuous. The sample size is tiny, and a small textual fragment in any case cannot prove the existence of the entire text of which it is a part. With some notable exceptions (mainly from Derveni, Dura Europos, Herculaneum, Nessana, and Petra as well as Qumran: cf. Leach and Tait 2000, 239; Tov 2003, 100–103), papyrus evidence is largely restricted to Egypt, where atmospheric conditions particularly favored its survival—and where many of the known extracanonical texts originated and thrived. (The only surviving noncanonical gospel-like text from outside Egypt is perhaps a Greek fragment of the *Diatessaron* from Dura Europos on parchment, that is, processed animal skin rather than papyrus: Yale P.Dura 10, formerly Dura Parchment 24; see below, p. 127.)

Except for the gospels of *Thomas* (P.Oxy. 1, 654, 655) and *Mary* (P.Ryl. 463; P.Oxy. 3525), no noncanonical gospel before 300 CE is extant in more than one copy. (P.Oxy. 2949 and 4009 are both sometimes assigned to the *Gospel of Peter*, but this seems unlikely in one and possibly both cases, for reasons discussed below.) No other gospel-like texts approach the manuscript dissemination of Matthew or John, nor for that matter the persistent breadth of attestation in extant early Christian literature of any of the four gospels that became canonical.

The statistics of extant manuscripts from the first three centuries coincide with those from literary sources in documenting Matthew and John as the most popular gospels by far, with Luke a relatively distant third. Mark was almost never copied at all: out of just over thirty known gospel papyri predating the year 300, at most three contain Mark ($\mathfrak{P}^{45}$; P.Oxy. 5073; and possibly $\mathfrak{P}^{88}$; see Hurtado 2013 [addenda], citing Barker 2009; also cf. Head 2012, 114–15, who points out that $\mathfrak{P}^{45}$ appears to punctuate and mark up the text of Mark, though not of the other gospels, for public reading).

While commentaries or scholia on Matthew, John, and Luke emerge in the second century, the first commentary on Mark appears only in the seventh, half a millennium later. (See, e.g., Wucherpfennig 2002 and Hill 2004 on John; Löhr 2003 on Luke; Cahill 1998 on Mark; also Kok 2015 on second-century reception of Mark.) In the preface to his commentary on Matthew, Jerome (345–420) could already claim to have benefited from extensive expositions by Theophilus of Antioch (late second century), Hippolytus (ca. 170–236), Origen (ca. 185–254), and numerous subsequent commentators in Greek and Latin (Jerome, *Commentary on Matthew*, Preface 4; cf. Scheck 2008, 19–20).

If one stops to think about it, the position of Mark's Gospel is perhaps the most surprising. After two centuries of New Testament scholarship's preoccupation with the priority of Mark, this gospel's virtual absence from the earliest manuscript tradition rightly strikes us as peculiar. What might explain this? At a time when manuscripts were beyond the reach of most private citizens, and even most churches could not afford the luxury of a complete four-gospel codex (for whose production expensive parchment rather than papyrus turned out to be more viable), perhaps there was less need for Mark: 90 percent of it does appear in Matthew, who provides a more satisfying introduction and conclusion for a biographical narrative.

That said, the intensive use of Mark by Matthew and Luke is itself eloquent tribute to this earlier gospel's importance for the Jesus tradition in the late first century. Moreover, several different second-century endings of Mark imply that *somebody* was engaging specifically with this gospel in the second century, and in the light of other gospel narratives. Distinctively *Markan* features of Tatian's gospel harmony (the *Diatessaron*) are difficult to substantiate with confidence and may not require that Tatian had at his disposal a specifically Markan *manuscript*, although the evidence does suggest knowledge of Mark 6:5; 10:18; and elements of the longer ending, 16:9–20 (see, e.g., Head 1992b, 130, 137). Further discrete second-century evidence for the use of Mark as one of the authoritative four is suggested by the mid-century *Epistle of the Apostles* (see below, p. 220 and cf. Kelhoffer 2000, 155).

The use of Mark along with the other gospels is also implicit in the emergence of four-gospel syntheses at this time: Theophilus of Antioch (fl. ca. 169–183) is said to have compiled an early example (Jerome, *Epistle* 121.6; *De viris illustribus* 25; cf. von Campenhausen 1972, 174–75). He was followed some decades later by the fourfold gospel synopsis that Ammonius of Alexandria (ca. 175–242) constructed on the basis of Matthew—and which Eusebius (ca. 260–340) refined in the system of gospel parallels known as the Eusebian canons (see Eusebius's *Letter to Carpianus*, lines 4–5 to *dia tessarōn . . . euangelion*; on Ammonius's synopsis see further Crawford 2015b). In the fourth century Ambrose of Milan knew (and heartily disapproved!) of a number of such attempts at synthesis, as he did of apocryphal gospels in the names of Basilides, Thomas, Matthias, or the Twelve (*Commentary on Luke* 1.2; CSEL 32.11).

Justin Martyr (ca. 100–165) indicates that Christians read "the memoirs of the apostles" at their weekly meetings (*First Apology* 67). He remains notoriously inexact about quite what texts he includes in this category, but it is clear that they are the writings of "the apostles and their successors" (*Dialogue* 103.8)—that is, at least two of each, and on one reading precisely four, which would coincide nicely with the fact that Justin includes among them Matthew

12

and (almost certainly) John as apostles, as well as Luke and Mark as apostolic students (for documentation, see Hengel 2000, 19–20 and nn.; more fully Hengel 2008b, 34–38; Stanton 2004; on Mark, see also Bockmuehl 2010, 84–86).

Despite some strongly suggestive passages especially in the *First Apology*, John's Gospel admittedly appears less prominent in Justin—possibly because it was at first less widely used in the West (as forcefully argued by Watson [2013, 473–93], who however fails to engage in appropriate detail with Hill 2004, 316–42, 191–204). Justin is familiar with a few "extracanonical" but widely influential traditions like the birth of Jesus in a cave or the fire appearing in the Jordan at his baptism (*Dialogue* 78, 88). Notably, however, the only apostolic gospels Justin explicitly acknowledges are those that appear in the New Testament—and no noncanonical gospel is either cited or mentioned. Leaving aside Justin and his pupil Tatian, other second-century writers of different stripes seem notably less familiar with Mark and cite Luke infrequently while foregrounding Matthew and John. Although individual sayings (agrapha) are indeed sometimes quoted as "gospel" or as words of the Lord (see below, page 45), identified noncanonical gospels do not appear to exercise a public liturgical role as analogous written sources alongside Matthew, Mark, Luke, and John. This observation applies even in Valentinian gnostic sources like Ptolemy's *Letter to Flora*, as Martin Hengel (2008b, 36–38) rightly notes, and is with very few exceptions further confirmed in the manuscript tradition. Important exceptions are the *Infancy Gospel of James* and the *Epistle of the Apostles*, which in some settings did exercise a relatively widespread liturgical role; but even these texts were not copied alongside the four gospels in ancient codices.

While both the terms "canon" (a rule or norm) and "New Testament" are used in the second century, the combination of these terms to designate a defined collection of writings appears only in the fourth century (cf. Markschies 2012g, 13–14; Nicklas 2012b).

As we shall see, however, this does not mean that any of the additional or alternative gospels ever achieved a comparable catholicity that might place them in competition with the four gospels, whether individually or as a fourfold whole. Conversely, even though Matthew and John were clearly more popular than Luke and especially Mark, none of the Four was ever seriously questioned as authoritative for the church.

13

Thus, the fourfold gospel status clearly emerged over the course of the second century and gradually gained in definition and exclusivity vis-à-vis some of the other permutations just described. This reality stands in contrast to occasional assertions that the distinctive status of the canonical gospels derived from a wholly unanticipated, "fictive" executive decision of fourth-century "theorizers" engaged in "suppressing or manipulating" others (Watson 2013, 454 and passim; contrast Watson 2016, 16–20). To be sure, in the late second century there is some limited evidence for the so-called Alogi, an anti-Montanist splinter group around a Roman presbyter who rejected the Gospel of John. But despite periodic assertions to the contrary the evidence is marginal at best, and recent scholarship has gone a long way toward demonstrating that there was no sustained opposition to the Gospel of John in the early church (see, e.g., Hill 2004 on Irenaeus, *Against Heresies* 3.2.9, and Epiphanius, *Refutation of All Heresies* 51.100).

Regional plurality and gradual convergence in the pattern of Christian gospel usage in no way detracts from the surprisingly early appearance of a widely acknowledged core of the fourfold gospel narrative, in both the East and the West. And as Christoph Markschies points out, signs of clear implicit reception and cross-referencing already *between* the four gospels themselves points to a first-century origin of this emerging core—even to the point that such material began to be quoted as "Scripture" alongside the Old Testament before the year 100 (Markschies 2012g, 26–27, 32–33, with reference to Matt. 10:10//Luke 10:7 in 1 Tim. 5:18; cf. *Didache* 13.2).

The (Re)Discovery of Noncanonical Gospels

So far, so straightforward, one might think. Does this not offer us a clear view of the canonical nest to which we may now contrast the noncanonical cuckoo as the hostile newcomer (so Wright 2013, 358)? It might seem so. But that assumption would be a mistake. Just when all seems order and clarity, the situation turns out to be confusingly interesting!

The existence of gospels—indeed, numerous gospels—other than the Four was well known in antiquity, although for long periods of church history our surviving mainstream Christian literature considered them a fringe phenomenon (an impression that, by

14

itself, could in theory reflect either de facto marginality or deliberate marginalization).

But then in the first half of the last century the inherited view
of these texts was dramatically transformed by extensive manuscript
discoveries in a landfill site in Upper Egypt at the ruined ancient
city of Oxyrhynchus ("The Sharp-Nosed Fish") beginning in 1896
and at Nag Hammadi (ancient Chenoboskion) in the late 1940s.

For our discussion in what follows, it will be worth noting that
these manuscripts are mostly written on either papyrus or parchment. Manuscripts of both kinds could be part of codices (singular:
codex), books formed by folding larger sheets and binding them
together. Although not entirely unique to Christians, this medium
of the codex, rather than the book roll or scroll, is widely recognized
as the preferred Christian book technology for authoritative texts.
On a papyrus page the front is typically called the *recto* while the
back is called the *verso*. (See Leach and Tait 2000; Hurtado 2006,
84–86; and note the definitions of terms offered in the glossary of
technical terms below, page 239).

Oxyrhynchus

Unlike most other newly found written sources from antiquity, the
treasure trove of manuscripts that first came to light at Oxyrhynchus in 1896 proved to be so vast that first editions of its contents
are still being published today. Bernard Grenfell (1869–1926) and
Arthur Hunt (1871–1934), two young archaeologists from Oxford,
joined work at an excavation that included the remains of an extensive ancient landfill site on the outskirts of the Egyptian village of
Al-Bahnasa, 200 kilometers (about 125 miles) south of Cairo.

Before long this ancient rubbish deposit yielded tens of thou-
sands of documents, of which even now only a minority have been
published. At the time of writing, over eighty volumes of papyri
are in print (most recently Gonis et al. 2016), representing about 5
percent of the total—though a good deal of the remainder is in very
small fragments. Most of the texts are in Greek, although there is
some material in Coptic, Demotic Egyptian, Latin, and (for the latest period) even Arabic. Among a wealth of classical literary as well
as scientific and documentary sources, there were large numbers
of biblical and other ancient Jewish and early Christian texts from
antiquity all the way to the seventh or early eighth centuries, with

15

the bulk of material clustered between the first and third centuries. (I will here for convenience designate all Oxyrhynchus fragments as they were officially published, even though subsequent scholarship has suggested not only that some extraneously acquired fragments also originated from this site, but also that some early published "Oxyrhynchus" finds may instead derive from the region of Fayûm, about 100 km [62 mi.] closer to Cairo; see Blumell 2012, 89–162, on the extensive epistolary networks and traffic patterns to and from Oxyrhynchus.)

All in all, the literary material from Oxyrhynchus appears to have comprised five major book collections, discarded at different periods during the lifetime of the site (Houston 2014, 130–79). Among the various Christian writings were about twenty examples of what are often somewhat imprecisely called "apocrypha," that is, quasi-biblical texts with subjects related to the New Testament. In addition to substantial parts of what we now know as the *Gospel of Thomas*, there were fragments of gospels in the names of Mary, Peter, and James, along with three or four other previously unknown gospel fragments. In the early decades of the twentieth century, this gave rise to a lively discussion about the significance of this seeming profusion of new and unknown gospels. Many other questions remain unanswered—not the least of which is why so many biblical, nonbiblical, and other manuscripts were consigned to an apparent rubbish dump (provocatively explored by Luijendijk 2010; cf. more recently Houston 2014, 130–79; and more generally Blumell and Wayment 2015, on the Christian texts from this site).

Nag Hammadi

Continued study of the Oxyrhynchus discoveries has had far-reaching consequences for our understanding of Greco-Roman culture in late antiquity, and of Christianity's place within it. But a generation later came a further Egyptian discovery that was tiny by comparison but at least initially seemed even more dramatic for an understanding of early Christianity.

In December 1945, farmers near the village of Nag Hammadi, several hours' drive farther up the Nile (540 km [335 mi.] by road from Cairo), discovered a collection of thirteen leather-bound ancient codices in a pottery jar concealed at the foot of a cliff. Reliable accounts of their discovery are hard to come by, and successive versions related by James M. Robinson and other editors seem to have gained in the telling and become notably contradictory (see Goodacre 2013). One of these volumes and part of a second one were destroyed before they could be studied, but the rest turned out to contain a wealth of mainly gnostic writings that were initially thought by some to have been part of the library of the nearby monastery founded by St. Pachomius (ca. 290–346), and possibly to have been discarded at a time of tightening canonical boundaries. The improbabilities surrounding both this Pachomian theory and the original discovery narratives have encouraged other, perhaps more likely explanations. Among these is the idea that the manuscripts were an eclectic collection of privately commissioned copies, buried as part of their owners' grave goods or Christian "books of the dead" (thus Denzey Lewis and Ariel Blount 2014)—a point rendered plausible by their discovery on the site of a large ancient burial ground.

17

The surviving fourth-century manuscripts are in Coptic translation rather than the original Greek, but they nonetheless represent writings that in some cases were composed as early as the second century. Several are presented as New Testament apocrypha. For our purposes the most significant ones may be those with these titles:

The Gospel of Thomas
The Gospel of Philip
The Sophia of Jesus Christ
The Gospel of Truth
The Dialogue of the Savior
The Apocryphon of James
The Book of Thomas [the Contender]
The Gospel of the Egyptians

These Coptic documents are now all available in accessible editions and English translations (see below, p. 52).

"Gnosticism"?—A Definition

Because the controversial terms "Gnosticism" and "gnostic" are frequently applied to texts like those found at Nag Hammadi, this may be an appropriate point at which to offer a brief definition. While the term itself derives from the Greek word for "knowledge" (*gnōsis*), its significance here is in relation to a highly fluid and diverse set of religious groups in the early Christian centuries. "Knowledge" may function as a technical term as early as the later writings of the New Testament (famously in 1 Tim. 6:20, where this concept already appears related to a preoccupation with "myths" and genealogies, 1:4). The noun's complete avoidance in the Johannine writings may also be significant.

Many key ideas about access to secret and otherworldly salvific knowledge for the few were anticipated in popular Middle Platonism and esoteric mysticism. In the most general sense they have a wide and almost timeless currency across diverse religious, philosophical, and even pseudoscientific manifestations, whether ancient, medieval, or modern. Specifically Christian gnostics experienced their heyday in the second, third, and fourth centuries. They developed sometimes elaborate mythologies influenced by

18

Christian and Jewish scriptural texts (not least the opening chapters of Genesis) as well as by Platonic philosophical ideas about the origin and nature of humanity and the cosmos. Scholars often distinguish Valentinians, on the one hand, from the more elaborate mythologies of Sethians, "Barbelo gnostics," and Ophites, on the other (e.g., Rasimus 2009); but there is still no consensus on these typologies. Certain gnostic ideas enjoyed a long and intriguing afterlife from late antiquity to the Middle Ages and beyond and are sometimes thought to have influenced such groups as the Manicheans and (much later) the Bogomils and Cathars.

As the name suggests, one of the key ideas uniting otherwise diverse and differentiated groups was the belief that the adherents were an elite gaining privileged access to *knowledge* of divinely revealed insights. This secret knowledge was understood to carry a saving significance in that it allowed the initiates to escape humanity's fleshly condition, liberating their true divine spark from its imprisonment in a corrupt materiality that is the evil design of an inferior creator (the workman or demiurge).

In view of the complexity of the evidence, few generalizations about gnostics or Gnosticism are likely to prove universally serviceable. Indeed there has been a lively debate about whether the "gnostic" terminology serves any useful purpose at all, with some scholars casting doubt on whether these terms can ever be meaningful (M. A. Williams 1996; cf. King 2003b; and more cautiously Marjanen 2005). Certainly an important upshot of such debates is the recognition that there was no single movement we could call "Gnosticism."

It is of course true that "gnostic" labels have often been deployed indiscriminately or polemically. For our discussion it matters that such terminology should not be invoked in order deliberately to load the critical dice when discussing the apocryphal gospels. The fact is that the terms "gnosis" and "gnostics" were indeed widely used in antiquity for certain philosophical schools or *haereses*, by Christian and non-Christian outsiders (e.g., Plotinus) as well as by insiders. Even mainstream writers like Clement of Alexandria and Origen implicitly acknowledged the validity of concerns for saving knowledge in their rather different adoption of the language of gnosis in the service of catholic theological ends. So the active use of the terminology is significant even if the term "gnostics" (*gnōstikoi*) is relatively rare as a self-designation.

19

"Gnosticism," by contrast, is a potentially misleading modern analytical construct (invented by the seventeenth-century commentator Henry More), which for the sake of clarity we will avoid in this book. (See further M. Edwards 1989; 1990; Layton 1995, 338; Markschies 2003, 10–11; also McGuire 2010, 203–5 with nn5–7.)

On a related note, recent scholarship has also repeatedly called into question whether several of the leading second-century founders of such groups were themselves gnostic in any distinctive sense. Martin Hengel, perhaps the late twentieth century's leading New Testament historian, acknowledged the profound influence such prominent teachers clearly exercised on subsequent developments, and he assigned the investigation of this problem to several of his doctoral students and others. Their publications include Winrich Löhr 1996 on Basilides (fl. 117–138), Christoph Markschies 1992 on Valentinus (d. ca. 165), Niclas Förster 1999 on Marcus (founder of the Marcosians, mid-2nd cent.), and Ansgar Wucherpfennig 2002 on the Valentinian commentator Heracleon. Similar work on Ptolemy, the author of *Letter to Flora* explaining the Valentinian approach to the Old Testament, remains desirable.

In a much-cited essay (2008a), Martin Hengel argues for the development of these gnostic movements around the year 100 CE out of Christian, Jewish apocalyptic, and Middle Platonic roots (cf. further Lahe 2012; Drecoll 2013). In particular, Hengel suggests that the attractiveness of gnostic ideas may have been in combining a deep disillusionment about apocalyptic eschatology in the wake of the catastrophic Jewish War with the educated Christian desire for a viable philosophy of religion in Greco-Roman intellectual culture (560–63, 589–92). Such a cultural aspiration may also animate Valentinian ethics: as an attempt to provide an intelligible Christian philosophical account of the good life, gnostic moral teaching stresses ideas like the escape from materialism to a spiritual transcendence, the control of emotions, and the rational elimination of excess—from preoccupation with sex to the union of alienated gender differences (see Dunderberg 2015; also Tite 2009).

This question of the origin and appeal of gnostic ideas is clearly a large and complex topic to which we cannot do full justice here. (For useful further reading, see Brakke 2010a; Logan 2006; Marjanen 2008; Markschies 2003; Pearson 2007; van den Broek 2013. The most comprehensive overview of Valentinianism remains Thomassen 2006.)

20

Gospels of the Original Jesus, Suppressed by an Authoritarian Church?

In Europe and North America, the third millennium of the Christian calendar began on a note of surprisingly widespread confusion about Christianity's origins, in the media and even in the churches. That confusion was fueled in no small part by several cleverly marketed new (or newly reinterpreted) discoveries of ancient artifacts, including a supposed bone box (ossuary) of James the brother of Jesus; a supposed family tomb of Jesus in Jerusalem, which somehow came to be rebranded and republicized as such several decades after its discovery; and a manuscript containing the so-called *Gospel of Judas*, whose existence had been rumored ever since its clandestine discovery in 1978, and which was published in 2006 to much fanfare by none other than *National Geographic* magazine. In 2012 Karen L. King of Harvard Divinity School caused a considerable stir when she announced (and later published, King 2014) a papyrus fragment mentioning Mary Magdalene as the "wife" of Jesus, although this was subsequently exposed as a modern fake (see below, p. 187).

We will return to these texts. But even before these finds one could not fail to notice the extraordinary media circus surrounding *The Da Vinci Code* (D. Brown 2003), a blockbuster novel predicated on wholly fanciful theories about the repercussions of Mary Magdalene's imagined marriage and children with Jesus. Swashbuckling tales of conspiracy and deception at the heart of religion or power retain a timeless potential to entertain the gullible while generating impressive streams of revenue for their promoters (not to mention for industries like Hollywood and tour guides from Saint-Sulpice in Paris to Rosslyn Chapel outside Edinburgh). More recently, comparable historical nonsense on stilts was in 2014 "discovered" to fresh media fanfare in the supposed "decoding" of a seventh-century manuscript paraphrasing *Joseph and Asenath*, an early Jewish or Christian apocryphal narrative about the conversion of Joseph's pagan Egyptian wife. Contrary to appearances, this "lost gospel" supposedly encodes the secret of Jesus' marriage to Mary Magdalene, who, like Asenath, gave birth to two sons (Jacobovici and Wilson 2014; cf. Gen. 41:45, 50; 46:20). And so it goes on. Given Christianity's accelerating and partly self-inflicted decline in public influence and credibility throughout many Western societies, the loss of old certainties unsurprisingly yields the stage to more fanciful counternarratives about Christian origins.

It is not sensationalist or misleading to point out that the ancient church was indeed aware of the existence of a large number of other gospels or gospel-like texts. The gradual acceptance of settled canonical boundaries in turn entailed a more confident demarcation of documents that as a result had *not* become canonical. (See Watson 2013; the more problematic notion of literature that "became" apocryphal or canonical has been particularly stressed by Lührmann 2004; Lührmann and Schlarb 2000; but see also the critique in Nicklas 2011.)

A pivotal twentieth-century contributor to this conversation was Walter Bauer (1877–1960). Known to students of New Testament Greek above all as the originator of a definitive lexicon (Danker, Bauer, et al. 2000), he also became ideologically influential in the 1920s for his depiction of Jesus as a "syncretistically softened" anti-Judean Jew who had grown up in a hellenized Gentile setting "in considerable freedom from the Law," disdainful of "levitical purity" and of the Temple—as a place of conflict rather than of worship (Bauer 1967, 102–3, 108). His sort of liberal Protestant Jesus was hardly original, but seemed before long to lend grist to the mill of "German Christian" New Testament scholars determined to discover a Jesus who was not Jewish at all (e.g., Grundmann 1940, esp. 175; cf. Ericksen 1985; Head 2004; Heschel 2008).

More significantly for our purposes, however, Bauer's book *Orthodoxy and Heresy in Earliest Christianity*, first published in 1934 (English translation, Bauer 1971), became particularly formative in postwar scholarship through its idea that "heretical" beliefs were not historically a deviation from singular Christian "orthodoxy," but rather were the dominant expression of a fundamentally diverse and plural faith from which "orthodoxy" emerged only at a later stage. This view, seemingly boosted by fresh discoveries like those at Oxyrhynchus and Nag Hammadi, commended itself to the study of gospel literature among the students of Helmut Koester and James M. Robinson, as well as among members of the late-twentieth-century North American Jesus Seminar (see Koester 1990; Koester and Robinson 1971).

22

In more popularizing scholarship influenced by the Bauer and Koester schools, conspiracy-minded interpretations have frequently asserted that these ancient texts were at first of the same status as, and at least in some cases earlier than, the canonical gospels, superior witnesses to the real essence of the Jesus movement, and freely proliferating in Christianity's charismatic infancy until they came to be brutally suppressed by authoritarian churchmen, perhaps at the emperor Constantine's beck and call.

Bauer's scholarly reception by Koester, Robinson, and their students encouraged the emergence of a view that the gnostic gospels in particular offered access to the authentic original genius of the Christian message—a view that has energized writers ranging from scholars like Elaine Pagels (1979) to racy fiction writers like Dan Brown (2003). Related to this are attempts to date the canonical gospels exceptionally *late* while insisting that certain noncanonical sources, including the *Gospel of Thomas*, grant exceptionally *early* access to the teaching of Jesus. That is the approach of a writer like John Dominic Crossan (1991, 427–30), who asserts no fewer than fifteen sources of "independent attestation" *predating* the Gospel of Mark, or of the optimistically titled volume *The Complete Gospels*, which conveniently presents "for the first time anywhere all twenty of the known gospels from the early Christian era," all of which are said to be "witnesses to early Jesus traditions" (Robert Miller 1994, cover, 3).

Certain observations are, however, important to bear in mind if we are to keep the second-century profusion and variety of Christian literature in perspective. One pertinent insight to be elaborated in the course of our discussion is this: while scholars from time to time postulate the existence of primitive texts like Q or early sources of *Thomas*, no extant alternative gospel forms or attestations predate the New Testament Four. Even a large and diverse collection of early Christian literature like that at Oxyrhynchus turns out to corroborate the popularity of the two mainstream apostolic Gospels of John and Matthew. These were evidently—there as elsewhere—the most widely read and copied.

As for the apocryphal gospels, at one level the overwhelmingly Egyptian evidence is what we would expect, given the extent to which the climate favored the survival of papyri. But there, to some extent, lies the rub for a good deal of the evidence on which Bauer's hypothesis draws: can the discoveries at Oxyrhynchus or indeed those at Nag Hammadi (which followed the publication of his book) really grant us representative insights into the nature of early Christianity *more generally*, or are they perhaps eloquent first and foremost *about themselves* and their own context—namely, at the core of the singular Nag Hammadi collection and nearer the periphery of the vast Oxyrhynchus finds? These discoveries do illustrate the rich diversity of theological approaches in early Christian circles of Upper Egypt—but they cannot straightforwardly establish the priority and predominance of heterodoxy in quite the way that Walter Bauer assumed. (Blumell [2012, 318–25] offers a valuable if incomplete inventory of Christian evidence from Oxyrhynchus published up to 2010, which implies a proportion of canonical to noncanonical gospel fragments in purely numerical terms at around 2.5 to 1, depending on which centuries are included. More significantly, only the dominant Gospels of Matthew [15x] and John [13x] seem to be attested consistently in every century up to the time of canonization, and they appear respectively five times and four times as often as the three confirmed fragments of *Thomas*, their nearest noncanonical rival; there are two fragments for *Mary* and arguably just single attestations for the nine other noncanonical gospel-like texts. Canonical and noncanonical gospels are not found together within the same manuscripts.)

In other words, even for Egypt the manuscript finds may help underscore the serendipitous and marginal or subsidiary character of what was discovered. Some readers at Oxyrhynchus were evidently interested in apocryphal gospel literature—but as we just saw, never to the extent that any of these texts competed with the preferred Gospels of Matthew or John, even if Luke and Mark are admittedly rarer. Nag Hammadi offers fewer statistical clues, but we have here a dozen books about whose status and representative currency we can have no assurance on the basis of this single find. This point becomes more significant if one considers how very few of these texts generated multiple copies or translations, let alone commentaries.

All in all, these observations certainly do not invalidate Bauer's thesis, but they do urge considerable caution. The appeal of authoritarian suppression theories casts a long shadow—not least for a Protestant romanticism that loves to lionize an imagined primitive charismatic anarchy being crushed by authoritarian institutions and orthodoxies. In such scenarios Hegel's philosophy of history, Adolf von Harnack's nineteenth-century rediscovery of Marcion, and a popular heroic mythology of Luther's battle against the pope are never far from the surface.

24

We must certainly take on board the important questions about early Christian diversity that were raised by the Bauer thesis and the Egyptian discoveries of the twentieth century. But this cannot make the evidence from the sands of Egypt yield answers as straightforward as either traditionalist or skeptical accounts would have us believe.

The idea of a fourfold apostolic gospel of Matthew, Mark, Luke, and John emerged during the first half of the second century and continued to gain in strength until it formally prevailed in the fourth. But other gospels and gospel traditions richly proliferated in the later second and third centuries, many of them informed—either directly or more often indirectly—by the narrative outline of the Four. Far from these documents being eliminated as "heretical" departures from a clear, uninterrupted orthodox line from the start, many appear to have coexisted happily with the protocanonical tradition and even taken it for granted.

Mainstream church leaders did indeed voice opposition to such alternative accounts in either written or oral form, whether or not they knew them at first hand. Such conflict began not in the fourth century but in the second, if not earlier. Several New Testament documents already explicitly discount false or inaccurate renderings of the ministry or teaching of Jesus (see, e.g., Matt. 5:17, 19; Luke 1:3–4; John 1:8; 6:66; 21:23–24; also 1 John 4:2–3; 1 Cor. 15:14–18).

But the idea that the noncanonical gospels disappeared from view simply or primarily because they were formally silenced by church authorities founders on several contrary facts.

First, the supposedly suppressed documents were evidently known and read by some, but—judging from the manuscript evidence—appear never to have gained widespread popularity, circulation, or acceptance. The following table illustrates this well.

Precise dates and therefore absolute manuscript statistics are admittedly always debatable; but it is now factually incorrect to claim that there are no pre-300 manuscripts of Mark (so, e.g., Watson 2016, 3–4; but note $\mathfrak{P}^{45}$, P.Oxy. 5073, and perhaps $\mathfrak{P}^{88}$), let alone that "papyri dating from 100 to 300 CE are equally balanced between canonical and non-canonical gospels" (Burke 2013a, 29, citing only Koester 1980, who was, among other things, unaware of at least eight as yet unpublished papyri on John [$\mathfrak{P}^{90}$, $\mathfrak{P}^{95}$, $\mathfrak{P}^{106}$, $\mathfrak{P}^{107}$, $\mathfrak{P}^{108}$, $\mathfrak{P}^{109}$, $\mathfrak{P}^{119}$, $\mathfrak{P}^{121}$], five on Matthew [$\mathfrak{P}^{101}$, $\mathfrak{P}^{102}$, $\mathfrak{P}^{103}$, $\mathfrak{P}^{104}$, $\mathfrak{P}^{110}$],

Table 1. Gospel Manuscripts prior to the Year 300

Matthew	13x
Mark	2–3x
Luke	7x
John	18x
Diatessaron?	1x
Thomas	3x
Protevangelium of James	1x
Gospel of Mary	2x
Gospel of Judas	1x
Various "Unknown" Gospels	5x

This table is adapted from Hurtado 2013, a fuller inventory than the list of papyri in the appendix to Nestle-Aland[28] (Nestle et al. 2012, 792–99).

one on Luke [$\mathfrak{P}^{111}$], and one or possibly two on Mark [P.Oxy. 5073; $\mathfrak{P}^{88}$?], all predating the year 300).

Those gospels that went on to become canonical in the fourth century are also the ones that were most frequently read and copied before 300, as well as most frequently cited and commented upon—Mark being a partial exception on both counts. It is a particularly telling additional observation that the early-third-century manuscript $\mathfrak{P}^{45}$, possibly our earliest unambiguous multiple-gospel codex, includes parts of four and only four gospels: Matthew, John, Luke, and Mark—in that order, plus Acts. (Skeat [1997] suspected an even earlier example in a compilation of $\mathfrak{P}^4$ + $\mathfrak{P}^{64}$ + $\mathfrak{P}^{67}$; this has not been widely accepted, but Gathercole [2012b, 218, 235] does suggest "the possibility (but no more)" that $\mathfrak{P}^4$ formed part of a codex containing both Matthew and Luke.)

Even if one counts *all* extant manuscripts prior to the invention of the printing press, the copies of gospels composed before 300 remain in single-digit numbers except in the case of the four New Testament gospels—and the *Infancy Gospel of James* (along with later translations of public texts like the *Diatessaron*).

Significantly, too, there are no extant manuscripts from antiquity (whether before or after canonization) that combine canonical with apocryphal gospels. The manuscript record does suggest that some or many early Christians knew both sorts of texts, and in some places like Rhossus or Oxyrhynchus some of them clearly read both sorts (see Hurtado 2015). But their manuscripts evidently

Table 2. Extant Manuscripts of Some Ancient Noncanonical Gospels

Gospel of Thomas	4x
Gospel of Philip	1x
Gospel of Mary	3x
Gospel of Judas	1x
Sophia of Jesus Christ (Wisdom of Jesus Christ)	1x
Gospel of Peter	1x
Infancy Gospel of James (Greek manuscripts only; numerous translations and derivatives exist)	Over 150x

distinguished between them. And Christians did *not* copy or read them as equivalents side by side, contrary to a twentieth-century scholarly prejudice in the wake of Walter Bauer that continues to be popularized to this day (nicely illustrated by collections like Robert Miller 1994 or for that matter Taussig 2013).

All this says a great deal about a process of dissemination and acceptance of popular authoritative texts that, especially in the early centuries, was far too diverse and widespread to be explicable in terms of structures of authoritarian imposition or censorship.

Official suppression is of course one possible explanation for this disparity of attestation—and for particular cases this possibility cannot be categorically excluded. But occasional efforts to blacklist various documents (for example, by Irenaeus of Lyons and Serapion of Antioch in the second century or by the Gelasian Decree in the late fifth or early sixth) appear for the most part to have had little effect. The effective replacement of the *Diatessaron* with the fourfold gospel in Syrian churches of the fifth and sixth centuries demonstrates that some "opposed" texts did disappear; but others, like the *Infancy Gospel of James* and various Pilate cycles, continued to go from strength to strength.

Until the sixth century—and perhaps until considerably later—the church simply did not have the power to make such texts go away. Of course it could merrily anathematize and in certain places sporadically take or threaten action; but it could not, it seems, successfully enforce. With the notable exception of para-canonical texts like the *Diatessaron* and the *Infancy Gospel of James*, the absence of noncanonical gospel literature from the Eastern and Western churches' public liturgical reading may be simply that—the

27

nonappearance of texts that failed to attract a sufficient communal readership to establish themselves as universal Christian "classics," that is, popularly received Christian texts that could garner consensus and stand the test of time and faith. As has been the case for popular religious literature and music through the ages, eventual success or failure was above all a function of their power to engage their subject matter credibly and authentically in the service of the faithful—and, at least partly as a result, their ability to weather occasional periods of local, popular, or official opprobrium.

An interesting early medieval confirmation of this view is provided by the discoveries in the genizah (storeroom for disused manuscripts) of the Old (Ben Ezra) Synagogue in Fustat near Cairo. These have long been noted to include palimpsests (scraped and recycled manuscripts) of the New Testament texts of Matthew, John, Acts, and 1 Peter. In addition to Greek Old Testament translations of Aquila and of Origen's *Hexapla*, the genizah also contained translations of New Testament texts and lectionaries into languages including Arabic, Judeo-Arabic, and Syriac (on which, see Niessen 2009; some may have been used in part for liturgical purposes). But aside from the well-known medieval *Toledot Yeshu* fragments (on which see below, p. 129), not a single apocryphal gospel has turned up among the Christian texts and palimpsests of the Cairo Genizah. (On a more speculative note, Piovanelli (2011, 92–96) nevertheless suggests close links between the *Toledot Yeshu* and the *Gospel according to the Hebrews* as well as the *Gospel of Judas*.) This absence of Christian apocrypha seems particularly notable since the Cairo Genizah's somewhat catholic selection of texts included a number of *Jewish* noncanonical or "apocryphal" writings like Hebrew Sirach, Aramaic Levi (a source for the *Testament of Levi*), and the *Damascus Document*—whether these attest a surviving ancient manuscript tradition or were later rediscovered, like the cache of Hebrew manuscripts found near Jericho at the end of the eighth century (mentioned in a famous letter by Patriarch Timothy I [780–823]; for text and translation, see Reeves 1999, 174–77).

The Design and Approach of This Book

28

As a deliberately brief and accessible guide to this complex and newly reinvigorated field of study, this book does not intend to break new ground or push the envelope on basic historical-critical questions of the authorship, date, and setting of the noncanonical gospels. The aim is to develop the argument in the context of a fairly middle-of-the-road approach to most critical debates, rather than to advance the field in this respect.

Five main emphases constitute the basic argument of this book.

1. First, the aim is to provide an introduction that is both *accessible* and *nonsensationalist* while offering a sympathetic account of these writings in relation to what became the New Testament. This involves taking the texts seriously on their own terms and in relation to a centrist range of assessments within mainstream critical scholarship. It will also relate them to their place within the reception history and formation of what was to become the canonical fourfold gospel.

2. This approach also favors the conviction that it is legitimate and instructive to read these texts *alongside* the New Testament gospels. In doing so we will find that their status can be usefully understood as *epiphenomenal* and supplementary to that gospel tradition. In relation to its narrative structure as well as its status as public and "apostolic," all noncanonical gospels presume that New Testament tradition's *existence*; many of them presuppose its substance or even its wording. In some sense, therefore, the apocryphal gospels occupy what at least in retrospect can be described as a "para-canonical" perspective—whether their intent is to supplement and reaffirm, to replace, or to subvert the four gospels that became canonical.

As I will suggest, this is routinely the narrative perspective they adopt, and sometimes their explicit self-understanding, whether or not they identify themselves (like the *Gospel of Thomas,* the *Gospel of Judas*, the *Apocryphon of John*, and others) as "apocryphal" or "secret"—and therefore whether or not they intend any bid for public ecclesial status at all. This para-canonical identity pertains even for texts that are formally or chronologically nearer the New Testament canon than others. (On this point it is helpful to consult the articulation by Luke Timothy Johnson [2008] of the respective "canonical" settings of John and *Thomas*, in contrast to the alternative account of that relationship offered by writers like Elaine Pagels [2003]. See also below, p. 42, for an attempt to define the slippery term "apocryphal.")

3. We will repeatedly find our attention drawn to one simple and obvious but easily overlooked feature of our source material, which in turn encourages this para-canonical way of looking at the

texts. Of the dozens of noncanonical gospel-like documents from antiquity, whether familiar from ancient citations or only through manuscript discoveries, not a single surviving text offers an alternative narrative account of the kind provided in the four New Testament gospels. That is to say, none of them trace what Jesus did and said and suffered from his baptism through his public ministry to his crucifixion and resurrection. Apparent exceptions to this rule are either closely dependent on the text of the four gospels, like the second-century synthesis known as the *Diatessaron*, or else belong in this form to a much later period, like the Jewish antigospel *Toledot Yeshu* or the Muslim *Gospel of Barnabas*.

It is true that quite a number of fragmentary texts *might* in theory have provided such an alternative narrative—including, for example, the *Gospel of Peter* or Papyrus Egerton 2. But none is extant—or even attested in the ancient literature. Nor did any alternative gospel-style narrative accounts of Jesus' mission and ministry from birth or baptism to death or resurrection experience significant attestation or circulation in antiquity. The canonical Four are thus notably distinctive in this regard; indeed their Markan outline appears in one way or another to have been the narrative reference grid for at least the large majority of noncanonical gospels.

4. Quite how that relationship between noncanonical and canonical gospels works intertextually will be a matter for repeated reflection in the following chapters. Most typically, we will encounter gospel-like texts showing a marked editorial *distance* from the New Testament gospels, while nevertheless revealing their own (and their readers') presupposed *consciousness* of the narrative framework and even the wording of those protocanonical gospels to a greater or lesser extent.

We will thus see that traditional scholarly notions of literary dependence, when narrowly understood in terms of scribes working with written texts, are rarely serviceable for this relationship between the fourfold gospel and the others. In trying to describe this clearly epiphenomenal but often somewhat loosely or indirectly articulated connection, it seems in many cases preferable to think in terms of *antecedence* and *influence* rather than a relationship of direct dependence on a written text. This accounts for the frequent presence of shared themes or phrases while also explaining the considerable literary freedom and *independence* which some of the noncanonical texts manifest at the same time. (Others, like Foster

[2010a, 116–17], prefer to maintain, e.g., for the *Gospel of Peter*, a somewhat extended notion of "literary dependence" that might include "drawing upon a literary work from memory." This is a conceptually helpful clarification, but it still presupposes the mediated antecedent to be a distinct written text rather than, say, an informal harmony or conflation.)

5. Finally, another occasionally useful frame of reference can be the concept of "social memory," which considers the social, cultural, ritual, and religious dimensions of how communities remember their past and understand their identity (see Dignas, Smith, and Price 2012; Fentress and Wickham 1992; the relevance for the gospel tradition is explored by Dunn 2007; Kelber 2002; Kirk and Thatcher 2005; Le Donne 2009). In a surprising number of cases the protocanonical pattern of attributing gospels to key apostles or their immediate disciples also characterizes the noncanonical gospels; and at least until the second century it remains in theory possible that such associations are informed in part by appeal to the often contested living memory of these apostolic figures or their students, as they were for Ignatius, Justin, and Irenaeus (see Bockmuehl 2010 and 2012b on Simon Peter).

How Many Apocryphal Gospels?

There is always something unquestionably exciting and intriguing about public announcements that an ancient text about Jesus has come to light—or perhaps even just a papyrus fragment of such a document. What if it contains genuine sayings or stories previously unknown about him? What if it reveals mysterious or secret truths about Jesus of Nazareth or his followers, authentic insights into the earliest Jesus movement?

But it is in the nature of this material that much of what we are dealing with is either highly fragmentary, lost, or perhaps even entirely hypothetical. This fragmentary nature of our texts is self-evident for papyri like those found at Oxyrhynchus and elsewhere, but it is also clear from a number of apparently well-known documents that are repeatedly mentioned in early Christian writings, but whose actual text is only ever cited in passing or quoted in occasional short snippets in the church fathers. So how do we study this confusing wealth of disparate material outside what is presented

31

to us so tidily in the four complete narrative gospels of the New Testament?

To arrive at a proper reading we must first find a serviceable way to describe what we are dealing with. How many texts are there? One reason the noncanonical gospels often seem particularly formidable and bewildering to the nonexpert is the sheer difficulty of even establishing how many sources we are talking about. It is one thing to discover that in antiquity more than the four biblical gospels were known, or perhaps that one of them was a text known as the *Gospel of Thomas* and another called the *Gospel of Judas*. What can be more confusing is to open one of several excellent recent volumes of translations to discover *quite how many* of these "gospel" documents there are, surviving either in their entirety or more often as fragments. One ballpark figure often cited is that there were approximately forty "other gospels" (e.g., Tuckett 2005; cf. Ehrman and Pleše 2011, viii); but the 1,500-page German work of Markschies and Schröter 2012 contains around twice that number (depending, inevitably, on how one counts). Ancient sources certainly cite or report dozens of other noncanonical gospels or gospel-related texts. For some of these we have fleeting descriptions or quotes, but no trace survives of many others.

It is easy to feel dismay or paralysis at the complicated mass of this material, much of which is either lost or fragmentary, and about whose original size and shape we can only speculate. The following two lists will help to illustrate the broad scope of the material, and the problems of taxonomy, by means of one ancient and one modern inventory of "apocryphal" gospels.

An Ancient Inventory of Noncanonical Gospels

Below is a list of prohibited texts in the so-called Gelasian Decree (*Decretum Gelasianum*), a Latin document of uncertain provenance and authority transmitted under the names of popes including Damasus I (366–384) and Gelasius I (492–496) but thought to have been compiled more unofficially in the sixth century. The list below (culled from Klauck 2003, 3–5) includes only the gospel-related texts, in the order in which they appear. The text of the decree explicitly identifies each item as "apocryphal" (and therefore rejected).

32

The Gospel under the name of Matthias

The Gospel under the name of Barnabas

The Gospel under the name of James the younger

The Gospel under the name of Thomas, which the Manicheans use

Gospels under the name of Bartholomew

Gospels under the name of Andrew

The Gospels that Lucian has forged

The Gospels that Hesychius has forged

The Book about the childhood of the Savior

The Book about the birth of the Savior and about Mary or the Midwife

The *Cento* about Christ, compiled in Virgilian verses [probably the *Cento Vergilianus de Laudibus Christi* by Faltonia Betitia Proba (ca. 315–ca. 366), which covers biblical history up to the ascension]

The Book which is called The Passage of Holy Mary (*Transitus Mariae*)

The Epistle of Jesus to Abgar

The Epistle of Abgar to Jesus

All amulets composed in the name not of angels (as those people pretend), but rather of demons

The inclusion of one or two of these items is admittedly doubtful and reflects the extent to which the term "apocryphal" was applied fairly liberally to suspect documents. Faltonia Betitia Proba's *Cento*, for example, however disagreeable to the author of the decree, is certainly not apocryphal in any sense either of secrecy or of supplementation or competition with the canonical gospels. In fact, it is a poetic composition that seeks to recapitulate them through the educated and aesthetically refined medium of Virgilian verse, which in turn facilitated a wealth of fresh allegorical associations (see Sandnes 2011, 141–80).

A Note on Amulets

While the final category, amulets, perhaps was included in this catalog somewhat whimsically (but in keeping with general early Christian opposition to magic), it does hint at a relevant point for

33

our purposes. Recent text-critical research has drawn attention to the neglected category of noncontinuous biblical texts. Among these are amulets containing or echoing biblical quotations, including, for example, P.Oxy. 5073, which is now by at least a century the earliest attestation of the text of Mark 1:1–2 (Head 2013, 439–43). As a number of these noncontinuous texts appear to redeploy gospel quotations in amulets or other unofficial formularies, they clearly constitute an interesting interstitial category between the customary ecclesial forms of biblical manuscripts and lectionaries, on the one hand, and popular praxis and belief, on the other. It is significant for our purposes that virtually all known examples of such talismanic gospel texts consist of authoritative *canonical* rather than apocryphal gospel excerpts—usually incipits (opening lines of works or passages) or the Lord's Prayer. (The main exception is the story of Jesus and Abgar, on which see below, p. 121; de Bruyn 2015, 156–60, 173–74.) Greek examples are conveniently cataloged in de Bruyn and Dijkstra 2011, nos. 4, 8, 19, 21, 22, 26, 36, 38, 44, 45, 50, 59, 70, 77, 84, 95, 105, 117, 122, 134, 146, 148, 156, 157, 182; there are many others in Coptic. See further de Bruyn 2010; Sanzo 2014; also Kraus 2004; 2007 on problems of classification and definition.

A Modern Inventory of Noncanonical Gospels

This section is adapted from the large collection edited by Markschies and Schröter (2012). For ease of reference it follows their sequencing of the material (see, e.g., pp. ix–xii), lightly adapting the structure for easier representation.

> Jesus Traditions
> > Words of Jesus (incl. Nag Hammadi, Arabic literature)
>
> Non-Christian Traditions about Jesus
>
> Traditions about Jesus' Ministry and Passion
> > The Legend of Jesus and Abgar
> > *The Gospel of Nicodemus*
> > *The Acts of Pilate*
> > *Christ's Descent to Hell*
> > Other Literature Associated with Pilate

Traditions about the Relatives of Jesus
>
> *The Dormition and Assumption of Mary*
> *The History of Joseph the Carpenter*

Gospels
>
> Papyrus Fragments of Unknown Gospels
>> P.Oxy. 840
>> P.Egerton 2 + P.Köln 255
>> P.Berlin 11710
>> P.Oxy. 1224
>> P.Cair. 10735
>> The Fayûm Gospel (P.Vindob. G. 2325)
>> The Rylands Gospel (P.Ryl. 464)
>> PSI XI 1200bis
>> The Strasbourg Coptic Papyrus (P.Argent.
>> Copt. 5–7)
>> P.Merton 51
>> P.Oxy. 210
>
> *The Secret Gospel of Mark*

Other Minor Gospel Fragments
>
> *The Gospel of Eve*
> *Questions of Mary*
> *The Birth of Mary*
> *The Gospel* (or: *Traditions*) *of Matthias*

Secondary Reports about Extracanonical Gospels
>
> *The Gospel of the Four Zones of the World*
> *The Gospel of Perfection*
> *The Gospel of the Twelve*
> *The Quqite Twelve Gospels/Gospel of the Twelve*
> *The Manichean Gospel of the Twelve*
> *The Gospel of the Twelve Apostles*
> *The Gospel of the Seventy*
> *The Memoir of the Apostles*
> *The Gospel of Cerinthus*
> *The Gospel of Basilides*
> *The Gospel of Marcion*
> *The Gospel of Apelles*
> *The Gospel of Bardaisan*

35

Sayings Gospels
>*The Gospel of Thomas:*
>>Nag Hammadi Codex II,2
>>P.Oxy. 654
>>P.Oxy. 655
>*The Gospel of Philip*

Narrative Gospels
>Fragments of Jewish Christian Gospels
>Fragments of the *Gospel of the Hebrews*
>Fragments of the *Gospel of the Ebionites*
>Fragments of the *Gospel of the Nazoreans*
>Textual Variants of the "Jewish Gospel"
>*The Gospel of the Egyptians*
>*The Gospel of Peter*
>*The Gospel of Bartholomew*
>*Questions of Bartholomew*
>The Coptic "*Book of the Resurrection of Jesus Christ Our Lord*"
>Infancy Gospels:
>>*The Protevangelium of James*
>>*The Infancy Gospel of Thomas*
>>*The Narrative of Justin* (in Hippolytus)
>>*The Arabic Infancy Gospel*
>>*The Gospel of Pseudo-Matthew*
>>The Gospel of the Arundel Manuscript (British Library MS Arundel 404)
>>An Extract from the Life of John the Baptist
>>*The Gospel of Mani*

Dialogue Gospels
>The Freer Logion
>*The Epistle of the Apostles*
>*The [Letter* or] *Apocryphon of James* (NHC I,2)
>*The Book of Thomas the Contender* (NHC II,7)
>*The Sophia/Wisdom of Jesus Christ* (NHC III,4/BG 3)
>*The Dialogue of the Savior* (NHC III,5)
>*The First Apocalypse of James* (NHC V,3/CT 2)
>*The Second Apocalypse of James* (NHC V,4)
>*The Letter of Peter to Philip* (NHC VIII,2/CT 1)

The Gospel of Mary (BG 1/P.Oxy. 3525/P.Ryl. 463)
Fragments of a Conversation between John and Jesus
The Gospel of Judas (CT 3)
The Book of Allogenes (CT 4)

"Gospel Meditations"
The Gospel of Truth (NHC I,3)
The Holy Book of the Great Invisible Spirit (NHC
     III,3/IV,2; sometimes erroneously identified as
     "Gospel of the Egyptians")
Unknown Berlin Gospel/Gospel of the Savior
Pistis Sophia
The Books of Jeû (CB 1/CB 2)
The Gospel of Gamaliel:
          Coptic Fragments of the *Gospel of Gamaliel*
          Arabic Version of the *Gospel of Gamaliel*
          Ethiopic Version of the *Gospel of Gamaliel*
     The Anonymous Apocryphal Gospel

It is not hard to find oneself multiply confused or overwhelmed by conflicting catalogs like these! For one thing, they suggest that the question of an overall document count may be the least of our problems. Much of what is known from ancient sources is not extant, while a good deal of what is extant is "unknown"—that is to say, we have no way of linking it either with other surviving texts or fragments or with sources mentioned in antiquity. There are of course occasional exceptions to this state of affairs. Once in a while a lost ancient text may indeed come to light (e.g., the *Gospel of Judas*); careful scholarly study may suddenly stumble upon a demonstration that one previously unconnected fragment of papyrus belongs with another, well-known text (e.g., P.Köln 255 with P.Eger. 2). But these are happy exceptions in what in many other respects remains a frequently perplexing state of affairs.

Then again, one cannot leaf through more than a few of the documents in the major collections without stopping to ask oneself in what sense some of these items can really be said to represent gospels, even on a broad nontechnical definition of that term. The *Oxford English Dictionary*, for example, characterizes apocryphal gospels as "certain ancient lives of Christ of a legendary character." Should we really count ancient texts that show no interest in the life of Christ, whether legendary or otherwise? If not, our inventory immediately becomes very much shorter. What is more, no two scholars' lists or taxonomies seem to agree: it is remarkably difficult even to describe, let alone to categorize, what we are dealing with.

It will help to begin our task by asking what defines an "apocryphal" gospel and questioning a few conventions that are likely to obscure rather than to clarify.

What Makes a Gospel "Apocryphal"?

The designation of texts as "apocryphal" often carries the negative connotation of an implied value judgment between apparently normative texts and others that are deemed extraneous and quite possibly suspect. The ancient church's usage of the term in relation to Jewish or Christian writings was overwhelmingly pejorative (for the Western church, see the documentation in Gallagher 2014). For this reason some interpreters prefer to speak only of "early Christian" texts without singling out some as canonical and others as inferior: the very notion that some gospels are canonical is on that view a late and somewhat arbitrary fourth-century imposition upon texts which until that point had happily coexisted and cross-fertilized each other (thus Watson 2013).

Yet one of the more intriguing aspects of the texts we are studying is precisely the question of their historic place, and sometimes even their literary presentation, as in some sense "hidden," *apokrypha*. This notion has had a variety of meanings in different contexts.

The Old Testament already implies the possibility of hidden secret knowledge that can be revealed only by God rather than by human inquiry: the God of Israel alone is the author and dispenser of wisdom (Prov. 1:7; 2:6; 20:27; cf. Job 12:22; Amos 3:7). A classically influential text in this respect was Deuteronomy 29:28 (29:29 in the Vulgate and most English translations), famously supplied in Masoretic manuscripts (and still in the standard modern critical edition, *Biblia Hebraica Stuttgartensia*) with ten scribal dots marked across particular words to warn against dangerous speculation: "The secret things belong to the LORD our God, but the revealed things belong to us and to our children forever, to observe all the words of this law." The "secrets" in this case may well denote the future, as the preceding context implies (so Fishbane 1985, 540), but for

Wisdom literature like Sirach 3:22 (cf. 20:30) or Tobit 12:7 there are other secrets of wisdom that should be kept concealed from the uninitiated. (See further Bockmuehl 1990, 66–68.)

Matters are once again different for the Christian texts related to the gospels, with which we are here concerned. Certainly it is true that anathemas or assertions of their "apocryphal" status (e.g., in documents like the Gelasian Decree, cf. above, p. 32) are denials of legitimacy or authority. This derogatory usage seems at least implicitly to be found as early as Hegesippus in the second century (cited in Eusebius, *Ecclesiastical History* 4.22.8: apocrypha composed by heretics) and Origen in the third (e.g., *Commentary on John* 2.31.188; *Commentary on Matthew* 10.18; *Epistle to Africanus* [Migne 1857–86, 11:65, 80]).

That said, some of the noncanonical gospels do indeed make explicit claims to contain material that is hidden, secret, or indeed—in that specific sense—apocryphal. Most obvious among these is the *Gospel of Thomas,* which famously begins with the words, "These are the *secret* words which the living Jesus spoke, and which Didymus Judas Thomas wrote" (incipit). A similar claim opens the *Gospel of Judas*, which claims to present "the *secret* discourse of revelation that Jesus spoke with Judas Iscariot" (Codex Tchacos 33). By implication the Lord's instruction to Mary Magdalene in the *Gospel of Mary* is similarly identified as secret by Peter within that text (*Gospel of Mary* 17; see Tuckett 2007, 127, 188). The gnostic library of Nag Hammadi contains several other examples.

So it is interesting that the term "apocryphal" crops up as a deliberate self-designation in the opening statement or framing narrative of (frequently gnostic) texts that propose their material by means of the literary fiction of an alternative, "hidden" tradition about Jesus. Such hiddenness may be intended to emphasize that this Jesus is not part of the mainstream gospel tradition on which the subsequent text draws and which it seeks to interpret, supplement, or occasionally to subvert. It is thus hidden in the sense of being unfamiliar or unknown to the mainstream public gospel tradition, but also—indeed already in the *Gospel of Thomas*—in the sense of conveying something deliberately concealed because it is intrinsically difficult to understand and requires insider knowledge for its explanation. Compare *Thomas* 1: "And he [Jesus? Thomas?] said: the one who finds the interpretation of these words will not taste death." In texts like *Thomas* that manifest gnosticizing sympathies, then, the

39

terminology of *apokryphos* may thus be deliberately adopted and endorsed to convey difficult saving knowledge for the spiritual elite, while attaching to this a claim (implicit or indeed explicit) of antiquity and authority. Both Hippolytus and especially Irenaeus take it for granted that what sets Valentinians and other gnostic "heretics" apart from catholic Christianity is that they emphasize the secrecy of their writings and their meetings (e.g., Hippolytus, *Refutation of All Heresies* 1, preface; 6.1, 4, 36, 37; 9.10; 10.8; Irenaeus, *Against Heresies* 1, preface; 3.2–4 and passim).

Jesus' private teaching of his disciples is as such, of course, a theme already familiar from the Gospel of Mark (most famously in 4:12); but the difference here is that the secret is evidently something to be publicly disclosed after the resurrection and publicly intended for all who respond in faith (contrast Mark 9:9; 14:9; cf. 16:15; Matt. 10:27).

In this sense, it turns out that the contrast between "apocryphal" gospels and mainstream sacred Scripture is at one level quite in keeping with the self-definition of such texts. Writings like *Thomas* that stake an explicit claim to secrecy appear deliberately to position themselves in competition with liturgically public, nonapocryphal Jesus tradition. Indeed their claimed superiority actually presupposes the prior givenness of *non*secret, accessible writings that already carry some sort of public authoritative character. And leaving aside the contested question of whether isolated sayings in (say) *Thomas* might indeed convey earlier strands of Jesus tradition, overall this self-identification acknowledges its own distance from the antecedent gospel literature.

In this sense, as H. Förster (2013, 144–45) also points out, while the New Testament gospels were indeed authoritative texts that in time "became canonical," it is rather more problematic to assume that other gospel-like texts, after originally occupying the same ground as the Four, had then necessarily "become" apocryphal only by an act of formal exclusion. This is sometimes claimed (e.g., by Lührmann and Schlarb 2000; cf. also the general argument of Watson 2013, e.g., 606). While such a scenario is of course conceivable and worth considering for any given case, in most of the more prominent instances (including *Thomas*, *Mary*, and *Judas*) a more accurate description would envisage texts that *remained* apocryphal, in their quite self-conscious and deliberate competition with those that became canonical.

40

It is perhaps also important that many other extracanonical texts do *not* claim to be in any sense hidden or secret rivals to the protocanonical gospels. Certainly this is true of second-century writings counted among the Apostolic Fathers or the Apologists, but it also pertains to certain infancy gospels, Jewish Christian gospels, and the gospel harmony known as the *Diatessaron*.

It is an interesting, if slippery, corroboration of this point that none of the New Testament writings one might deem pseudonymous makes any analogous claim to preserve a secret, alternative connection to Jesus or to the church's apostolic origins. All these texts claim on the contrary to stand within the same public, "catholic and apostolic" tradition.

Importantly, moreover, there are no known *gospel* texts, either extant or otherwise attested, that became apocryphal after having once been widely normative or authoritative—let alone canonical. The Synoptic Sayings Source Q, if it existed, could potentially be an exception; but quite apart from any intrinsic questions about Q it matters that no assertion of normativity for this hypothetical document can be found in antiquity (see further discussion on p. 89 below). Another exception to prove the rule is the widely popular *Diatessaron*, a harmony of the protocanonical gospels that eventually gave way to the discrete canonical Four. But no known individual gospel, inside or outside the canon, *began* in a normative ecclesial mainstream and *then* became unequivocally apocryphal.

This observation tends to lend further credence to the impression that the apocryphal gospels are instead—often indirectly and in part—*epiphenomenal* on the gospel tradition that became canonical. In other words, contrary to the impression frequently conveyed in some popular media (and occasionally reinforced by scholarly constructs), *the fourfold gospel is not the endpoint of centuries of complete uncertainty about which of many gospels might be normative*. Even while debate continued about certain minor epistles and Revelation, no such sustained doubt ever affected Matthew, Mark, Luke, or John either in the early manuscript tradition or in preserved second-century discussions like those of Serapion, Irenaeus, Justin, and Papias. We have previously cited in this connection Theophilus of Antioch, the *Epistle of the Apostles*, and other second-century sources. But it is worth adding here the much-debated but probably late-second-century list of authoritative writings known as the Muratorian Canon, which survives only in a fragmentary translation into a barbaric pidgin Latin. This puzzling document, too, never-theless references precisely four gospels: the text begins in midsen-tence with a conclusion on Mark before introducing Luke as the third gospel and John as the fourth. (Its certainty about the four gospels seems particularly telling in view of the omission of New Testament documents like Hebrews, 1–2 Peter, and James along with the apparent inclusion of the Book of Wisdom, the *Apocalypse of Peter*, and possibly the *Shepherd of Hermas*.)

Should We Use the Term "Apocryphal"?

On the subject of terminology, common usage does not necessarily distinguish between "noncanonical" and "apocryphal" gospels. The second of these terms is more widely known and often preferred, and is therefore retained in the title of this book for pragmatic rea-sons; its continuation has similarly been advocated by Ehrman and Pleše (2011, vii) and Markschies (1998; 2012g, 18–21).

That said, there are reasons to be cautious and circumspect about this terminology and to note the advantages of the more neutral term "noncanonical." First, while "apocryphal" in its Greek etymology derives from the word *apokryphon*, meaning sim-ply "hidden," in time it acquired a more ambivalent significance. "Apocryphal" writings might then be hidden either in the sense of communicating a knowledge reserved only for the few, or else per-haps as concealing secretive or conspiratorial knowledge as opposed to (and perhaps subversive of) the received public teaching of the church and its Scriptures.

Both of these meanings might function either as a posi-tive claim on the part of a book's advocates or as a negative value judgment about a text whose opponents deem it to be damaging, defamatory, and perhaps wholly fictitious. Neither of these over-tones seems appropriate to the noncanonical gospels. Many are not obviously "hidden" at all, whether in an elitist or a subversive sense. Conversely, as we saw earlier, a handful of these texts actually claim hiddenness or secrecy for themselves as a *positive* quality—beginning arguably with the incipit of the *Gospel of Thomas*. So the term "apocryphal" might seem to skew the discussion, one way or another, from the start.

42 As applied to books often called "apocryphal" by Protestants and "deuterocanonical" by Roman Catholics in relation to the *Old*

Testament, the significance of the terminology is rather different, and indeed almost equivalent to "noncanonical." In the narrowest sense, the "apocryphal" label is here a Protestant designation implying that books contained in the Greek (Septuagint) or Latin (Vulgate) but not in the Hebrew Old Testament carry no canonical authority. In this case, their "apocryphal" status pertains not to any secrecy but to a perceived lack of authority—though the deuterocanonical books are in fact liturgically used in Roman Catholic and (with slight variations) Orthodox Churches, as well as by some Anglicans.

By contrast, *none* of the so-called apocryphal gospels appear in the canon of any major Christian tradition (though see below on the *Epistle of the Apostles*, p. 215).

"The" Apocryphal Gospels?

Given the lack of any agreed-upon inventory, even the frequently encountered definite article "*The* Apocryphal Gospels" turns out to be misleading. It seems to imply the existence of an identifiable set of texts. But in reality it may be impossible to create a definitive list. Not only are we confronted with numerous fragments that may or may not be part of larger documents, but the textual traditions themselves often appear to be highly unstable and volatile compounds of which each new manuscript, and each new translation, may in fact be the creation of a new or secondary apocryphon. The so-called infancy gospels are a particularly accessible case in point (see Voicu 2011, 408–11), but various "gnostic" and "Jewish Christian" traditions present comparable challenges.

This point about the volatility of our texts becomes even more problematic if we recognize that comparable documents continued to be produced throughout antiquity into the Middle Ages and beyond. Does any and every literary retelling of the life of Jesus qualify, even once the New Testament's canonical boundaries are firmly drawn?

For this reason, too, neither forty nor some other figure can offer a definitive or exhaustive total count of "the" apocryphal gospels.

"Fragmentary" Gospels?

Another problem of taxonomy in inventories like the above is that so much of what we have is either highly fragmentary or indeed known to us only from brief citations or allusions in other ancient

43

texts. In many cases at Oxyrhynchus, in patristic citations, or elsewhere, the surviving fragments do not amount to enough material to give us confidence about the shape of the original document. For any given text, are we dealing perhaps simply with a single narrative episode or set of sayings, or even with a longer but still strictly limited set of passion or resurrection material? Or must we think of it as either a part or the whole of an integral composition, whether a continuous narrative account of the ministry of Jesus or a complete collection of sayings? What if the fragments we have are in fact all there ever was? Since in many instances the extant fragment may be the only one of its kind, these supposedly "fragmentary" gospels often leave us with more questions than answers.

Among the relevant examples are several Jewish Christian gospels, which are mentioned numerous times in antiquity but are known only from brief snippets of text. Some of these papyri and patristic citations *are* de facto fragmentary in their extant state. But in many cases it is impossible to be certain about the overall nature and shape of the document concerned—for example, whether it was only a sayings collection or also a narrative, and whether that narrative covered the entire ministry of Jesus or only one aspect of it. Were some of them perhaps only ever intended to *supplement* the retelling of an existing (canonical or harmonized) gospel outline rather than to constitute part of an entire alternative account? As we will see, there are reasons to think this may have been the case for the so-called Jewish Christian gospels. Perhaps the best-known example of such an "intruded" episode is the story of the adulterous woman that eventually attached itself to the end of John 7 (7:53–8:11) in the third century, perhaps to answer the Pharisees' challenge of 7:15 (but in some manuscripts it follows 7:36; 7:44; or Luke 21:38; see further Keith 2009). That said, the actual number of such "intrusions" in the textual tradition of the gospels remains remarkably small.

Or there are the discourse collections—including short fragments, more extensive texts like the gospels of *Thomas* or *Philip,* and, for that matter, the sayings source Q, if it ever existed. And there are episodic narrative texts, including somewhat more extensive ones like the infancy gospels of *James* and *Thomas* and passion accounts like the gospels of *Peter* and (much later) *Nicodemus.*

44

But it concentrates the mind to consider that we do not have a single surviving alternative ancient narrative account of Jesus'

ministry ranging from the baptism of Jesus to his death and resurrection. Is it possible that this narrative structure, which is held in
common by the four canonical gospels, was by the noncanonical
writers either ignored or else (and more typically) used as a rough-
and-ready scaffold in which to insert supplementary or substituted
episodes of "rewritten gospel" (somewhat in analogy to the "rewritten Bible" or "rewritten Scripture" technique attested in the Dead
Sea Scrolls and other ancient Jewish and Christian texts)? We will
need to revisit these questions (see, e.g., p. 87).

Agrapha

A related question concerns the so-called agrapha or "unwritten"
sayings of Jesus, which surface in a wide range of early Christian
writings, in certain variant New Testament manuscripts (e.g., Codex
Bezae, or D in the standard text-critical designation), and even in
the mainstream text of the New Testament itself (esp. at Acts 20:35,
where Luke has Paul quote a saying of Jesus that appears nowhere
in his gospel).

The problematic nature of agrapha as originally conceived has
become increasingly clear in a number of respects. Most obvious
is the paradox that this material survives by definition in literary
sources and is therefore not unwritten in any meaningful sense.
Further, the distinction between agrapha and fragmentary gospels
is sometimes a matter of degree rather than of kind: some isolated
sayings might in theory be excerpted from larger sayings collections
(like the *Gospel of Thomas*) while, conversely, some of the collections may be anthologies of such individual sayings. There is also
the less compelling objection to any definition of agrapha based on
a distinction between canonical and noncanonical sayings, which
Ehrman and Pleše (2011, 351) in a somewhat curious dichotomy
deem "a decision that involves theological rather than historical
judgments."

Relevant inventories therefore vary considerably, but involve
at a minimum a number of New Testament sayings not recorded
in the gospels (e.g., Acts 20:35, "It is more blessed to give than to
receive") and undesignated variants in the textual tradition (e.g.,
in Codex D: Mark 9:49, "Every sacrifice will be salted with salt,"
and Luke 6:4, where Jesus says to a man working on the Sabbath,
"Man, if you know what you are doing, you are blessed; but if you

45

do not know, you are cursed and a transgressor of the law"). Among the many other sayings, the most notable include several in *2 Clement*, such as a brief dialogue with Peter in which Jesus encourages the disciples to be as sheep even in the midst of ravenous wolves (5.2–4; cf. P.Oxy. 4009 below, p. 148) as well as an enigmatic statement that the kingdom will come "when the two will be one and the outside like the inside, and the male with the female will be neither male nor female" (12.2–6, also echoed in *Gospel of Thomas* 22; also *2 Clem.* 4.5).

Clement of Alexandria also cites a number of logia ("sayings"; singular: logion) like "Ask for the big things, and the small things will be given to you as well" (*Stromateis* 1.24.158) and "My mystery is for me and the children of my house" (5.10.63, also in Pseudo-Clementine *Homilies* 19.19–20, and several other writers); Origen quotes "Be clever bankers" (*Commentary on John*, 19.7.2).

Some of these isolated sayings could in theory feature among the oldest parts of the Jesus tradition. But the majority seem more clearly the derivative product of reported speech, paraphrase, expansion, or quotation from memory. They are sometimes placed on the lips of Jesus in edifying or homiletical settings or indeed as devotionally experienced, rather than necessarily intended as recording authentic pre-Easter sayings.

Illustrations of this point abound from the earliest to the latest examples in Christian antiquity. The memory of what "he said to me" in prayer is already part of the apostle Paul's spirituality: 2 Corinthians 12:8–9. In the fifth or sixth century, the recently published P.Monts.Roca IV 59 (inv. no. 996), in an apparently homiletical or meditative context, includes a saying of the Lord that might be rendered as "it has been kept to pronounce sweet words" (see Torallas Tovar and Worp 2014, 164–67).

It is significant that, as Jens Schröter has demonstrated, the gospel tradition's "recollection" of Jesus is from the start articulated within an integrated complex of sayings *and* narrative. Individual agrapha and short dialogue units are in that connection much more likely to "emerge secondarily to the already existing gospels" (Schröter 2013b, 130–32, 262). This is an important corrective to formerly widespread views that imagined the gospels growing instead "from bare sayings" to full narrative lives (so again recently Hägg 2012, 148–86 and blurb).

46

Recent scholarship has tended to restrict the number of texts being considered under this heading—in particular by omitting clearly derivative or misattributed material, sayings of the pre- or post-incarnate Jesus, and non-Christian sources.

The most recent German edition (Markschies and Schröter 2012) for the first time considers these sayings under the three categories of (1) noncanonical sayings of the (earthly) Jesus (Hofius 2012; on this somewhat minimalist reading just seven early sayings are not derivative); (2) Jesus logia from Nag Hammadi texts other than apocryphal gospels (Plisch 2012b: five units from *Testimony of Truth* [NHC IX,3] and *Interpretation of Knowledge* [NHC XI,1]); and (3) sayings of Jesus in Arabic and Islamic literature (Eissler 2012: ten logia from the Qur'an and thirty-one traditions from post-Qur'anic sources of the seventh and later centuries).

While Otfried Hofius (2012; following his teacher Jeremias [1964]; cf. Hofius 1991) focuses on potentially "authentic" sayings of the "historical Jesus," recent scholarship has been more open to the development of such material from the perspective of the reception history of both canonical and noncanonical gospel traditions. As Elliott (1993, 26) rightly notes in critique of Hofius's minimalism, notions of "authenticity" and "originality" are not normally thought pertinent to the selection of apocryphal gospels. That said, Elliott himself opts for a relatively sparse account (26–30), while Ehrman and Pleše (2011, 351–67) argue for an economical but more "representative" identification of agrapha as "sayings allegedly spoken by the historical Jesus that are recorded in documents other than the surviving gospels (canonical or non-canonical)." (Contrast further the more expansive collections of Morrice 1997 and Stroker 1989.)

"Lost" Gospels?

Another category problem is presented by documents whose existence is asserted by either ancient or modern authors, but which may be either fictive or hypothetical. Most famous among the latter is the so-called Q source of sayings material shared by Matthew and Luke, which is still widely affirmed in Synoptic Gospel scholarship. We will return to this in a separate section (p. 89).

Several other hypothetical "lost" gospels have been postulated from time to time. Among these are first editions of the existing

47

canonical gospels (Proto-Mark, Proto-Luke, etc.), as well as miscellaneous other narrative or sayings sources adduced to explain certain parts of the gospel tradition. John Dominic Crossan, for example, proposes a text called the "Cross Gospel" that he believes to underlie the canonical passion narratives as well as the noncanonical *Gospel of Peter* (Crossan 1988, 1991, 2007; cf. p. 137 below), while Francis Watson (2013) more recently has substituted a source he calls SC (Sayings Collection), which in his view predates the canonical gospels and is most conservatively preserved in the *Gospel of Thomas*.

None of these other hypothetical sources have been found compelling by a significant number of scholars, and not one is a document whose real existence, let alone whose ancient identity as a gospel, has been demonstrated.

Even so, this is not to deny that some gospels were indeed lost in antiquity: the list above from the Gelasian Decree contains a number of plausible examples, and Markschies (2012c) discusses others (cf. above, table 2, p. 27), several of which our discussion references in passing. All in all, however, we have no reason to think that lost gospels constitute a literary category in their own right. Rather than being unique, such texts are far more likely to belong to one or another familiar genre. Even many of the apocryphal gospels we will discuss survive only in a single copy and were "lost" until they were rediscovered.

How to Organize the Texts: A Taxonomy

How then should we structure the available evidence, using what we know to be an inevitably partial inventory of (so-called or self-styled) gospels, along with numerous other ancient texts and fragments that present gospel-like narrative or teaching about Jesus of Nazareth?

A quick comparison of the tables of contents in recent editions and textbooks illustrates the reality of the problem by showing a variety of often incompatible organizing principles. Some, like Christopher Tuckett, Hans-Josef Klauck, Paul Foster, and Christoph Markschies, recognize the difficulty of consistent classification and try to address it by variously mixing historical, literary, and linguistic categories with narrative or even geographic ones (e.g., for Nag Hammadi). This unfortunately leaves us with an unwieldy hybrid. Markschies and Schröter (2012) have compiled the most comprehensive collection but are left with an even more impenetrable taxonomy, the rationale for which is inadequately elaborated in an otherwise magisterial and wide-ranging introduction.

A number of serviceable schemes exist, including some that sort the texts by theological orientation and others by literary or geographic criteria. In the end, a degree of eclecticism is probably inevitable in choosing which particular documents to focus on. Here I will adopt a fourfold taxonomy patterned loosely on elements of the New Testament gospels' narrative typology, developing insights drawn from Christopher Tuckett and Paul Foster. Tuckett (2005, 243–48) suggests four categories:

- Narrative gospels
- Sayings gospels
- Birth and infancy gospels
- Resurrection discourses

As Tuckett points out, the fragmentary nature of much of our material inevitably leaves our judgments about these categories provisional, and certain texts arguably belong to more than one category. But perhaps this is not the best we can do. There is a certain awkwardness in juxtaposing essentially *literary* categories of narrative and sayings genres with essentially *narrative* ones relating to the infancy and resurrection of Jesus. In terms of literary genre, Tuckett's third category could arguably fold into the first, and the fourth into the second. Some editors in fact simply distinguish two headings, sayings and narratives (e.g., Cameron 1982, 7).

Paul Foster (2009) produces similar categories but introduces an additional twist:

- "Gospels" from Nag Hammadi
- Infancy gospels
- Gospels during the earthly life of Jesus
- Secret revelations and dialogue gospels

Once again there is a certain clash of literary and biographical categories. Clustering the Nag Hammadi texts together under

49

a separate heading of their own (an archaeological or perhaps geographical one) has a certain neatness about it, and at least in this case contextualizes like with like. And yet, as Foster acknowledges, these texts are vastly different from one another in form and substance, so it seems better not to prejudge the question of whether in origin, intent, or function they belong together. In any case the remainder of Foster's outline seems tethered to a biographical sequence, especially when one realizes that the last genre is almost exclusively cast in a post-resurrection setting.

Genre distinctions are quite often somewhat crude and arbitrary. On the other hand, the attempt to offer finer distinctions very quickly turns unwieldy. Compare, for example, Hans-Josef Klauck's taxonomy of no fewer than twelve categories, deployed in his introduction to the apocryphal gospels (2003):

- Agrapha (unwritten, "scattered" words of Jesus)
- Fragments
- Jewish Christian gospels
- Two gospels of the Egyptians
- Infancy gospels
- Gospels about Jesus' death and resurrection
- Gospels from Nag Hammadi
- Dialogues with the risen Jesus
- Nonlocalized dialogues with Jesus
- Legends about Mary's death
- Lost gospels
- An antigospel

Large collections like that of Markschies and Schröter (2012) resort to even more complicated and cumbersome lists (above, table 2, p. 27; cf. previously Schneemelcher 1991–92, vol. 1). Complex mixtures of literary and biographical categories are deployed by Elliott (1993) and Robert Miller (1994), while Ehrman's 2003 book gives no account of order or taxonomy at all (though he remedies this in Ehrman and Pleše 2011; 2014).

We clearly need to start somewhere. Tuckett's attractive breakdown of narrative, sayings, infancy, and resurrection quite reasonably points in a direction that is largely guided by the explicit content and setting of these documents themselves, without unduly prejudging questions of context, literary criticism, or interpretation.

Further along this line, I suggest, the most promising and least prejudicial taxonomy of these documents is therefore quite reasonably *narratival* rather than literary-analytical. In other words, it seems advisable to map the extracanonical sources onto the basic structure of the New Testament's narrative gospels, in relation to which they most often position themselves. Among recent writers this decision is, for example, similarly adopted with minor variations by Ehrman and Pleše (2011), who follow the threefold division of (1) infancy gospels, (2) ministry gospels, and (3) passion, resurrection, and post-resurrection gospels.

This is also the approach we will take in the present volume. It seems best to structure the documents under four broadly biographical headings:

- Infancy
- Ministry
- Passion
- Resurrection

Similar or related finds from an important geographic location (e.g., Nag Hammadi) will also fit this scheme without undue difficulty—sometimes because interest in one or another of these headings predominates. Fragmentary gospels on papyrus, too, tend to be identifiable along these lines. The scheme arguably remains serviceable even where the writers apparently do not know, or do not accept, a biographical account of Jesus' life: the focus in such cases is often on one *aspect* of the Jesus tradition that implicitly functions in a way that in other sources forms part of a narrative whole—be it the instruction of the risen Jesus or the parable-like sayings of his earthly teaching.

Where to Read the Noncanonical Gospels Today

Given the lively interest and controversy the noncanonical gospels have generated since at least the nineteenth century, it is puzzling that for quite a long time these texts nevertheless remained relatively difficult for the general public to access. Until the late twentieth century, English translations were often partial, expensive, and not always up to date (e.g., James 1924; the two editions of Hennecke, Schneemelcher, and Wilson 1963; Schneemelcher 1991–92). The mid-1990s produced a couple of more serviceable but still partial translations, Elliott 1993 as well as Robert Miller 1994. Elliott 2006 additionally contained a useful "synopsis" specifically of the infancy gospels. At the time of writing the most accessible and reasonably priced collection and translation of non-canonical gospels, in both paper and e-book versions, is Ehrman and Pleše 2014. (This is also available in a useful four-language edition with facing pages in Greek, Latin, or Coptic [Ehrman and Pleše 2011]. The 2014 edition updates their translation of the *Gospel of Judas* and additionally includes the *Unknown Berlin Gospel* [*Gospel of the Savior*] and the *Discourse on the Cross* [the Stauros Text from Qasr El-Wizz].)

For the gospel-like texts from Nag Hammadi, several editions still advise readers to consult the exhaustive but expensive and unwieldy five-volume *Coptic Gnostic Library* (Robinson 2000). A more recent and handier, if still costly, bilingual Coptic-German edition is Nagel 2014, which contains specifically gospels and Acts material from Nag Hammadi. The most accessible English translation is that of Meyer 2007.

The most complete translation, with an outstanding monograph-length critical overview by Christoph Markschies as well as individual introductions to the texts, is at present available in German only (Markschies and Schröter 2012). Its translation into English seems highly desirable but also liable to prove a complex undertaking in view not only of the volume of material but also of the often contested and rapidly shifting lines of scholarly debate.

In what follows I will take as my base texts Ehrman and Pleše 2011/2014 wherever possible, as theirs is a widely available set of translations. Students of the original languages are strongly encouraged to consult the 2011 multilingual volume. Since the available space does not permit us to do full justice to all thirty-seven of this edition's "gospels," we will foreground the most important and supplement this with brief treatments of texts not included by Ehrman and Pleše, particularly a number of dialogue gospels from Nag Hammadi (drawing on the translation of Meyer 2007). For each document, I offer a brief historical introduction and survey of the content, concluding with an analysis in relation to some or all of the five interpretive emphases outlined above (see pp. 28–31).

52

Suggested Further Reading

Texts

Ehrman, Bart D., and Zlatko Pleše, eds. 2011. *The Apocryphal Gospels: Texts and Translations*. New York: Oxford University Press.

———, eds. 2014. *The Other Gospels: Accounts of Jesus from Outside the New Testament*. New York: Oxford University Press.

Meyer, Marvin W., ed. 2007. *The Nag Hammadi Scriptures: The International Edition*. New York: HarperOne.

General

Foster, Paul. 2009. *The Apocryphal Gospels: A Very Short Introduction*. Oxford: Oxford University Press.

Hengel, Martin. 2000. *The Four Gospels and the One Gospel of Jesus Christ: An Investigation of the Collection and Origin of the Canonical Gospels*. Trans. J. Bowden. London: SCM Press.

Hurtado, Larry W. 2006. *The Earliest Christian Artifacts: Manuscripts and Christian Origins*. Grand Rapids: Eerdmans.

———. 2013. "Christian Literary Texts in Manuscripts of Second & Third Centuries." http://larryhurtado.files.wordpress.com/2010/07/second-third-century-christian-texts1.pdf.

Markschies, Christoph. 2015. *Christian Theology and Its Institutions in the Early Roman Empire: Prolegomena to a History of Early Christian Theology*. Translated by W. Coppins. Baylor-Mohr Siebeck Studies in Early Christianity. Waco, TX: Baylor University Press.

Nicklas, Tobias. 2011. "'Apokryph Gewordene Schriften'? Gedanken zum Apokryphenbegriff bei Grosskirchlichen Autoren und in einigen 'Gnostischen' Texten." In *"In Search of Truth": Augustine, Manichaeism and Other Gnosticism; Studies for Johannes van Oort at Sixty*, edited by J. A. van der Berg et al., 547–65. Leiden: Brill.

Tuckett, Christopher. 2005. "Forty Other Gospels." In *The Written Gospel*, edited by M. Bockmuehl and D. A. Hagner, 238–53. Cambridge: Cambridge University Press.

Watson, Francis. 2016. *The Fourfold Gospel: A Theological Reading of the New Testament Portraits of Jesus*. Grand Rapids: Baker Academic.

53

CHAPTER 2

Infancy Gospels

In keeping with the narrative outline suggested above, we begin by looking at gospel-like texts associated with the birth and childhood of Jesus and with the family origins especially of his mother, Mary.

Multiple ancient and medieval texts are associated with the birth and childhood of Jesus and its antecedents, in a host of different languages and manuscripts. Among these, the best known are the *Infancy Gospel of James* and the *Infancy Gospel of Thomas*, each in several different text forms; the *Arabic Infancy Gospel* and the *Gospel of Pseudo-Matthew* with several alternative versions or variants dependent upon it (including the so-called Arundel form and numerous other medieval translations); and the so-called *History of Joseph the Carpenter*. (See Ehrman and Pleše 2011, nos. 1–6 [pp. 3–160]; cf. Markschies and Schröter 2012, 1.2:886–1029; 1:308–42.) In this chapter we will foreground the two most important and influential of these texts, the *Infancy Gospel of James* and the *Infancy Gospel of Thomas*, before going on to comment more briefly on others.

Why Infancy Gospels?

Whether by design or inadvertently, the canonical gospels implicitly invite the thought that the origin and youth of Jesus perhaps harbored rather more of interest than is recorded in the relatively economical accounts of Matthew and Luke, let alone in the even more taciturn Mark and John.

Given the New Testament nativity stories' pervasive influence on the history of Christianity, it is easy to forget that only two of its gospels offer us birth and infancy narratives at all. Mark's interest in the background of Jesus extends only to his spiritual home in the ministry of John the Baptist, while John's Gospel finds the origin of Jesus emphatically in his incarnation as the eternal Logos of God. Mark introduces Jesus at the point of his encounter with John the Baptist, but without any prior biographical information (Mark 1:9). John's Gospel, by contrast, speaks of his origins in philosophical and theological rather than biographical terms and otherwise leaves the reader guessing—even in the face of repeated insinuations on the part of Jesus' enemies about the identity of his father or his place of birth (John 1:46; 6:42; 7:42; 8:19, 41).

Mark and John thus provide few answers about where Jesus came from, or indeed what he did for the first thirty years of his life. Explanations for this silence have not infrequently been sought in Mark's ignorance and John's rejection of any birth or infancy traditions of Jesus, including perhaps the Lucan and Matthean claim about Joseph not being his real father. For Mark and John, "high" Christology appears not to require a miraculous nativity (see Frey 2011).

But what accounts for this silence in two of the four New Testament Gospels? Absence of evidence is not of course evidence of absence; and omission may or may not imply ignorance, let alone denial. We may recall that just as Paul asserts only a derivative role in the transmission of Jesus tradition (1 Cor. 11:23; 15:3), so too Mark's Peter and John's Beloved Disciple are staged and remembered by their literary executors in terms of what they saw and heard—by implication sidelining other matters. An interest in Davidic and other family lore about exceptional paternity may well have played little part in that construal, even if these evangelists were aware of it (and, in John's case, might be ironically implying just that: John 7:42; 8:19, 41; and in that light 1:46 and 6:42). Yet despite John's stirring and formative identification of Jesus' origin as the divine Word made flesh, evidently no one looked to either John or Mark for encouragement to think more deeply about Jesus' childhood, birth, and family background.

56

Even Matthew and Luke, of course, offer quite differently pitched accounts both of Jesus' family tree and of the circumstances surrounding his birth and infancy. Neither of them appears particularly interested in the life of Joseph or of Mary, Jesus' mother. And neither offers much information about his childhood or youth until he emerges from the shadows in his late twenties as a follower of John the Baptist.

Particularly in view of the ground they concede to narrative interest in the birth of Jesus, both Matthew and Luke seem to invite speculation about his family origins and infancy almost by design. Matthew tantalizingly abandons his economical narrative of the boy Jesus not long after his return from Egypt perhaps not yet three years old, resuming only with the thirty-year-old's baptism by John (cf. Matt. 2:16, 19–21; 3:13).

Luke never asserts, nor ever attracted, a close literary association with the name of an apostle; but he claims that he consulted eyewitnesses—and that the contemporary who thought more about the nativity than anyone else was Jesus' mother, Mary. Luke introduces the motif that Mary's story matters even before Jesus is born, and that it is she who synthesizes the theological significance of the annunciation and birth of Jesus—perhaps above all in the Magnificat (Luke 1:46–55). The Lukan stories of the nativity and of the boy Jesus in the Temple at Passover are each followed by the assurance that "Mary treasured all these words and pondered them in her heart" (2:19, 51). And these two stories bracket a childhood of Jesus about which the evangelist tells us not once but twice that "the child grew and became strong, filled with wisdom; and the favor of God was upon him" (2:40; cf. 2:52). In this way he unabashedly implies that there was a great deal more to think about than he records. Luke returns to the story just once, with the twelve-year-old Jesus' visit to the Temple at Passover and his subsequent adolescence in submission to Joseph and to Mary at Nazareth, where he "increased in wisdom and in years, and in divine and human favor" (2:51–52).

It is little wonder, then, that devout Christian imagination and reflection on these texts should find itself led to ask what *else* might have characterized that birth and childhood. Interest in the family origins of Jesus, and more particularly in his relatives, was certainly widespread and influential among Jewish Christians and others in the early church (see, e.g., Bauckham 1990; Lambers-Petry 2003). Examples include the second-century traditions about the grandsons of Jesus' brother or half-brother, Jude, documented by the fourth-century writers Eusebius and Epiphanius. Assertions about

57

his virgin birth and descent from David garnered extensive interest and debate on the part of Christians themselves and, more skeptically, of their enemies (see further Bockmuehl 2011).

It is significant that both Matthew and Luke articulate a *public* dimension for these otherwise sketchy childhood stories: we read about magi, shepherds, a presentation in the Temple, correlations to public historical events or figures, and so on. And for both Gospels these events are profoundly relevant to the identity of Jesus as the scripturally adumbrated Messiah who emerges fully in the later narrative.

All that, we may suppose, provides a fertile soil for the emergence of gospel-like stories elaborating the family background, birth, and childhood of Jesus. Devout imagination found plenty of food for curiosity in the evocative but minimally sketched infancy narratives of Matthew and Luke (If a similar provocation was constituted by Mark's silence about the past of a Jesus who appears out of nowhere to be baptized by John, Matthew and Luke may already attest precisely the eloquent fertility of such reserve about Jesus' origin.)

Such stimulus to textual development was not just light entertainment. Early Christians clearly recognized in the infancy stories an invitation to prolific devotional and theological engagement with the nature of the incarnation—and thus with some of the most basic challenges of Christology. How human was this man? How divine? And in what sense could he be fully the son of David, yet also born of a virgin, the eternal Son of God?

The Infancy Gospel of James

The *Infancy Gospel* or *Protevangelium* (Protogospel) *of James* is unfamiliar and relatively unknown to most modern readers. It has received little media attention in recent discussion, compared with the gospels in the names of Thomas and Judas. Dan Brown's *The Da Vinci Code* leaves books like this well alone, and even conservative critics like Bock (2006) and Jenkins (2001) find little need to discuss it. (Text and English translation are readily accessible in Ehrman and Pleše 2011; 2014.)

In fact, however, this text astonishingly towers above all other apocryphal gospels in its effect and influence on subsequent

Christian tradition. Quite unlike any other noncanonical work, this infancy gospel has profoundly shaped how most Christians through the ages and into the twenty-first century have understood and imagined the Christmas story—regardless of whether they have ever even heard of this text.

The *Infancy Gospel* concerns the events leading up to the birth of Jesus and the events immediately following it. It extends the New Testament stories significantly and makes Mary, the mother of Jesus, its central character, notably beginning with narratives about her own family background, birth, and childhood. It is called a proto-evangelium because in a way it tells the gospel *before* the gospel. To help gain a sense of what it is about, we will begin with an overview of its content before asking about its origin and textual tradition.

Content

The first seven chapters of the work deal with the conception, birth, and childhood not of Jesus but of Mary, the daughter of devout and well-to-do Jews by the name of Anna and Joachim, who until that time had been childless. In reflecting on his childlessness, the *Infancy Gospel*'s Joachim is confronted with a belief that childless Israelites are accursed (which also surfaces repeatedly in Origen, Jerome, Augustine, and other church fathers on the basis of a questionable extrapolation from the Old Testament). Joachim seeks anxiously to probe the reasons for his exclusion, fasting for forty days and nights in the wilderness. Anna similarly expresses bitter lament about her condition.

After two visions of angels announcing Mary's birth, Anna in her joy vows to offer the child to the service of God. Great rejoicing follows the birth of Mary, who grows precociously and walks at six months. From the age of three, Mary grows up in the Temple—a motif strikingly similar to Anna's Old Testament namesake Hannah, whose divinely given child Samuel is also given back to God's service in the Israelite shrine at Shiloh (1 Sam. 1).

In chapters 8–16, Mary reaches adolescence and is engaged to her guardian Joseph, a widower with several children from a previous marriage. In Joseph's absence Mary joins a team of virgins weaving a curtain for the Temple. During this time the angel Gabriel visits her at a well and announces the birth of Jesus—despite its fuller narrative detail, this episode shows

59

particular similarities with the Lukan infancy narrative (1:26–38; cf. Matt. 1:21).

As in Luke, Mary soon goes to visit her relative Elizabeth for three months; Elizabeth's husband, Zechariah, is here presented as the high priest. Joseph's return and discovery that Mary is pregnant brings considerable consternation despite Mary's protestations of innocence. Here the narrative introduces and expands a number of motifs from Matthew's narrative. Joseph agrees to shelter and protect Mary after an angel visits him in a dream. Jewish priestly authorities take a probing and critical interest in the irregular pregnancy.

Chapters 17–24, finally, present the story of the birth of Jesus, following the synoptic narrative. Thus Joseph and Mary travel to Bethlehem (though it is not clear if they are coming from Galilee). Mary rides on a donkey that is led by Joseph's older son, perhaps the James who is identified as the older brother of Jesus and the author of this document. Mary gives birth to Jesus in a cave while Joseph is out looking frantically for a midwife. At this point, chapter 18, he relates a vision in which suddenly the whole of time stands still—with clouds and birds paused in midair, animals and people in frozen suspense as the Savior is born.

The baby Jesus is born in Joseph's absence, and in chapters 19–20 Mary's virginity even after the birth is verified by a recklessly nosy Salome, whose hand is burned in the process and then healed by the baby Jesus. The focus then turns to the familiar narrative of the magi and the Holy Family's flight to Egypt to escape Herod's massacre of the children, which here threatens even John the Baptist and results in the murder of his father, Zechariah, by Herod's soldiers (chap. 23). The text ends with the appointment of a new high priest named Simeon and the concluding statement from the author about the circumstances of the document's composition by James in Jerusalem during upheavals following the death of Herod, presumably either Herod the Great in 4 BCE or perhaps more likely Herod Agrippa I in 44 CE, whose brief reign had included a severe persecution of Christians (see Acts 12:1–23).

The work has been designated by different titles throughout history, although the earliest manuscript (Codex Bodmer V of the third or fourth century) identifies it as "Birth of Mary—Revelation of James" (Ehrman and Pleše 2011, 32).

60

Origin and Setting

In order to engage this material sympathetically and critically, we do well initially to suspend judgment about questions such as whether what we find here has any historical bearing or is pure fancy, whether the text is theologically orthodox or not, whether it intends to edify or to unsettle its ecclesial audience, and whether it seeks to enhance or to subvert the reader's confidence in the protocanonical gospel tradition it annotates. In this case, as it happens, we will find the *Infancy Gospel* surprisingly close to quite early orthodox interests in both Mariology and Christology, several of which are clearly present in other second- and third-century Christian sources.

But here we may begin by asking about the document's origin and manuscript tradition. Scholars have long since recognized that this text is dependent on numerous details in the final form of *both* Matthew and Luke—or at least on redactional elements of *both* their narratives. As I suggested in chapter 1 (p. 30), in dealing with non-canonical gospels it is often impossible to prove any *literary* dependence on the canonical gospels or indeed whether such dependence may reflect these two New Testament gospels in aggregate, perhaps via an informal oral harmony. This dynamic of secondary orality or reoralization has been the subject of a number of studies of the gospels, and it will surface repeatedly in this book. (See classically Ong 1982, 136 and passim; cf. esp. Byrskog 2000, 138–44, on the canonical gospels; and Kirk 2007 on the *Gospel of Peter.*)

For purposes of dating, it will be helpful to bear in mind that the *fact* of dependence on the synoptic tradition shows the implied link with the figure of James to be fictional. This "James" is evidently James the Just, the brother of Jesus, who was martyred in 62 CE, potentially two or three decades before the composition of Matthew and Luke. Our document's composition is therefore unlikely to predate the second century.

But the *Infancy Gospel* in any case makes remarkably little of its alleged connection with James the Just: he appears only in the first-person postscript of chapter 25 and in the two-part title at the end. (That colophon's reference to the "Revelation of James" sits awkwardly with "Birth of Mary" and not seem to relate easily to the document's content.) In the Greek, James is identified by the Hebraizing form of the Old Testament name "Jacob" (*Iakōb*) rather

61

than in the hellenized New Testament form translated as "James" (*Iakōbos*). Only in chapter 18 does any speaker or narrator use the first person—and then that person is not James but Joseph. It is in a sense only the reception history of this document that firmly identifies the speaker of chapter 25 with the brother of Jesus.

Such a secondary attribution is of course not dramatically different from the named authorial associations of the canonical Gospels. Nevertheless, most interpreters agree that what the title intends is indeed an attribution to James the Just, the brother of Jesus. He is known (from the New Testament, from the Jewish historian Flavius Josephus, and from second-century Christian authors like Hegesippus) to have been held in great affection as the respected leader of the Jesus movement in Jerusalem and Judea during the 40s and 50s of the first century. Several other surviving documents from diverse points on the early Christian spectrum are associated with his name, including the New Testament Epistle of James and sources incorporated in the late second or early third-century Pseudo-Clementine and Nag Hammadi collections (the *Epistle of James to Peter*, the *Apocryphon of James*, and the *Second Apocalypse of James*). So the *Infancy Gospel* follows a familiar path in appealing to this important apostle. More specifically, we may speculate that for our author and his community this particular attribution might even be said to have carried a certain biographical plausibility in relation to this nativity setting: unlike most other figures of the apostolic generation, James could be envisaged as having had uniquely personal access to the childhood of Jesus.

We have no real certainties about the time of composition, let alone the place. Our author seems notably sympathetic to Palestinian Jewish piety of the period, although only superficially and inaccurately acquainted with its particularities of belief and practices, or even its geographic setting. There are, for example, some odd ideas about Jewish ritual and legal praxis, and the author seems a little unclear about whether Bethlehem is in Judea or outside it. Vaguely Palestinian sensitivities combine with an unsophisticated Septuagintalizing Greek to produce a perspective that shows some cultural proximity to the milieu of Matthew, the *Didache*, and the Lukan infancy stories.

62   Christianity's Jewish origins are of considerable theological importance for our author—and this point is sometimes overlooked by attempts to classify the text as a popular Greco-Roman novel

or perhaps a historicizing encomium, that is, an accolade or florid expression of praise (for examples, see Hock 1995, 10, 15–20). Our text, whether of Syrian or perhaps Egyptian origin, relates to Christianity's Palestinian Jewish origins with distinctly greater interest and sympathy than most other Christian literature of its time, between the late first and the early third century. (A broadly second-century date seems required by dependence on Luke and Matthew on the one hand and the citation in Origen on the other; the earliest manuscript evidence appears ca. 300.)

The *Infancy Gospel of James* is often moving and enthusiastic in its affection for the Holy Family. At the same time, its hagiography rarely if ever comes across as crassly exaggerated or apologetic (except perhaps in its stress on the miraculous circumstances of the birth, 18–19).

Any apologetic notes remain at a relatively simple and popular level. For this reason, they cannot be seen as any kind of concerted late-second-century response to the attack on Christianity's origins by the second-century pagan scholar Celsus (fl. ca. 170–180?), as has sometimes been claimed (e.g., by Ehrman and Pleše 2014, 21). It seems just as plausible that Celsus's learned and well-informed attack was itself prompted in part by a distaste for florid popular Christian hagiographies, including views about Jesus' infancy (cf. Origen, *Against Celsus* 1.28, 32). The *Infancy Gospel of James* may instead anticipate or forestall the sorts of allegations about the origins of Jesus and Mary that Celsus picks up from his Jewish source. The level of engagement or response is certainly too popular and unspecific to suggest any explicit awareness of Celsus.

The question of composition is complex but not particularly enlightening for our purposes. Nineteenth-century scholars proposed a number of sophisticated source and composition theories. But in the absence of textual evidence, confidence about elaborate literary hypotheses is today less common. Although many would still allow for the possibility of multiple sources, the general consistency of style and vocabulary probably does at least favor a single editorial hand in overall charge (so already de Strycker 1961).

Readers sometimes wonder if there can be any kernel of historical reference here. Most scholars regard this infancy gospel as historically worthless, except as a source of second-century piety, and that does seem the safest point of departure. Our text may be assumed to document primarily the second century rather than the

63

first. It illustrates how the family background of Jesus and of his mother were understood in second-century Christian circles sympathetic to Jewish faith and practice.

A standard critical objection to the notion of any early tradition here is that the document's knowledge of first-century Judaism appears romantic and clichéd as well as full of wildly implausible factual errors about the realities of Jewish daily and religious life. In particular, Mary growing up in the Temple, the priestly authorities strangely requiring Joseph to undergo the ordeal of drinking "water of refutation" (cf. Num. 5:11–28 for the woman suspected of adultery), the influential notion of Mary's continuing virginity even after the birth of Jesus, and Zechariah the father of John the Baptist being murdered by Herod the Great have all seemed legendary, implausible, and fanciful.

This judgment is certainly a useful default position. One should not, however, dismiss the possibility that while the writer has no independent access to earlier sources, he seems occasionally to be drawing on traditions that were already popular and indeed largely unquestioned by the early second century. In one or two cases these traditions might conceivably have been nourished by a living memory of the apostolic generation. Among these are ideas like the birth of Jesus in a cave, which church fathers like the Palestinian-born Justin (ca. 100–165) and the Bethlehem-based Jerome (ca. 345–420) both accept. Another pertinent motif is that Mary too is connected to the Davidic line, a belief widely attested from the second century onward and eventually linked to a particular exegesis of Luke (1:27; see more fully Bockmuehl 2011).

More tentatively, attention has also been drawn in recent study of this text to the extraordinary claim noted earlier—that the young Mary, like Samuel at Shiloh, grew up in and around the Temple. It is possible that in this instance, as in one or two others, the vitality of free-ranging legend is interwoven with a slightly better understanding of first-century circumstances than is sometimes allowed for. An interesting case in point is the priestly decision in chapter 10 to assign Mary to a team of young virgins employed in spinning precious thread used to manufacture a new curtain for the Temple. This has struck many a modern interpreter as charming and far-fetched in equal measure. But Jewish sources repeatedly acknowledge the existence of teams of young girls continually involved in weaving replacements for the numerous curtains in the

Temple (including, but not limited to, the *parochet*, the main curtain separating the ark and the holy of holies from the main hall of the Temple, veiling it from sight). Evidence for this is suggested in a late-first-century text like *2 Baruch* 10:18–19 and confirmed in rabbinic literature (e.g., Tosefta *Sheqalim* 2:6 and possibly as early as Mishnah *Sheqalim* 8:5; cf. Babylonian Talmud *Hullin* 90b; *Tamid* 29b; see discussion in Ilan 1997, 139–43).

One insightful recent treatment notes the intriguing correlation between Mary's threefold role as (1) consecrated to the service of God, (2) accused of sexual immorality, and (3) a virgin involved in producing the Temple curtains. This triad of identities corresponds to the only three groups of women who filled an official function in the Temple: female Nazirites, accused adulteresses seeking vindication, and virgins who made the Temple curtains. By connecting all three motifs to the Temple, the writer managed to offer Christians a narrative of origins that remains rooted in Israel's Scripture while also answering Jewish attacks on Mary (cf. Nutzman 2013, 553–54, 578, and passim). This does not of course establish anything at all about historicity, but it does perhaps suggest a religious and hermeneutical setting of this protogospel in closer awareness of Palestinian Jewish realities than has often been acknowledged.

Interpretation

The text often called the *Infancy Gospel of James* has almost nothing to do with James and very little even with the birth and infancy of Jesus. It is instead clearly concerned with Mary first and foremost, and only then with the incarnation and birth of her son— although of course for this author the importance of the former is clearly a function of the latter. As a result, the alternative designation *Protevangelium* is highly appropriate. This work tells the story of Mary; it is the gospel *before* the gospel, articulating the spiritual context into which Jesus is birthed and praising the unique integrity of his divinely favored mother.

The unfolding of this story entails a great deal of implicit Christology. Aside from the emphasis on Mary's virginity, along with her Davidic and Temple connections, perhaps the most poignant confirmation of this is the moment of the incarnation itself, when in Joseph's vision time stands still and creation pauses in worshipful astonishment at the divine birth. Subsequent Christian reflection

65

on the nativity was often captivated by Joseph's vision; among the more striking twentieth-century interpretations is Norman Nicholson's 1951 poem "A Turn for the Better," which takes its opening line from the paradoxical statement in 18:2, "I, Joseph, was walking, and I walked not." (The broader motif of signs and wonders at an important birth had many parallels in other ancient religious contexts: see Bovon 1991, 399; Pellegrini 2012, 924n139. According to Suetonius, miraculous signs and favorable dreams and omens also attended the birth of the poet Virgil: *Virgil* 3–5.)

It is possible that the birth narrative's implicit christological theme carries twin apologetic implications, on the one hand safeguarding the authentically Jewish birth of Jesus from the line of David, while on the other hand ruling out a purely human, adoptionist Christology of the sort that was apparently current in some more sectarian Jewish Christian circles. The primary and explicit focus is at any rate very much on Jesus' birth as the gift of a pure, obedient, and miraculously graced mother.

The *Infancy Gospel* is an early example of Marian theology in the service of Christology. This Marian emphasis is explicitly foregrounded in the document's title as given in 25.4: "Birth of Mary—Revelation of James." One important overarching aspect of this appreciation of Mary is that of her *purity* (words like *katharos* [clean, pure] and *amiantos* [undefiled] are used frequently), developed with a threefold emphasis on Temple purity, menstrual purity, and sexual purity (see Vuong 2013). The narrative reiterates this theme from the story of Joachim and Anna to Mary's birth, childhood, and virginal motherhood of Jesus.

Another reason the Marian connection is so important is because this text explicitly affirms that Mary too is of the "tribe" of David, as we saw (10.1). This intriguing and highly charged conviction is never mentioned in the New Testament, but came to be of key importance for Jewish Christians and others concerned to stress Jesus' true status as Messiah of Israel—grounded in his biological descent from David, as the prophets had envisaged.

The New Testament gospels notoriously fail to resolve a problem at the heart of their genealogies of Jesus: they focus on the Davidic descent of *Joseph*, a man who was for all of them emphatically *not* the father of Jesus. Modern critical commentators tend to assume this problem is solved by Joseph's adoption of Jesus as his son. But in ancient Judaism it was not possible to acquire a

valid genealogy by adoption (see Levin 2006)—a point not lost on
Christianity's second-century Jewish critics, who sometimes liked
to assert that Jesus' doubtful paternity concealed his true origin as
the bastard son of a Roman soldier. (These were among the polemical accusations picked up by the accomplished pagan critic Celsus
in his anti-Christian treatise *The True Discourse* [cited in Origen,
Against Celsus 1.28, 32].)

The *Infancy Gospel of James* thus sets a highly influential precedent for Christian doctrine when it draws so heavily on Mariology
in support of its Christology. While Christology is at the heart of
the fifth-century Nestorian controversy about Mary as "mother of
God" (*theotokos*), the *Infancy Gospel*'s appeal to Mary in relation to
Christology is not without parallel in the second century. Another
early writer to hint at this is Ignatius in his letter *To the Ephesians*
(19.1; cf. 8.2, "son of Mary and Son of God"), and Luke's Gospel of
course implicitly identifies Mary as instrumental through the narrative of the annunciation and the Magnificat (Luke 1:31–35, 48–49).
But the *Infancy Gospel* does seem to be the first text to give explicit
narrative articulation to her unique role. On this, as on one or two
other fronts, it seems at least conceivable that our text incorporates
preexisting Christian traditions.

Transmission and Influence

One of the effects of the *Infancy Gospel* is to accentuate even
further the concern in Matthew and Luke to tether the gospel of
the incarnation to an account of the origins and infancy of Jesus.
Although our text is only about 25 percent of the length of Matthew, that still enormously inflates the sheer bulk of the infancy
traditions (which constitute less than 5 percent of Matthew).

More telling for this text's outstanding prominence and influence among the documents we are discussing in this book, the
Infancy Gospel generated a far larger manuscript tradition than any
other noncanonical gospel. The standard critical edition of Émile
de Strycker 1961 (cf. de Strycker 1980) was able to draw on over
140 mostly medieval Greek manuscripts, of which the earliest dates
back to the third century; today the inventory extends to over 150
manuscripts (cf. Pellegrini 2012, 910).

The Greek textual tradition also generated translations into at
least eight other ancient languages, including Armenian (see Terian

2008) and especially Arabic, which in turn may have had some influence on the considerable prominence of Mary in the Qur'an and traditions of the hadith. Scholarship has increasingly noted the possible influence of pre-Islamic Jewish Christianity in the Arabian Peninsula (e.g., Gnilka 2007). In this respect it is interesting to recall the widely cited tradition of Muhammad protecting the icon of Mary and Jesus when the Kaaba in Mecca was purged of idolatrous images (according to the ninth-century Meccan writer Al-Azraqi's *Kitab Akhbar Makka*, in Wüstenfeld 1861, 105).

No early Latin translation of the *Infancy Gospel of James* survives. Its relative eclipse in the Western church is explicable partly by its explicit (but hardly successful) rejection in documents beginning possibly as early as the *Letter to Exsuperius* by the early-fifth-century pope Innocent I (paragraph 7; cited somewhat too confidently in Ehrman and Pleše 2011, 32) and explicitly around the end of that century in the so-called Gelasian Decree (discussed above on p. 32). More influentially, perhaps, it was displaced by becoming extensively reused by other infancy gospels in Latin. In this way, before long it reentered the Western tradition by spawning several *secondary* apocrypha (note Voicu 2011, 406–8, on this intriguing phenomenon). Of these, *Pseudo-Matthew* alone accounts for over two hundred extant manuscripts (see this and related texts in Ehrman and Pleše 2011, 73–155). Other important derivatives include the so-called Arundel recension of *Pseudo-Matthew* ("Latin Infancy Gospels") and the *History of Joseph the Carpenter*. Several Marian narrative themes from the *Infancy Gospel* exercised a profound influence on the development of Christian art (Cartlidge and Elliott 2001; Jensen 2015).

Christmas and the Infancy Gospel of James

To illustrate the *Infancy Gospel*'s influence, we will briefly consider some of the ways in which this narrative has irreversibly influenced basic aspects of Christianity's celebration of Christmas. My suggestion here is that the *Infancy Gospel*'s effect on the Christian imagination has been so pervasive that it has become difficult to envisage the Christmas story without certain distinctive aspects of its articulation in this extracanonical tradition.

68

Ten points may here be singled out, presented roughly in the order in which they appear in the text. Some of these may well be familiar to most readers, while others are a staple only in certain Christian traditions.

1. The overall frame of the work takes for granted that Mary's parents were a devout Jewish couple called Joachim and Anna. This is a theme important to Catholic piety through the ages: both Catholics and Anglicans, for example, commemorate the feast day of Saints Joachim and Anna on July 26; most Eastern churches, on September 9. Further in relation to the interest in Mary's parentage, we may mention prominent Catholic feasts like those of Mary's immaculate conception on December 8, her birth on September 8, and her presentation in the Temple on November 21. In the West, by the early fourteenth century it seemed wholly unproblematic for Giotto's (1266–1337) famous frescoes in the Scrovegni Chapel at Padua to include several scenes from the lives of Joachim and Anna.

2. We have already noted the affirmation in 10.1 that Mary was of the "tribe" of David. It is this (and only this) conviction that provided a genealogically credible explanation of the infancy narratives' identification of Jesus as descended from David.

3. A theme less familiar to Protestants is that the annunciation occurred while Mary was fetching water, perhaps from a well (11.1–2). Whether (as here) in Jerusalem or in Nazareth, a well associated with the annunciation has long featured in icons and narrative accounts—possibly already in an early-third-century fresco at the Christian baptistery of Dura Europos in Syria (see Peppard 2012, 545–56). Such a site has been pointed out to pilgrims through the ages, and still to this day, at the Orthodox Church of the Annunciation in Nazareth.

4. At 17.2 Mary rides a donkey to Bethlehem. This especially is a theme without which Christmas pageants or even Hollywood movie representations like *The Nativity Story* (2006) are unthinkable. Adults and children alike tend to take this as integral to the biblical Christmas story. A motif more surprising to Western Christians is that in the *Infancy Gospel* the donkey is driven along by James (one of several older sons of Joseph from a previous marriage, 18.1). Coptic and Eastern Orthodox icons often feature James as well as Joseph in scenes like the Holy Family's flight to Egypt.

5. Notably, at 18.1 we are told that Jesus was born in a cave. This tradition was accepted by Justin Martyr in the second century (*Dialogue with Trypho* 78), and the associated site was regarded as historical and identifiable by Origen in the third (*Against Celsus*

1.51) and Jerome in the fourth (e.g. *Letter* 46.11; 58.3; 108.10). It is a standard feature of Orthodox iconography. By contrast, the popular notion that there was no room in the "inn" at Bethlehem derives from a common misreading of Luke 2:7 KJV, where the Greek word *katalyma* probably means the guest room of a house—perhaps in this case the vestibule of a cave dwelling. The emergence of wooden stable structures is a late feature of Western Renaissance art. Interestingly, the *Infancy Gospel* makes little of the notion that the infant Jesus was laid in a manger—seeing here mainly a device to help Mary hide Jesus from the persecution of Herod (22.2).

6. Strikingly, Joseph is absent at the birth because he has gone out to find a midwife. This is a perspective also retained in the standard Orthodox icon of the nativity (18.1).

7. Not just one but apparently two midwives are eventually located (19.1, 3), one of them called Salome. Although they arrive too late to witness the birth, they do assist in its aftermath. In the nativity icon the two midwives are often seen washing the baby as a way of illustrating the physicality of the incarnation.

8. It is perhaps also worth noting the theme of a bright light appearing inside the cave (19.2). This was a familiar staple of innumerable paintings of the adoration of the shepherds or the magi, including in Western art: the light illuminating the faces of the shepherds and wise men typically emanates from the baby Jesus himself.

9. In an affirmation of considerable consequence for subsequent Christian doctrinal reflection, Mary is said to have remained a virgin even after the birth—a fact verified to alarming effect by the midwife Salome (16.1–8; 19.8; 19.19–20.12). The concept of perpetual virginity has a partial Jewish antecedent in Philo's description of Sarah (*Prelim. Studies* 7; *Posterity* 134) and may possibly have Jewish Christian associations (so Horner 2004). It became christologically important for John Chrysostom, the Cappadocian fathers, and Augustine, and may be implied in the creeds. It was explicitly affirmed at the sixth ecumenical council (Constantinople, 681 CE) and continued to be upheld even by Martin Luther (e.g., Luther 1883–2009, 6:510; 11:319–20; Luther 1955–86, 22:23; 45:206; *Table Talk* no. 4435). As we saw, the *Infancy Gospel* thus already supports the ancient tradition that the brothers and sisters of Jesus mentioned in the gospels are half siblings: Joseph is explicitly said to be an older man with sons from a previous marriage (9.2

70

and passim). This is also affirmed in the *Infancy Gospel of Thomas* 16.1–2 (cf. Origen, *Commentary on Matthew* 10.17, apparently confusing the *Gospel of Peter* with the *Infancy Gospel of James*); Richard Bauckham (1994) is among those who have argued that it could be historically factual.

10. Finally, the *Infancy Gospel* also affirms that the star of Bethlehem was explicitly the brightest in the sky and dimmed all other stars (21.2). This is nowhere stated in Matthew's Gospel but came to be assumed by iconographers of the nativity. Although perhaps an understandable extrapolation from the Matthean text, it clearly received explicit support from the *Infancy Gospel*.

Many of these points are usefully illustrated by reference to the history of Eastern and Western Christian art. Here we have noted a number of themes attested in the classic Orthodox icons of the nativity; a fuller discussion can be found in Cartlidge and Elliott 2001.

In its devout engagement of early Christian beliefs about Mary and the birth of Jesus, the *Infancy Gospel of James* shaped mainstream Christian piety both East and West. While it always remained extracanonical, the *Infancy Gospel* rarely, if ever, became apocryphal in any sense—either of secrecy or of heresy. Its popularity well outside scribal circles is also documented in the important fact that in the Eastern churches it went on, like other Marian apocrypha, to be read liturgically at various distinctive feasts of the Virgin (see, e.g., Shoemaker 2010, esp. 155, 161–62nn8–11). This influence continues today at the Orthodox feasts of the nativity of Mary and of her entrance into the Temple.

All in all, this *Infancy Gospel*'s impact on later Christian theology, spirituality, and artistic expression was enormous—more than one interpreter has said that its importance "cannot be overestimated" (Hock 1995, 27, citing Quasten 1950, 1:122). Its manuscript tradition and circulation far exceeds that of any other noncanonical work discussed in this book. Indeed one may say without exaggeration that the *Infancy Gospel of James* along with its later derivatives is the *only* ancient noncanonical gospel text to have enjoyed such a wide and long-lasting influence (even if the public reading of the *Diatessaron* in the Syrian churches made it for several centuries an important quasi-canonical exception to this rule). Other, lately famous and controversial gospel texts in the popular limelight are, by contrast, known from at best a handful of manuscripts—more often just a single one.

The Infancy Gospel of Thomas

We turn next, and more briefly, to a very different text that strikes many readers as a puzzling and perhaps, in aesthetic or spiritual terms, less attractive document. Although it has received renewed scholarly attention in recent years, its historical influence has been far less extensive and can be discussed more briefly. (For text and translation, see Ehrman and Pleše 2011, 3–17; 2014, 25–26.)

Content

In its most commonly encountered form (the longer Greek recension), the *Infancy Gospel of Thomas* promises this apostle's report for a Gentile audience of what it calls "extraordinary childhood deeds" of Jesus (1.1, *paidika kai megaleia*). The Jesus we encounter here may well strike contemporary readers as an obstreperous and contrarian little boy, mischievous if not malicious, who acts defiantly both in the exercise of his miraculous powers and in demonstrating his argumentative superiority to three Jewish teachers.

Although the rather episodic nature of the extant material suggests no clear overarching outline, the narrative progression is nevertheless fairly straightforward. Having identified himself as "Thomas the Israelite," the author introduces Jesus not as an infant but as a five-year-old boy. The first episode is perhaps the most famous and influential in this document. On a Sabbath, Jesus is playing with water and mud by a creek. When his father, Joseph, rebukes him for shaping a dozen sparrows out of the mud on the Sabbath, Jesus simply claps his hands and the sparrows fly away (2.1–5). This story came to be frequently cited, including in the Qur'an (3:49; 5:110)—perhaps via the *Arabic Infancy Gospel* (36), a text that also supplies the idea of the infant Jesus speaking from his cradle (1: cf. Qur'an 3:46; 19:28; see further Josua and Eissler 2012a, 976–77).

Somewhat more disturbing scenes of conflict follow. Jesus' playmate, the son of a scribe named Annas, uses a branch to make the dammed-up creek water drain away. Jesus is so enraged that he causes the boy's body immediately to wither away and die (chap. 3). Another boy collides with Jesus in the village and falls over dead. When his parents complain to Joseph, Jesus punishes them with blindness (4.1–5.1). Joseph attempts to discipline Jesus, who

72

responds evasively. Unsurprisingly, these actions provoke recurring consternation at the fact that every statement of Jesus appears instantly to turn into reality (5.3; 17.4).

Chapter 6 introduces an exchange with a Jewish teacher called Zacchaeus, who has taken on the task of teaching him the alphabet. In an episode also known from other early Christian sources, such as the *Epistle of the Apostles* (4), Jesus explains to his teacher the mystic meaning of the triune lines of the letter *A* (or alpha) joined in a single stroke—a theme that echoes ancient Jewish speculation on the first letter of the book of Genesis (see discussion in Bockmuehl 2012a). Zacchaeus cannot cope and excludes Jesus from his classroom as unteachable—and perhaps not even human (7.2, 4; cf. 17.2). As in a number of gnostic gospels (e.g., the *Gospel of Judas*), Jesus simply laughs—and explains his status as having come from heaven.

At this point, all who were previously struck by his curse are healed (8.2). Perhaps somewhat to the reader's relief, chapters 9 to 13 now temporarily turn a narrative corner by substituting redemptive miracles in place of the earlier vindictiveness. When a boy playing with Jesus on the roof of a house falls off and dies, he restores him to life, and the boy's parents praise God and fall down before Jesus. He also heals the foot of a young man who injures himself while splitting wood, which prompts the crowd to recognize the spirit of God in him. When Mary sends the six-year-old Jesus to fetch water, his clay jar is accidentally smashed but he manages to carry the water home in the folds of his garment. Aged eight, he joins his father in the field and sows a single grain of wheat that yields a harvest large enough to feed not only his own family but all the poor of the village. When Joseph the carpenter lacks a plank long enough to complete the assignment of building a rich man's bed, Jesus quickly stretches a shorter plank to make it fit.

Although Jesus appears for the moment to have changed his ways, he has not resolved his anger management problems completely. In chapters 14–15 the exasperated Joseph hires another tutor to instruct the boy in Greek and Hebrew. Faced with the same puzzle about the letter alpha, this teacher gets annoyed and hits Jesus over the head; the boy angrily curses his teacher, who falls unconscious to the ground. Not long afterward another teacher recommends to Joseph that he should instead have Jesus attend his school (chap. 15). Jesus turns up and by the Holy Spirit gets up and

73

teaches the law. This time, the teacher recognizes the child's grace and wisdom, and as a result the earlier tutor awakes from his coma.

Further miracles follow in chapters 16 to 18. While Jesus and his brother James are gathering wood, a venomous snake bites James on the hand, and he is saved from death only by Jesus breathing on the wound and instantly healing his brother. When a neighbor's baby dies, Jesus is alerted by the mother's loud wailing and comes to touch the infant's chest and summon it back to life—the child immediately awakes with a laugh and is returned to his mother's breast. A year later Jesus brings to life a construction worker who has fallen to his death. As on a number of other occasions the author places considerable importance on the marvelling reaction of the crowd: "This child is surely from heaven, since he has saved many lives from death and is able to go on saving throughout his life" (18.3).

The longer Greek text concludes in chapter 19 with the Lukan episode of the boy Jesus in the Temple at Passover (Luke 2:41–52), embellished mainly by placing on the lips of the astonished scribes Elizabeth's words declaring Mary blessed among women because of the fruit of her womb (Luke 1:42). As in Luke, Jesus then follows his parents and grows up in obedience and learning.

A brief doxology concludes the text, although the Slavonic version has the secondary addition of three further chapters of anti-pagan and anti-Jewish flavor (including a gratuitously offensive episode of turning Jewish children into pigs, chap. 22). The Latin and one variant Greek version also feature additional material associated with Jesus as a toddler in Egypt, including an episode of resurrecting a pickled fish in a pool (a motif that in another form also appears in the late-second-century *Acts of Peter*).

Origin and Setting

If the story and its purpose leave one puzzled, critical study of this text soon proves to be even more complex and confusing.

We begin with the manuscript tradition. Four separate and remarkably different Greek recensions of varying lengths make it difficult to be sure that there was ever a single underlying original text, although the tradition appears to have begun in Greek. Fourteen extant Greek manuscripts are known, all of them from the late Middle Ages.

Translations into other languages are attested in Ethiopic, Syriac, Latin, and Georgian. Some of these translations predate the earliest Greek manuscripts and are widely regarded as a better clue to earlier forms of the text, which may have consisted only of chapters 2–9, 11–16, and 19. (For the manuscript tradition, see Burke 2004; 2010; Kaiser 2012a.)

The bewilderingly diverse length of the transmitted texts may itself be the result of the document's episodic character, which presents not a taut story line but an almost interchangeable pastiche of self-contained episodes from the childhood of Jesus ages five to twelve. Narrative continuity is achieved somewhat stereotypically by the repetition of motifs like Jesus' age, his ability to best a Jewish teacher or another boy, and the amazing power of his words. (Interestingly, there is no equivalent noncanonical narrative tradition covering the period of Jesus as an adolescent and young adult. This could be because in antiquity boys were assumed to reach maturity and responsibility at the age of thirteen—a point marked in later Judaism by the bar mitzvah ceremony; but we are in any case faced with a gap of fifteen years or so that is left vacant in these and all other early Christian texts.)

Given the subject matter, the connection with the canonical infancy traditions is understandably much less developed than in the case of the *Infancy Gospel of James*: even the longer Greek recension links to the New Testament narratives only at the single point of the Passover visit to Jerusalem by the twelve-year-old Jesus (Luke 2:41–52; cf. *Infancy Gospel of Thomas* 19; the later Recension C echoes elements of Matthew's and the *Infancy Gospel of James's* interest in the Holy Family's flight to Egypt). A number of scholars see in this Lukan story the catalyst for this entire document: the author fills the gaps in Luke's account with a cameo collection of astonishing tales about Jesus' childish exploits (*paidika*). Similarly, the theological and cultural background of this document is far less concerned with Jewish or Old Testament motifs than the *Infancy Gospel of James*. In these and other respects, the *Infancy Gospel of Thomas* certainly plows distinctive furrows.

Occasional sayings or teaching elements have been thought to represent a more distinctive, possibly gnosticizing character. It is true that Irenaeus claimed to find the story of Jesus' precocious interpretation of the letter alpha in a gnostic source (*Against Heresies* 1.20). A gnostic origin of this document is, however, unlikely in

75

the view of most scholars. More specifically, it is also worth pointing out that the attribution to Thomas does not in any way link this text ideologically with the better known and perhaps more gnostic *Gospel of Thomas*: indeed the name Thomas only came to be attached to this text at a later stage.

Given the puzzling characteristics of this document and the late date of the extant manuscripts, we can say little more about its geographic setting other than that it must have originated in the Greek-speaking Eastern Mediterranean. The date also seems to most scholars very difficult to pin down, with estimates ranging from the later second century to the fourth or fifth and sometimes allowing for lengthy oral elaboration and development. (Eastman [2015, 205–7], for example, suggests that the motif of the cursing of opponents owes something to the narratives of Syrian Christian ascetics of the fourth century.) The earlier proposed dates seem in considerable measure a counsel of convenience, which may relate simply to the second-century *attestation* of motifs included in this text rather than to its compilation as an infancy gospel.

Interpretation

The literary character, ethos, and orientation of the *Infancy Gospel of Thomas* are clearly different from the *Infancy Gospel of James*. Here, the boy Jesus seems repeatedly to be angry, malicious, flippant, and arrogant in turn. He appears as a mystery and a menace to his family, friends, and acquaintances alike. The depictions of his miracles seem at times troublingly amoral or one-dimensional, and almost gratuitously exaggerated. Readers may be reminded of some of the themes in Saturday morning children's cartoons.

If that seems at one level a wholly off-putting assessment, it is only fair to acknowledge that cultural expectations in antiquity might well be different from our own. Ancient biographies of great men sometimes presaged and foreshadowed their heroes' mighty words and deeds in traditions about their childhoods. For the decades before the birth of Jesus Suetonius reports that the baby poet Virgil was born with a blissful expression on his face and did not cry (*Virgil* 4), while the Emperor Augustus's birth and infancy were accompanied by astonishing portents and feats foretelling his future greatness (*Augustus* 94). From antiquity to the Middle Ages, children were commonly understood as mini-adults and sometimes depicted with such features in art. Scholars have discussed the well-known ancient character motif of *puer senex,* the old man hidden in the boy (cf., e.g., Carp 1980; Wiedemann 1989, 76, 79, and passim)—or, in a more familiar proverb popular with nineteenth-century poets like Wordsworth and Hopkins, "The child is father to the man."

Such convictions facilitated the generation of powerfully emblematic childhood tales of both the great and even the not so great. As one recent specialist study puts it, "It seems that any child of note, whether an Emperor, a hero, a saint, or simply one's prematurely deceased child, did not act like children do. And [the *Infancy Gospel of Thomas's*] Jesus is no exception" (Burke 2008, 136; cf. Kaiser 2012a, 938). To that extent one might even say that the *Infancy Gospel of Thomas* found its exemplar and precedent in the Lukan infancy narrative's wise and precocious Jesus in the Temple.

Despite all this, it is difficult to get beyond the impression that the text seems relatively devoid of theological insight and morally vacuous in its handling of inexplicable miracles. Its intention is evidently to entertain and amuse a fairly unsophisticated, immature audience. Can we say more about why and for whom this cycle of texts was composed? One contemporary scholar welcomes the human appeal of a text she imagines addressed to parents of challenging youngsters (Kaiser 2010, 269), while another wonders, less reassuringly, if the intended audience may themselves have been children (Aasgaard 2009)!

Such undoubtedly interesting and attractive scenarios may in the end beg more questions than they answer. The problem remains that the *Infancy Gospel of Thomas* rejoices in a number of cheap shots to assure its readership of Jesus' effortless triumph over his opponents. One can of course feel sympathy for how this might encourage a marginalized or disenfranchised social group, or indeed entertain its children and their long-suffering parents, perhaps even allowing the latter a momentary wry relief at the possible normality of their offspring's challenging behavior.

That said, one need not subscribe to sugary Victorian Christmas carol sentiments about the "wondrous childhood" of Mary's son as "mild, obedient, good" to find this document's narrative resolution somewhat troubling. The story lines here generally seem to operate at the level of populist one-upmanship found in *Dennis the Menace* or *Superman* comic books. Perhaps that is both the strength and

77

the Achilles' heel of our text, and a pointer to one plausible type of audience. In the absence of Saturday morning television, one could here indulge youthful and perhaps parental imaginations about a Jesus whose humanity made him not only a baby and a man like us, but also "all boy."

This infancy gospel's themes of arbitrary violence and amoral miracles nevertheless strike a note at once disturbing and reminiscent of two-dimensional cartoon heroes. Modern readers may be forgiven for supposing that the boy Jesus is an enfant terrible, a menace who "leaves a trail of havoc wherever he goes" (Foster 2009, 63)—drawn perhaps as a strongly gendered figure, "all boy" in that sense too (cf. Aasgaard 2009). On the other hand, this strange collection of stories may well match the concern of other ancient biographical writers to find distinctive evidence of the adult's greatness in the child. After all, even Luke already looks to Simeon in the Temple as prophesying conflict and controversy: this child would be a sign opposed, for the rising and falling of many, and causing his mother anxiety and pain (Luke 2:34–35). In one sense the *Infancy Gospel of Thomas*'s provocative narratives may not be very far from that mark.

Transmission and Influence

A recent study of this tradition's medieval reception and derivative literature has suggested that readers even in the Middle Ages differed in their assessment. Some considered this material blasphemous because of its implication of Jesus as an aggressive and ill-tempered bad boy playing havoc with the boundaries of a mild-mannered Joseph's discipline, while others saw instead a testimony to the humanity of a Jesus who (like Paul, 1 Cor. 13:11) behaved in childish ways when he was a child (see Dzon 2005, 157 and passim).

This certainly suggests a familiar dilemma between high and low Christology faced by ecclesial interpretation of the gospels through the ages—that is, the contested identity of a Jesus who risks being estranged from devotion because his character appears either too detached and divine or too flawed and ordinary. In its own way, our text certainly represents elements of Christology from above as well as below, a boy both divine and human—yet medieval and modern readers alike may be forgiven for wondering if in the end it strikes a plausible balance.

That said, the lowbrow appeal of the text and its readership also means that it is not patently aligned with either sectarian or mainstream political interests. The diversity of the manuscript tradition and of the document's reuse in later infancy collections demonstrates that it was versatile enough to reach a variety of audiences. The late antique and medieval flowering of so many *Infancy Gospel of Thomas* traditions and translations makes it permissible to wonder if, despite the undeniably early date of certain individual episodes (like the sparrows of clay and the encounter with Jesus' teacher), the fully compiled written work can significantly predate the early Byzantine period.

In terms of the document's later footprint and reception, most of the stories seem understandably to have had quite limited impact. In addition perhaps to the boy Jesus' discussion about the alphabet with his rabbinic teacher, one episode in particular stands out for its influence on subsequent piety and imagination, both Christian and Muslim (see Davis 2014): the story of Jesus creating one or more live birds out of clay. That said, however, this narrative's exceptional influence usually appears without reference to any other part of the *Infancy Gospel of Thomas*—which may characterize the latter as the compilation of a loose set of thematically associated narratives that also circulated independently.

The scene not only recurs in numerous translations (e.g., Syriac, Ethiopic, Latin, Georgian, Slavonic, Irish) but also was widely included in other texts like the *Arabic Infancy Gospel* as well as recycled independently in the Qur'an (3:49; 5:110) and elsewhere—deriving quite plausibly from the independently transmitted memorable narrative motif rather than from a complete *Infancy Gospel of Thomas*. Similarly, and again unlike the rest of the gospel, this particular motif also inspired occasional artistic representations, ranging from the spectacular painted wooden ceiling at the medieval church of St. Martin at Zillis, Switzerland (see Cartlidge and Elliott 2001, 107–8 and fig. 4.21; Davis 2014, 196, 211–20), to the twentieth-century British Catholic poet Hilaire Belloc's (1870–1953) striking poem "The Birds":

The Birds

When Jesus Christ was four years old,
The angels brought Him toys of gold,
Which no man ever had bought or sold.

And yet with these He would not play.
He made Him small fowl out of clay,
And blessed them till they flew away;
Tu creasti Domine.

Jesus Christ, Thou child so wise,
Bless mine hands and fill mine eyes,
And bring my soul to Paradise.

Other Infancy Texts

Recent scholarly editions of the noncanonical gospels often include other texts, including some or all of the following nine works. Since almost all of these date from the Byzantine period or later and depend on the canonical narratives along with the infancy gospels of *James* or *Thomas*, we will mention each one only briefly—enough, perhaps, to vindicate our decision to concentrate our efforts on the *Infancy Gospel of James* and the *Infancy Gospel of Thomas.*

Papyrus Cairo 10735

The first of these additional texts, P.Cair. 10735, consists of a single page of papyrus leaf inscribed on both sides; nine highly fragmentary lines of Greek are visible on the recto and nine on the verso. Usually dated to the sixth or seventh century, it has been variously interpreted as either a separate "unknown" gospel or, perhaps more plausibly, as a slightly expansive harmony or homiletic paraphrase on the infancy narratives of Matthew and Luke. The underlying narrative on the two sides of papyrus features motifs that may have been orally familiar to the writer from Matthew (2:13 and the flight of the Holy Family to Egypt, on the recto) and Luke (1:36 and the Annunciation of John the Baptist, on the verso).

However one reads the text, it provides a brief glimpse of the evident popularity of infancy motifs even in literary settings that did not generate texts of enduring circulation. The papyrus was (like the first of the Oxyrhynchus papyri) discovered and first published over a century ago (1903) by Grenfell and Hunt; it may quite possibly derive from Oxyrhynchus too. While there is limited verbatim dependence, the language seems sufficiently derivative to suggest

80

a *relecture* or "rewritten scripture" approach, perhaps relying on a gospel harmony. As Adolf Deissmann and other early critics of the original publication pointed out, we cannot be sure that it was ever part of any complete "gospel"—even an infancy gospel. (See Deissmann 1904; 1927, 430–34; for text and translation, see Kraus 2009, 240–252; Ehrman and Pleše 2011; 2014.)

An Infancy Narrative from Justin the Gnostic's Book of Baruch

The *Book of Baruch* appears to be a gnostic work of the late second or early third century quoted by Hippolytus (ca. 170-236) in his treatise *Refutation of All Heresies* (5.26, 29–32; cf. Kaiser 2012b). It narrates a brief angelic visit to the twelve-year-old Jesus in Nazareth to advise him to preach the true message of the Father Elohim and of the highest, Good God—the one to whom he returns after his body is crucified.

The "Birth of Mary"

In his inventory of heresies known as the "Medicine Chest" (*Panarion*) or *Refutation of All Heresies*, Epiphanius (ca. 315–403) includes a brief paraphrase of a short document identified as the "Birth of Mary" (36), which despite Epiphanius's characterization seems unlikely to be of gnostic origin. We hear little of its content, although Epiphanius does mention its assertion that John the Baptist's father, Zacharias, was killed in the Temple because during his sacrifice he saw a vision of a human in the form of a donkey. The intriguing link between John the Baptist's father and the Zacharias (or: Zechariah; NRSV) killed in the Temple at Matthew 23:35 is already taken for granted in *Infancy Gospel of James* 23–24 and in Origen's commentary on the passage. Some scholars have identified additional dependencies on the *Infancy Gospel of James,* which would potentially confirm the latter's early date and add to the history of its second-century effects. (See the discussion in Markschies 2012b.)

The Arabic Infancy Gospel

A substantial *Arabic Infancy Gospel* exists in two Arabic and three Syriac medieval manuscripts. This apparently pre-Islamic work of fifty-four chapters expands on the *Infancy Gospel of James*'s story line of the birth and infancy of Jesus with an extensive collection of additional fanciful narratives of healings, exorcisms, and other magical exploits associated with the Holy Family's residence in Egypt and with childhood tales reflecting traditions in the *Infancy Gospel of Thomas*. The original compilation may date from the sixth century. (See Josua and Eissler 2012a, 963–65.)

The Gospel of Pseudo-Matthew

The *Gospel of Pseudo-Matthew* essentially represents the translation and reconception of the *Infancy Gospel of James* for the Latin West, with certain distinctive emphases. The latter include not only an extension of the narrative to encompass the Holy Family's flight to Egypt, but also a more patrician Joachim and a less emotionally volatile Joseph. The name of the text derives from the fact that it is prefixed in some manuscripts by a fictitious correspondence in which Bishops Chromatius and Heliodorus ask Jerome to translate the evangelist Matthew's secret Hebrew infancy gospel into Latin. The work exists in two main textual forms, each with a manuscript tradition dating to the beginning of the ninth century; the original composition is thought to be no earlier than the seventh century. (See Ehrman and Pleše 2011, 73–77; 2014; Ehlen 2012a, 983–86.)

The Infancy Gospel of the Arundel Manuscript

A number of French and English medieval manuscripts contain another birth narrative closely related to *Pseudo-Matthew*. Its most influential form is a compilation sometimes called the J Composition or the Arundel Gospel after the major British Library Manuscript (MS Arundel 404). The document also appears to date from the seventh or eighth century and is heavily dependent on a Latin translation of the *Infancy Gospel of James* and on the *Gospel of Pseudo-Matthew*. Other sources may also be used, and perhaps even quoted, in an extended account of the two midwives' alarming experiences relating to Mary's postpartum virginity (77–80). (See Ehlen 2012b; Ehrman and Pleše 2011; 2014.)

The History of Joseph the Carpenter

An extensive Egyptian text called *The History of Joseph the Carpenter* is sometimes included under the heading of infancy narratives (Ehrman and Pleše 2011; 2014; Elliott 1993; 2006). Its explicit intention, however, is to present a biography (*bios*: prologue; 1.9) of Joseph rather than a story of the dominical nativity or its immediate context. Significantly, the text dwells rather longer on the death of the 111-year-old Joseph (chaps. 12–29; his "testament," chap. 30) than on his life leading up to the birth of Jesus. Jesus himself intriguingly functions as the narrator for large parts of the biography, and the author frames the entire biography as a dialogue (chaps. 1, 30–32) partly resembling post-resurrection discourse gospels of the sort we will encounter in chapter 5.

The Dormition of the Virgin Mary

Another strand of Egyptian influence has been detected in the "Passing" or "Dormition" of the Virgin Mary. The text survives today in nine medieval Egyptian manuscripts ranging from tenth-century Sahidic Coptic, via Bohairic Coptic to Arabic (parts of which reappear in a fourteenth-century Latin translation); its diversity is sufficiently complex to make even the recovery of the Sahidic archetype unlikely, let alone an occasionally postulated seventh-century Greek original. In the West, the document only achieved a certain influence on piety about the Holy Family after about the fifteenth century.

A Syriac Homiletical Work on the Life of John the Baptist

Finally under this heading, a Syriac homiletical extract on the life of John the Baptist was first published in 1927 using two Syriac manuscripts from the sixteenth and eighteenth centuries. The author deploys considerable freedom in an account that largely relies on the opening chapters of Luke and Matthew, with some awareness of the *Infancy Gospel of James*, but leads beyond the biblical accounts of John's life and death (including a brief encounter with Jesus at the baptism, chap. 20) to a lengthy concluding narration of his body's

83

removal four centuries later from Palestine to Alexandria, where a church was built to house it and it occasioned five significant miracles. Since the text references figures like the emperors Julian the Apostate (332–363) and Theodosius the Great (347–395) as well as the Egyptian bishop Serapion (fl. 339–360), scholarly inquiries have plausibly suggested that its portrayal of John the Baptist may represent popular Egyptian piety of the late fourth century. Unlike other infancy gospels here under consideration, this text has not yet attracted the attention of a significant body of secondary literature (see Josua and Eissler 2012b).

Conclusion: Infancy Gospels

The infancy gospels may be said to take their cue from an implicit invitation in the eventually canonical texts themselves. Matthew and Luke are somewhat more forthcoming about Jesus' origins than John and Mark—in their provision of a family tree, narratives of his family and birth, and glimpses of his infancy. Matthew implicitly abandons the story when Jesus is still a toddler and even Luke provides only a single narrative of the boy Jesus at the age of twelve.

But as the infancy gospels of *James* and *Thomas* demonstrate, interest in these matters was already flourishing in the second century. The *Infancy Gospel of James* quite understandably takes up the question, with a particular emphasis on the role of Mary before and during the birth of Jesus. Although not intimately familiar with Palestinian Judaism, the author is perhaps more so than has sometimes been supposed, and is in any case attentive to several key concerns of the infancy narratives in both Matthew and Luke, including their Jewish setting. As we saw, the *Infancy Gospel of James* reflects widespread second-century traditions such as Jesus' birth in a cave and Mary's descent from David. And it supplies a range of other supplementary details, from the mundane (like the virgin riding to Bethlehem on a donkey) to the supernatural (like the Creator's human birth causing creation and time themselves to pause).

The *Infancy Gospel of Thomas* develops a different narrative focus. Covering the boyhood of Jesus between the end of Matthew's infancy narrative and the end of Luke's, it shows us Jesus between the ages of five and twelve. For perhaps understandable reasons, despite its keenly popular subject matter this text circulated less widely and left less of a footprint in the history of Christian piety and reflection—though it is significant to note its reworking in the *Arabic Infancy Gospel* (and the Qur'an) and also as an appendix to later Latin manuscripts of the *Gospel of Pseudo-Matthew*. One singularly popular episode was the scene of the boy Jesus creating birds out of mud, which also occasionally appears in artistic representations.

The infancy gospels do not presuppose a clearly delimited canon of four canonical gospels. Indeed at least the original composition of the two foregrounded in this chapter must predate the New Testament's formal canonization. Nevertheless, both of them distinctly presuppose written or at least oral knowledge of the Gospels of Matthew and Luke, without whose larger narrative they make little sense on their own.

In that sense, therefore, the two influential infancy gospels we have highlighted also constitute useful initial case studies for the principle I aim to develop in this volume: the apocryphal gospels are in an important sense supplementary and para-canonical. That is to say, they make sense above all in relation to implied readers already familiar with at least an outline of the ecclesial story of Jesus that went on to become canonical in fourfold form. The infancy gospels speak *alongside* that larger narrative outline, whether that is encountered as a written gospel manuscript, a public liturgical gospel reading, or perhaps more diffusely in a second- or thirdhand oral form.

Suggested Further Reading

Bockmuehl, Markus. 2011. "The Son of David and His Mother." *Journal of Theological Studies* 62:476–93.

Bovon, François. 1991. "The Suspension of Time in Chapter 18 of Protevangelium Jacobi." In *The Future of Early Christianity: Essays in Honor of Helmut Koester*, edited by B. A. Pearson, 393–405. Minneapolis: Fortress.

Burke, Tony. 2008. "The *Infancy Gospel of Thomas*." In *The Non-Canonical Gospels*, edited by P. Foster, 126–38. London: T&T Clark.

Foster, Paul. 2009. *The Apocryphal Gospels: A Very Short Introduction*. Oxford: Oxford University Press.

Nutzman, Megan. 2013. "Mary in the *Protevangelium of James*: A Jewish Woman in the Temple?" *Greek, Roman, and Byzantine Studies* 53:551–78.

Vuong, Lily C. 2013. *Gender and Purity in the Protevangelium of James*. Wissenschaftliche Untersuchungen zum Neuen Testament 2:358. Tübingen: Mohr Siebeck.

CHAPTER 3

Ministry Gospels

Continuing our biographical sequence of gospel-like texts relating to the story of Jesus, we now turn to a number of almost entirely fragmentary ancient works. Most of these have only come to light in papyrus discoveries over the last century or so, but a handful of others are known to us by name and from citations in the works of early Christian writers.

In one sense it is these texts concerned with Jesus' teaching ministry that most closely emulate the main substance and form of the canonical gospels. Another interesting feature of this material is that it includes all of the texts traditionally, if rather misleadingly, identified as "Jewish Christian gospels," and which are known to us exclusively from often-critical citations in early Christian writings. By contrast, as chapter 5 will demonstrate, texts like those at Nag Hammadi show relatively little investment in the narrative of Jesus' embodied earthly life, and therefore contextualize his teachings rather differently.

The Problem of "Fragmentary" Gospels

One particularly challenging question we touched on in the introduction (p. 31 above) is whether the noncanonical texts here gathered under the "ministry" heading ever existed in anything other

87

than fragmentary form, even if some of these textual units may originally have been more numerous or more extensive. We will have occasion to reconsider this question when looking at some of the texts in more detail below. For now, it will be useful to observe simply that *no extended alternative narrative outline of Jesus' ministry survives outside the canon.* Given that quite a number even of the partially extant texts in other categories (like the infancy gospels) run to numerous chapters, it does seem significant to note the absence of any extended extracanonical narrative of teaching, dialogue, and miracles between Jesus' baptism and resurrection—the material, in other words, which in all four of the canonical gospels constitutes at least 80 percent of the proceedings.

There could in theory be any number of reasons for this significant absence. Might it simply confirm what advocates of both Q and the sayings collection known as the *Gospel of Thomas* have long since proposed—that key early Christian groups treasured traditions of Jesus' teachings but had little or no investment in stories about his life or death? As we will see in chapter 5 below, such a preference for discourse and sayings over particular pre-Easter narrative traditions did indeed attract some interest in certain Christian communities, especially in Upper Egypt, as is illustrated with particular clarity in gnostic gospel-like writings.

But these texts belong overwhelmingly to the second or third century, not the first. And like the *Gospel of Thomas*, they are in several cases significantly dependent on sayings of Jesus in a form characteristic of the gospels that became canonical. That tradition, however, assigned saving significance not only to the teachings of Jesus but also to his deeds, and not only to his post-Easter discourses but also to his Palestinian ministry, crucifixion, and resurrection. The idea that *first*-century Christians were uninterested in the life of Jesus is therefore not the most compelling explanation for the lack of any alternative biographical narratives. On the contrary, it may be precisely the widespread familiarity and acceptance especially of Matthew and John which accounts for the intriguing fact that no known ancient Christians appear to have created or preserved any wholesale rival narratives of Jesus' ministry—a point we will explore more fully below.

88 Nevertheless there were supplementary stories and sayings in circulation. Some of these were transmitted independently, while others appear to have been appended to the transmission of the

familiar gospel tradition, whether in oral or manuscript form. In what became the canonical four, the most famous examples of such narrative "peripheral attraction" include the peripatetic story of Jesus and the adulterous woman, which eventually settles at John 7:53–8:11 (see p. 44 above). Another case in point (though not part of the "ministry" narrative) may be the resurrection narratives included in the longer ending of Mark, 16:9–20, which dates from the early decades of the second century. While it remained absent from key early manuscripts, it soon became part of the only version of Mark known to some later second-century writers like Irenaeus and the author of the *Epistle of the Apostles*. The composition draws extensively on motifs known in all three of the other protocanonical gospels, but it also features prophecy about apostolic miracles found in the book of Acts as well as in one tradition about apostolic immunity from poison (for discussion, see Black 2008; Kelhoffer 2000; also Heckel 1999, 281–86).

That said, the nature of our evidence usually prevents any certainty about the size of the original text complex of which surviving fragments may have formed a part. Since some such texts might in principle have included material related to the passion and death of Jesus, our distinction here between ministry and passion gospels is clearly to some extent a matter of structural convenience. In some cases (including the *Gospel of Thomas*), the boundary lines between ministry and discourse gospels may also be blurred.

A Note on Q

Some readers might expect the famous hypothetical Synoptic Sayings Source Q to take pride of place as a ministry gospel. If it existed, this would indeed have constituted a collection of sayings of Jesus covering his entire ministry, from his baptism by John to the eschatological announcement of Q (= Luke) 22:28–30—though with a narrative frame at best implicit and with little or no explicit interest in the birth and infancy, death and resurrection of Jesus. Assuming such a reconstruction to be correct, one could then proceed to potentially interesting textual comparisons with several cognate texts that also compile isolated sayings—including of course the *Gospel of Thomas*, whose link with the earthly ministry of Jesus is not always equally evident. As we have already seen, however, that construal depends substantially on several increasingly contested assumptions, including not only Q's existence but also the priority or at least the editorial independence of *Thomas* vis-à-vis the final forms of the canonical gospels.

Q was first asserted in nineteenth-century Germany by C. H. Weisse (1838, 1:56) and most influentially by H. J. Holtzmann (1863) and others who observed the substantial verbal overlap between canonical Matthew and Luke. This hypothesis, systematically developed in Anglophone scholarship by B. H. Streeter (1924), seemed for much of the twentieth century to be the definitive account of Synoptic Gospel origins. At the height of confidence about Q, leading scholars could declare without irony that the Synoptic Problem had been "solved" with "completeness and elegance" (Dodd 1936, 10, 25). Even at the end of the century it was still possible for a self-styled International Q Project to publish "the critical edition" claiming to "reconstitute" the text of this "lost Gospel" accurately "word by word" (thus Robinson 2006; Robinson, Hoffmann, and Kloppenborg 2000—though it hardly flatters such methodological bravado that Q's "word by word" reconstitution *changed* between the first and second publications of this critical text: see Neirynck 2001 and cf. the sympathetic caution in Tuckett 2002, 219 and 219n24).

Thus "reconstructed" and placed alongside the *Gospel of Thomas*, Q also became extremely important to the work of the so-called Jesus Seminar in the 1990s, whose members famously decided the authenticity of individual sayings of Jesus by majority vote and claimed on the basis of Q and *Thomas* to construct an alternative account of early Christianity that all but eliminated passion and resurrection accounts along with most apocalyptic or eschatological teaching.

Viewed as a distinct and independent written gospel source, Q has unexpectedly fallen on somewhat harder times in recent years, in the wake of a number of attempts to redescribe gospel origins without recourse to this hypothesis. Increasing numbers of scholars have nursed doubts about the idea that a document of such presumed apostolic authority and enormous importance to the formation of the gospels could really have disappeared without a trace, leaving no knowledge even of its existence in any ancient literature. Luke the evangelist, supposedly a major user of Q, explicitly acknowledges his own use of preexisting written sources, at least

90

some of which are in his view apostolic—but these are identified as *narrative* accounts (*diēgēsis*, 1:1), that is, emphatically not sayings collections like Q or *Thomas*. Implausibly maximalist accounts of Q eventually had the effect of soliciting alternative explanations.

At present, the most successful of these alternative theories is based on an idea of Austin Farrer (1955) that was then developed in various ways by Michael Goulder, Mark Goodacre, and others (see, e.g., Goodacre 2002; Goodacre and Perrin 2004; Goulder 1996, 1999). This view accepts Mark as the first gospel, but then envisages a more linear development in which Matthew used Mark, perhaps alongside other traditions, while Luke used Mark and Matthew and possibly John and other traditions. Other, less successful alternatives to Q include proposals by Martin Hengel (Matthew used Mark and Luke; 2008b; cf. Hengel 2000) and previously by David Dungan (1999), William Farmer (1993), and other supporters of a revived Griesbach Hypothesis (Mark wrote after Luke used Matthew). The most substantial and comprehensive recent critique of the Q hypothesis has been put forward by Francis Watson (2013), who rightly casts doubt on its excessive reliance on "coincidences" between the gospels (but rather less convincingly substitutes in its place an alternative "Sayings Collection" based largely on a close predecessor to the *Gospel of Thomas*).

Here is not the place to resolve this argument. Q as a "lost gospel" is a hypothesis that has played a useful explanatory role but is today by no means universally accepted. Even its advocates tend to be more modest in their claims than their predecessors and to accept the need for sustained engagement with serious alternative views (cf., e.g., Christopher Tuckett and others in Foster et al. 2011; more vigorously, Viviano 2013).

More importantly, whether or not Q in some form existed, it seems appropriate to note in the face of occasional scholarly bluster that no ancient source or modern reconstructed text attributes to it the claim of being a gospel. Q was never in any identifiable sense a rival, analogue, prototype, or supplement to other gospels. Nor does any ancient source identify anything like it (even the supposed Matthean collection of logia reported by Papias of Hierapolis) as secret or apocryphal in the sense that *Thomas* and several other texts claim this for themselves. Here, therefore, we take note of the hypothesis, but without including Q more fully as an apocryphal or noncanonical gospel in its own right. Q is never attested

91

prior to nineteenth-century scholarship, and it survives in no extant fragment. If on the other hand it did exist, its substance could potentially make it a kind of ministry gospel, not least since it omits consideration of the infancy, passion, and resurrection.

"Jewish Christian" Gospels?

Diverse early Christian writers like Papias, Clement of Alexandria, Origen, Eusebius, Epiphanius, and Jerome refer repeatedly either to a text identified as an original Hebrew Gospel of Matthew (possibly a collection of sayings) or to another gospel or gospels variously designated either as "the Hebrew" (*to hebraikon*) or *of the Nazoraeans*, *of the Ebionites*, or *of the Hebrews*. Despite numerous attestations and citations of what were evidently known passages, the early Christian references to these gospels remain remarkably vague, isolated, and discontinuous. Ancient citations often seem to multiply sources that are elsewhere conflated (and have sometimes even been suspected to go back to a single original Hebrew gospel collection, e.g., by J. Edwards [2009]). As a result, standard editions and translations list an inventory of isolated, discretely numbered traditions that do not self-evidently point to a continuously authored document or documents. The most commonly accepted number of attested Jewish Christian gospels is three—but this is not unproblematic, as we will see. (For the various texts collected together, see Ehrman and Pleše 2011, 2014.)

Who Might "Jewish Christians" Be?

In recent years the term "Jewish Christian" has come in for fresh scrutiny and debate. What groups of people might this term designate, and did they really exist in significant numbers? Does the term include Jesus-believers who are (1) ethnic Jews, and are they (a) observant or nonobservant, (b) religious or nonreligious? Does it denote more broadly (2) those whose ethnic or cultural identity may be ambiguous but who are identified as Jewish either by themselves or by others? Or might it also include (3) any or all ethnically Gentile believers who see their identity as in some sense constituted in Israel and who may conduct their lives to a lesser or greater extent in keeping with perceived Jewish praxis on such matters as diet, calendar, ritual immersion, burial of the dead, magic or exorcism, vows, prayer and worship, or participation in public office? The sum of these categories certainly included very substantial numbers of Christians not only in Palestine and Greater Syria, but also in Egypt, Asia Minor, Mesopotamia, the Arabian Peninsula, and farther afield.

In the most straightforward sense, all the very earliest Christians were Jews who had become believers in Jesus as Messiah. This much is not in question; indeed, it seems quite possible that Jewish believers remained in the majority among the early Christian communities at least for the duration of the first century. But there is considerable uncertainty about what happened to Jewish communities of Jesus-believers over the subsequent centuries. One standard scholarly narrative assumes that during the years following the first (66–73) and especially the second (132–35) great Jewish wars against Rome, Christians' nonmilitant stance and refusal to acknowledge the quasi-messianic cause of the rebel leader Simon Bar Kokhba accelerated their marginalization from the center of Jewish religious life—sometimes perhaps reinforced by overtly hostile or exclusionary Jewish religious rulings. A so-called parting of the ways between Christianity and Judaism used to be invoked by scholars as having achieved some definitive finality not later than the first half of the second century (so, influentially, Dunn 1991, 2006, 1992).

Vigorous recent study of Jewish Christianity has, however, drawn fresh attention to the considerable vitality and diversity of Christian groups, whether or not visibly Jewish in ethnicity, who continued for centuries to straddle the seemingly exclusive boundaries between normative Jewish and Christian self-definitions—falling afoul of the eventual tidy consensus of rabbinic and episcopal authorities that no Christian could be a Jew, and no Jew a Christian. This in turn requires not so much an abandonment, but certainly a much more nuanced and diversified account of whether, how, why, and where certain Christians continued to be Jews.

Amid the fog and ambiguity, noteworthy evidence for the scale and persistence of the Jewish Christian question surfaces three and a half centuries later when Jerome (347–420), himself no friend of Judaizing faith, grudgingly reports to Augustine (354–430) that

93

to this day there is among the Jews, throughout all the synagogues of the Orient, the so-called heresy of the Minim, which is condemned even by the Pharisees until now. Popularly they are known as the Nazarenes, who believe in Christ as Son of God, born of the Virgin Mary, and they say that he who suffered under Pontius Pilate and rose is he in whom we too believe. (*Letter* 112.13; my trans.)

The question of quite what it might mean for Jews to *cease* to be Jews is intrinsically complex and contested. The issues are only in part about religious convictions, but also (and at least as importantly) about cultural and ethnic boundaries. And the latter are complicated by large numbers of Gentile sympathizers and partial adherents of Jewish belief and practice in antiquity, including the many Christians of Gentile and Jewish extraction who continued a variety of Jewish practices—from attendance at the local synagogue to the observance of ritual practices. The fact that church fathers like Jerome in Judea and Chrysostom in Antioch were skittish about the continuing presence of such phenomena serves to confirm their prevalence.

For these and other reasons, the definitional problems around the terminology of Jewish Christianity are likely to exceed our grasp here. Indeed, as James Carleton Paget argues in a major study, the term "Jewish Christian" is itself a modern construct of convenience that was never used in antiquity and should perhaps be laid to rest (2010b, 316–20). Messianic Judaism or "Jewish believers in Jesus" (Skarsaune and Hvalvik 2007 and others) may be less tendentious terms, even if not unproblematic. The phenomena we are considering involve some combination of belief in Jesus as Messiah, observance of at least some Jewish law, and a corporate identity that in some (possibly complex) way involves continuing membership in the elect people of Israel.

This Jewish witness to Jesus never entirely disappeared. And so throughout the early centuries there were such believers who related their emphatically Jewish self-identity and praxis to their understanding of Jesus, some within the creedal parameters of the emerging orthodox tradition and others outside it. (For recent work on Jewish Christians and their literature, see esp. Carleton Paget 2010a, 2010b; Luomanen 2012; Skarsaune and Hvalvik 2007; key critiques of the "parting of the ways" paradigm include Becker and Reed 2003; Boyarin 2004, 2009; also Broadhead 2010; Nicklas 2014c.)

Jewish Christian Gospels

The claim that this Jewish witness included written tradition about Jesus surfaces from time to time in early Christian writings and also, perhaps, in the rabbinic references to *gilyonim* as scrolls of the gospel (e.g., Tosefta *Shabbat* 13:5; Babylonian Talmud *Shabbat* 116a–b; *Sifre Numbers* 16).

Thus defined, the possible scope of Jewish Christian literature is considerable. At least the canonical Gospels of Matthew and John clearly fall into this category and are in that sense Jewish Christian gospels. A good many other New Testament documents would arguably require consideration under a Jewish Christian label.

The Jewish character of certain noncanonical gospels is complicated by the fact that these documents do not survive. We know the texts and their titles only from citations in the work of other early Christian authors, some of which include serendipitously preserved quotations. This makes it extremely difficult to speak with confidence about the nature and literary shape of these texts—and helps to keep alive the question of the extent to which we are dealing with Jewish Christian "gospels" that were ever discrete and distinctive texts in their own right. And yet, regardless of this pertinent and significant uncertainty, it is precisely the cognate identification of these texts in a variety of ancient sources that makes it appropriate to discuss this material as a group under the present heading.

From the surviving evidence it is far from clear whether these gospels could be described as heretical or even in any obvious sense subversive or resistant to aspects of the canonical gospel tradition. Leaving Epiphanius aside, Alexandrian church fathers like Clement and Origen quote a *Gospel according to the Hebrews* quite positively—as if presuming that, although not perhaps fully authoritative, it was nevertheless known and respected. Origen, for example, repeatedly prefaces his quotations with a phrase like "if one is willing to accept it"—though explicitly only as a pertinent source, not as an authority (e.g., *Commentary on John* 2.12 on John 1:3; *Homilies on Jeremiah* 15.4; *Commentary on Matthew* 15.14). Eusebius includes this text among the disputed writings rather than the heretical ones (*Ecclesiastical History* 3.25.5).

On the other hand, the survival of Jewish Christian literature was perhaps not helped by the fact that Jesus-believing Judaism itself lacked an ecclesial or theological center after the destruction

95

of Jerusalem. By the fourth century it was increasingly forced into the religious underground by both rabbinic Jewish and catholic Christian authorities united in the disastrous irony of agreeing about one key point: one cannot be both a Jew and a believer in Jesus. As Jerome tragically but typically concludes at the end of the passage cited above (*Letter* 112), "Since they want to be both Jews and Christians, they are neither."

How Many Jewish Christian Gospels?

Quite how many such gospels, then, might we be dealing with? Neither rabbinic nor early Christian sources are clear on this point, or indeed on what these texts were called in antiquity: while some church fathers refer to a gospel according to the *Hebrews*, other materials are variously attributed to the *Nazarenes* or *Nazoreans*, or to the *Ebionites*. Contemporary scholarship tends to allow for between one and four, but most commonly three, distinct Jewish Christian gospels (sometimes referred to as the "three-gospel hypothesis"). One reason for this latter number is that there appear to be three differing traditions attesting the baptism of Jesus. A few scholars consider all the early Christian references to be in principle reducible to a single Hebrew gospel (e.g., J. Edwards 2009).

The notion of an identifiable *single* Hebrew gospel text is difficult to substantiate. A recent study suggests instead that the best way to understand these discrete but related texts is as belonging to a harmonized "post-synoptic" stage of the gospel tradition in Syria, resembling but predating Tatian's so-called *Diatessaron* and drawing on the gospel tradition (including Q, if it existed) in a form represented both in writings like the Epistle of James and also, possibly, like the *Gospel of Thomas* (so Luomanen 2012, 236–39 and passim). Epiphanius is aware of a view that identifies the *Gospel of the Hebrews* with the *Diatessaron* (*Refutation of All Heresies* 46.1). Even though erroneous, this opinion is perhaps nevertheless telling about the synthesized nature of the documents we are dealing with.

Citations of one or more "Jewish Christian gospels" continue unabated in late antiquity and the Middle Ages, and seem to have encouraged proliferating and sometimes polemical narratives (see Klauck 2002, 69–72). Among the latter, we must certainly note the interesting narratives about Jesus in rabbinic literature, which have in some recent scholarship been thought to reflect primarily the rhetoric and social setting of newly confident Babylonian Jews outside the influence and authority of Byzantine rule (Schäfer 2007, 2012; contrast Murcia 2014).

For the present discussion, however, it seems wise to focus on texts that are actually attested in antiquity. Extensive similarities suggest considerable overlap and dependence on some form of the canonical narratives, even if there may be occasional traces of earlier traditions. The surviving citations of the Jewish Christian gospels appear to offer a series of glosses and insertions that would fit around a broadly canonical narrative gospel outline—a character that could account for the tendency of both patristic and manuscript traditions to cite isolated traditions rather than any longer passages. Once again the passage about the adulterous woman in John 7:53–8:11 may be instructive: although initially circulated as an independent tradition, it soon became attached to either Luke or John among the larger gospel narrative constructs—and its anchor in John's Gospel proved canonically determinative.

This may suggest the answer to another, more puzzling question. Why do we not encounter more extensive sections of these texts? The surviving citations and reports of Jewish Christian gospels tend to supplement a largely synoptic outline with additional traditions, rather than producing an entire gospel of their own. That, at any rate, could explain why the texts cited by early Christian writers are so consistently brief and disjointed.

In short, it seems entirely possible that these gospel traditions were never transmitted in a form wholly separate from that of the canonical gospels. Since we cannot be certain about the original literary shape of what the ancient sources refer to, some favor the more "neutral" nomenclature of "the Jewish gospel known to Origen," "to Epiphanius," or "to Jerome" (so Evans 2007). Nevertheless, while taking due note of this caution, the following discussion will follow the current scholarly preference of tentatively distinguishing three main gospel-like texts traditionally labeled as "according to the Hebrews," "the Nazoreans," and "the Ebionites" (Frey 2012a and passim; Ehrman and Pleše 2011, 197–200; Gregory 2014, 41).

We begin, however, with a comment on the related 97 phenomenon of Jewish Christian variant readings in the canonical gospel manuscript tradition.

Jewish Christian Manuscript Variants

At least five Greek New Testament manuscripts (Gregory-Aland nos. 4, 273, 566, 899, 1424) reference alternative readings from a textual source designated "the Jewish [gospel]" (*to ioudaikon*; on which cf. Klauck 2003, 48–49; Evans 2007; Frey 2012d; texts and translations also in Ehrman and Pleše 2011, 201–2, 208–9). The fact that these sporadic variants occur *only* in relation to Matthew helps underscore the possibility that at least these cases represent a set of *supplementary* traditions to Matthew rather than an integral alternative gospel account.

It would seem that a series of traditional marginal glosses or supplementations to a scriptural text has been gathered into a collection sequentially structured by the run of that parent document, yet without constituting an integral part of its manuscript transmission. (Among a number of possible ancient parallels one might compare the similarly sporadic Jewish Palestinian Aramaic paraphrases of the Torah known as the *Fragment Targum*.)

Such a "paratext" model has several explanatory advantages. It would on the one hand help account for the surprisingly sympathetic reception of readings in the "Jewish gospel" (or gospels) by a number of early Christian writers who are otherwise decidedly unsympathetic to "apocryphal" Christian documents. Jerome and Alexandrian Christian writers like Origen and Didymus match their relatively favorable reception of Jewish Christian "variants" to the gospel tradition with a similar selective acceptance of alternative Jewish textual revisions of the Old Greek text of the Old Testament by Aquila, Symmachus, and Theodotion, whenever this helped secure the text's "fuller sense." On the other hand, such a reading also comports well with textual criticism's increasing recognition of the importance of marginalia and other paratexts for understanding New Testament manuscripts in the context of their use, reception, and interpretation. (At the time of writing, the University of Basel hosts a major European collaborative research project on Greek biblical paratexts [www.paratexbib.eu], while related work is envisaged at Birmingham and elsewhere.)

Some editions of the apocryphal gospels explicitly include these textual variants in their reconstruction specifically of the *Gospel according to the Nazoreans*, which they regard as closely related or identical (e.g., Schneemelcher 1991–92, 1:150; also Ehrman and Pleše 2011, 208–9).

The Gospel according to the Hebrews

The Gospel according to the Hebrews is the only such gospel whose title is so used in antiquity, and it appears to have been familiar particularly in Alexandrian Christianity. Nevertheless there is much confusion about the relationship between this and the other supposedly Jewish Christian gospels, which in turn makes it difficult to be certain about the content. Key quotations appear in Clement of Alexandria, Origen, and Jerome. They include the saying, "He who marvels shall be king and he who is king shall rest," or perhaps more fully, "He who seeks will not stop until he finds, having found he will marvel, and having marveled he will reign as king, and having reigned as king he will rest" (fragment 4a/b; Clement of Alexandria, *Stromateis* 2.45.5; 5.96.3). This is also echoed in the opening words of the *Gospel of Thomas*, and it is not clear how to understand the relationship with that text.

A very different saying appears in Origen (*Commentary on John* 2.12; *Homilies on Jeremiah* 15.4): "Just now my mother, the Holy Spirit, took me by one of my hairs and carried me away to the great Mount Tabor." Once again it is difficult to know what to make of this saying in isolation. The idea of the Holy Spirit as a mother is suggested by the feminine gender of the word *ruach* (breath, wind, spirit) in Semitic languages including Hebrew and Aramaic (but not in Greek or Latin), and it is a familiar theme in Syriac Christian literature. Like Proverbs and other Jewish texts, the gospel tradition, including Matthew, envisages a female figure of Wisdom (another grammatically feminine word, in Hebrew as well as Greek). Mount Tabor was sometimes regarded as the site of the transfiguration (Matt. 17:1–9) and perhaps also the mountain of the resurrection appearance in Matthew 28:16. The theme of the Holy Spirit carrying people suddenly to another location may also be implied in the narrative of Philip and the Ethiopian eunuch in Acts 8:39–40.

Jerome (*De viris illustribus* 2) also cites from the *Gospel according to the Hebrews* a striking narrative of the risen Jesus handing his burial shroud to "the servant of the priest" before appearing to James the Just and breaking bread with him (fragment 7)—thus filling an evident blank in the New Testament text, which records such an appearance (1 Cor. 15:7) without describing it. The narration of such an encounter would be of obvious importance to the diverse communities for whom James the brother of Jesus was a particularly prominent apostolic figure. Didymus the Blind (ca. 313–398) illustrates the idea that one person may have two names by attributing to the *Gospel according to the Hebrews* the confirmation that Matthias, the disciple who replaced Judas, is the same as the disciple called Levi in the gospels (*Commentary on the Psalms*, 184.8–10).

Eusebius may be somewhat less knowledgeable. He knows this text as a disputed document, and somewhat confusingly claims it is the gospel read by the Ebionites (*Ecclesiastical History* 3.27.4; cf. also 3.39.17, citing Papias).

Given the few clearly attributable quotations, we cannot be certain about the shape and structure of this text. In addition to a handful of sayings, there appears to have been some reference to the baptism and temptation of Jesus, the Last Supper, the resurrection, and the appearance to James. The story of Jesus and the adulterous woman (John 7:53–8:11) is occasionally also associated with this gospel (e.g., again by Eusebius, citing Papias: *Ecclesiastical History* 3.39.17) but this seems difficult to verify. All in all, the evidence does not suggest a complete and coherent alternative narrative ranging from the baptism to the cross and resurrection (and to that extent it is far from clear that these texts constitute narrative gospels, *pace* Markschies 2012a).

The Gospel according to the Nazoreans

The Gospel according to the Nazoreans is known from Epiphanius and especially from Jerome, who seems to distinguish it from the *Gospel according to the Hebrews*—although, as previously indicated, the demarcation lines seem decidedly blurred (see esp. Frey 2010, 2012a, 2012b, 2012c, etc.). Jerome also gives the most extensive extracts and claims to have translated them from Hebrew (or perhaps Aramaic) into Greek, using a manuscript he discovered in the library at Caesarea—although he himself is at times inconsistent in how he identifies and discusses these sources (Ehrman and Pleše 2011, 199). Several of the episodes resemble synoptic narratives, especially as in Matthew—indeed Jerome adduces several of his citations specifically as variations or additions to the Matthean text. (Others, however, suspect dependence on something rather more like a gospel harmony: see Klauck 2003, 45; Luomanen 2012.)

In this connection it is worth noting the continuing scholarly debate about whether a manuscript tradition of Matthew in Hebrew may in some circles have survived from antiquity until the Middle Ages. The discoveries in the genizah of the Old Synagogue at Cairo (see p. 28 above) have long been noted for their Jewish reuse of several Greek New Testament manuscripts in palimpsests; these included parts of Matthew (chap. 10) along with John, Acts, and 1 Peter. A more interesting case, however, is the reproduction of a complete text of Matthew (and parts of Mark) in Hebrew in a fourteenth-century polemical treatise by the Jewish writer Shem Tob ben Isaac (also known as Ibn Shaprut). This shows signs of Jewish Christian translational usage relating to the divine name, matters of halakah or law observance, a messianic understanding of Elijah, and the view of the Gentiles. From these features it has sometimes been thought that Ibn Shaprut could be indebted to a much earlier Jewish version of the Gospel of Matthew from antiquity (see Evans 2007, 267–70; Howard 1995). Horbury (1997), however, has shown that a number of the "Jewish" features of this text actually reflect inner-Jewish polemics (including the *Toledot Yeshu*, on which see below, p. 129), while other distinctive textual variants are just as likely influenced by earlier Christian gospel traditions in different languages (but not particularly Hebrew).

Relevant stories include Jesus healing a builder with a withered hand and the assertion that at the death of Jesus, instead of the Temple's veil being torn, its enormous lintel was smashed. Scholars often agree that the flavor of these stories is synoptic, but it is very difficult to know what more we can say about the origin and setting. It remains worth considering if they are perhaps just intermittent alternative readings or annotations to a Matthean gospel outline.

The Gospel according to the Ebionites

The document known to contemporary scholarship as the *Gospel of* (or: *according to*) *the Ebionites* is also untitled in antiquity. While Jerome appears to think that Ebionites and Nazoreans read the same Jewish Christian gospel (*Commentary on Matthew* 23.35), a distinctively Ebionite gospel finds its most explicit ancient witness

101

in the fourth-century antiheretical work of Epiphanius known as the "Medicine Chest" (*Panarion*) or *Refutation of All Heresies*. Epiphanius claims (30.13.2–3) that the group called the Ebionites were related to but distinct from the Nazoreans, were named after a heretical teacher called Ebion, and read an Ebionite gospel related either to Matthew or to the *Gospel according to the Hebrews*.

Overall it is fairly clear to most scholars that Epiphanius (drawing on Irenaeus, *Against Heresies* 1.26.2) conflates and confuses a number of early Christian traditions both about Hebrew gospel material associated with Matthew and about a group called the Ebionites, whose name derives not from an arch-heretic but from the Hebrew word *ebyon*, meaning "poor." (Origen, who was more aware of the term's Hebrew or Aramaic meaning, instead mocked the group for the eponymous "poverty" of their intellect [*First Principles* 4.2] or of their Jewish law observance [*Against Celsus* 2.1].)

But regardless of Epiphanius's multiple confusion about the nature and identity of his source, the seven quotations he gives from it hold considerable interest and suggest that he had at least partial access to a genuine Jewish Christian source.

Three units about John the Baptist are given, including an unexplained omission of locusts from his diet and an expanded vision of the dove at the baptism of Jesus. Fragment 5 introduces Jesus as about thirty years of age and entering the house of Simon Peter when he first comes to Capernaum. There Jesus narrates his call of the disciples in the first person singular, partly reflecting a third-person narrative in the Synoptic Gospels. After comments about Jesus' family that resemble the account in Mark 3, a further fragment (6) attributes to Jesus the intention to abolish sacrifice ("I have come to do away with sacrifices, and if you do not stop sacrificing, the wrath of God will not depart from you"). In the final fragment, Jesus denies that he wants to eat meat at his final Passover—perhaps representing an attempt to explain the absence of any reference to a sacrificial Passover lamb at the Last Supper. (This is a theme that, together with the substitution of honey cakes for locusts in John the Baptist's diet, has sometimes been thought to indicate support for vegetarianism—see, e.g., Kelhoffer 2004, 139–40.) The text evidently ranges in synoptic fashion across different parts of the ministry of Jesus, but it is again not clear to what extent we may presume that it formed part of a comprehensive narrative.

102

Epiphanius seems to assume that this document is basically a corruption of Matthew—a point that would chime in well with our earlier observation about Matthean paratexts. But although the material looks vaguely synoptic, it cannot be straightforwardly associated with any one canonical tradition; indeed Gregory (2008, 63–64) suggests that its portrayal of the Baptist shares elements with the canonical gospels more generally. If that is correct, this would once again support the idea of a somewhat indirect, perhaps oral dependence on the Synoptic Gospels, quite possibly by way of an informal gospel harmony conflating elements from different Synoptic Gospel narratives (so also Ehrman and Pleše 2011, 210; cf. more fully Gregory 2014).

The *Gospel of the Ebionites* evidently operates within a well-attested Jewish and Jewish Christian cultural space, in which the cessation of sacrifices was regarded as a potential problem and a matter of dispute. In that context, the attribution to Jesus of a saying about this matter could become important for Jesus-believers and others as they articulated ways of Jewish life without the Jerusalem Temple (for this problem more generally, cf. Ego, Lange, and Pilhofer 1999; K. Jones 2011; Stroumsa 2009).

All in all, the so-called Jewish Christian gospels are not only fragmentary but also surprisingly disparate in flavor and substance. Frey (2010, 137) wisely concludes that they give us no access to early gospel tradition, except potentially in liturgically rooted expressions like certain phrases connected to the Lord's Prayer (e.g., "Give us today the bread you will give us in your kingdom," attested in Jerome, *Commentary on Psalm* 85).

Were There Other Jewish Gospels?

A Christian or even non-Christian Jewish origin of several other texts has sometimes been suggested. As we will see, several of the papyrus fragments about the ministry of Jesus could potentially be related to Jewish Christian traditions. This does not of course constitute evidence for a multiplicity of such gospels, but it does suggest something of the potential diversity of gospel-like texts that might be identified as Jewish Christian.

Claims for certain later documents are even more complex and controversial. An alternative Coptic version of much of Matthew 5–28 is known from a papyrus dating from the first half of the

103

fourth century (Codex Schøyen 2650). Although its initial editor saw here an alternative noncanonical version of Matthew characterized by a more consciously Jewish reading (Schenke 2001), more recent critical study suggests a rather free and perhaps harmonizing translation, with annotations and minor abridgment, of what may have been a relatively high-quality Greek text of Matthew (see the important critique in Leonard 2014). On that account there is insufficient evidence here to identify this Coptic text as a Jewish Christian gospel.

We will return below (pp. 129–32) to two much later documents that do represent alternative gospels originating respectively from a Jewish and an Islamic context.

Ministry Gospels on Papyrus

In addition to the so-called Jewish Christian gospels preserved only in ancient citations, a number of more recently discovered texts about the ministry of Jesus survive on papyrus. All of these finds are, like several texts discussed above, fragmentary parts of what might at one time have been a larger whole.

While in most cases it seems clear that additional material must have preceded or followed the surviving extract, here too the extent and nature of such absent text is almost invariably unknown to us and impossible to reconstruct. (When these documents first came to light, more than one of them was unhelpfully named "Unknown Gospel," an analytically vacuous designation that is still occasionally deployed in contemporary editions—e.g., for the *Unknown Berlin Gospel* in Markschies and Schröter 2012.)

As discussed earlier (above, pp. 31, 43), the fragmentary nature of these texts sheds light on important critical questions surrounding many of the texts discussed in this book. It is right to insist that the existence in antiquity of full noncanonical gospel narratives remains entirely conceivable. However, given that not a single one survives, we will do well to continue weighing the possibility that some, most, or even all of these texts were perhaps only ever attestations of select traditions, and therefore *inherently* partial or fragmentary, at least as gospels. That likelihood seems greater still for magical or amulet-like texts (e.g., P.Oxy. 1384; see the discussion of

104

amulets above, p. 33), as it does for many other fragmentary texts of doubtful or hybrid literary genre. Even in apparently gospel-like texts we simply cannot be certain whether an extant fragment represents part of a larger continuous gospel.

This question is rendered more difficult by the fact that most of these fragments are only attested in single copies. Circular arguments from silence abound. Scholars therefore sometimes wisely step back to acknowledge that what they like to term a "gospel" might just as easily have been part of a paraphrase, homily, or commentary. Certainly only a small handful of the extant ancient texts claim to be gospels, and a few more were thus identified in antiquity, but most others were not.

In his large German edition, Markschies (2012f, 1239–40) rightly acknowledges not only the familiar subgenre distinctions between "sayings" gospels, "narrative" gospels, and "dialogue" gospels, but also the blurred boundaries between these and a collective category that he identifies as "gospel meditations." Markschies illustrates that category with reference to Nag Hammadi's *Gospel of Truth*, the *Gospel of Gamaliel* (a Marian "lament" homily, perhaps from Oxyrhynchus), and the so-called *Anonymous Apocryphal Gospel* as examples. Markschies's appropriate methodological nuance stands in contrast with a continuing tendency in some circles to extrapolate from oblique or unusual gospel echoes to a proliferation of apocryphal "gospels."

"Gospel meditations" of this sort manifest a degree of familiarity with elements of the New Testament gospels and aim to combine reflection about the gospel message of Jesus with quasi-homiletical appropriation and—particularly in gnostic circles—with the disclosure of additional saving knowledge. Markschies's examples derive overwhelmingly from gnostic literature, where the prevalence of epiphanic as well as didactic dialogue texts makes definitional boundaries particularly difficult (cf. Nagel 2014, vi; also Markschies 2012f). But the problem of bloated and distended gospel genres is arguably no less acute for the fragmentary "ministry gospels."

Most recent introductions agree that two ministry gospel discoveries stand out as particularly important: Papyrus Egerton 2 (newly reconnected to Papyrus Köln 255) and Papyrus Oxyrhynchus 840. We begin with these, followed by a few others that will be covered more briefly.

Papyrus Egerton 2 (+ Papyrus Köln 255)

Papyrus Egerton 2 was named after a benefactor who enabled the British Museum to purchase a number of Egyptian papyri, subsequently first published in 1935. Among them were four leaves of a papyrus codex, written on both sides, two of which remain quite legible and contain five episodes of noncanonical Jesus tradition.

Like many other such discoveries, this was at first identified as an "unknown gospel." As in virtually every other case, it is impossible to tell whether this formed part of a larger gospel narrative or not—scholarly claims to the contrary notwithstanding. On the one hand, reference to "the hour of his being handed over" (fragment 1, line 8) certainly suggests awareness of a larger context of narrative which, notably, is once again reminiscent of the frame of the canonical gospels. But what seems wholly unclear from the extant fragment is whether *for this particular case* that context did in fact constitute an entire "Egerton Gospel" life of Jesus or rather a more limited, perhaps homiletical or metatextual "rewritten gospel" excerpt composed in awareness of an existing larger narrative outline resembling that canonical frame. (Writers like Crossan [1991, 428] and more recently Nicklas [2009, 104–5] and Watson [2013, 334 and passim] somewhat too confidently assume the former.)

The sequence of pages is unclear, and in at least one place an important reconstruction of the text remains contested. A missing part of the first leaf has turned up separately in a papyrus collection in Cologne (P.Köln 255), and editions of the text since the 1990s have reintegrated this fragment (see Nicklas 2009).

In recent scholarship the manuscript itself is said to date from around the year 200—possibly a little later, based on the use in P.Köln 255 of a scribal apostrophe (separating two consonants) that became more common in the third century. The original text could have been composed a few decades earlier. We cannot tell whether this was in Syria, Egypt, or elsewhere, although the fact that no copies, quotations, or even references to it appear to survive may suggest that its influence was confined to Egypt—and that even there it did not circulate widely.

In any case it is striking that here one of our earliest surviving noncanonical gospel manuscripts is already presented in the physical form of a codex rather than a scroll—a technological shift characteristic of early Christian writing. And like other early Christian

106

texts, this papyrus also uses a familiar scribal convention of abbreviating important holy names like God, Lord, Jesus, and Christ but also, unusually, prophets like Moses and Isaiah (see Nicklas 2009, 17–18, and more generally on these *nomina sacra* Hurtado 2006).

The subject matter concerns the encounter between the teaching of Jesus and certain Jewish opponents. As is also sometimes supposed for the Gospels of Matthew and John, this could double as a cipher for this conflict in the experience of the apostolic church, potentially mirroring later experiences.

The two legible fragments of P.Eger. 2 are inscribed on both sides. Only fragment 1 provides significant amounts of text; the verso and recto sides of P.Köln 255 clearly continue the verso and recto of P.Eger. 2, fragment 1, and are now generally treated as such (although confusingly still given separate entries in some recent editions, including Markschies and Schröter 2012). Text and translation of both papyri are presented together in Ehrman and Pleše 2011, 2014; also Bernhard 2006, 84–97 and plates 18–25.

Content

Fragment 1 (with P.Köln 255) shows Jesus in conversation with Jewish opponents. The fragment opens with the concluding response to a preceding episode, the rest of which is lost. Next, Jesus addresses Jewish leaders on the subject of Israel's Scriptures and the extent to which they testify to him, in language that looks closely reminiscent of, and in some fashion literarily dependent on, the similar "search the scriptures" controversy in John (5:39, 45–46; 9:29; cf. Nicklas 2014b, 18–19). This is followed by the audience's attempt to seize Jesus and stone him. As in John 10:39 (cf. 7:30 and Luke 4:30), however, Jesus departs because the "hour" of his surrender has not yet come. In the next episode a leper comes to Jesus for healing, in an abbreviated parallel to Mark 1:40–44 that opens with the interesting narrative embellishment that the patient had contracted his leprosy by eating with lepers in their hospice (an unlikely scenario in first-century Palestine, as a number of interpreters point out). The miracle almost seems a reward for the man's selfless conduct. In addition to the Markan instruction to show himself to the priests as prescribed in the law, Jesus also warns the healed leper to sin no more (as in John 5:14; cf. 8:11; and see Nicklas 2013; cf. Watson 2013, 323–24).

Fragment 2 begins with a flattering overture from the Jewish leaders introducing a version of the dispute about paying taxes to Caesar from Mark 12:13–17. Instead of the familiar answer, however, Jesus replies angrily on a note of prophetic protest, quoting Isaiah 29:13 about the people's unwillingness to honor God with their hearts rather than merely with their lips (cf. Matt. 15:7–9// Mark 7:6–7). The reverse of fragment 2 is more damaged, but seems to contain two episodes that are otherwise unknown from the gospel tradition. Some reconstruct an opening saying about seeds and harvest, though even that seems a little optimistic given the state of the text. The second half of the page shows Jesus by the shores of the Jordan stretching out his hand and either sowing or sprinkling something—possibly hinting at a miracle story. The reading here again seems uncertain at best.

Interpretation

The gospel-like text constituted by P.Eger. 2 and P.Köln 255 relates extensively to traditions found in the New Testament gospels, and there is a widely held (although still debated) critical view that it reflects at least indirect knowledge of something like the canonical text of John. A maximalist view of clear *literary* dependence on all four canonical gospels was favored in some older editions (e.g., Schneemelcher 1991–92, 1:97) and is still sometimes cited approvingly (e.g., Porter 2013, 56).

Against this view it is occasionally claimed that our text represents instead an *earlier*, more Jewish Christian form of quasi-Johannine tradition (Watson [2013, 330–40] calls it a "Mosaic stratum"), which the Gospel of John then assimilates and alters in the direction of a more radical Christology and a firmer separation from Judaism. While it is indeed true that fragment 2 incorporates significant noncanonical traditions or supplementations, most readers would regard fragment 1 as more closely conversant with prior Johannine concerns. Although not by itself decisive, the early and persistent evidence of John's dissemination and overwhelming influence (cf., e.g., Hill 2010a; others cited in Rasimus 2010) might seem prima facie to favor the Fourth Gospel's priority over a text that disappeared without trace. For John to have used P.Eger. 2 would, moreover, require the implausible technique of singling out

108

precisely its Johannine-sounding elements while taking care to omit the synoptic ones (see Hill 2004, 304–5).

Here, as in many other cases we have encountered, the language of a *literary* dependence of texts like this on the New Testament gospels may underplay the extent to which the protocanonical four exercise an influence that is often not strictly literary, but could just as easily be in terms of a secondary *oral* familiarity (so, e.g., Klauck 2003, 25, on P.Eger. 2; Labahn [2000, 272–75] believes the same may also characterize John's relationship to the Synoptics). To the extent that the writer may have knowledge of a written copy of John, Tobias Nicklas shrewdly suggests that its "dependence" is of a sort that nevertheless takes significant liberties with a Johannine text whose Palestinian world it does not inhabit and whose wording it does not regard as definitive (2014b, 19; cf. further Nicklas 2009, 97 and passim; contrast the reassertion of a more straightforwardly literary dependence on John in Bauckham 2014, 193–96).

On balance, we find here an extract from a gospel-like narrative about Jesus that was either a short vignette or possibly part of a longer narrative. The wording is both derivative and yet to an extent autonomous of the gospels that became canonical—whether or not one chooses to portray that relationship as competitive. There is certainly no evidence suggesting knowledge of each of the Four as discrete works (as Jeremias and Schneemelcher [1991, 97] thought). But nor, on the other hand, is this a harmony. Nothing in the text requires us to see here a deliberate substitute for the canonical Fourth Gospel, even if the writer's departure from John's text perhaps allows for that possibility.

Papyrus Egerton 2 stands on the margins of the emerging fourfold gospel tradition, which it may not know as such but on which it depends—and without which, significantly, its episodic narrative awareness of Jesus would look substantially diminished, not to say incomprehensible. The very reason that this Jesus is of interest as standing in conflict with Jewish leaders, both about the law and about his own identity, must be because he was already familiar to the writer and his audience as the singular protagonist within a larger saving narrative.

This text shares John's keen awareness of the complex and at times conflictual relationship between Jesus, the Jewish leaders, and the Jewish people, even if the extant text does not cover the

109

Johannine passages of the sharpest hostility. Some have seen behind this toned-down language an apologetic context which, while much less familiar with John's Palestinian setting, nevertheless required a Jesus who could be seen as more compatible with Moses (e.g., Zelyck 2013, 46–47, citing Erlemann 1996; cf. further Watson 2013, cited above). Somewhat unusually, the text abbreviates the name Moses as a sacred name (*nomen sacrum*).

In the absence of additional information we cannot be sure about this document's original extent. Nothing points to extensive circulation or any authoritative afterlife.

"Papyrus" Oxyrhynchus 840

The document cataloged as "papyrus" Oxyrhynchus 840 is in fact a leaf of parchment (i.e., prepared animal skin). It originates from a miniature codex dating from the fourth or fifth century, which due to its size (but for no other compelling reason) is sometimes thought to have served as an amulet. The Greek text is fragmentary but extends to forty-five lines over two pages. It begins and ends in the middle of a sentence. After the concluding phrase of the previous paragraph, which is otherwise lost to us, the text begins its intriguing story of Jesus in controversy with a Pharisaic priest. (For text and translation, see Ehrman and Pleše 2011, 2014; Kruger 2005, 2009; Blumell and Wayment 2015, No. 77; Bernhard 2006, 120–25 (plate 27 provides only an illegible image of the verso)

Content

Jesus takes his disciples into what is called the place of purification in the Temple. He is challenged by an opponent, somewhat unusually described as a Pharisaic chief priest (perhaps by the name of Levi, line 10). This man engages Jesus on questions of purity and ritual washing by pointing out that only a person who has ritually bathed his feet and changed his clothes is permitted to see the Temple's holy implements. In answer to Jesus' counterquestion of whether his opponent is himself clean, the priest replies that he has indeed bathed in the pool of David, entering it by one set of stairs and exiting by the other, and putting on white clean clothes before entering the holy precinct to gaze on the sacred vessels.

110

Jesus, now identified as "the Savior," then launches into a statement of woes which contrasts outer and inner purity in a manner similar to Matthew 23:25–28. The content of these woes is to chastise the spiritually blind who take pains to bathe in the requisite running water even though dogs and pigs may have previously frolicked in it, or who scrub their skin just as prostitutes and flute girls do before they put on makeup to satisfy men. Such outward beauty conceals internal scorpions and unrighteousness, but, by contrast, Jesus and his disciples have bathed in the water of eternal life.

Interpretation

The significance of this text remains debated and depends to a considerable extent on its context and setting, as extensive recent study has shown (most fully Kruger 2005; cf. Kruger 2008, 2009). While the central narrative represents a tradition independent of the protocanonical gospels, its proximity especially to synoptic passages like Matthew 7–8, 15 is nevertheless worth noting.

Like Matthew, this writer clearly deploys a thinly veiled anti-Gentile polemic in highlighting the impurity of dogs and pigs, used in antiquity and indeed in the Jesus tradition as a metaphor for people who, like Gentiles, were regarded as invariably careless about purity. The point here seems to be that the stale water (literal or symbolic) in which the Pharisaic chief priest has bathed was contaminated by those (animals or people) who disregard purity. This is in addition to the less overtly racial motif of contempt for prostitutes and flute girls (cf. Matt. 7:6; 15:26–27; and parallels). Despite scholarly claims to the contrary, this text's anti-Pharisaism need not equate to anti-Judaism.

While terms like "water of life" might seem at first sight to evoke similar language in texts like John 4:14; 7:38, a number of other aspects of this fascinating text link it more specifically with Jewish Christian concerns about purity. Water as such cannot convey purity, except as "living" water, especially when immorality remains unaddressed.

Leaving aside that particular question, it is clear nevertheless that this document retains a surprisingly specific awareness of issues surrounding Temple purity and ritual washing. Although it is nowhere mentioned in the New Testament gospels and would no longer be anyone's contemporary experience in the second century, until 70 CE

111

Jews did indeed immerse in a *miqvah* (a ritual bath) before entering the Temple precinct. Dozens of such baths have been uncovered in archaeological excavations around the southwestern corner of the Jerusalem Temple precinct, and the early rabbinic legal anthology known as the Mishnah seems to confirm that postbiblical convention (e.g., Mishnah *Yoma* 3:3). A few of these excavated baths did turn up with separated steps for entering the water in an unclean state and exiting after immersion; and the construction of partitioned steps into and out of these pools is similarly found at Qumran. The habit of changing into a clean set of clothes after ritual immersion is also well attested (including, it seems, in New Testament texts like Gal. 3:27; cf. Rom. 13:12–14; Eph. 4:22–24; Col. 3:9–14). The reference to "poured out" water in the *miqvah*, possibly understood as running into it from a cistern some distance away, where it was subject to contamination, may allude to the standard Jewish halakic requirements for a supply of fresh water to ritual baths (e.g., Mishnah *Mikwa'ot* 4:4; 5:5). Jesus and his disciples, by contrast, have bathed in "living water"—the text here is only partly legible, but this could indicate a polemical requirement for fresh running water as more appropriate and symbolic of baptism.

The surprising emphasis on *seeing* the holy implements seems to some commentators to document the author's ignorance of Second Temple Judaism. And yet Judaism both before and after the destruction of the Temple took very seriously the command of Exodus 23:17, which called on every male in Israel to appear before the Lord God three times a year. In rabbinic teaching it was recognized that the Hebrew word meaning "he shall appear" could just as easily be translated "he shall behold." Indeed, Josephus (*Antiquities* 3.127–28) and rabbinic sources make it clear that one of the features of the Festival of Tabernacles in particular was that at a certain point the curtains were rolled back to permit the people to observe the Temple furniture as representing this beholding of the Lord (see Schwartz 1986; Anderson 2009, 172–82; also Kruger 2009). Even after the Temple's destruction, Roman Jews had a continuing consciousness of the Temple furniture's presence in their city (Noy 1998, 116), while rabbis were said to visit all the way from Palestine in the late first century in order to view the Temple implements on public display in the Senate building (see, e.g., Tosefta *Yoma* 2:16; Jerusalem Talmud *Yoma*, 4:1, 41c; *Genesis Rabbah* 10:7; with discussion in Fine 2007; Fraade 2009).

All this is not of course to argue for the historicity of this narrative episode (although Jeremias [1947] and others thought this plausible). But it might nevertheless represent the sort of historicizing aggiornamento that one also encounters in the Mishnah's representation in the third century of Temple proceedings in the present tense, in vivid colors and considerable detail.

Other features, however, fit a later setting more easily. The contrast between outer ritual and inner moral purity (lines 35–41) is striking, but it has an antecedent in Matthew 23:16–28. More significant for the date of this tradition, perhaps, is the historical credibility of the idea that Jesus meets a chief priest who is also a Pharisee: no high priest (*archiereus*) called Levi is known at any time in the first century, and chief priests were overwhelmingly Sadducees (although it is worth bearing in mind the apparent integration into the rabbinic movement of figures like Rabbi Hanina the deputy high priest, *segan ha-kohanim*: e.g., Mishnah *Avot* 3:2).

More significantly, recent years have seen a gathering scholarly argument that the composition of the text as it stands may not date much earlier than the extant fourth- or fifth-century manuscript, since it appears to allude to the substance and terminology of liturgical developments that first came into use at that time. In particular, some have seen connections with significant church-synagogue contestations about the validity of their respective ablutions (Zelyck 2014), while others suspect a backdrop of disputes about baptism and purity between gnostics and Manicheans on the one hand and "orthodox" groups on the other (e.g., Bovon 2000; followed by Klauck 2003, 27; Lindemann 2011, 776–77; Stewart-Sykes 2009).

Only in the fourth century did the use of two distinct sets of steps for entry and exit become a feature of Christian baptismal architecture, as is here supposed (25–26, *di' heteras klimakos*); at Qumran and at the Temple Mount, by contrast, the separation between unclean entry and pure exit was achieved by a (twin) ridge down the middle of the *same* single set of steps. On the other hand, the apparent concern about the potentially defiled source of the running water required for immersion (32–34) relates more specifically to Jewish or Jewish Christian halakah than to wider Christian debates or critiques of baptism (cf. *Didache* 7.1–3; Pseudo-Clementine *Contestatio* 1.2; *Apostolic Tradition* 21.2). Others also point out that the viewing of holy implements became a renewed controversy toward the end of the fourth century following the introduction of

113

curtains or screens to veil the climactic moments of the eucharistic liturgy (echoing partly Old Testament sentiments and partly the experiences of mystery religions); and around this time the eucharistic implements began to be identified as "holy vessels" (cf. Buchinger and Hernitscheck 2014, 122–23 and nn.).

A fourth-century date is therefore increasingly entertained in recent scholarship on P.Oxy. 840. Given the somewhat inconclusive evidence, it seems on balance best to recognize that this text may well be developing a Jewish Christian tradition that could have carried contextual frisson in more than one historical period. Disputes about the significance of purity, baptismal praxis, and sacramentality not only had their place in the first and second centuries (as the *Didache*, the *Epistle of Barnabas*, and early Pseudo-Clementine traditions attest) but continued to matter in late antiquity.

If P.Oxy. 840 did have roots in the second century, its milieu was one in which concerns for the Temple were to some extent still alive, but in which its demise had created sharp disagreements about the spiritualization or abiding significance of purity laws, some of which had become impossible to maintain without the Temple. This question of the relationship between the Old and New Testaments occupied Gentile Christian circles too, including followers of Marcion and Valentinus (among the latter notably the author of *Ptolemy's Letter to Flora*, preserved by Epiphanius). Second-century Jewish believers in Jesus, on the other hand, may naturally have asked these Temple-related questions of the Jesus tradition with a greater degree of existential urgency.

The story could thus fit a number of contexts sensitive to Jewish or Judaizing Christian concerns during the first five centuries. In its opposition to any literal observance of purity it may represent some of the more radical positions: an increasing alienation from mainstream Judaism, expressed through an articulation of the Jesus tradition in possibly indirect and nonliterary awareness of the protocanonical gospels.

Other Papyrus Fragments

In addition to these two particularly important and well-known texts, the past century's discoveries have brought to light a number of mostly smaller fragments on papyrus that seem appropriate to include under our heading of ministry gospels. In the scholarly literature they are sometimes still identified as "unknown gospels," although this designation arguably begs the question of their genre and textual intention from the start. These documents are invariably intriguing in their attestation of a time and place when a rich diversity of Christian textual expression continued to flourish alongside copies or harmonic conflations of one or more of the gospels that became canonical. Although a number of these texts are too fragmentary to detain us here, the following are worth considering in brief.

Papyrus Berlin 11710

This text of two tiny leaves of a sixth-century papyrus is written in a semiliterary hand in Greek, with a Coptic colophon (a concluding scribal note). It appears to offer a narrative development and expansion of an episode resembling Jesus' encounter with Nathanael and draws on motifs encountered in John 1:29, 49. The extant text permits very few conclusions, although the small page size (with a surviving short piece of thread used in the binding) and the concluding Coptic words "Jesus Christ, God" have widely been taken to indicate an amulet or book for personal use, rather than a gospel manuscript in the conventional public sense (see further Bernhard 2006, 102, 126–27 and plates 28–31; Kraus 2009, 228–39; Porter 2012; also Ehrman and Pleše 2011, 2014).

Papyrus Oxyrhynchus 210

Two further third-century Greek papyri from Oxyrhynchus merit inclusion in this chapter. The first, P.Oxy. 210, cannot be confidently connected to the ministry of Jesus, but may instead be a paraphrase or homily loosely based on gospel themes. Despite the absence of a clear narrative frame, we include it here under the ministry heading because its two poorly preserved and awkwardly inscribed fragments reference several pre-Easter motifs, including Jesus' teaching about the good tree bringing forth good fruit (Matt. 7:16–20; 12:33–35), although other New Testament allusions appear to range well beyond the gospels. (The theme of good fruit versus bad fruit, although doubtless a commonplace, also resurfaces in other noncanonical fragments, including P.Merton 51, discussed below.) Some have suspected a potential allusion to a nativity theme in the reference to an angel on the mostly illegible recto. Nothing in the

115

text offers assurance that the document to which these fragments belonged constituted a gospel (despite occasional bold claims to the contrary—e.g., Porter 2013, 57–58 and 58n42). The document is omitted from the "gospel fragments" in Kraus, Kruger, and Nicklas 2009, but text and translation are included in Ehrman and Pleše 2011, 2014; Blumell and Wayment 2015, No. 63; Bernhard 2006, 108–13 and plates 24–25.

Papyrus Oxyrhynchus 1224

Six pages of gospel-like material from a fourth-century codex have been brought together under the single identification P.Oxy. 1224, combining one small two-sided fragment and one larger bifoliate (folded two-sheet) leaf. Only fragment 2, presented in double columns, allows for substantial reconstruction.

Explicit page numbers 139 and 174, respectively, at the top of fragments 1 recto and 2 verso (col. 1) suggest that at least thirty-two pages are missing between them (fragment 2 recto appears to be p. 173, while fragment 1 verso could be p. 140; my inspection of the fragments in 2015 confirmed this interpretation of page numbers, although in the case of p. 139 the ink had notably deteriorated compared to the photographic plates published in Kraus 2009). This sizable gap in pagination would either imply a substantial original document or else, and perhaps more likely, cast doubt on whether the two fragments really constitute part of the same work rather than, say, part of a relatively extensive anthology. (Significantly, too, the often haphazard circumstances of the original excavations at Oxyrhynchus permit very little certainty about the proximity of these two fragments *in situ*.)

Four narrative units can be identified in fragment 2. First, Jesus appears to the first-person speaker explicitly in a vision (recto col. 2). Next (verso col. 1), the speaker or another person addresses Jesus (?), reproving opponents who accuse him of "new teaching" and a "new baptism" (cf. Mark 1:27). Thirdly (verso col. 2), scribes, Pharisees, and priests are angry at Jesus for keeping company with sinners (cf. Mark 2:15–17 and parallels). And finally (recto col. 1), there is a composite instruction to pray for one's enemies, expanding on motifs found in texts like Matthew 5:44//Luke 6:28 and Mark 9:40.

116

Neither narrative continuity nor the presence of any "gospel" outline can be assumed; the text ranges freely from teaching to controversy to visionary encounter. Like other noncanonical gospels, this document is clearly familiar with synoptic-like Jesus tradition, although once again that familiarity is not best seen in terms of a direct literary dependence. Most scholars see here a mid-second-century composition that continues a process of reception in its loose—possibly secondary oral—knowledge of a hybrid Markan and Matthean tradition. As has often been pointed out, in its handling of issues like martyrdom or Christology, this oral engagement seems "saturated . . . in ecclesiastical conditions and practices of the second century" (Kirk 2007, 157; following Head 1992a and Lührmann 2004). A few others, like the contributors to Miller 1994, prefer instead to find here support for their notion of proliferating mid-*first*-century gospels.)

The fullest recent treatment is Foster 2010c; the best critical edition is perhaps Kraus 2009, 264–80, with good photographs at plate 15; cf. Blumell and Wayment 2015, No. 75 and plate 26. Introduction and translation are also included in Ehrman and Pleše 2011, 2014.

Papyrus Merton 51

Papyrus Merton 51, a single small leaf of papyrus, is generally dated to the third century. The Greek text is written on both sides of the page; scholarly editions and translations present it extensively reconstructed from canonical parallels—an interpretative approach that seems, in the nature of the case, both plausible and defensible. The document is a paraphrase (or, as the original editors surmised, a homily) concerned with Jesus' teaching about repentance in Luke 6–7. The extant material reflects familiarity with Luke 7:29–30, 36 on the recto side and with Luke 6:45–46 (and possibly *Thomas* 45?) on the verso. Scholars generally acknowledge that nothing in the text hints at the context of a larger contiguous gospel account, as opposed to a shorter treatise or homily. (See text, translation, and discussion in Ehrman and Pleše 2011, 2014; Kraus 2009, 2012b; also Bernhard 2006, 106–7)

PSI XI 1200bis

In the early 1970s, a researcher at Florence's Laurentian Library was working on a second-century papyrus roll from Oxyrhynchus containing a manuscript of Plato's *Gorgias*. He discovered that a tiny, almost unreadable fragment had been mistakenly filed with this text, even though the notable presence of *nomina sacra* suggests instead a certain proximity to early Christian texts. Attempts at a more specific reconstruction, particularly its identification as part of an apocryphal gospel, remain rather speculative; Blumell and Wayment 2015, No. 79 identify it as a "patristic text" of eschatological orientation, perhaps a sermon. Nicklas (2012a) suspects among related Christian texts the unidentified source that is apparently quoted in *Epistle of Barnabas* 6.13: "Enter into a land flowing with milk and honey, and rule over it." (Cf. further Lührmann and Schlarb 2000, 178–79.) Although it is included in several recent apocryphal gospel collections, neither the fragment, labeled PSI XI 1200bis, nor the cited passage from *Barnabas* suggests a dominical saying, let alone part of a gospel.

Papyrus Oxyrhynchus 5072

A late-second- or early-third-century gospel fragment from Oxyrhynchus labeled 5072 was first published in volume 76 of the official edition, and has since been the subject of additional discussion in print as well as on the Internet (Chapa 2011, 2012; Blumell and Wayment 2015, No. 54; cf. Nicklas 2012c). The fragment extends to twenty-four broken lines on both sides, and may have been part of a larger codex. A scribal paragraph marker and several punctuation marks have been thought indicative of possible public reading, although this is hardly conclusive. The document's antiquity is impressive, and it may be "the second earliest [unidentified *non-*canonical] gospel fragment" after P.Eger. 2 (Chapa 2012, 382). (It is worth recalling here that a dozen or more manuscripts of the canonical gospels are earlier or roughly contemporary, including $\mathfrak{P}^4$, $\mathfrak{P}^5$, $\mathfrak{P}^{52}$, $\mathfrak{P}^{64+67}$, $\mathfrak{P}^{66}$, $\mathfrak{P}^{75}$, $\mathfrak{P}^{77}$, $\mathfrak{P}^{90}$, $\mathfrak{P}^{103}$, $\mathfrak{P}^{104}$, and possibly Aland 0171.) There are interesting parallels with P.Eger. 2 (including uncommon *nomina sacra*); other comparably early apocryphal fragments include at least P.Oxy. 2949 and 4009 and the possible *Diatessaron* fragment P.Dura 10, all of which are discussed elsewhere in this book.

118   On the recto side, the manuscript presents parts of a story resembling the exorcism of the Gadarene demoniac(s) (Matt. 8:28–34//Mark 5:1–20//Luke 8:26–39). The language generally

echoes Matthew and Luke rather than Mark, but does not closely follow any one gospel. The document appears to conflate this story with exorcisms of the man in the Capernaum synagogue (Mark 1:23–28//Luke 4:33–37) and of the boy healed immediately after the transfiguration (Matt. 17:14–21//Mark 9:14–29//Luke 9:37–42). The demon-possessed man "tears" his chains (cf. Luke 8:29; Mark 5:4) or possibly his clothes, but also shouts and objects that the "son" has "come before the time" (Matt. 8:29), before Jesus "rebukes" him (a feature of other synoptic exorcisms, e.g., Mark 1:25//Luke 4:35; Mark 9:25//Matt. 17:18//Luke 9:42; cf. Mark 8:33) and apparently casts the demon out. Interestingly, however, the missing space on the page appears insufficient to accommodate the actual expulsion of the demon(s) and their transfer into a herd of pigs stampeding to its demise in the lake. All in all, we may assume familiarity with something resembling the synoptic Gadarene demoniac story (and not necessarily an alternative version without swine, as is sometimes claimed). But as Chapa (2012, 385) rightly notes, the extent of the surviving text makes it impossible to ascertain whether we are dealing with an informally garbled or compiled rendition of identifiable synoptic narratives or instead with a fresh composition from existing narrative building blocks. (For P.Oxy. 5072, as for other apocryphal papyri, some critics have warned against excessively reconstructing from gospel parallels what might instead be a fresh composition rather than a *relecture* from memory. See also Ponder 2016 for a revised reconstruction and translation.)

The verso features an apparently unconnected dialogue of Jesus with a current or potential disciple, although neither name is mentioned. Echoes of related passages (like Matt. 19:21–23 and parallels) are relatively distant, although one finds similar contrasts between "confessing" and "denying" Jesus in Luke 12:8–9// Matthew 10:32–33, and the call not to love anything above Jesus in Matthew 10:37–38//Luke 14:26. The final few lines are impossible to decipher but include a mention of Jerusalem, as well as of scribes (*grammatikoi*, rather than the more common *grammateis*) and sages. Matthew 23:34, 37 speaks of Jesus sending wise men and scribes to a recalcitrant Jerusalem, while the idea of Jesus' teaching being hidden from the "wise" and "understanding" is present in Matthew 11:25//Luke 10:21. But this could just as easily be an otherwise unattested logion.

119

There appear to be no distinctively Markan features, and no signs of direct literary dependence on the Synoptic Gospels. At the same time, Chapa (2012) and Nicklas (2012c) rightly note that partial reuse of synoptic language and narrative without any clear literary dependence is also characteristic of other texts (e.g., P.Eger. 2; P.Oxy. 1224). Although a possible parallel to the unusual contraction *baleia* for *basileia* (verso line 9, a *nomen sacrum*) is found in P.Eger. 2, nothing here requires any connection with that text. All in all P.Oxy. 5072 appears to illustrate the informal and creative oral awareness of familiar gospel narratives in shaping many of the noncanonical gospels.

A *Secret Gospel of Mark*?

At one time in the later twentieth century, it would have seemed appropriate to devote a careful section to the so-called *Secret Gospel of Mark*. This is a document whose existence is affirmed in a manuscript letter supposedly discovered in 1958 by the Jewish scholar Morton Smith at Mar Saba monastery, in what was then the Palestinian West Bank of Jordan. This text, allegedly copied onto the endpapers of a seventeenth-century printed edition of the letters of Ignatius of Antioch, was eventually published in Smith 1973a, 1973b. The manuscript was repeatedly verified and even photographed in the 1970s and early 1980s, although its disappearance since that time has complicated the potentially vital task of paleographical analysis.

The text's author, writing as Clement of Alexandria, claims that after Peter's death Mark the evangelist moved to Alexandria and added to his earlier public text a second, secret and more "spiritual" gospel intended for the elite of those who are becoming perfected. This second gospel, strictly guarded by the church in Alexandria, is said to have been illicitly procured by the Carpocratians (a sect bitterly opposed in Clement's writings) and put to inappropriate use in support of their heretical views. Two closely related quotations from the book are offered by way of illustration, the second being merely a brief allusion to the first. This main episode, added after 10:34, is a story resembling the raising of Lazarus in which the young man appears to fall in love with Jesus and Jesus goes with him to his home before later teaching him about the kingdom

120

of God. The text is widely recognized as incorporating themes or phrases present in all four canonical gospels.

The authenticity of this document has long been seriously questioned. Among those prepared to accept it, some have suspected Clement to be in error about this supposed supplementary Markan gospel, while others (like Helmut Koester) have been prepared to accept the existence of an early "secret" alternative version of Mark whose text may even predate canonical Mark. Skeptical voices were also raised from the beginning, including some who suspected it to be a twentieth-century fake. In the current century, the weight of scholarly discussion has swung quite decisively in favor of the view that the work is a modern forgery. The content of the text and the narrative of its "discovery" appear to match many of Smith's own documented preferences and contemporary experiences since he first visited Mar Saba in 1941. Among these are a novel about a Lord Moreton [*sic*] investigating a forged Greek manuscript that was planted at Mar Saba's library and concerned a resurrection account (Hunter 1940); the combination of an affected style that seemingly "out-Clements" Clement with the counterintuitive idea of his affirming a secret gospel; the anachronistic rendering of same-sex love; and Smith's own penchant as early as his 1944 Hebrew University dissertation for linking the phrase "the mystery of the kingdom of God" (Mark 4:11) with rabbinic discussion of illicit sexuality (Tosefta *Hagigah* 2:1). (See, most emphatically, Carlson 2005; Jeffery 2007; Piovanelli 2013; Watson 2010; and others.)

That said, one still encounters occasional attempts to rehabilitate this document's credibility—not only by intemperate bloggers but also more seriously: for example, S. Brown 2005 (as well as Brown and Pantuck 2013; Meyer 2013 and others in Burke 2013b; Rau 2010a, 2010b). At the time of writing, however, *Secret Mark* is increasingly omitted from new editions or textbooks on the noncanonical gospels—or is included only in order to be exposed as a fake (so, e.g., Merkel 2012; Foster [2008c, 2013b] rides the fence).

The Abgar Legend

We must make at least brief mention of recurring ancient references to a correspondence between Jesus and a first-century king of Edessa. This tradition is attested in Eusebius (*Ecclesiastical History* 1.13), in a Syriac document known as *Teaching of Addai* (or *Doctrina Addai*), and in numerous papyrus fragments that in some cases served as amulets. Despite occasional attempts to condemn it as apocryphal (e.g., in the Gelasian Decree), the legend became popular in both the Eastern and Western church; it circulated in more than half a dozen languages and came to be recycled in various secondary legends, including the so-called *Acts of Thaddeus*. (For the text, see Ehrman and Pleše 2011, 2014.)

In this narrative, King Abgar V of the northern Syrian city of Edessa (reigned 4 BCE–7 CE as well as 13–50), suffers from an incurable disease and sends Jesus a letter by his servant Ananias to ask for healing, offering him refuge in Edessa from Jewish plots against his life. In his reply, Jesus praises the king's faith and promises that while his present mission does not permit him to come in person, he will send the king a disciple to heal him and bring his people the message of life. Eusebius explains that after Jesus' ascension, Thomas (also called Judas) dispatched the apostle Thaddeus to Edessa to heal the king and others and to preach the word of God powerfully. (The *Doctrina Addai*, which may reflect a fifth-century elaboration of the legend, reports an oral rather than a written reply, carried back to Edessa by Ananias with a portrait of Jesus made by the impression of his face on a handkerchief; it calls the city's apostle Addai [= Thaddeus].) Eusebius insists that Edessa's archives preserve the relevant documents to his own day, a claim also echoed by the fourth-century pilgrim Egeria (*Ecclesiastical History* 1.9.4; cf. Egeria, *Itinerary* 17.1).

Scholars agree that the story as such must be legendary. That said, Ramelli (2015, 205–13) has recently attempted to rescue a historical reference in the alleged correspondence between Abgar Ukkama and the emperor Tiberius (which she suspects may have mentioned the execution of Jesus due to a collusion between Pilate and the party around Caiaphas).

Such tenuous possibilities aside, the later legend may well reflect an attempt to link the second-century conversion of Edessa and its royal dynasty back to the apostolic era, while invoking upon this kingdom a special dominical protection. In that sense this material certainly has more in common with apocryphal apostolic acts than with gospel-like writings. Some have argued for a later, more polemical (possibly anti-Manichean) intent. But while this narrative clearly stands in some supplemental relation to gospel traditions about the ministry of Jesus, it was arguably never composed as a freestanding narrative work nor received as a gospel. Indeed, while Abgar's letter may well predate the present narrative, the *Teaching of Addai* certainly understands "the gospel" explicitly as the *Diatessaron* (Howard 1981, 71). The Abgar narrative served Edessa's influential proto-orthodox church as a way to link the gospel narrative to its local patriotism about the city's Christian royal dynasty before Constantine. (For further discussion, see, e.g., Horn and Phenix 2009, 545–51; Mirkovic 2004; Wasmuth 2012.)

Alternative Whole Narrative Gospels?

As previously noted, only a small handful of extracanonical texts and collections offer a complete account of the ministry of Jesus from his birth or baptism to his death or resurrection. All of these appear to be closely indebted to one or more canonical gospels. None require extensive discussion here, but four should at least be mentioned.

Marcion's Gospel

One of the most celebrated and most influential of all Christian heretics, Marcion (ca. 85–160) was the wealthy and possibly wayward son of a bishop of Sinope, a prominent port and Roman colony on the Black Sea in the province of Pontus (modern-day Turkey). Little is known of his early life, but he arrived in Rome not long before the year 140 and, according to Tertullian (ca. 160–225; *Prescription* 30), presented the Christian community there with a very large donation, 200,000 sesterces (brass coins worth a quarter of a silver denarius, which was the average daily wage during the early Empire). Before long his characteristically binary views about the antagonistic relationship of the new Christian faith to the Scriptures and practices of Judaism attracted growing numbers of followers. Any favor this bought him in the Roman church was, however, short-lived: by the year 144 he was excommunicated and his money

123

was returned to him. Nevertheless Marcion's alternative vision of Christianity continued to prosper among his followers for a century or more and thereby provoked vigorous orthodox opposition until it was apparently superseded by Manicheism and other movements.

The text of Marcion's (revised) Lukan gospel does not survive, but a significant amount can be inferred from its treatment among his opponents, particularly Tertullian, Epiphanius, and the fourth-century *Dialogue of Adamantius*. At present the most up-to-date discussion and critical reconstruction is Roth 2015 (text, 410–36; cf. further Roth 2010; Lieu 2015, 183–233). Given that we know him primarily through the lens of his opponents, any general reconstruction of his views remains fraught with difficulty.

Marcion apparently regarded—and rejected—the Creator and God of Israel as a harsh God of law, unmerciful, erratic and impulsive, angry and vindictive. He contrasted this sharply with the very different Lord God of grace and love, revealed in the radically novel, unforetold, and discontinuous gospel of Jesus Christ for the purpose of vanquishing the inferior God of the Old Testament. A keen-eyed reader who consistently privileged literal over against allegorical interpretation, Marcion thought that Paul alone had grasped the true implications of this antithesis of law versus grace, with Galatians therefore taking pride of place in his interpretation. Paul's altercation with Peter at Antioch (Gal. 2) seemed to Marcion to establish beyond question that the original apostles were so mired and compromised by their Jewish background that their writings could not be accepted as authoritative—unlike the Letters of Paul. As a guide to the message of Jesus, therefore, only Paul's companion Luke could be trusted—and even this gospel required a fresh edition purged of Judaizing corruptions in order, as Marcion thought, to recover the pristine original text. Thus it is stripped, for example, of its infancy narratives and instead represents Jesus as appearing "suddenly" to begin his ministry in Capernaum, but not as any promised Messiah or with any Jewish prehistory. As he had no need for birth narratives, so also the crucifixion of Jesus had become for Marcion merely a bodily death exacted by the evil Creator, which redeemed the faithful from his clutches.

We have at best murky and elusive historical knowledge about Marcion's direct or indirect influence on the canon formation of the New Testament (a term Kinzig [1994] attributes to Marcion's invention). The situation is again complicated because our information

124

about Marcion and his gospel is so largely extracted from the hostile comments of his critics. In the absence of clear evidence, the history of scholarship has witnessed many a tall speculation. There are hotly debated questions about the relationship between Marcion's gospel text and the different manuscript traditions of the Gospel of Luke, with the latter occasionally alleged to depend on the former—a theory promising even to resolve the Synoptic Problem (thus Klinghardt 2006, 2008, 2015; Vinzent 2014; see also Tyson 2006)! Given the apparent elasticity of the second-century Lukan text, however, serviceable answers are bound to require greater suppleness and sophistication, whether or not connected to straightforward Lukan priority (thus contrast, e.g., C. Hays 2008; Moll 2010; Roth 2008, 2015; BeDuhn 2013 revives the proto-Luke hypothesis of Knox 1942).

In practice Marcion's substantive impact on the canon formation—possibly as distinct from the *text*—of the New Testament was minimal, as "a figure of wonderful interest but no clear consequence" (Gamble 2006, 211; contrast the influential earlier view of von Campenhausen [1972, 147–209], who interpreted the emergence of the New Testament canon overwhelmingly as a reaction against Marcion).

Marcion's rejection of Mark, Matthew, and John may well have encouraged incipient tendencies among catholic Christians, in Rome and elsewhere, to recognize the apostolic gospel as both unitary and yet plural—indeed quite possibly fourfold, as my next section will suggest. The ease and speed with which Tatian's gospel synthesis (the so-called *Diatessaron*) gained wide acceptance in Greater Syria and beyond suggests that his appeal to the pluriform attestation of an essentially single apostolic narrative was pushing on open doors. That said, although radically contrarian vis-à-vis Judaism in the Old Testament, Marcion's concern for an identifiable and reliable *text* of this "new testament"—both in his edition of "the apostle" and in his purged Luke as "the" true (i.e., Pauline) "gospel"—might be understood as motivated by a conservative and repristinating rather than an innovative impulse. In the eyes of Marcion's younger critic and contemporary Irenaeus, by contrast, the effect of what he did was so radical that what remained was not the (fourfold) gospel but merely a fragment of it (*Against Heresies* 1.27.2).

In its twin emphases on "the gospel" and "the apostle," Marcion's project is in some respects reminiscent of Luke's own. Unlike

125

Tatian or even Justin, Marcion preferred a rigorous hermeneutic of sanitized reduction to the emerging fourfold synthesis. His quest for a viable literalism of "original writings," purified of later "traditional" (i.e., Judaizing) accretions, may have made him perhaps the first Christian biblical fundamentalist (cf. Barton 1998, 43; Moll 2010, 78, 83–84; also Gamble 2006, 212; Hengel 2008b, 59–63). Marcion's enmity against Judaism, indeed, is deep-rooted: his Jesus, like his Paul, is fundamentally at war with Judaism, in defiance of the Jewish God and his law. In this respect the impetus for Marcion's version of Luke is not a meticulously exegeted Pauline law-grace dichotomy so much as the "vulgar Platonism" undergirding his fundamental contempt both for the physical world and for what he deemed the intellectually crude and morally questionable Scriptures of Judaism (cf. Ritter 2012 on a cognate point by Moll 2010). Perhaps this also explains a little of his appeal to those who, like Adolf von Harnack (1851–1930), thought they recognized in Marcion something of the genius of Protestantism (Harnack 1924, 2003).

The Diatessaron

The most influential noncanonical gospel in antiquity was the Syrian apologist Tatian's harmonizing composition known as the *Diatessaron*. This text, which Tatian composed in either Greek or Syriac during the final third of the second century, after his return from a sojourn in Rome, rapidly gained enormous popularity and became the standard lectionary in many churches throughout Greater Syria until the fifth century. Its popularity may be due in part to its transmission of authoritative gospel tradition in the Syriac language at a time before translations of the individual gospels were available (and perhaps before the rise of a significant monastic scribal culture made it possible and affordable for most churches to own discrete copies of the gospels that became canonical).

Tatian's method of conflating the texts appears not to have been motivated by an apologetic concern to eliminate contradiction, but instead typically selects one of the parallel accounts in a given pericope with the aim of weaving together a coherent narrative without significant additions of his own (and amounting to a little under three-quarters of the four gospels in length). A few omissions appear to be more substantial, as for example in relation

126

to the genealogies. As is often rightly pointed out in this connection, Tatian is an important witness to the authoritative, pluriform if not necessarily fourfold, gospel prior to Irenaeus—developing more explicitly the posture of his teacher Justin, whose mode of gospel knowledge and citation tended to remain more vague and perhaps indirect (see Hill 2004, 312–42, on Justin and John; more generally Hill 2010b, 123–50; Hengel 2008b, 45–46 and 45n133 quotes Leloir 1966, 16, in support of the idea that John's Gospel had become the key to the synoptics for Tatian, as for the school of Valentinus). At the same time, recent study of Ephrem's fourth-century commentary on the *Diatessaron* (which he simply calls "the gospel") suggests a degree of caution about the extent to which the underlying text of "the gospel" was actually, properly speaking, a harmony of four discrete gospels, rather than a composition based primarily on Matthew and Luke interwoven with John (see Crawford 2013, 2015a). Mark's explicit role is less clear, but his relative silence does not negate the *Diatessaron's* importance as a "precanonical" synthesis of the gospels that had in fact become authoritative (see further, pp. 10–14 above).

In late antiquity and the Middle Ages, the *Diatessaron's* influence continued as it was translated into other languages. In its native Syrian environment, however, it was eventually displaced by the canonical four gospels—a development accelerated particularly after Bishop Theodoret of Cyrrhus (ca. 393–460) campaigned instead for the Syriac Peshitta translation of the canonical gospels. The *Diatessaron* came to be seen as tainted by its author's supposedly heretical views.

No Syriac manuscripts of the text survive. Nevertheless, later translations into Arabic and Persian, and especially the extant Syriac portions and Armenian translation of the commentary attributed to Ephrem (see Leloir 1966; McCarthy 1993, 25–34), permit some insight into its original sequence and structure. Medieval Western translations into Latin and French also used to be commonly cited, but are now recognized as based on a gospel harmony included in the sixth-century Codex Fuldensis, and of little use for reconstructing Tatian's original.

A single Greek, rather than Syriac, parchment fragment of fourteen lines from Dura Europos (destroyed 231 CE), covering part of the passion narrative (Matt. 27:55–61 and parallels), was identified by its original editor (C. H. Kraeling) as belonging to the *Diatessaron* (Yale P.Dura 10, formerly Dura Parchment 24). Although some initially questioned if it might instead be a non-Diatessaronic passion harmony, subsequent scholarship tended to accept the identification (including Lührmann and Schlarb 2000, 102–5; Ehrman and Pleše 2011, 231–35; 2014, 120–22; cf. Petersen 1994, 196–203, for the early history of the fragment's interpretation). Given the proliferation of informal hybrid gospel compilations in subsequently published Christian papyri, however, that confident identification now looks rather more tenuous—especially when dealing with a fragment in Greek rather than in Syriac. (This point was also rightly stressed in an important critique by Parker, Taylor, and Goodacre [1999], whose comparison of the text, structure, and wording with the extant translations led them to conclude that Yale P.Dura 10 must be a gospel compilation from someone other than Tatian.)

The *Diatessaron*'s compositional technique and surprisingly wide liturgical influence is evident testimony to the authoritative standing of the increasingly fourfold gospel not long after the middle of the second century. This point, which is also confirmed by other late second- and early third-century syntheses well before the Eusebian canons (see p. 12 above), is too often underrated by those who imagine instead a proliferation of undifferentiated "gospel writing" until a much later imposition of canonical boundaries. Here we may note that the *Diatessaron* bears eloquent witness both to the acceptability of textual conflation and yet to the authority of the gospels that went on to become canonical.

Some biblical critics snidely dismiss Tatian as a harmonizer. But to do so underplays the fact that harmonization presupposes existing authorities worth synthesizing and rewriting. Following his predecessor Justin (and probably texts like the hybrid longer ending of Mark [16:9–20] and the *Epistle of the Apostles*), Tatian's *Diatessaron* raises significant questions for any theory that "the fourfold gospel remained a work in progress until well into the fourth century" (thus Watson 2013, 453–54; cf. critique in Bauckham 2014; Bockmuehl 2014). Significantly, it does so in the company of other explicit fourfold affirmations of Theophilus of Antioch, Irenaeus, Ammonius, and Origen.

128   Evidently the authority of these gospels was still deemed compatible with a "rewritten gospel" mode of engagement with the apostolic narratives—to adapt nomenclature commonly used for

quasi-biblical texts in the Dead Sea Scrolls. (Henderson [2011, 32–43 and passim] applies this particularly to the *Gospel of Peter*.)

To be sure, this same mode of rewriting an authoritative textual predecessor already pertains to a significant extent in the mutual relationships among the Four. In Tatian, however, we see this task undertaken with an unprecedented concern for accuracy that appears to reveal his commitment to a single, and at least in some sense fourfold, apostolic gospel testimony to Jesus Christ (even if his discrete use of Mark may be minimal). Since Tatian spent formative years in Rome, this commitment may well intend a superior and more faithful alternative to Marcion's fateful prior attempt at a unitary gospel (so Hengel 2000, 31–32). In the history of the emerging New Testament canon (as also previously at Qumran), such "rewritten scripture" before long gave way to scholia and commentaries as the preferred mode of engagement (cf. Bockmuehl 2005, 2009).

Finally, in two respects the *Diatessaron* offers an interesting counterexample to the apparent lines of distinction we have observed between apocryphal and canonical gospels. First, unlike all of the noncanonical gospels, the *Diatessaron*'s proximity to the Four and its quasi-canonical standing in the Syrian church encouraged a notable commentary in the name of Ephrem of Edessa (ca. 306–373)—simply identified as a commentary on "the gospel." Nothing equivalent is known or referenced for any other noncanonical gospel. Second, it is again worth recalling that aside from Marcion's gospel and the *Diatessaron* we know of no other ancient noncanonical gospel that traces the life and teachings of Jesus from his infancy or baptism to his death or resurrection. Although (eventually) noncanonical, the *Diatessaron* was therefore never in any obvious sense "apocryphal," and certainly neither secret nor reserved for an elite.

Toledot Yeshu

Finally in this section, two other texts also represent "whole gospel" treatments of the ministry of Jesus, but are composed at a much later date and engage with this ministry from a more hostile perspective.

During the Middle Ages a Jewish antigospel known as the *Toledot Yeshu* (Generations/Biography of Jesus) enjoyed a wide

129

circulation. Given that it is neither ancient nor Christian, nor indeed in any conventional sense either apocryphal or a gospel, it is understandably not included in most editions and textbooks. (See, however, Klauck [2003, 211–20], who rightly notes that it shares more of the gospel genre's formal features than do many of the other texts usually discussed as noncanonical gospels; cf. Alexander 2011, 604 and n37.)

At the same time, this text is one of the very few complete narratives purporting to give an account of the life of Jesus from birth and infancy to death. Its polemic follows a narrative outline very vaguely resembling that of the Gospel of Matthew, but with numerous insertions drawn from elsewhere. Although the text itself is a parody not generally thought to predate the Middle Ages, it notably recycles a number of anti-Christian polemical tropes that were already known in antiquity, including several that the second-century pagan critic Celsus already appears to have derived from a Jewish source (see discussion above, p. 63).

Jesus is here born during the reign of the Jewish Hasmonean king Alexander Jannaeus (103–76 BCE) as the illegitimate son of Pandera, who seduced or raped Mary. (In some manuscripts, Pandera is identified as a Roman soldier.) Jesus' illegitimate birth is exposed by the rabbinic sage Simon ben Shetach (ca. 120–40 BCE). He grows up to be an attractively impressive and talented person who is in reality a sorcerer and false prophet whose pernicious influence continues even after his execution. The emphasis is on a Jesus who is offensive to authority, performs spectacular miracles by the illegitimate invocation of the secret divine name, and publicly self-identifies as messiah and son of God. Other material reflects a knowledge of popular Christian legends like the clay birds Jesus causes to fly away (from the *Infancy Gospel of Thomas*) and a lethal Quidditch-like flying contest against Judas Iscariot (drawn apparently from the narrative cycle of Peter's contest with Simon Magus in the *Acts of Peter*). (See further, e.g., Horbury 1970, 75–151; Piovanelli 2011; Schäfer 2011; Schlichting 1982.)

The Gospel of Barnabas

130   The *Gospel of Barnabas* is another, even later, text that has sometimes been discussed in connection with the noncanonical gospels, most popularly in Muslim-Christian polemics of the nineteenth

and twentieth centuries (see Schirrmacher 1992). We do know of one or two ancient documents attributed to Barnabas—above all the early-second-century *Epistle of Barnabas* and a much later book, the *Acts of Barnabas*, but an otherwise unknown *Gospel according to Barnabas* is anathematized in the sixth-century Gelasian Decree, as we saw above. By contrast, the extant *Gospel of Barnabas*, composed in the fourteenth or fifteenth century in Italian and then translated into Spanish, has continued to be popular in Arabic (as *Injil Barnaba*) and other languages in the Muslim world, where it is still often presented as an authentic first-century text rebutting Christianity and demonstrating Islam as its rightful replacement. (In English, the Oxford translation Ragg et al. 1907 continues to be widely reissued both electronically and in print. For the likely date and origin of the *Gospel of Barnabas* see also Joosten 2010.)

This text has, however, nothing directly to do with our subject matter of ancient apocryphal gospels. It is a substantial document of 222 chapters and presents itself as the "true gospel" of Jesus the Prophet, as composed by Barnabas. Like the *Toledot Yeshu*, but unlike all ancient noncanonical gospels, it approximates a complete narrative of the life of Jesus.

The status of Barnabas as an apostle in his own right might at first seem surprising in view of his description as a prophet and teacher distinguished from the apostles in the early chapters of Acts (4:36; 13:1; etc.), but Luke does designate Barnabas as an apostle in Acts 14:14, and there may have been scope for confusion with Matthias, for whom, together with Joseph "Barsabbas," lots were cast in the endeavor to identify the apostle who would replace Judas among the Twelve (Acts 1:23–26; cf. also 15:22; cf. esp. Pseudo-Clementine *Recognitions* 1.60). This apostolic Barnabas here appears as the enemy rather than the friend of Paul, who is held responsible for what are seen, in a familiar Muslim critique, as the errors of a church that regards Jesus as the Son of God although he was a mere prophet, and that abandons circumcision along with all discretion about the impurity of food.

In substance, the book extensively rephrases the fourfold gospel into a harmonized whole. In keeping with an ancient docetic motif reaffirmed in the Qur'an (4:157) and later Muslim conviction, Jesus does not die on the cross; rather, another man resembling him is crucified in his place—in this case Judas. Indeed the text

131

polemicizes against what it deems to be Paul's chief error, the sote-riological interpretation of the cross as a sacrifice—quite possibly a way of making the hated apostle to the Gentiles the creator of a dis-tinctively Western form of Christianity (as Klauck [2003, 210] sur-mises). Significantly too, Jesus himself is not the definitive Prophet; instead, emulating a characteristic feature of the New Testament's John the Baptist, he points explicitly beyond himself to Muham-mad as the one whose sandal he is not worthy to untie (chap. 44). Jesus reveals to the disciples that it was Muhammad's name that the expelled Adam saw written on the gate of Paradise in the words of the Muslim confession or *shahadah*: "There is only one God, and Muhammad is his messenger" (41). In this way Jesus is found to affirm Islam as the only appropriate heir and fulfillment of both Judaism and Christianity.

Conclusion: Ministry Gospels

Just as the rich and varied story of Jesus from his baptism to his arrest takes up the bulk of the New Testament gospels, so the apocryphal ministry gospels provide the most diverse material under consideration in this book. Under this heading we have encountered a fascinating collection of papyri fragments, scat-tered sayings sometimes called agrapha, and "Jewish Christian gospels" cited by early Christian writers. We also encountered a narrative cycle about Jesus' supposed correspondence with King Abgar of Edessa, which turns out to be intended less as a gospel than as a foundation legend of the apostolic mission to that city, complementing or in some sense besting the account of other such missions in canonical and other apostolic acts. Additionally this chapter has considered several ancient attempts at homogenizing the existing protocanonical gospel tradition into a more definitive unitary gospel—in Marcion's case by singling out a version of one gospel (Luke) and excluding the rest, and in Tatian's *Diatessaron* by an inclusionary integration of both synoptic and Johannine tra-dition (to which can be compared Ammonius of Alexandria's syn-opsis of the fourfold gospel based specifically around Matthew: see p. 12 above).

132   The sheer material and literary diversity of these sources is cer-tainly striking. At the same time, we have repeatedly encountered

an apparent structural reliance on something rather like the canonical gospel outline, if perhaps rarely a direct literary dependence on those protocanonical gospel texts themselves. This presupposition of a shared gospel outline appears even more pronounced than in the case of the infancy or dialogue gospels. That said, a certain methodological caution in this question remains advisable in view of the fragmentary nature of so many of our texts (whether extant on papyri or quoted in early Christian writers). As we saw in the discussion of the famous Egerton papyrus (P.Eger. 2 + P.Köln 255), even this potentially more extensive narrative gospel text appears on balance most likely to represent a partial rewriting of existing Johannine (and perhaps synoptic) tradition rather than an alternative gospel composition.

What accounts for this wealth of material? In the chapter on the infancy gospels, I suggested that such sources take up an evident narrative omission on which the canonical gospels almost seem to invite the reader's reflection—for example, those memories of the Lord's childhood that Mary repeatedly "treasured in her heart" (Luke 2:19, 51). A similar generative dynamic could be at work in relation to the post-resurrection discourse gospels, to be discussed in chapter 5. There too, the gospel narratives that became canonical almost appear to invite reflection on Luke's somewhat taciturn account of what Jesus said and did during the forty days before his ascension (Acts 1:3–11; cf. Luke 24), let alone the infinite number of books that *could* be written about Jesus' other signs and deeds (John 20:30; 21:25).

By contrast, the ministry (and passion) of Jesus occupies the vast majority of the canonical gospel material, which as a result presents fewer explicit or implicit invitations to generate altogether fresh compositions. Virtually all the gospel-like texts we have encountered here are in some sense epiphenomenal, representing either rewriting or supplementation (*Fortschreibung*) of existing protocanonical gospel narratives—whether these are engaged as integral literary texts or via a written or informal oral harmony.

The intended aim of some such compositions is often less clear than their effect: a text like P.Eger. 2 arguably produces not so much a new authoritative text but rather a fresh theological appropriation and rereading of known gospel tradition to address the social or rhetorical needs of a new situation. Although cast in the form of a

133

fresh narrative, P.Oxy. 840 likewise seems to reflect existing (perhaps orally known) gospel tradition in the service of subsequent inner-Christian or Christian Jewish disputes about baptism. The so-called Jewish Christian gospels and textual variants also represent episodic supplementations of the Matthean outline that in some cases may service narrative, liturgical, or halakic concerns of specific later communities. The intended authority of many shorter fragments is even more elusive.

For certain other gospels discussed in this chapter, however, it seems difficult to avoid the impression of a quasi-canonical aim to create a formally authoritative text. Marcion, for example, claimed to recover the true and original gospel, while Tatian synthesized the fourfold (mostly Matthean, Lukan, and Johannine) apostolic testimony into a similarly definitive composition that became "the gospel" of the Syrian church for several centuries. An implicit claim to comprehensive authority for a complete account also attaches to two much later polemical antigospels we discussed, the Jewish *Toledot Yeshu* and the Islamic *Gospel of Barnabas*—both of which, like the earlier Christian examples, rely on their predecessors in the texts that were or became canonical.

Suggested Further Reading

Crawford, Matthew R. 2015b. "Ammonius of Alexandria, Eusebius of Caesarea and the Origins of Gospels Scholarship." *New Testament Studies* 61:1–29.

Edwards, James R. 2009. *The Hebrew Gospel and the Development of the Synoptic Tradition*. Grand Rapids: Eerdmans.

Evans, Craig A. 2007. "The Jewish Christian Gospel Tradition." In *Jewish Believers in Jesus: The Early Centuries*, edited by O. Skarsaune and R. Hvalvik, 241–77. Peabody, MA: Hendrickson Publishers.

Kraus, Thomas J., Michael J. Kruger, and Tobias Nicklas. 2009. *Gospel Fragments*. Oxford Early Christian Gospel Texts. Oxford: Oxford University Press.

Luomanen, Petri. 2012. *Recovering Jewish-Christian Sects and Gospels*. Vigiliae Christianae Supplements 110. Leiden: Brill.

Roth, Dieter T. 2015. *The Text of Marcion's Gospel*. New Testament Tools, Studies, and Documents 49. Leiden: Brill.

Skarsaune, Oskar, and Reidar Hvalvik, eds. 2007. *Jewish Believers in Jesus: The Early Centuries*. Peabody, MA: Hendrickson Publishers.

Watson, Francis. 2013. *Gospel Writing: A Canonical Perspective*. Grand Rapids: Eerdmans.

CHAPTER 4

Passion Gospels

The decision to treat gospels about the passion of Jesus here under a separate heading is essentially a counsel of convenience. As it happens, for a handful of texts—including the *Gospel of Peter*—all that survives concerns the events from the Last Supper to the crucifixion and beyond to the morning of the resurrection. One could in principle include this material in the previous or to some extent in the following chapter. That said, we cannot be sure that any of the ministry gospels also included passion material or vice versa. Indeed, that some forms of Christianity were decidedly uninterested in the passion and death of Jesus is clear from gnostic texts and has been equally suspected for the *Gospel of Thomas* and for Q.

In this chapter, then, we will initially foreground the so-called *Gospel of Peter* along with two other papyrus fragments sometimes associated with it, before turning to a more rapid discussion of a number of other texts concerned with the passion.

The Gospel of Peter

We turn first and most notably to the *Gospel of Peter*, which in recent years has attracted lively scholarly debate. In 2010 it was the subject of a large edition and commentary by Paul Foster (2010a). After several preparatory publications, a further commentary is expected from Tobias Nicklas. (See previously Kraus and Nicklas 2004, 2007; also Vinzent and Nicklas 2012.) The critical text and a translation of the Akhmim Codex are offered by Foster 2010a, 177–205; Kraus and Nicklas 2004; Ehrman and Pleše 2011, 371–87 (cf. Ehrman and Pleše 2014, 191–200); see also Bernhard 2006, 56–81 and plates 8–16.

At the site of Akhmim (ancient Panopolis) in Upper Egypt, excavators in 1886–87 discovered a substantial parchment codex containing a brief text that was soon identified with the "Gospel according to Peter" cited in ancient Christian sources, along with a second text identified as the *Apocalypse of Peter* in the same scribal hand and similar style, parts of Greek *1 Enoch* 1–27, and (on a separately inserted sheet) a martyrdom of St. Julian. The manuscript tends to be dated between the sixth and ninth centuries, with perhaps a majority of scholars content to settle on the seventh century. The text itself, by contrast, is often thought to have been composed in the later second century (Foster [2010a, 172] suggests 150–190 CE).

The Akhmim codex (P.Cair. 10759) of sixty-six pages contains the longest extant text we have, but even this remains a fragment. Interestingly, the clear spacing and ornamentation immediately before and after the manuscript's incomplete opening and closing sentences suggests that even this seventh-century scribe had access only to a fragment; his copy of it, by contrast, is preserved intact. Evidently this noncanonical text had continued to be valued by some members of this particular monastic community, perhaps because of its claimed association with Peter; but it had not attained sufficient circulation, let alone regular congregational use or a commentary tradition, to ensure the survival of a complete text.

The manuscript itself has been missing from Cairo's Egyptian Museum for some time, but we do have serviceable photographic images taken around 1981, which are freely accessible online from Oxford's Centre for the Study of Ancient Documents (http://ipap .csad.ox.ac.uk/GP/GP.html; cf. Foster 2010a, 1; Henderson 2011, 13n22). Unfortunately even the circumstances of the text's discovery (supposedly in a monk's tomb) now seem less clear than they were once assumed to be.

Content

138

The subject matter of the *Gospel of Peter* concerns the story of Jesus' trial and crucifixion and especially the subsequent events.

Although the original text must have included more material both before and after the narrative contained in the surviving fragment, there is (despite occasional claims to the contrary) little or no evidence that the text originally encompassed a full account of Jesus' life or ministry.

The extant story opens with the refusal of Herod, his officials, and "the Jews" to emulate Pilate's example in washing his hands (cf. Matt. 27:24). Herod Antipas now takes center stage, determining the outcome of the trial and handing Jesus over to "the Jews" who act as a lynch mob in precipitating the killing. Joseph (presumably of Arimathea) asks Pilate for Jesus' body before the crucifixion takes place. Meanwhile the mob continues to drive Jesus to the site of the crucifixion, mocking him as they go. In the entire discourse Jesus only speaks once, in a striking alteration of the Markan or Matthean cry of dereliction from the cross: "My power, the power, you have left me behind" (19).

This is a theme that older scholarship tended to link to gnosticizing or docetic theologies in which the Holy Spirit—or indeed the divine Son of God!—abandons the apparently human Jesus precisely at the crucifixion ("orthodox" accounts attribute a more developed form of this view to Cerinthus: see, e.g., Myllykoski 2008). Similarly the theme of Jesus being silent "as if he had no pain" (10) has often been thought to suggest a docetic Christology. But in fact this motif is not consistently applied (the crucified thieves observe him suffering like them, 23; cf. 9–10), and in any case it is not so far removed from the more serene Lukan or Johannine picture of Jesus speaking and praying on the cross. More difficult, perhaps, is the idea that when Jesus dies he is "taken up" (19), though even here one should not underrate the analogy with Johannine language about the cross of Jesus as his "lifting up" or exaltation (e.g., John 3:14; 12:32–33).

Most of the text, however, is concerned with events that happen *after* the crucifixion. Matthew's story of the Roman guards at the tomb (Matt. 27:62–66; 28:4, 11–15) is expanded and developed in more elaborate fictional detail, which reports the name of the centurion (Petronius), the attachment of seven seals to the tomb, the presence of Jewish elders and priests with the guard, and the nature of the night watch arrangements. All of this supports scholarly views of the *Gospel of Peter* as an epiphenomenal composition, manifesting clear signs of awareness of the Matthean narrative, if

139

not literary dependence on it, and dating from the second century rather than the first.

Unlike in any of the canonical gospels, the soldiers and other Jewish observers actually watch the angels rolling away the stone on Sunday morning. When the two angels come out of the tomb supporting a third man and followed by a moving cross (!), their height reaches to the heavens and his height reaches *above* the heavens. The three are addressed by a heavenly voice asking Jesus if he has proclaimed to those who are asleep (41). The emphatic yes is given not by Jesus but by the cross—in an allusion to the tradition of Christ preaching to the imprisoned souls of Hades (the "harrowing of hell"), which has a similar Petrine connection in 1 Peter 3:19 (cf. Eph. 4:8) and later appears in the creeds.

A number of other post-resurrection accounts then follow, involving the conclusion of the episode relating to the Roman guard and a resurrection appearance to Mary Magdalene and her friends. The angel they encounter assures them that "the crucified one" is not here but has risen and returned to the place from which he was sent. Interestingly, the women are not told to report to the disciples, and even on the last day of the Feast of Unleavened Bread the disciples are apparently still in mourning and perhaps have not yet seen the risen Jesus. They return to their homes; Peter, Andrew, and Levi go back to fishing (58–60). The narrative breaks off here—leaving us to speculate whether a further resurrection appearance like that at the Sea of Galilee in the Gospel of John may have been intended to follow. (John 21 is widely regarded as an originally separate tradition attached to this gospel as an appendix at a late stage of composition.) In any case it seems that the missing sections preceding and following our extant extract contained additional narrative material.

Interpretation

Thirty years ago it was fashionable to regard the *Gospel of Peter*, or a source contained within it, as predating and shaping the New Testament gospel passion narratives (see, e.g., Crossan 1988; Koester 1980). Since then, the balance of critical opinion has rightly swung in favor of the view that this noncanonical gospel renarrates the death and resurrection of Jesus on the basis of one or more existing synoptic or synoptic-like accounts, supplementing them with additional narrative detail but apparently at some remove from the social and historical setting of the events (e.g., Foster 2008a, 2010a; Henderson 2011; cf. Nicklas 2010). This is not to assert straightforward dependence on each of the four gospels (thus perhaps R. Brown 1987, 335–36 and passim: by secondary orality; cf. much earlier C. H. Turner 1913, 173: literary dependence). Nor, on the other hand, need we deny the *Gospel of Peter*'s distinctive lines of interpretation or tradition (esp. in relation to the Old Testament: Nicklas 2010). But in general this text clearly does presuppose and supplement elements of the New Testament crucifixion and resurrection stories, enhancing the miraculous aspects of the resurrection and heightening the canonical narrative's potential for anti-Jewish sentiment.

The existence of a gospel in the name of Peter was already well known prior to the nineteenth-century manuscript discovery at Akhmim. The best-known source is a reference in Eusebius to Bishop Serapion of Antioch (ca. 190), who had come across such a document in the nearby church of Rhossus and, after initially regarding it as harmless for private reading, developed concerns about it when he discovered what he thought were problematic ideas associated with "docetists" (Eusebius, *Ecclesiastical History* 6.12.3–6; critical comments also at 3.3.2; 3.25.6).

Twentieth-century scholarship tended to accept an identification of the Rhossus *Gospel of Peter* with the work discovered at Akhmim (and therefore a date of composition no later than the second century). Recent studies, however, have been far less confident about this identification. If it were correct, a second-century origin for the Akhmim *Gospel of Peter* at least *in some form* would be assured. It would in that case also be interesting to wonder if the date must be relatively late in the second century, since Serapion had evidently never come across this text before, or even heard of it—indeed he claims to know that, in relation to Peter, "such things we have not received." (This latter affirmation may carry additional frisson in relation to the *Gospel of Peter*'s projected discourse in the first-person voice of the apostle, a phenomenon that some critics regard as the telltale artifice of relatively late-vintage pseudepigraphy: so Vinzent and Nicklas 2012, 689.)

Theologically, there is little to suggest any clearly defined position, whether docetic or otherwise. The consistent devout reference to "the Lord" rather than "Jesus" does provide a degree of

141

christological emphasis: it is worth comparing a similar move away from "Jesus" to titles like "the Savior" in gnostic texts as well as in apologetic writers like Tatian (after 160) and Minucius Felix (perhaps early third century). Here, preference for "the Lord" may also relate to Christ's apparently painless suffering and a toned-down cry of dereliction that is apparently not addressed to God and certainly demands no explanation ("My power, the power, you have left me behind"). Most scholars agree that the Christology of this text is neither orthodox nor heretical in any technical sense, as was sometimes supposed to be the cause of Bishop Serapion's association of it with the group he calls *dokētai*. Instead, the *Gospel of Peter*'s Christology is diverse and unrefined without subscribing to any particular "heretical" view.

There has been much debate and perplexity about the striking visual imagery of the cross emerging from the tomb behind Jesus and the two angels reaching up to the heavens. Some have proposed emending the text in order to avoid the paradox of a walking, talking cross (but note the counterarguments of Foster [2013a]; also Combs [2014], who sees the personified cross as an expression of the *Gospel of Peter*'s Christology). The figures reaching to heaven have been plausibly thought to reflect a theme of Jewish mysticism, influential in both rabbinic and gnostic texts, in which encounters with the divine are visualized in terms of the gigantic dimensions of the bodies of angels or of God (*shi'ur qoma*: see, e.g., Rowland and Morray-Jones 2009, 507–15; cf. Swartz 2006, 413). In the early third century, Hippolytus polemicizes against an apocalyptic *Book of Elchasai* that was used by the Jewish Christian heretic Alcibiades of Apamea and supposedly revealed by a male angel called "the Great King" who was ninety-six miles tall (*Refutation* 10.9; 13.2–3; 15.1; cf. Luttikhuizen 1985, 86–87; 2006; 2008).

The idea of seeing the risen Christ in different forms is fairly well attested even in the canonical gospels. Anticipated in the transfiguration narratives (Mark 9:2–9 and parallels), it is explicit in the longer ending of Mark (16:12) and implicit in the other gospels' recurrent theme of the disciples' difficulty in recognizing or identifying Jesus (e.g., John 21:4, 7, 12; Luke 24:16, 31, 35, 37–40; cf. Matt. 28:17; Acts 1:3). Early Christian literature repeatedly features the idea that encounters with Christ show him taking on the appearance of an old man to some and a boy or a youth to others (see already Dan. 7:9–14 with Rev. 1:14; also, e.g., *Acts of John* 89,

142

91; *Acts of Peter* 20–21; *Acts of Andrew* 18—although it is true that the same polymorphous feat is elsewhere attributed to Satan: *Acts of Thomas* 43).

The Akhmim *Gospel of Peter* has had an enormous signifi-cance for a number of key modern scholarly debates about early Christianity (see Foster 2010a, 7–39; Foster 2011 for the history of research). In debates about the New Testament canon, there has understandably been much controversy about the significance of Bishop Serapion's resistance to the *Gospel of Peter*—a problem complicated by the question of whether he was really concerned with the same document at all.

Debate has also raged over the question of the document's relative popularity and influence in antiquity. Its discovery in a seventh-century parchment manuscript from Egypt suggests a certain staying power, although this is balanced by the fact that even the scribe seeking to preserve it was able to copy only a frag-mentary extract. Citations in other early Christian writers certainly seem at first sight to reinforce the impression of a relatively wide-spread familiarity: a document by the same title is referenced, for example, by Origen, Eusebius, Jerome, Theodoret, and Didymus the Blind.

What is perhaps more striking than this awareness, however, is the increasingly vague and distant knowledge these patristic authors appear to have of the text itself. There is little or no awareness of its content—even leaving aside the question of whether they are in any case referring to the *Gospel of Peter* we have before us (note Foster 2010a, 90–91). The third-century theologian Origen, for example, had a lively interest in pseudepigraphical and other extra-canonical sources, and briefly mentions a *Gospel of Peter* in *Com-mentary on Matthew* 10.17. In fact, however, it is far from clear that the same text is meant or even whether Origen personally knew it at all. He attributes to "the Gospel of Peter *or* the Book of James" the idea that Mary's husband Joseph had children from an earlier marriage—a suggestion that seems indeed much better grounded in the *Infancy Gospel of James* (Origen's "Book of James"?) than in any attested version of the *Gospel of Peter*. Origen's passing mention certainly yields no evidence that he knew the *Gospel of Peter* to contain not just a passion narrative but a complete life of Jesus, as is sometimes asserted. It seems on the contrary that the actual text of the *Gospel of Peter* may not have been available at all

143

to third-century scholars working in Alexandria or Caesarea (see Vinzent and Nicklas 2012, 686–87).

Further echoes have been postulated in other early Christian texts, including the *Pseudo-Clementines* (e.g., F. S. Jones 2007), Melito (Karmann 2007), Justin Martyr (e.g., Greschat 2007; Ehrman 2013, 324–27; Pilhofer 1990), the *Epistle of the Apostles* (Hills 2008, 79–82 and passim), and numerous others (Meiser 2007, 185–87). But what these cases document is shared or overlapping traditions rather than the presence specifically of the *Gospel of Peter*. A parallel as such demonstrates neither literary use nor dependence (Vinzent and Nicklas 2012, 688). In the end it seems significant that explicit references to this text in early Christian literature are not only vague but almost invariably critical, identifying it as *rejected* rather than merely (like 2 Peter) as disputed.

As noted earlier, an important scholarly voice in this document's interpretation around the turn of the twenty-first century was that of John Dominic Crossan (1988; cf. more recently Crossan 2007), who argues that the *Gospel of Peter* was substantially early and dependent on a first-century source he calls the "Cross Gospel." By eliminating sections that seem to show unambiguous dependence on the canonical gospels, Crossan isolates a hypothetical, very early source to which he then assigns great authority in postulating an alternative origin of the passion narratives. This and similar theories have failed to persuade many scholars. A majority of interpreters instead see the *Gospel of Peter* as a document that elaborates on and fills in a familiar synoptic-type narrative. *Peter*'s awareness of that predecessor may be oral or literary, direct or indirect. But leaving aside the recurrent verbatim agreements especially with Matthew and Luke, Foster (2008a, 39) notes in relation to Crossan's hypothetical source that "even the reconstructed kernel of the Cross Gospel appears to represent a theological development of canonical traditions."

The *Gospel of Peter* as a whole seems, rather, an appropriation and *relecture* of protocanonical synoptic tradition, not necessarily in written form. Placed in the mouth of Peter, who speaks as the narrator in the first person singular, in a sense the *Gospel of Peter* fictionalizes what the tradition had always asserted for the Gospel of Mark, and what is also implicitly affirmed in 1 Peter 2:21–25; 5:1 (cf. Gal. 1:18; 2 Pet. 1:16–18): the gospel passion narrative derives its authority from the witness of Peter.

144

In terms of the *Gospel of Peter's* relevance for later Christian reflection on the passion, perhaps the most important consideration is that in this text responsibility for the actual execution of Jesus lies not so much with Pilate or the Romans but, it seems, with "the people" or "the Jews" to whom he is surrendered by Pilate (1, 5–6, 14, 23).

In the New Testament, for all the responsibility borne by the scheming Jerusalem high priesthood or by the hostile complicity of pliable crowds (whom John too calls "the Jews"), it is Roman soldiers who carry out the crucifixion itself. Even so, the ambiguity of reference to the Jewish authorities in certain passages evidently engendered a well-known and notorious aftermath in the accusation that Jews—"the Jews"—murdered Christ. Mark 15:15–24// Matthew 27:26–35 has Pilate hand Jesus over to "the soldiers," who carry out the mockery and execution. But the grammar of Luke 23:13, 25–26 already appears to envisage the executioners as "the chief priests, the leaders, and the people," while John 19:15–18 less ambiguously has Pilate delivering Jesus over to "the chief priests" who take him out to Golgotha where "they" crucify him. As early as 1 Thessalonians 2:14–15 (and thus well before the composition of the New Testament gospels), we already find the affirmation that "the Jews . . . killed the Lord Jesus."

Pilate, by contrast, is often virtually absolved of responsibility—it seems easy to see how subsequent Christian legend might go on to paint him in an even more positive light as a convert or even a saint (both anti-Judaism and the whitewash of Pilate are taken further in the cycle of Pilate and Nicodemus literature discussed below). That said, it has rightly been noted that he appears in the second part of the *Gospel of Peter's* narrative to become a much more problematic figure who offends against his own conscience in order to satisfy political expediency (Augustin 2015, 282–84; cf. Omerzu 2007).

The impression of heightened anti-Jewish sentiment does at one level appear to derive an uncomfortable degree of encouragement from the New Testament itself. At the same time, the *Gospel of Peter* liberally inserts the Johannine-sounding "the Jews" alongside Pharisees, scribes, and elders as protagonists of Jesus' death throughout the narrative, while in part accelerating the exoneration of Pilate. The intensification of hostility especially to the Jewish authorities here has been identified as a plausibly apologetic

145

motif characterizing this later-second-century reappropriation of the Synoptic Gospel narratives (see Henderson 2011, 221–24 and passim; Nicklas 2001; Foster 2007b, 324; Johnston 2016 proposes similar second-century apologetic motifs in the depiction of Jesus' resurrection).

Despite these tendencies the picture of "the Jews" in the *Gospel of Peter* remains somewhat ambivalent: unlike in the New Testament, it is precisely the people of "the Jews" who beat their breasts in the face of the coming judgment as they acknowledge how evil their actions have been (25, 28; cf. Luke 23:48), since the executed "Son of God" was "righteous" (6, 9; 29). The enemies of Jesus appear to recognize that their attempt to repress the truth of the resurrection is a "great sin before God," which they are prepared to prefer to being stoned by "the Jewish people," who would otherwise realize that Jesus is the Son of God (45–48). Some scholars allow in this text for a continuing distinction between the Jewish people and their leadership (so most fully Augustin 2015, 279–82 and passim; cf. further Nicklas 2014c, 35–47; Shoemaker 1999; and Tomson 2001 on anti-Jewish tendencies in other ancient Christian gospel-related apocrypha).

Is there a particular significance in the choice of Peter as the chief witness for this text? Peter's centrality to the protocanonical gospel narrative in general, and his pivotal role for Mark and Matthew in particular, is well known and much discussed (see, e.g., Bockmuehl 2012b, 67–88, 131–41). Part of the reason for the continuing authoritative status of the Markan framework (and Matthean development) of the life and death of Jesus appears to be the traditional conviction that its witness was rooted in the testimony of Peter—and also, for Mark, in the evangelist's status as Peter's interpreter. Strikingly, however, all four New Testament gospels *remove* Peter from the narrative as a witness both of the crucifixion (after leaving the house of Caiaphas he is absent until at least Easter Sunday) and of Jesus' emerging from the tomb (a resurrection appearance to Peter is affirmed but not narrated in Luke 24:34 and 1 Cor. 15:5).

The *Gospel of Peter*, by contrast, clearly *reinserts* the Petrine stamp of authority into this narrative, perhaps particularly in relation to its innovative features. Peter functions not necessarily as an eyewitness of the crucifixion and the resurrection, but certainly

146

as a participant of the events on Good Friday (26–27) and as the implied first-person narrator throughout (59–60). The gravitas of Peter's testimony seems further highlighted through an implied appeal to other New Testament motifs like the apostle as a witness of the passion (1 Pet. 5:1) or Christ as preaching to the souls in Hades (1 Pet. 3:19; cf. *Gospel of Peter* 41–42). In the political and rhetorical setting of increasing anti-Judaism in the second century, Peter's authority may even serve to enhance the idea of Jewish responsibility for the death of Christ (cf., e.g., *Kerygma Petrou* = *The Preaching of Peter*, fragment 6; Clement of Alexandria, *Stromateis* 6.15.128).

Another observation underscoring the Petrine theme arises from the fact that part of an *Apocalypse of Peter* was placed with the *Gospel* in the Akhmim manuscript P.Cair. 10759, evidently to be read together—and according to one scholarly view even understood as part of a single integrated text (so Nicklas 2005; cf. Nicklas 2010, 225–26). This theory is not widely followed; indeed it has been argued that neither this text nor those mentioned below form part of the *Gospel of Peter* (esp. Foster 2010a, esp. 57–91; cf. Foster 2008a, 40).

Nevertheless, linguistic and theological similarities make it possible that both the *Gospel* and the *Apocalypse of Peter* arose in a comparable context. If so, this confirms a tendency in second-century Petrine memory to juxtapose the idea of Peter as bearer and pillar of the Jesus tradition with that of him as a conduit of apocalyptic heavenly disclosure—*both* of which already appear important in the Gospel of Matthew (Matt. 16:17–19; cf. also Bockmuehl 2012b, 94 and passim).

Papyri Oxyrhynchus 2949 and 4009—Additional Manuscripts of the Gospel of Peter?

Two Oxyrhynchus papyri (P.Oxy. 2949 and 4009), considerably earlier and in their origin unrelated to the Akhmim parchment P.Cair. 10759, have also sometimes been controversially associated with the *Gospel of Peter* (particularly by Lührmann 1981, 1993; Lührmann and Schlarb 2000, 72–93; cf. Myllykoski 2009a, 2009b). The case for a potential link is stronger for P.Oxy. 2949 than for P.Oxy. 4009.

147

P.Oxy. 2949

Although discovered over one hundred years ago with the other Oxyrhynchus papyri, P.Oxy. 2949 was not published until 1972. There are two papyrus fragments written on one side only, which suggests their origin not in a codex but in a papyrus roll, perhaps to facilitate private study. (By contrast, New Testament gospel manuscripts are virtually always in codex form.) A date in the later second or early third century is widely accepted.

The content is highly fragmentary, and its interpretation must guard against excessive reconstruction from canonical parallels and the Akhmim *Gospel of Peter*, to avoid loading the historical dice with a good deal of circular reasoning.

The text clearly concerns Joseph (of Arimathea), described as a "friend of Pilate" who asks for the body of Jesus after the crucifixion; Pilate consults his friend, possibly Herod (conjecturally reconstructed in line 9), before granting the request. A proposed connection with our text is established by the parallel in the Akhmim *Gospel of Peter* 3–5: Joseph is the friend of both Pilate and Jesus who asks for the body *before* the crucifixion, and his request is granted after consultation with Herod.

As we will see below, it may be that P.Oxy. 2949 represents an early text form of the document that eventually surfaces at Akhmim. (For text and translation, see Ehrman and Pleše 2011, 2014; also Blumell and Wayment 2015, No. 56; Bernhard 2006, 82–83 and plate 17.)

P.Oxy. 4009

The manuscript P.Oxy. 4009 is on a single sheet of papyrus, inscribed on both sides, and generally dated to either the late second century or the early third. This too is in a highly fragmentary state of preservation. Reconstructions by Lührmann and Parsons (1994), Lührmann and Schlarb (2000), and others rely heavily upon supplementation from the Synoptic Gospels (for text and translation, see also Ehrman and Pleše 2011, 2014; Blumell and Wayment 2015, No. 53; Bernhard 2006, 54–55 and plates 6–7). Enough original text remains, however, to permit the confident identification of an individual extracanonical saying (agraphon) of Jesus. This is attested elsewhere in a conversation between Jesus and Peter in

2 Clement 5.2–4, but here recounted—perhaps by Peter?—in the first person (recto, lines 9–14, trans. mine):

> I said to him, "What if
> we are torn apart?"
> He answered and said to me, "After the
> wolves tear apart the
> lamb they can no longer
> do anything to it. . . ."

Most scholars regard the other side of the papyrus (the verso) to be unreadable, although Myllykoski (2009a) has somewhat optimistically identified a narrative parallel to Luke 7:36–50.

While the subject matter has no evident connection to the extant text of the Akhmim codex P.Cair. 10759, the combination of gospel-like material with a narrative voice (quite possibly Peter's) in the first person singular persuaded Lührmann to identify this as part of the *Gospel of Peter*.

Assessment

Recent years have seen considerable debate about these two manuscripts, with scholars taking firm positions on both sides.

Paul Foster in particular has argued strongly against the practice of extrapolating from just one or two undoubted (but potentially incidental) thematic and stylistic *similarities* to an *identification* of either of these texts. He notes that the limited overlap should be seen in the context of late antiquity's proliferating Petrine apocrypha: there are, for example, no direct connections between at least three extant texts all titled *Apocalypse of Peter* (Foster 2008a, 40; 2010a, 89–91; cf. 2006, 2007a, 2010b).

More generally, as we have seen, Lührmann's case for an association with the *Gospel of Peter* has found greater scholarly support in the case of P.Oxy. 2949 than in that of P.Oxy. 4009. For the latter, significant objections have repeatedly been raised by leading scholars (e.g., Foster 2006, 2007a, 2010b, and Kraus and Nicklas 2004, 59–68, with replies by Lührmann 2006, 2007; contrast more favorably Myllykoski 2009b; Ehrman and Pleše 2011, 283, 289–90). No part of the text can be reliably restored from the Akhmim codex P.Cair. 10759; and aside from the hypothetical connection with the Peter of *2 Clement*, the text has no

149

demonstrable link or overlap with the *Gospel of Peter* (cf. Blumell and Wayment 2015, 201–2).

In the case of P.Oxy. 2949, by contrast, more scholars are prepared to grant that the identifiable overlap does provide a cognate text that should indeed be discussed alongside the *Gospel of Peter*, helping to locate it in the late second or third century (e.g., Nicklas 2010, 224–25; Vinzent and Nicklas 2012, 688). Even if one sets aside the large amount of textual reconstruction from the Akhmim Codex, the verbal and syntactical agreements still require explanation. Two basic options could account for the verbal similarities: (a) they may reflect different but closely related traditions of *Gospel of Peter* material, alternatively, (b) P.Oxy. 2949 represents either a literary source specifically reused in the Akhmim document or perhaps a different recension of the same work. Given the extensive textual reconstruction required for the small sample represented by P.Oxy. 2949, the evidence supporting (b) seems insufficiently substantial and (a) should probably be preferred pending further discoveries. An important consideration here is that talk of "text types" or "manuscript witnesses" makes little sense when all we have are two fragmentary texts with limited overlap, written nearly half a millennium apart. Neither of these fragments establishes a larger narrative canvas for the *Gospel of Peter*.

The Fayûm Gospel (P.Vindob. G 2325)

A related question arises in relation to the Fayûm Fragment or Fayûm Gospel (Papyrus Vienna/Vindobonensis G 2325), a very small third-century papyrus fragment that came to light in the Rainer collection of the Austrian National Library in the late nineteenth century. Text and translation are available in Ehrman and Pleše 2011, 2014; also Bernhard 2006, 104–5.

Parts of seven lines of Greek text are legible on one side of what could potentially have been part of a papyrus roll. It seems unwarranted, however, to take for granted that the fragment must therefore ("of course," Ehrman and Pleše 2011, 295) have belonged to a much larger manuscript or consecutive gospel-like document.

The physical manuscript production is significant because, unusually, the scribe wrote a Greek three-letter abbreviation *PET*, for Peter's name in red ink—a phenomenon occasionally deployed

150

in other manuscripts (see, e.g., Kruger 2005, 48–49; Kraus 2009, 224–25; and Foster 2010, 82; with reference to P.Oxy. 840). It would seem that this text, which assigns a special significance to Peter, may be some sort of informal paraphrase or excerpt of Matthew and Mark—or possibly just of their passion narrative.

In terms of its subject matter, the fragment fits easily into a discussion of noncanonical passion narratives. The extant text closely resembles the synoptic Jesus' prediction of the flight of the disciples and the threefold denials of Peter (see esp. Mark 14:26–30//Matt. 26:30–34). This has again encouraged successive editors to restore the text extensively from those canonical parallels, despite a notable lexicographical difference (discussed below) and the omission of Jesus' assurance that after his resurrection he would go before the disciples to Galilee (Matt. 26:32//Mark 14:28).

The text clearly synthesizes elements of both Matthew and Mark, but is in other respects not straightforwardly dependent. In particular, the vocabulary of the Greek phrase "before the rooster crows twice" (*[pri]n alektryōn dis kok[kysei]*) differs notably from that in the Synoptics (*prin alektora phōnēsai*). Together with the omission of the prophecy of a post-resurrection reunion, this suggests a somewhat abbreviated recompilation based on an informally remembered (secondary oral) form of the synoptic text rather than either an independent formulation or for that matter a literary redaction.

As noted earlier, the fragment's importance for the present discussion derives in part from the fact that Dieter Lührmann postulated here a lost fragment of the *Gospel of Peter* (Lührmann and Schlarb 2000, 80–81). He based his argument partly on the remarkable red-letter appearance of Peter's name and on the omission of a Galilean resurrection appearance from the *Gospel of Peter*, but this was combined with his alternative reconstruction of the text, transforming Peter's reply from the third to the first person singular (line 5: *[emo]u Pet[rou]* instead of *[to]u Petrou*, i.e., "*I Peter* said, 'Even if they all stumble, I will not'"). This suggestion has been deemed implausibly speculative both intrinsically and for reasons of scribal technique; and this text is now not generally considered relevant to the *Gospel of Peter*, even if it may have broader relevance for Petrine reception in late antiquity. (See further Porter and Porter 2008, 291–94; Kraus 2001, 2012a.)

"Peter" Ostracon (van Haelst 741)

Brief mention may also be made here of a sixth- or seventh-century ostracon (inscribed pottery fragment; plural: ostraca) carrying an image of Peter and (possibly) the words "Peter, the saint, the evangelist: let us revere him and accept his gospel." Inscribed ostraca with fragments of gospel incipits (opening words) or other text evocative of the gospels are not as such unparalleled (cf. P.Aberdeen 3, Kraus and Porter 2012, 355; see further the list of de Bruyn and Dijkstra 2011). More problematic is the occasionally voiced suggestion that the notion of Peter as an "evangelist" (or preacher) with a "gospel" here denotes specifically his authorship of the *Gospel of Peter* (Lührmann and Schlarb 2000, 72–76)—a theory that was the subject of a lively critical exchange (Kraus 2003; Lührmann 2005) but has not been widely accepted. Nor of course is there any link with the passion narrative.

The Unknown Berlin Gospel/Gospel of the Savior (P.Berl. 22220)

A more compelling and plausible connection with the *Gospel of Peter* has been argued for fragments of a sixth-century Sahidic Coptic codex on parchment, inscribed in two columns. This codex was acquired by the Egyptian Museum of Berlin in 1961 but did not come to public attention until the 1990s, when it was briefly sensationalized in the media and then became the subject of two quite different critical editions (Hedrick and Mirecki 1999, now regarded as defective; corrected by Emmel 2002, 2003). The latter of these editions proposed a more convincing sequence of fragments and argued for a close integration with the Strasbourg Coptic Papyrus (see below). The title *Gospel of the Savior*, a modern editorial artifice, has not been universally accepted and a number of textbooks (esp. outside North America) refer simply to the *Unknown Berlin Gospel* (UBG). (See also the translation in Ehrman and Pleše 2014, though without corresponding bilingual presentation in Ehrman and Pleše 2011.)

152   The surviving material (three double sheets, two single sheets, and twenty-eight smaller fragments) pertains to the passion narrative and presents Jesus offering extended farewell discourses and dialogues with the apostles. The setting resembles the Farewell

Discourses of the Gospel of John, although the material draws loosely on a range of both Johannine and synoptic motifs from the Last Supper to the crucifixion. It also converts a number of narrative elements into prophetic or other verbal articulations by drawing them into Jesus' discourse. Most dramatically, the Gethsemane scene is cast as a mountaintop vision (perhaps on the Mount of Olives?) in which Jesus and the disciples rise with spiritual bodies all the way to the seventh heaven, where in the presence of the angels and the twenty-four elders (cf. Rev. 5:8, etc.), Jesus falls on his knees before God and his Gethsemane prayer becomes the substance of an extended dialogue between the Father and the Son.

This is followed by an extended scene in which Jesus offers a number of lapidary sayings in the first person singular, to each of which the disciples respond quasi-liturgically with the word "Amen": e.g., "I am in your midst like a little child [cf. *Gospel of Thomas* 82]. . . . I am only with you for a short time. . . . I am the King. . . . I am the son of the King. . . . I am the fountain of water. . . . I am your only helper." In this litany-like responsory, Jesus also repeatedly addresses the cross as the key to eternal life, and he predicts several events due to occur during his crucifixion (e.g., being given gall and vinegar, being pierced with a lance).

Heated controversy has swirled around this text, for example as to whether it is translated from a Greek original dating from the middle of the second century or was originally composed in Coptic no earlier than the fourth century. (Thus the recent German edition of Markschies and Schröter 2012 includes a critical "correction" to Hans-Martin Schenke's earlier conception in that volume: Schenke 2012c, 1282; contrast also Nagel 2003 and Piovanelli 2012, 236–39, who see here a Coptic novelistic composition from late antiquity. Ehrman and Pleše 2014, 218, following Plisch 2005, favor the late second century.)

Echoes of the *Gospel of Peter* seem relatively distant or indirect, although a number of scholars have been willing to recognize *Peter*'s influence on the *Unknown Berlin Gospel*. This has been seen particularly in the first person plural voice of the apostles (cf. the *Epistle of the Apostles*, discussed below, p. 215), in the strong focus on the Jewish people's responsibility for the death of Jesus, in his predicted task of preaching to the dead, and in the personification of the cross—here as a living, emotional being repeatedly addressed by Jesus (so, e.g., Schenke 2012c, 1279). That textual

153

distance also seems confirmed by the fact that in the *Gospel of Peter* Jesus still remains identified as "King of Israel" and as "the Lord," whereas here he has become consistently "the Savior."

Much stronger connections exist with the four New Testament gospels, whose influence is here at times skillfully and almost homiletically blended. This is clear, for example, when Jesus integrates the prediction of his disciples' desertion when their Shepherd is struck (Matt. 26:31 and parallels) with the Johannine theme of him as their Good Shepherd who gives his life for them (John 10:11; *Unknown Berlin Gospel* 13–21; cf. Zelyck 2013, 126–42). In addition, certain aspects of the canonical passion and resurrection accounts are here repeatedly not narrated but voiced as prophecies on the lips of Jesus, as passion predictions integrated into the character of this blended Johannine farewell discourse.

The most distinctive element, perhaps, is the representation of the Gethsemane scene as a heavenly transformation and ascent in which both Jesus and the apostles participate. His Gethsemane prayer becomes the substance of an extended dialogue between the Father and the Son. (The inner-trinitarian dynamism of the Gethsemane episode came to be widely explored by early Christian writers, culminating perhaps in Maximus the Confessor [ca. 580–662]; cf., e.g., Jenson 2008; McFarland 2005, 424–26.)

There is a decided tendency to privilege discourse over narrative, and in that sense the text shares characteristics with the discourse gospels to be discussed in the next chapter. That said, however, the clear focus on the redemptive significance of the cross suggests very clearly that we are not dealing with a gnostic text.

Finally, other significant relationships have been suggested with two other texts: the Strasbourg Coptic Papyrus and the *Discourse on the Cross*. Although the latter dates from the Middle Ages and therefore falls outside our primary frame of reference, connections with both texts are sufficiently interesting to merit brief discussion.

The Strasbourg Coptic Papyrus (P.Argent. Copt. 5, 6, 7)

154   The Strasbourg Coptic Papyrus survives in the form of badly torn fragments from two pages of a substantial papyrus codex that came to light at the beginning of the twentieth century. The precise

nature of the text is difficult to establish. Fragment 5, containing the largest portion of text, appears on the recto side to reference a scene of the Son's heavenly enthronement and intercession, while the verso portrays Jesus' farewell to his disciples in verbal and thematic proximity to Matthew 26:38, 41, 45 as well as John 15:20; 16:33; 17:1, and so on (including hints at Gethsemane themes, lines 6–8). Fragments 6 and 7 are more sparsely preserved and difficult to place, although it is possible to recognize a first person plural recollection of the commissioning of the apostles in the context of a vision of God's glory, possibly on a mountaintop.

The substance and narrative voice of this text has led some to attach it confidently to the *Unknown Berlin Gospel* (or *Gospel of the Savior*: see previous section) as a new apocryphal *Gospel of the Twelve Apostles* (Schenke 2012c, 1277–79; cf. Emmel 2003, 2005). But comparable conflations of motifs from the passion, resurrection, and ascension narratives are in fact rather common, and attested in a variety of early Christian genres, as we have seen. In that connection it is probably telling that the treatment here involves no heavenly vision substituting for Gethsemane, and that there is no address to a personified cross.

That said, either a literary connection or at least a context closely cognate with the *Unknown Berlin Gospel* looks to many scholars plausible. Fragment 5 recto contains hints of a similar "amen" litany, while the verso carries parts of a farewell discourse combining synoptic and Johannine elements. Yet in neither case do the surviving fragments suffice to confirm the identification of a "gospel" (cf. rightly Wucherpfennig 2012, 382, with reference to the Nag Hammadi documents).

The Discourse on the Cross
(Nubian Stauros Text)

A ninth- or tenth-century papyrus came to light in the 1960s during excavations in Upper Egypt near the Sudanese border. This text, known as *The Discourse on the Cross*, appears to share a number of ideas with the *Unknown Berlin Gospel* (= *Gospel of the Savior*) and further develops them. In particular, here we find Jesus apparently offering a farewell discourse on the Mount of Olives, in which his prediction of the saving function of the cross is central.

155

He then turns to a responsive litany in praise of the cross, some of which is addressed to the cross itself; to each of its affirmations the disciples respond with "Amen." Interpreters generally agree that this text is a later development of the text represented in P.Berl. 22220. As a result, it is problematic that some scholars significantly reconstruct the text of the *Unknown Berlin Gospel* from the *Discourse on the Cross*, including, for example, this later text's notion of Jesus dancing around the cross (thus, e.g., the revised translation of the *Unknown Berlin Gospel* in Ehrman and Pleše 2014; cf. Piovanelli 2012, with reference to the second "hymn to the cross" in the *Discourse*).

Passion Gospels Associated with Pilate, Nicodemus, and Joseph of Arimathea

A large cluster of mostly medieval manuscripts attests a number of documents traditionally grouped by scholars under the heading of the *Gospel of Nicodemus* or the *Acts of Pilate*. That a number of literary entities of this sort may have existed already in antiquity seems possible from occasional vague (and mutually incompatible) references in writers like Justin, Tertullian, and Epiphanius. Justin (twice: *First Apology* 35.9; 48.3) and Tertullian (*Apology* 21.24) refer to an official file supposed to have been submitted by Pilate to the emperor Tiberius to account for the legal proceedings around these events. Tertullian claims more specifically that Tiberius was so taken by reports he heard that he proposed the inclusion of Christ among the gods of Rome (*Apology* 5), and also that the Roman archives confirm an eclipse of the sun during the crucifixion (*Apology* 21).

That a Roman report or dossier might have existed does not seem impossible and may even be plausible. And that a genuine or (more likely) rhetorical appeal to such a thing might suit second-century Christian apologists also seems entirely credible, regardless of whether they themselves had ever laid eyes on it. According to Epiphanius, a document he identifies as *Acts of Pilate*, and to which he evidently attaches some credence, was invoked by the Quartodecimans (second-century defenders of a Jewish Passover date for Easter) in favor of dating the crucifixion to March 25 (*Refutation* 50.1).

It was not only Christians who found the idea of Pilate's report to Rome beguiling and politically expedient. Eusebius claims that during the final brief but fierce persecution under Maximinus Daia (311–12 CE) the church's enemies at Tyre and elsewhere forged defamatory and blasphemous *Acts of Pilate* to be publicly disseminated against the Christians (*Ecclesiastical History* 9.5.1; 9.7.1), thereby obtaining a favorable rescript from the emperor. Something of the intense hatred and animosity of this period speaks in this attempt to turn a favored apologetic trope against the Christians themselves. Yet although undoubtedly a fascinating chapter in the early church's articulation of its relationship with Rome, quite clearly none of this represents the documents more commonly included in editions of the apocryphal gospels.

The extant Christian literature under this heading is extensive and well attested, but also subject to a highly complex manuscript tradition that variously includes and recombines material identified as *Acts of Pilate*, the *Gospel of Nicodemus*, *Christ's Descent to Hell*, the *Report of Pontius Pilate*, Letters of Pilate to Claudius and Herod as well as of Herod and Tiberius to Pilate, the *Handing Over of Pilate*, and so forth. The material is remarkably extensive, and it found astonishingly wide distribution in about five hundred medieval manuscripts in more than twenty European languages (see, e.g., Schärl 2012a, 2012b; Ehrman and Pleše 2011, 419–585; cf. Ehrman and Pleše 2014). The *Gospel of Nicodemus* both deploys and substantially supplements the four canonical gospels. But it also quite evidently belongs to a late period of conception, composition, and circulation—perhaps taking shape around the fifth or sixth century. There is unlikely to have been a single "original" text, merely the vitality of successive rewritings and adaptations (*Fortschreibung*), in which texts continue to generate secondary metatexts. Ehrman and Pleše (2011, 465) rightly note "how fluid and utterly malleable these traditions were."

One occasionally finds Justin Martyr's testimony (cited above) encouraging some to fancy a second-century date of origin, but it has long seemed to most scholars more plausible that the hostile fourth-century concoction and circulation of anti-Christian *Acts of Pilate* was itself decisive in the development of a Christian tradition along these lines. Most pertinently for our purposes, perhaps, it was not until the thirteenth century that a combination of that *Acts of Pilate* tradition with a narrative of Christ's descent to hell first came to be designated

157

as the *Gospel of Nicodemus*. This text, therefore, does not fall under the present volume's rubric of ancient noncanonical gospels.

That said, the sheer bulk and complexity of this manuscript tradition eloquently attest its astonishing popularity, especially in the Middle Ages, when it developed into a rich treasury of source material for a proliferating piety concerned with the passion of Jesus, including Veronica's facecloth that became one of the eventually fourteen stations of the cross (associated with multiple relics beginning in the eighth century) as well as Christ's descent to Hades to proclaim release to its captives in keeping with 1 Peter 3:19 (the "harrowing of hell").

The latter part of the Latin Acts of Pilate (Tischendorf's Version A) is narrated by Leucius and Carinus, two recently deceased sons of the Simeon who had taken the baby Jesus in his arms in the Temple (Luke 2:25–35) and who were among those restored to life after Christ's resurrection (Matt. 27:52–53; cf. Klauck 2003, 95—also noting the puzzling confusion with the nebulous Leucius Charinus, traditionally the editor of a Byzantine collection of apostolic acts). More particularly, the *Gospel of Nicodemus* went on to become a key resource for the development of European mystery plays as well as of legends surrounding the Holy Grail and the travels of Joseph of Arimathea. A *Narrative of Joseph of Arimathea* is sometimes included as a separate document in editions of apocryphal gospels (e.g., Ehrman and Pleše 2011, 569–85), but elsewhere this corresponds to chapters 12–16 of the *Gospel of Nicodemus/Acts of Pilate* (thus, e.g., see Klauck 2003, 88, 93–94; Schärl 2012b, 236–37, 248–53).

Gospels of Gamaliel?

A cluster of Gamaliel stories came to light in 1904 with the publication by the French National Library of two pages of parchment that were inscribed in the Sahidic dialect of Coptic and apparently formed part of a larger manuscript dating perhaps to the later fifth century. The material in this text appears to be part of a wider passion complex that was integrated into a homiletical "Lament of Mary" by the possibly sixth-century Bishop Cyriacus of Behnesa (i.e., Oxyrhynchus). No ancient attestation confirms the existence of a *Gospel of Gamaliel*, and the similarities with the *Gospel of Bartholomew* and more generally with the Pilate/Nicodemus cycle suggest that this material should be understood as part of the same burgeoning cycle of passion literature (Schenke 2012d, 2012e). Extensive portions of a passion lament cycle associated with the name of Gamaliel also survive in Arabic (Josua and Eissler 2012c) and Ethiopic (Burtea 2012). (Although excluded from most editions of the apocryphal gospels, in Markschies and Schröter 2012, 1307–47, the relevant sections of translation and discussion amount to a full forty pages.)

Conclusion: Passion Gospels

This brief chapter has focused on gospel-like texts concerned exclusively or predominantly with the events surrounding the passion of Jesus. Martin Kähler's (1835–1912) clichéd (and admittedly exaggerated) identification of the canonical gospels as "passion narratives with extended introductions" had by the late twentieth century fallen on harder times (Kähler 1964, 80n11; cf., e.g., Kee 1977, 30–31; Lemcio 1991, 135–36n42; Broadhead 1994). But there can be no doubt that the crucifixion-resurrection sequence is, for the Gospels as for the rest of the New Testament, the pivotal moment by which the identity of Jesus stands or falls. It is this that helps explain the impetus for apocryphal passion gospels, and the extraordinary influence which the Pilate cycle in particular exerted in due course on the development of medieval passion plays.

The outstanding ancient document in this chapter is clearly the *Gospel of Peter*. While this is a freestanding text that shows little or no straightforward *literary* dependence on the canonical gospels, it does seem to renarrate known synoptic Jesus traditions (perhaps familiar by way of secondary orality), combining the essentially Markan (or Matthean) outline with fresh elements that could either be new legendary creations or otherwise unattested traditions.

The effect of the narrative is to emulate but heighten Matthew's latent potential for anti-Judaism and his connection of the crucifixion with the resurrection narratives. (Indeed it is a recurring feature of passion gospels that they thematically and narratively seem to link forward to the resurrection more than backward to the ministry of Jesus.)

It is worth considering the edifying homiletical potential some early Christians found in distinctive themes like the *Gospel of Peter*'s walking, talking cross on Easter morning. Other passion

159

gospels like the *Unknown Berlin Gospel* (*Gospel of the Savior*) and the *Discourse on the Cross* also suggest something of the inherent liturgical appeal and capacity of such reflections on the cross.

Finally, the *Gospel of Peter*'s evident desire to underwrite the passion narrative more explicitly with Peter's authority also seems apparent in both the content and the scribal presentation of the Fayûm Gospel fragment. Yet apart from the passing (and quite possibly unconnected) second-century episode involving Bishop Serapion, there is little evidence that the *Gospel of Peter* or any other passion gospel either sought or secured any formal ecclesial acceptance prior to the later popular developments around the Pilate traditions.

Suggested Further Reading

Bockmuehl, Markus. 2012b. *Simon Peter in Scripture and Memory: The New Testament Apostle in the Early Church.* Grand Rapids: Baker Academic.

Emmel, Stephen. 2002. "Unbekanntes Berliner Evangelium = The Strasbourg Coptic Gospel: Prolegomena to a New Edition of the Strasbourg Fragments." In *For the Children, Perfect Instruction: Studies in Honor of Hans-Martin Schenke on the Occasion of the Berliner Arbeitskreis für koptisch-gnostische Schriften's Thirtieth Year*, edited by H.-G. Bethge, 353–74. Nag Hammadi and Manichaean Studies 54. Leiden: Brill.

———. 2003. "Preliminary Reedition and Translation of the Gospel of the Savior: New Light from the Strasbourg Coptic Gospel and the Stauros-Text from Nubia." *Apocrypha* 14:9–53.

Foster, Paul. 2010a. *The Gospel of Peter: Introduction, Critical Edition and Commentary.* Texts and Editions for New Testament Study 4. Leiden: Brill.

Henderson, Timothy P. 2011. *The Gospel of Peter and Early Christian Apologetics: Rewriting the Story of Jesus' Death, Burial, and Resurrection.* Wissenschaftliche Untersuchungen zum Neuen Testament 2:301. Tübingen: Mohr Siebeck.

CHAPTER 5

Post-Resurrection Discourse Gospels

Most of the more substantive noncanonical gospel-like texts discovered over the last century or so fall into our fourth main category, post-resurrection discourse and dialogue gospels. These are repeatedly associated with a Jesus who teaches his disciples in private (and usually in secret) after the resurrection, although at other times the specific narrative setting is more tenuous. A post-resurrection or temporally indeterminate setting has often been thought to reflect a gnostic preference for direct, unmediated, and indeed secret spiritual knowledge without the need for an earthly incarnate narrative, let alone for stories of an uncomfortably human Jesus' birth, infancy, or passion.

Even more than in the earlier chapters, many of the lines of textual, ideological, and genre identification are here patently blurred. This mercurial fluidity and diversity of the documents, and typically their lack of wider circulation, may be a function of their emergence from experientially vibrant but elite and ecclesially separate groups that tended to develop outside the mainstream Christian tradition of worship and faith. (Within the New Testament, a comparable and perhaps increasing tendency to segregation has sometimes been thought to pertain for the Johannine epistles, esp. 2–3 John.)

A surprising proliferation of texts could be included under this heading. Quite a few present themselves as a somewhat timeless dialogical engagement between Jesus and the disciples, with or

161

without clear narrative characteristics. Unambiguous examples of a post-resurrection setting include the *Epistle of the Apostles* and several of the Nag Hammadi texts (*Sophia of Jesus Christ*, the *Letter* and *First Apocalypse of James*, and the *Letter of Peter to Philip*). Other documents, like the *Gospel of Mary* and the *Second Apocalypse of James*, strongly presuppose or imply such a narrative setting, even if they do not describe it overtly.

New Testament Origins?

Increasing interest in the post-Easter Jesus' *teaching* of his disciples begins to be evident as early as the New Testament gospel tradition. Under this heading one could consider the expansion of Luke 24 or of Matthew 28 over against Mark 16:1–8, the supplementation of John 20 with chapter 21 (or indeed of Luke 24 with Acts 1), and of course the secondary canonical ending of Mark 16:9–20 (on which see p. 89 above).

While the collective terminology of "discourse gospels" or "dialogue gospels" has in recent years become increasingly influential for good reason (so esp. Hartenstein 2012a), its application is not always unproblematic. To cite just one example, a strictly dialogical insertion into that canonical ending of Mark famously appears in the so-called Freer Logion attested in Codex Washingtonianus (W), which probably dates from the fourth or fifth century (see Frey 2012e, 1060, also citing Kelhoffer 2000) and among ancient writers appears to be known only to Jerome (*Against the Pelagians* 2.15). Here the disciples try to excuse their timidity by blaming Satan's power over an age of unbelief and lawlessness, but Jesus instructs them that the years of Satan's power are fulfilled and they are to call sinners to repent and inherit the eternal glory of righteousness. At one level this looks straightforwardly "dialogical." And yet Frey (2012e, 1060) rightly notes that as an expansion deliberately composed to extend Mark 16:9–20 when this had already become part of the gospel, the Freer Logion never existed apart from the Markan manuscript tradition and thus cannot be regarded as a dialogue gospel. In one sense its status resembles that of the episodic "Jewish Christian" fragments transmitted with the Greek manuscript tradition of Matthew (cf. p. 98 above).

Boundaries of genre, then, may be extremely fluid here. A comprehensive inventory of related discourse texts in this category should probably include dominical discourses (like the *Gospel of Thomas*) that may or may not have a post-Easter setting, others that relate more compatibly to the Easter narratives but might be more appropriately seen as apostolic acts, and others still that (like the *Gospel of Philip*) affect a timeless mode of instruction that may only be tenuously identified as the teaching of Jesus.

As a result our discussion in this chapter must inevitably be somewhat discriminating. That said, several key texts undoubtedly do represent the "discourse gospel" here in view, whether or not they clearly fit a post-Easter setting. These include the *Gospel of Mary*, the *Gospels of Philip* and *Judas* (along with several other texts discovered at Nag Hammadi), the *Epistle of the Apostles*, and above all the well-known *Gospel of Thomas*, which has enthralled over a century of critical debate around the so-called Synoptic Problem of gospel origins. It is to this text that we will turn first of all.

The Gospel of Thomas

The past century's most celebrated and controversial noncanonical gospel discovery is undoubtedly the *Gospel of Thomas*, whose text had been unknown in manuscript form until a fragment was published as the first of the Oxyrhynchus papyri (P.Oxy. 1). Here we encounter a Jesus who is above all a sage teacher and guide to secret divine knowledge—rather than, as in the Synoptic Gospels, a prophet or martyr, one who "went about doing good and healing all who were oppressed by the devil" (Acts 10:38). Nor, interestingly, does he appear as Israel's Messiah, the Son of God, or one who taught his disciples to pray to God as "our Father." But he provides a radical guide to wisdom, self-knowledge, and a discipleship of visionary ascent, without the constraints of apostolic tradition or ecclesial order (let alone theological problems of sin and atonement). In addition to its important role in scholarly debates about the origin of the synoptic tradition, the *Gospel of Thomas* has in recent years been promoted at the popular level as a newly recovered resource facilitating a more direct access to Jesus and a

163

largely churchless spirituality (e.g., Ron Miller 2003, 2004, by an ex-Jesuit; cf. Ross 1998, 2010, by a Quaker; cf. further Pagels 2003; Taussig 2013).

In substance, the *Gospel of Thomas* comprises 114 sayings of Jesus, with only rare elements of narrative context or even of genuine dialogue. The sayings are also almost devoid of apocalyptic flavor: the document's eschatology is largely personal, realized, and anti-apocalyptic (with rare exceptions like logia 11 and 111; cf. Gathercole 2011, 286–99 and passim). Instead of miracles, exorcisms, apocalyptic eschatology, passion, cross or resurrection, we find a considerable emphasis on wisdom and proverbs, sapiential prophecy, words of Jesus in the first person, parabolic statements and word pictures, blessings and woes, and a few statements about the law and about the Christian life. (For text and translation see Ehrman and Pleše 2011, 2014; Meyer 2007; Blumell and Wayment 2015, nos. 57, 64, 65. Translations of *Thomas* in this book follow Gathercole 2014a except where noted.)

Content

It is patently difficult to offer a meaningful summary of the 114 sayings, given that there is virtually no story line and little evidence of progression aside from certain pairings or groupings of logia related by theme or language. A few logia appear more than once (e.g., 2/81; 2/92/94; 10/82; 13/108; 56/80). Glimpses of a narrative setting are exceedingly rare and indirect (see, e.g., logia 22, 60).

The gospel opens with the statement, "These are the secret sayings which the living Jesus spoke, and Didymus Judas Thomas wrote them down" (prologue). Commentators sometimes suggest that the phrase "the living Jesus" is a formulation that in gnostic texts became popular as a reference to the heavenly, eternal as opposed to earthly Christ (see, e.g., Nag Hammadi's *Revelation of Peter* NHC VII,3 81.3–82.3; *Holy Book of the Great Invisible Spirit*, NHC III,2, 64.1–3). And given its juxtaposition with texts like the *Gospel of Philip* at Nag Hammadi, the *Gospel of Thomas* evidently lends itself to being understood in connection with postresurrection discourses, despite the fact that it shows little or no explicit concern with either the death or the resurrection of Jesus. (This is a question to which we will return below, p. 178). Significantly, perhaps, the only passing mention of the cross is in logion

55, where it denotes the cross-bearing of the true disciple (cf. Luke 14:27 and parallels), rather than the death of Jesus.

After the prologue, most of the logia are introduced with the phrase "Jesus says" (in the present tense), although logion 2 may instead continue the author's voice introducing the text: "Whoever discovers the meaning of these sayings will not taste death." That is to say, from the start of the book it is vital that the sayings of Jesus are not self-interpreting but require the sort of secret knowledge and understanding that belong to an initiated elite. This is a theme underscored for this text by appeal to a saying familiar from Mark 4:9 and parallels: "He who has ears, let him hear" (logia 8, 21, 24, 63, 65, 96). The *Gospel of Thomas* is rightly seen as first and foremost a text concerned with radical and sometimes contrarian wisdom.

This importance of understanding and interpretation is perhaps further explored in the first of several sayings about seeking and finding (logia 2, 58, 90, etc.). The object and purpose of this seeking is implicitly "the kingdom." Logion 3 makes clear that this kingdom of God is a present and interior reality rather than being distant either spatially in heaven or temporally in the future:

> Jesus said, "If your leaders say to you, 'Look, the kingdom is in the sky,' then the birds of the sky will precede you. If they say to you, 'It is in the sea,' then the fish will precede you. But the kingdom is within you, and it is outside you." (Trans. Ehrman and Pleše 2011)

This is a point that seems to reflect and adapt the synoptic Jesus' teaching that the coming of the kingdom of God cannot be discerned in externally visible signs (Mark 13:21–22; Luke 17:20–21). The nature of this kingdom is for *Thomas* on the one hand subjectively internalized in terms of self-knowledge—an important principle in ancient thought more generally, which was emblematically connected with the famous motto of the temple of Apollo at Delphi (*gnōthi seauton*, "Know yourself") and associated with various other ancient philosophers. And yet the kingdom is also transcendent and emphatically not localized—whether geographically or ecclesially or in terms of a historical eschatology (see esp. logia 51, 113; cf. Gathercole 2011, 300–302). In place of an ecclesial context, the *Gospel of Thomas* depicts salvation as an individual quest for knowledge.

165

Another recurrent theme rightly highlighted by April DeConick (1996, cf. 2001) is a distinctly ascetic consciousness in *Thomas*, which in her view serves to prepare the initiate for visionary experience. This asceticism comes to expression initially in the works of piety known from Matthew 6 as fasting, prayer, and almsgiving (logion 6). The theme of fasting recurs on several occasions—sometimes critically (logion 14), but more often in a general commendation of abstinence: for example, "Unless you fast from the world, you will not find the kingdom. Unless you observe the Sabbath, you will not see the Father" (logion 27; cf. 21.6, "Be on your guard against the world"). A further aspect of this ascetical orientation is the dissolution of gender distinctions in favor of the union or reduction of male and female into a unitary asexual or androgynous state (logia 11, 22, 114; the union of diametrical opposites or the exchange of one thing for another is a common refrain, and the elimination of gender has many parallels in gnostic and Platonic writings; cf., e.g., Meyer 1992, 109–10; Gathercole 2014a, 613–14).

There has been much debate about whether *Thomas* envisages celibacy as mandatory for discipleship (so, e.g., DeConick 1996, 87, 190, and passim, with reference to repeated emphases on "singlehood"). Even if not formally mandated, the recurrence of the theme nevertheless suggests a strong presumption in favor of celibacy, whether for the present or for the eschatological age (cf. Gathercole 2014a, 159–61). It also resonates with the theme of an individualistic, elitist, and ascetical rather than ecclesial spirituality. (On the other hand, it raises further questions about the speculative suggestion that the Nag Hammadi finds were linked with the nearby Pachomian monastery, which was founded on orthodox principles around an influential and explicitly communal rule of life; see also above, p. 17.)

The general theme of detachment most famously surfaces in logion 42, which commands the disciples to become "passersby"— a theme reminiscent of Epicurus and his advice to "live obscurely" (*lathe biōsas*), that is, without drawing attention to yourself. Proverbial Hellenistic wisdom also appears in other places, for example, in the allusion to Platonic imagery about taming anger by reason in the contrast between a lion-eating man and a man-eating lion in logion 7.

166

Platonic ideas of image and likeness appear to bear on the interpretation of creation (83–84). One may also wonder here about the origin of the pantheistic-sounding statement in logion 77, in its later Coptic context: "I am the light that is over all things. I am the all: from me all has come forth, and to me all has reached. Split a piece of wood: I am there. Lift up the stone, and you will find me there." Unless perhaps one wanted to find here a coded reference to the cross and the tomb (in which *Thomas* elsewhere shows little interest), it seems feasible to understand this as a more abstract and universalized version of John's incarnate Logos: Christ is the light that shines on (or in) all the elect. The Greek P.Oxy. 1 notably links this saying with logion 30, which may oppose the more ecclesial understanding of Christ's presence in Matthew 18:20 (cf. Gathercole 2014a, 340, with reference to a similar gnosticizing polemic known to Clement of Alexandria, *Stromateis* 3.10.68–70).

Another interesting feature of the *Gospel of Thomas* is its sometimes unusual characterization of the twelve disciples known to us from the New Testament gospels. In particular, it is James the Just (the brother of Jesus) who is promoted and singled out as the authoritative leader of the disciples after Jesus' departure (logion 12). Thomas, unsurprisingly, is privy to secret wisdom (logion 13) and in this respect surpasses the role of Peter in Mark and Matthew.

Peter himself, by contrast, is rebuked in the final logion, 114, for his desire to exclude Mary (Magdalene) because she is a woman (cf. 22.6; also 13 on Thomas's superiority). Yet if that sounds like the well-deserved demotion of a chauvinist, modern ears may be no less taken aback by Jesus' reply: his no less striking solution to the "problem" of Mary's femininity is not to exclude her but to make her male, since "every female who makes herself male will enter the kingdom of heaven." Misogynistic tendencies like this were, of course, far from exceptional in some ancient Christian circles, and may conceivably have appealed to certain monastic communities (so Klauck 2003, 120–21). On the other hand, one needs to contrast this with the more egalitarian, androgynous, or asexual ideal of logion 22, including its affirmation of nursing infants. The apparent contradiction here may be reducible to an Adamic anthropology whose default position is invariably male, whether this is construed from "female + male" or "neither male nor female" (cf. Gathercole 2014a, 614, also with reference to Gen. 2:22). Mary Magdalene's appearance here is also echoed in other Nag Hammadi texts, like the *Gospel of Philip* and the *Gospel of Mary*.

167

Thomas likes parables, some familiar from the Synoptic Gospels and others otherwise unknown. The parable of the Sower appears here without interpretation, perhaps to enhance the appeal to secrecy and seeking understanding (logion 9). Nonsynoptic parables explaining what "the kingdom is like" are found in logia 97 and 98: the handle of a jar filled with flour breaks while a woman is walking on the way, but she remains unaware of the flour spilling out behind her along the road until she returns home to find the jar empty. And similarly the kingdom is like an assassin who rehearses his task at home by plunging his sword into the wall. Scholars sometimes speculate about the authenticity of these parables, and we cannot rule out the possibility that they derive from early tradition. While there is very little substantive evidence to support such a claim, one might say they do attest well-known gospel themes like the danger of inattentiveness and the need for resolve (e.g., Luke 14:31–32; Mark 3:27; Matt. 25:1–13).

Ancient Attestation and Modern Rediscovery

Prior to the twentieth-century discoveries, the *Gospel of Thomas* was known primarily from occasional but persistent and geographically widespread references in early Christian literature (several dozen explicit attestations and citations of the content are presented in Gathercole 2014a, 35–61 and 62–90, respectively; cf. more briefly Schröter 2012, 484–86). A somewhat confused quotation from the late-second-century Hippolytus of Rome (*Refutation* 5.7.20) ascribes the use of a *Gospel of Thomas* to a gnostic group he calls the Naassenes. The saying Hippolytus quotes is "He who seeks me will find me in children of seven years and up; for there, hidden in the fourteenth aeon, I am revealed." Although not identical, the saying has a certain parallel (however remote) with logion 4 of the *Gospel of Thomas* ("The man old in days will not hesitate to ask a little child seven days old about the place of life, and he will live"). The Manicheans also read a *Gospel of Thomas* that may be closely related to the one we now know, and a number of Syrian writers are familiar with individual sayings (which may or may not indicate familiarity with *Thomas* as such). Beyond this, subsequent centuries exhibit numerous attestations either of the existence of a *Gospel of Thomas* or of individual sayings of Jesus contained in it, beginning perhaps with parallels to logion 22 in texts like *2 Clement*

168

12.2. Nonetheless, the isolated nature of such citations, along with the numerous variations on this saying in second-century sources, suggests that literary dependencies are exceedingly tenuous and the traditions concerned may have circulated independently of the text as a whole.

This relatively limited and often indirect knowledge of the text throughout history changed dramatically with the late-nineteenth-century discovery of three Greek fragments at Oxyrhynchus, followed most importantly by the Coptic Codex II at Nag Hammadi in 1946. In fact it only became possible to identify the Oxyrhynchus fragments with the *Gospel of Thomas* in the light of the Nag Hammadi discoveries (P.Oxy. 654 = *Thomas* 1–7; P.Oxy. 1 = *Thomas* 26–33; P.Oxy. 655 = *Thomas* 36–39). The Coptic Codex shows a number of textual alterations that indicate the Greek text is older, although in the case of P.Oxy. 655 the Greek presents in dialogue form what in the Coptic appears abbreviated as isolated sayings (cf. Gathercole 2014a, 14–34; Schröter 2012, 488–92). Since the oldest Oxyrhynchus copy dates from around the year 200, this secures a date of composition no later than the second century.

All three of the early Greek fragments (P.Oxy. 1, 654, 655) are from a single location (Oxyrhynchus), and we cannot be certain how much more of the *Gospel of Thomas* they contained beyond the surviving few lines, which do not entirely match the sequence or substance of the Nag Hammadi text: P.Oxy. 654 contains *Thomas* 1–7 (with numerous lacunae reconstructed from the Coptic); in P.Oxy. 1 sayings 26–33 are continuous with part of 77; and P.Oxy. 655 has *Thomas* 36–39 together with a barely legible fragment (d) usually taken to represent logion 24.

Some have suspected a quasi-scriptural formality in certain scribal features of the three Oxyrhynchus manuscripts, including the presence of punctuation and (in the case of P.Oxy. 655) the use of double columns. (See further Luijendijk 2011.) That said, the small size and lack of other indicators of public use make it difficult to know how much these features can really tell us about any communally authoritative usage. The Coptic manuscript at Nag Hammadi, at any rate, does not share these formal characteristics. On balance even the Greek manuscripts may be extracts for personal "religious edification, reflection, and/or study" rather than parts of complete copies for liturgical reading by identifiable "communities" (thus Hurtado 2008, 30–31 and passim; cf. Gathercole 2014a, 5–7).

Interpretation

Critical study of the *Gospel of Thomas* has become a booming industry over the past half century, and the sheer volume of publications now eludes anyone but specialists. The latest definitive commentary runs to well over seven hundred pages (Gathercole 2014a; other recent commentaries include DeConick 2007a; Plisch 2008; Pokorny 2009; Grosso 2011; cf. Fieger 1991). Despite this document's undoubted importance, therefore, we must here restrict ourselves to a handful of key issues.

Origin, Setting, and Relation to the New Testament Gospels

Thomas raises interesting questions of comparison and source criticism in relation to the New Testament gospels. The text includes a large number of sayings resembling synoptic teachings of Jesus' public ministry both in Galilee and to a lesser extent in Jerusalem.

An agreed critical assessment of this gospel's setting continues to be particularly elusive because of the strikingly different evaluations it has attracted in the scholarly literature. Following Helmut Koester, American scholars in particular have often argued for a very early (first-century) date and postulated that we have here a reflection of the earliest form of Christianity in Syria. Unlike anywhere in the canonical gospels, Koester saw in the sayings of *Thomas* evidence of "a direct and almost unbroken continuation of Jesus' own teaching . . . —unparalleled anywhere in the canonical tradition" (1965, 301; cf. 1980, 118–19). And even if subsequent claims to direct continuity were a little more circumspect, one still frequently encountered the claim that *Thomas* gives us possibly our earliest access to the mainstream of the Jesus movement, in a gospel that is said to have influenced its closest parallel, the presynoptic sayings collection Q (cf., e.g., Patterson 1993). A variation on this approach has taken the *Gospel of Thomas* as closely linked with the emergence of Johannine Christianity, which displaced the thought world of *Thomas* (so, e.g., Pagels 2003; but cf. critically Dunderberg 2006, 2013). April DeConick, one of the best-known American *Thomas* scholars of the current generation, continues to lead the charge for the idea that this document developed from mid-first-century origins and was quite possibly first composed in Aramaic (DeConick 2008b, 28: "our earliest text showcasing a very old form of 'Orthodox' thought"; cf. more fully DeConick 2005).

From a slightly different perspective, Francis Watson has argued that a close predecessor of *Thomas* served as a source for Mark and Matthew and was subsequently excerpted by Luke, without being in any way dependent upon synoptic antecedents. Watson considers that evidence for the influence of synoptic final-form redaction on the text of *Thomas* must therefore be a case of "secondary assimilation" to the Synoptics on the part of this sayings tradition that stands in close proximity to the earliest form particularly of some of the parables (Watson 2013; curiously his sequel volume Watson [2016] mentions *Thomas* briefly in passing but makes no reference to this earlier theory).

Other scholars, by contrast, tend to see *Thomas* as a mid-second-century text that has been extensively redacted in a gnosticizing direction, shows a dependence on redactional (i.e., final-form) elements of the synoptic tradition, and reconfigures Jesus' originally eschatological and apocalyptic message of the arriving kingdom of God to suit the preference for additional secret knowledge and for a timeless and immediate apocalypse of the mind. This line of thought has been supported by a range of scholars, some of whom nevertheless leave open the question of whether *Thomas* might at the same time accommodate some individual elements of tradition from an earlier stage of gospel development. By contrast, scholarship has tended to resist occasional efforts to push *Thomas* even later toward the end of the second century, for example, in dependence more specifically on the Syriac gospel harmony known as the *Diatessaron* (thus Perrin 2002 and more cautiously Perrin 2007; on the *Diatessaron*, see p. 126 above). On this account a dependence on the New Testament gospels would be not just broadly plausible but consistently demonstrable, even in cases where the relationship is more loosely construed or mediated through reoralization.

Analysis is further complicated by the additional editing that took place between the Greek form attested in the papyrus fragments and the later Coptic translation: some would even argue that the extent of the differences makes the Nag Hammadi Coptic text in a sense a different work (so, e.g., Eisele 2010). To date there is no scholarly consensus about these matters, and disagreement seems likely to continue for some time—indeed, some recent scholarly analysis of the state of discussion voices a note of quite comprehensive inconclusiveness (e.g., Skinner 2012, 28, 56; Eisele 2010, 36; Popkes 2010, 292).

The reasons for the entrenched critical alternatives relate in part to the question of whether and how this document affects the genesis of the New Testament gospels. Those who want to see here the key to the earliest character of the Jesus movement unsurprisingly opt for a date in the middle of the first century (sometimes with a gradually expanding "rolling corpus" until ca. 120: so DeConick 2005, 55–56, 97–99, and passim), while those who detect dependence on, or awareness of, canonical gospel traditions naturally find a date in the mid-second century much more plausible.

We may not be well served by stark polarizations between *Thomas* as representing either the very earliest layer of gospel tradition in the mid-first century or else a substantially dependent, late and gnostic stage of development. Straightforward dependence can only be demonstrated in some cases, just as independence from the synoptic tradition could be demonstrated for at most a small handful of sayings.

That said, the scholarly momentum does seem for the moment to lie with those who favor *Thomas*'s composition in the second century under the influence, at times perhaps indirect, of final or near-final versions of the Synoptic Gospels. Christopher Tuckett (1988, repr. 2014) and others have long since noted that this frequent dependence is not merely on synoptic traditions in general but in several cases on *redactional* (i.e., editorial) elements in the text of the canonical gospels. In recent years this view has been argued most articulately by Mark Goodacre (2012) and Simon Gathercole (2012a, 2014a), both of whom responded to their critics in a joint forum (Gathercole 2014b; Goodacre 2014). This view of *Thomas* as, broadly speaking, dependent on the synoptic tradition is also largely shared by the editors of the recent 1,500-page German edition of the apocryphal gospels in translation (e.g., Schröter 2012, 2013a).

Simon Gathercole, perhaps at present the leading commentator along these lines, presents a powerful argument that *Thomas* is clearly influenced by both Matthew and Luke at every notional stage of its development (and in his view also by Paul, esp. Romans, in logia 53.3 and 17; see Gathercole 2008a; 2012a, 221–23, 227–49; also 2014a, 120–21, 178–80). If true, this rules out the possibility that *Thomas* predates *any* of the Synoptic Gospels (a point further corroborated by indications of its composition in Greek rather than in Aramaic or Syriac). Gathercole further suggests that there is no evidence to suggest *Thomas*'s versions of sayings or parables are more original than those in the Synoptics, although in a few individual cases this remains in theory possible. Schröter (2012, 492–97) also allows for the possibility of independent early tradition in principle but sees no positive evidence in its favor; indeed, he finds the evidence suggests that sayings collections as such already *presuppose* the existence of narrative gospels.

Might the Q hypothesis help clarify the relationship? At a superficial level of comparison, it is clearly the case that Q (if it did exist) may well have consisted primarily of sayings, although it apparently included more apocalyptic material than we now find in *Thomas.* But this partial analogy cannot by itself sustain the weight of demonstrating a supposed primitive Christianity that cared only for Jesus' sayings and was uninterested in a basic narrative engagement with his ministry, death, and resurrection—let alone their specifically religious significance. The mere existence of sayings collections does not mean that the communities hypothetically associated with them knew *nothing else* of the Jesus tradition other than what is contained in these texts. More convincing is the suggestion that *Thomas*'s tendency to abstract and contract synoptic teachings (often by leaving out the middle) allows this gospel to "authenticate" its Jesus through the deliberate reframing of known Lukan or Matthean sayings (thus Goodacre 2012, 126–27, 180; cf. also Foster 2013c, 299).

That said, some second- and third-century communities in Egypt may indeed have favored a more timeless account of the teaching of Jesus. At Oxyrhynchus the Greek *Thomas* material turns up in the company (broadly speaking) of other Christian texts, predominantly canonical or previously known to us. But there are very few clear indicators of *Thomas*'s use and function in that setting, let alone how this gospel may have related to the use and function of the canonical texts. At Nag Hammadi, by contrast, the codex discoveries are clearly more ideologically defined and distinctive; but this singular find of what may have been grave goods also permits few generalizations about its use, whether public or private.

If we then accept the argument that the direction of influence seems to run overwhelmingly from the New Testament gospels to *Thomas* rather than vice versa, two key issues nevertheless remain

173

somewhat underdeveloped in Gathercole's otherwise persuasive account and could usefully be given a little more nuance. Both concern the likely second-century context of *Thomas*'s composition. The first is the *vehicle* by which synoptic influence was delivered: should we assume an author who drew alternately on manuscripts of Matthew and Luke at his disposal, and occasionally on a text of Romans? Or might much of the apparent knowledge of the Synoptics derive from familiarity with something like a gospel synthesis or harmony, whether oral or written? (This question should be disentangled from Perrin's [2002] specific but improbable suggestion of a Syriac *original* closely dependent on Tatian's *Diatessaron*.)

A second, perhaps more interesting question is why, given the scope and importance of synoptic influence, *Thomas*'s development of the sayings of Jesus is at once so similar and yet so markedly different from their function in Matthew and Luke. After all, something like 50 percent of the *Thomas* material has no verbal parallel in the New Testament. Schröter (2012, 494–95) rightly draws attention to the decidedly second-century "shift of meaning" that key first-century Jesus traditions undergo as *Thomas* puts them to new and different uses—for example, in relation to ideas like the kingdom of God or the Son of Man (logion 86; see also Gathercole 2014a, 145–46, 520). What is most significant, then, may be not so much the synoptic influence itself but the particular ways in which that influence is creatively reconfigured and subverted in the service of distinctively *second-century* Gentile cultural presuppositions, casting a significant contextual light on the collection as a whole. (On a similar note, Denzey Lewis [2014] has rightly called for scholars to pay closer attention to the fourth-century setting of the developed Coptic text, rather than to continue pressing it into service in relation to first-century gospel origins.)

A number of scholars have suspected a possibly polemical relationship between *Thomas* and the New Testament's Gospel of John (Gathercole [2014a] lists some key contributors). There is no doubt that interesting comparisons can be drawn. For John, too, the disciples appear to enjoy closer access to potentially saving knowledge for a privileged community—although the noun *gnōsis* ("knowledge") itself is notably and perhaps studiously avoided in the Fourth Gospel. One may also usefully compare and contrast the apparent timelessness of John's loquaciously self-referential, supratemporal, descended, and perhaps already ascended Son who

seems—particularly in the Farewell Discourses of chapters 14–17—
to speak almost from a viewpoint outside history.

When it comes to specifics, however, the connections between
John and *Thomas* seem far less clear and in some ways implausible. "Doubting" Thomas is indeed (gently) chided in John's Gospel—though not for his antidocetic insistence on physical evidence
but for his refusal to trust the attestation of such evidence by the
apostolic eyewitnesses. It is of course theoretically possible that
the *Gospel of Thomas* reacts against such Johannine ideas, but the
arguments for specific influence or reaction either way seem to
most scholars inconclusive.

We know that the early second century saw the first attempts at
a thoroughly Hellenistic cultural synthesis of Christianity, notably
by Basilides and his school in Alexandria, who also paid close exegetical attention to the gospel tradition. And the fact that the Greek
original of the *Gospel of Thomas* found a welcome resonance at
Oxyrhynchus and in later Coptic-speaking gnostic circles of Upper
Egypt does seem eloquently suggestive for its cultural setting and
orientation.

Several major recent publications, then, have clearly injected a
new momentum into the previous critical stalemate on these issues;
indeed it may be right to regard them as "changing the field" (Denzey Lewis 2014; contrast Skinner 2012, 17, who still claims to find
few scholars willing to defend a second-century date). But questions remain, and it is perhaps too early to conclude that the evidence has ceased to look knotty and intractable.

Date and Place of Composition—and Authorship

A date of composition around or soon after the middle of the second century has been widely advocated in recent years. Gathercole
(2014a, 117–20, 477–79) confidently accepts the argument that
Jesus' irreversible destruction of the Temple predicted in *Thomas*
71 requires a post-135 date because it was only then that Christian sources began to capitalize on the Temple's demise. He opts
somewhat expansively for a date during "the Antonine era," that
is, 138–192 CE (see also his survey table, pp. 125–27). While this
broad time frame seems plausible for a variety of reasons, by itself
logion 71 may be a less compelling starting point than is sometimes
supposed. Old Testament prophecies of wholesale devastation were

175

a well-established trope (e.g., Jer. 9:11–16; 50:3) susceptible to repeated reappropriation at times of crisis. Just as importantly, several earlier Christian and potentially even Jewish sources envisage a context of worship that neither has nor requires a physical temple (e.g., John 2:20–21; 4:20–24; *Sibylline Oracles* 4.4–11, 27–30; cf. further Ego, Lange, and Pilhofer 1999). This therefore renders logion 71 rather less conclusive as a basis for dating *Thomas*.

Recent German scholarship has also tended increasingly to date the Greek original to the middle or even "the final decades" of the second century and the Coptic translation to the early fourth (thus, e.g., Nagel 2014, 102). While it remains possible that this composition incorporated both early and late traditions, some of which depend on the Synoptic Gospels while others do not, the composition as a whole seems to belong to the second century rather than the first.

Considerations of literary genre also militate against the idea of a first-century sayings collection's continuous transmission and reception, as Jens Schröter has shown. No collection of contextless sayings shows up in any extant manuscript or literary attestation prior to the third century. This in turn implies, first, that pure sayings collections seem to belong to a later stage than the narrative tradition; and second, that as a sayings collection this text *presupposes* the narrative gospel tradition (Schröter 2012, 495–96, also citing the genre research of Hezser 1996).

Much greater uncertainty attaches to the place of composition, whether Egypt or (as perhaps a majority think) Syria, let alone to any meaningful identification of the author. It may be significant for questions of origin, use, and circulation that no manuscripts of the *Gospel of Thomas* survive outside Egypt, and no ancient translations other than Coptic—although the relatively extensive secondary attestation suggests that at least indirect awareness of this text was widespread.

But Is It a "Gospel"?

A brief word is in order on the question of title and genre. Although the work was known as the "Gospel according to Thomas" to a variety of Christian writers, beginning with Greek sources of the third century (Gathercole 2014a, 35–61), the manuscript evidence only attests that title in the concluding colophon to the fourth-century Coptic manuscript from Nag Hammadi.

This title places *Thomas* alongside other gospels in the name of an apostle, among which are certainly the four New Testament gospels but by the late second century also gospels in the name of Peter and eventually Philip. (The *Gospel of Judas* is not "according to" but "of" Judas, in the sense of "about" him. Perhaps the *Gospel of Mary* is comparable: here too, unlike in *Thomas*, the name appears not to designate the implied author or scribe—although in the case of *Mary* the extant title in the Berlin Gnostic codex does include "according to," 19.4.)

There are striking differences between a document like *Thomas* and the four canonical gospels. The synoptics and John offer an account of Jesus' ministry of teaching and healing in an arc of narrative from his first public appearance to his cross and resurrection. *Thomas* has none of this. Should we then describe this text as a gospel, even though it lacks many of the key narrative, structural, and substantive features that readers of the New Testament might expect to find? It does of course parallel a substantial portion of the synoptic tradition. More significantly, perhaps, the "gospel" title is not only claimed by the Coptic text for itself, but in the third century it was already used by adherents and acknowledged by proto-orthodox detractors too.

The fact that both groups affirmed or at least tolerated the "gospel" designation suggests that popular usage of the terminology may have been broader than is supposed in scholarly debates about whether a gospel must necessarily belong to the literary genre of ancient biography or *bioi* (so, e.g., Burridge 2004, 2013; also cf. Burridge 2015 in reply to the critique of Hägg 2012, 152–56). *Thomas* is not biographical in orientation but was called a gospel in antiquity. What our discussion in this book suggests is not so much that a text called a gospel is necessarily a *bios*, but that almost invariably it either emulates or presupposes the biographical narrative associated with the Gospel of Mark.

Is the *Gospel of Thomas* Gnostic?

In addition to the fraught question of the literary relationship with the canonical gospels, another ideologically charged issue has been the extent to which *Thomas*'s theology should be characterized as gnostic or gnosticizing in the sense discussed in the introduction (p. 18). Certainly *Thomas* as a whole shows no evidence of a fully fledged gnostic system or mythology: the creation of Adam, for example, is seen in positive terms (logia 46, 85) and there is no sign of a gnostic demiurge-creator. Most scholars agree that we should resist the temptation to slot any given saying into a preconceived framework of gnostic ideology.

At the same time, *Thomas* features certain themes that would prove congenial or even vital to second- and third-century gnostic writings. These include the emphasis on secrecy, on saving knowledge, on a transcendent life, and on an internalized rather than a material eschatology, among others. And certain sayings do make better sense if interpreted in the framework of broadly gnosticizing presuppositions: the knowledge that Jesus conveys to bring about salvation can be seen to favor a Platonizing, incipiently gnostic function and intention. For this sayings collection, the world of matter is a useless cave of darkness, poverty, and death within which the spirit's "wealth" has been imprisoned (logia 29, 56). Salvation is reserved for an elite who have only entered this material world temporarily from their true home, to which they will return—a separate, otherworldly "kingdom" of light whose citizens live as fully spiritual beings without being trapped in a split identity of spirit and matter (logia 49–50, 11). The carnal inhabitants of this world, by contrast, are drunk and blind to the truth unless they give up their drunkenness (logion 28). Jesus' secret teachings provide the knowledge of oneself that alone can rescue the individual from death. This theme of saving knowledge abounds throughout (e.g., logia 1–5, 16, 18, 38–39, 46, 56, 67). By contrast, there is little sign of community or church: it is instead the solitary (*monachoi*) and elect whom Jesus blesses (logion 49).

Whatever such themes might be taken to mean individually or in isolation, for a gnostic worldview the *Gospel of Thomas*'s Jesus clearly articulates framing presuppositions that in concert facilitate rather more than is spelled out. Its conceptual and indeed physical placement between the *Apocryphon of John* and the *Gospel of Philip* in Codex II from Nag Hammadi appears to confirm that this is indeed how *Thomas* was heard and received by those who valued it (cf. also Gathercole 2014a, 13). In a sense this shows that while in its original setting and content *Thomas* was not properly gnostic, it certainly went on to become so—and was perhaps predisposed to being read in this fashion. (See further useful discussion in Marjanen 1998; Gathercole 2014a, 168–75.)

178

Thomas *and Scripture*

One characteristic of the *Gospel of Thomas* that has elicited frequent comment is its almost complete disregard for the Old Testament. *Thomas* does not quote Scripture explicitly, and one might say it systematically erases it from synoptic passages that do (Goodacre 2012, 187–90; R. Hays 2014, 9–11 and 114n17; cf. Hays 2016). That said, in the parable of the Vineyard, *Thomas* 65 (+ 66?) does appear, perhaps inadvertently, to retain motifs from Psalm 118:22–23—although without acknowledging Mark's explicit quotation of his biblical source: "Jesus said, Show me the stone that the builders rejected: that is the cornerstone" (contrast Mark 12:10–11).

Klauck (2003, 158) speculates that this removal of the explanatory quotation formula might be part of a wider trend in *Thomas* to present parables *without interpretation*. Another related feature of this preference for a certain literalism is the surprising absence of any allegorical interpretation. Since these are the "secret words of Jesus" that demand the discovery of their meaning reserved for the elect, their significance understandably cannot be disclosed by conventional allegory or "spiritual" interpretation (cf. Schröter 2012, 497). It also necessarily sets this gospel not only over against the Old Testament but by implication in opposition to the earlier gospels as well, since they evidently fail to disclose Jesus' "secret" teaching.

Benignly anodyne neglect of the Old Testament turns to explicit disdain in logion 52: "His disciples said to him, 'Twenty-four prophets spoke in Israel. And did all of them speak about you?' He said to them, 'You have neglected the living one in front of you, and spoken of the dead.'" Some have attempted to downplay this criticism of Jewish Christianity or the Jewish Bible; and one might wish to compare the tone of fulfillment-oriented gospel passages like Matthew 12:6 or John 5:39. But the fact is that *Thomas* nowhere allows a more positive estimation of the Old Testament to counterbalance the rejection of the twenty-four prophets (probably reflecting the number of the books of the Hebrew Bible) as "dead" and their messianic prophecy as irrelevant. And as Gathercole (2014a, 415) points out, the preceding and following logia both mirror this categorical rejection of Jewish Christian beliefs. Even more systematic criticisms of the Old Testament are familiar from other second-century sources: one thinks not just of Marcion but of gnostic or gnosticizing texts like the *Apocryphon of John* and the

Second Treatise of the Great Seth (with more restrained examples in the Pseudo-Clementine *Recognitions* and the *Letter of Ptolemy to Flora*). But although mild by comparison with these extreme examples, it remains the case that *Thomas's* thoroughgoing aversion to and neglect of the Old Testament is without parallel in the New Testament gospels.

On a different intertextual note, we find in logion 17 a statement apparently influenced by 1 Corinthians 2:9 (cf. also Gathercole 2014a, 283–84): "what eye has not seen and ear has not heard, nor the human understanding conceived, what God has prepared for those who love him." But whereas Paul affirms this as an Old Testament quotation (a widely encountered midrashic reformulation of Isa. 64:3), *Thomas* emphatically converts it into a saying of Jesus. Might this reinforce the general avoidance of the Old Testament?

A Post-Resurrection Discourse?

The sayings in the *Gospel of Thomas* overwhelmingly lack any narrative frame that might link them to a particular earthly setting, whether before or after Easter. So does *Thomas* have an implied "narrative camera" that might be said to envisage for its readers a distinct pre-resurrection or post-resurrection setting? Some scholars (e.g., Hedrick 2010, 19; Tuckett 2005, 248) detect a presumed post-Easter setting in the apparent timelessness of much of the material, combined with the extent to which the Jesus here in view seems untroubled by historical events and simply speaks in the present tense as "the living one" (prologue), evidently exercising an omnipresent "God's eye view" (cf. logion 77, quoted above). On that account the *Gospel of Thomas* might constitute a post-resurrection discourse comparable to a number of those discussed in this chapter.

Other scholars, however, insist that nothing in the text hints at an Easter narrative, let alone a resurrection dialogue (e.g., Klauck 2003, 146). On the contrary, occasional if rare narrative intrusions into the text (logia 22, 60–61; cf. 12, 100) seem to reflect a perspective from within the ministry of Jesus, confirmed perhaps by Thomas's envisaged role as an eyewitness (logion 13). Unsurprisingly, such allusions to the earthly career of Jesus of Nazareth also appeal to those who continue to favor *Thomas* as a source for the Synoptic Gospels.

A third possibility worth considering is that the pre-Easter versus post-Easter question is itself moot. On this view, *Thomas* exemplifies a form of Christianity that quite simply has no interest in the narrative of Jesus' life, crucifixion, or indeed resurrection. If this is true, it is again plausible that *Thomas* might resemble the hypothetical sayings source Q, assuming that this too privileged individual logia without regard for narrative context, let alone for the life of Jesus. In a different sense, such atemporality may at the same time evoke passages in John's Gospel that seem to leave unclear whether it is the earthly or the ascended Jesus who is speaking (e.g., John 3:13; 17:11). On this third reading, *Thomas* would resemble other noncanonical gospel texts of the later-second and third centuries that deploy loosely characterized resurrection settings to frame what are essentially timeless discourses or dialogues between Jesus and the disciples for the purpose of "supplementary" instruction (cf. Hartenstein 2000, 2007).

Conclusion

Thomas raises many interesting questions of comparison and source criticism in relation to the New Testament gospels, not least through a large number of sayings that resemble synoptic teachings of Jesus' public ministry both in Galilee and to a lesser extent in Jerusalem. Several major recent scholarly studies have cited its inclusion of synoptic *redactional* elements as evidence for the chronological priority of Matthew, Mark, and Luke. That said, it is much less clear whether *Thomas*'s apparent dependence on them is literary or oral, direct or indirect, or indeed if such preexisting gospel sayings material was even known in a textually discrete or harmonized form.

Much remains uncertain about the circumstances of *Thomas*'s literary genesis. Experts are divided; and several persist, against the drift of other recent specialist treatments (e.g., Gathercole 2014a; Goodacre 2012; Schröter 2012), in asserting a likely mid-first-century origin of this text or its predecessor (thus, e.g., DeConick 2007a, 2008b; Watson 2013; cf. Nicklas 2014a, 222).

Nevertheless, the balance of recent argument seems to favor a reading of *Thomas* as, in some sense, epiphenomenal on the synoptic Jesus tradition, and in that respect comparable to the ministry and passion gospels discussed above. More specifically, many of its central concepts appear to lie on a second-century trajectory to fully fledged gnostic profiles of Jesus. More to the point, perhaps,

181

the *Gospel of Thomas* was clearly understood in such terms, as its embedded function in the Nag Hammadi codices suggests.

At the same time, for purposes of this book we do well to observe that *Thomas* does *not* seek to present itself as either a restatement or a supplementation of widely shared Jesus tradition. Instead, and unlike most or all of the other gospel-like texts we have surveyed thus far, it sets out deliberately to present an *alternative* and in some sense *rival* account. These teachings of Jesus are emphatically characterized as "secret" (prologue), as they also are in a number of other texts (including the *Gospel of Judas* as well as Nag Hammadi's *Book of Thomas the Contender*, *Apocryphon of John*, and *Apocryphon of James*). Given the obvious familiarity of many of the sayings, it seems more likely that the secrecy attaches not to their wording so much as to the disclosure of their saving significance, which is elusive and reserved for the initiated (so logion 1).

What this means is that *Thomas* manifests no ambition to be accepted as ecclesially canonical; quite to the contrary, *it explicitly sets out to be apocryphal* (see Nicklas 2014a, 224). This deliberate posture of an individual, rival "apocryphicity" could explain why there appears to be no evidence of any ancient public liturgical use or commentary tradition around the *Gospel of Thomas* (contrast, e.g., the *Infancy Gospel of James*). It may also shed interesting light on the nature of the manuscript tradition and circulation.

It remains in any case significant that like the Oxyrhynchus fragments, the *Gospel of Thomas*'s only other surviving manuscript also turned up in the same general region of Upper Egypt, as part of Nag Hammadi Codex II. In other words, there is no evidence for a vibrant tradition of pervasive manuscript dissemination, commentary, or other metatext, as one might expect for a communal sacred scripture. The sheer absence of any wider public currency and familiarity explains why *Thomas* never remotely attained the status of a "fifth gospel" (*pace* Patterson 2013; Patterson and Robinson 1998).

At the same time, ancient and medieval *mentions* or references to the contents of *Thomas* are relatively abundant across a wide geographic and chronological range, with the *Acts of Thomas* perhaps being the document most patently and significantly influenced by the *Gospel of Thomas* (Gathercole 2014a, 35–90, 78; cf. further Grosso 2012). This wider attestation of certain Thomasine sayings seems, however, to demonstrate not so much its breadth of circulation as a complete text but rather the highly eclectic adaptability of its contextless logia to the needs of diverse publics (so Gathercole 2014a, 89). In other words, in assessing its influence it is important to distinguish between *Thomas* as a text that is known and one that is only known *about*—and perhaps in many cases mentioned and rejected simply as an antiheretical trope.

The Gospel of Philip

Following on immediately from the *Gospel of Thomas* in Codex II of Nag Hammadi is the *Gospel of Philip*, again in a Coptic manuscript dating perhaps from the fourth century and widely presumed to represent a translation from a lost Greek original. Unlike for *Thomas*, however, the Nag Hammadi codex represents the only surviving copy of this text. A gospel under this title is attested and indeed quoted in Epiphanius's inventory of heresies (*Refutation of All Heresies* 26.13.2–3), but its content shows no apparent overlap with the text from Nag Hammadi. Two later Byzantine authors reference a *Gospel of Philip* among the Manicheans, but again with no clear correlation (cf. Schenke 2012a, 529).

Unlike the adjacent *Gospel of Thomas*, Nag Hammadi's *Gospel of Philip* stands at a considerable distance from the canonical and even the noncanonical gospel tradition, with much of which it has at best tenuous connections. While the scribal colophon at the end of the sole surviving manuscript copy does identify it unambiguously as "The Gospel according to Philip," that concluding flourish may well reflect a desire to link the text with Philip as the only one of the twelve disciples mentioned in the text (91 [73.9][1]). In substance and genre, however, *Philip* seems remote from most of the other texts

---

1. Several incompatible (and therefore confusing) citation schemes are in use in the literature, the most influential being a simple paragraph numbering originally devised by Martin Schenke (still deployed in Schenke 2012a; cf., e.g., Ehrman 2003; Klauck 2003; Lapham 2003) and the other (now the most common) based instead on manuscript page and line numbers. Contrary to Meyer (2007, 157) it is not (yet?) true that Schenke's paragraph division "is rarely followed today." Here, in keeping with the practice of Nagel (2014), I will give both notations. (Note that both Nagel [2014] and Layton [1987] additionally use paragraph schemes of their own that differ from Schenke's.)

In relation to Nag Hammadi and other Coptic manuscripts more generally, there is also some divergence in the literature between scholars following a "continental" convention of citing page and line numbers separated by a comma (e.g., 73,17) and the more familiar American or British notation using a decimal point or a colon. For reasons of consistency with other ancient sources, I have here retained the latter usage.

discussed in this book—including even *Thomas* or, for that matter, the *Gospel of Truth*.

At the same time it must be significant that two such noncanonical gospels are here bound together in the same volume, and indeed that the text of *Philip* begins without any intervening new title. Nothing in this juxtaposition implies a liturgical usage of these texts in worship, let alone the formation of a Valentinian gnostic canon. But on the other hand it does presumably indicate that the fourth-century compiler had come to see these documents as in some important sense belonging together and sharing a common outlook—whether or not that was explicitly perceived to be gnostic. Since the *Apocryphon of John* with its elaborately gnostic mythology is prefixed to this codex as well as to Codices III and IV, a few scholars suggest—somewhat speculatively—that it may be that document which functions as a Valentinian (or perhaps Sethian) interpretative key to unlock the meaning of *Thomas, Philip*, and other texts (so, e.g., Foster 2008b, 69, also citing Logan 2006, 6; cf. previously Thomassen 1997).

The *Gospel of Philip* supports characteristic Valentinian ideas about the ascent of the soul and about salvation as the individual's saving knowledge of oneself and one's otherworldly home, attained through a mystical union of opposites. And *Philip* represents a more fully fledged expression of gnostic views than *Thomas*: the point of Christology and of salvation is not rescue from evil or from sin, but rather the liberation of the inner divine spark from earthliness, and the attaining (and reunion) of true being.

Again somewhat characteristically of the gnostic setting, the *Gospel of Philip* incorporates a good deal of sexual imagery in articulating this process of liberation and reunion in terms of a bridal chamber. Some have suggested that such language may reflect the sort of sexual libertinism associated with certain later branches of Valentinianism (notably by their opponents). But the case for this rests entirely on ambiguities, and in fact the text strongly indicates instead a metaphorical and spiritual perspective that is explicitly ascetic and hostile to sexuality.

There is certainly little or nothing to support the interpretation popularized by Dan Brown (2003), according to which 55b (63.33–34) furnishes proof positive that Jesus married Mary Magdalene: "The [Savior loved] Mary Magdalene more than [all the] disciples, and he kissed her of[ten] on her [mouth]." Worth noting first, perhaps, is the obvious point that the word "mouth" is in fact supplied

184

for a gap in the text, indicated by the square brackets in the quote: the text in no way identifies where the Savior kissed Mary; kissing the hands or the forehead seems culturally at least as plausible, although conversely the mouth might seem to suit the metaphor of the bridal chamber. As scholars have rightly noted, paragraphs 30b–32 (58.34–59.11) introduce a familiar apocryphal trope of a composite three-Marys-in-one figure (in this case, mother, sister, spouse: see Klauck 1992; Shoemaker 2015, 188–89; cf. also, controversially, King 2014, 146–48). The text explains the spiritual kiss by which those who are "perfect" receive nourishment and conception: "For the perfect conceive and give birth by a kiss. It is for this reason that we also kiss one another: we receive conception from the grace that we have in each other." Paul Foster (2008b, 74–76) suggests that on this reading of the "holy kiss" Mary Magdalene "becomes the matriarch of the form of Gnosticism which practices the bridal chamber sacrament of reunification" (76).

The *Gospel of Philip*'s general expression of gnostic mythology and cosmology also points to a more advanced stage of Valentinian ideological development, with its emphasis on escape from the world and the body, and on ascent to transcendent levels of being. For this and related reasons, a compositional date in the first half of the third century is normally thought plausible.

Like *Thomas*, *Philip* shows an interest in broadly sapiential material that is not subject to any particular narrative or logical flow of argument. While the arrangement may strike us as rambling and disjointed, this is not uncommon for ancient wisdom texts.

In substance, the *Gospel of Philip* communicates neither an account of any part of the life of Jesus nor a collection of his sayings. Instead, as is now increasingly agreed in the burgeoning scholarly literature, it appears to represent a fairly unstructured anthology of aphorisms and commonplaces—possibly, but by no means necessarily, gathered from a larger body of gnostic teaching or catechesis. As a result, in a sense each excerpt constitutes its own unit of meaning, even if some of these may be seen to establish internal topical connections (cf. Schenke 2012a, 536). Analogies have also sometimes been noted with the organizing principles governing other ancient notebooks of excerpts (e.g., M. Turner 1996, 62–63, 254, and passim) or indeed collections of sentences (including the 185 famous *Sentences of Sextus*, a Coptic version of which turned up in Codex XII at Nag Hammadi; cf. M. Turner 1996, 106). Klauck

(2003, 124), among others, suggests that it is possible to discern recurring "link-words and thematic groups," especially perhaps in relation to sacramental language.

Even prior to the Nag Hammadi discoveries, a *Gospel of Philip* was known to Epiphanius and later Byzantine writers who associated it with libertine Egyptian gnostics as well as with the Manicheans. Epiphanius (*Refutation of All Heresies,* 26.13.2–3) does quote from such a gospel; but while this supports the compatible idea of the soul's liberation by ascent to heaven, its wording has no match in the text from Nag Hammadi. The document in question might theoretically represent either an alternative or supplemented text, or else a different gnostic *Gospel of Philip* altogether (cf. Schenke 2012a, 530; Klauck 2003, 123).

In our Nag Hammadi document, Philip is the only named apostle, who claims that the cross was made from a tree planted by Joseph the carpenter (91 [73.9–15]). The notion of Philip as a writer of the secret teachings of Jesus is, as we noted before, explicitly affirmed in the document known as the *Wisdom of Jesus Christ* (*Sophia of Jesus Christ* 1.42–44; see p. 192 below). There, significantly, Philip is singled out with Thomas (and Matthias) as charged by the risen Jesus to write down his "discourses" (1.42).

Content

The lack of argument or narrative progression makes any representative summary nearly impossible, but we may select a few themes (see also the attempt at a table of contents by Foster [2008b, 72]).

Philip begins with a series of reflections on Hebrews, proselytes, Gentiles, and Christians—with "Hebrews" being the polar opposite of Christians. We then find an exposition of the work of Christ in the context of a dualistic cosmology, a statement about deceptive words and names, Truth versus the archons or rulers, and the abolition of sacrifices (14b [55.1–5]). Contrasting the rulers against the Holy Spirit, the text polemicizes against the idea that a female Holy Spirit could possibly have brought about Mary's conception. The polarity of soul and body is then developed, followed by Christ's many forms and the possibility of union with him. The text highlights three Marys as being particularly close to Jesus: his mother, his sister, and Mary Magdalene, called his "companion." Various similarities and contrasts between the Father, the Son, and

186

the Holy Spirit follow, with a focus on both their interrelationship and their interaction with the human sphere. We hear of the names of Jesus and their meanings—the Lord, the Nazarene, the Messiah, and the Christ—and then the contrast between ordinary human names like Jew, Roman, Greek, barbarian, slave, or free over against the powerful name "Christian." The text says that "the Eucharist is Jesus" (53 [63.22]), a significant point in relation to numerous other passages suggesting a sustained sacramental interest relating to baptism, anointing, Eucharist, salvation, and the mystery of the bridal chamber.

In 55b (63.33–34), Mary Magdalene, Jesus' most loved disciple, whom he "kisses on her [mouth]," appears in connection with the frequent recurrence of the bridal chamber as a sacramental metaphor.

Some scholars and journalists have sensationalized Mary's role here in relation to the so-called "Gospel of Jesus' Wife." This is an ancient papyrus fragment that in 2012 enjoyed worldwide media coverage and was giddily endorsed by academics from Harvard, Princeton, and New York University as "impossible to forge" (Goodstein 2012). By the time of its eventual publication (King 2014), however, the fragment had already been successfully exposed as a modern fraud, copied from a twentieth-century publication onto an apparently eighth-century scrap of papyrus (see, e.g., Askeland 2014; Emmel 2015; Watson 2012). Despite the continuing absence of concessions or disclaimers from Harvard Divinity School's Web page on the subject (King 2015), the identification of a quite recent forgery was further confirmed by contributors to a dedicated issue of the flagship journal *New Testament Studies* (Bernhard 2015; Schenke Robinson 2015; and others), before the likely perpetrator was exposed by an investigative journalist (Sabar 2016a) who appeared at last to persuade even Karen King (Sabar 2016b). Gathercole (2015) points out that far from shedding light on our passage in *Gospel of Philip* 63.33–34, the "Jesus' Wife" fragment owes far more to a patchwork of the Coptic *Gospel of Thomas* from which the forger ostensibly plagiarized it.

While *Philip*'s conception of the bridal chamber at times invokes sexual imagery, it is also the case that the text explicitly *rejects* carnal, sexual "marriage of defilement" over against the ascetical and sacramental marriage chamber sheltered from the power of the archons. The author lays stress on the pure rather than fleshly restoration of a primal mystical, androgynous union (esp.

187

122 [82.5–10]: "If even the marriage of defilement is hidden, how much more is undefiled marriage a true mystery! It is not fleshly but pure, a matter not of lust but of the will, not of darkness or night but of the day and the light"). Above all the sacrament of the bridal chamber (the "Holy of Holies," 76a [69.15–21]; 125a [84.24–31]) is related to the Father's heavenly begetting of the Son (e.g., 81–82 [70.35–71.14]), as indeed it appears to be the function of Jesus to reunite the gendered brokenness and division in humanity. An androgynously restored union emerges as a result.

The document goes on to praise the superiority of anointing over baptism, the eternal mystical union in perfect light and knowledge of the truth, and the development of Christlike perfection. Jews and "Hebrews" (possibly Jewish Christians) are spiritually inferior, "psychic" beings who may advance to become Christians (e.g., 6 [=52.21–24]; 16.2 [=55.27–33]); Jewish symbols like the Temple, High Priest, Sabbath, circumcision, and Abraham are appropriated in positive but radically gnostic ways (e.g., 8 [=52.34]; 76a [=69.15–25]; 123a [=82.26–29]; cf. Heimola 2015). A variety of other metaphors are deployed—including children resembling their (legitimate or illegitimate) fathers (112 [78.13–25]), becoming one in mystical union as light with light or spirit with spirit rather than as animal with animal (113 [78.26–79.13]), and God's spiritual agriculture through the elements of faith, hope, love, and knowledge (115 [79.20–25]).

Assessment

Few of the *Gospel of Philip*'s strong but unusual metaphors seem obvious or self-interpreting, although several scholars have attempted to detect liturgies or rituals of initiation. (Indeed the text as a whole has been described as a "tract about rituals" of salvation by Schmid [2010, 299].) It may be significant that "baptism," "anointing," and "resurrection" have here all become stages of initiation through which the individual passes *before death* on the path to enlightenment (90a [73.1–9])—just as, indeed, the Lord himself rose before he died (21 [56.17–20])! This reversal of death and resurrection is one of a number of themes in which scholars have suspected a clear resistance to the theology of Pauline and other New Testament texts (e.g., 1 Cor. 15; cf. 2 Tim. 2:18) associated with the mainstream of Christian belief and praxis. That said, it is

188

of course true that even some New Testament texts already anticipate or elide the sequence of death and resurrection, particularly
as related to baptism (e.g., Col. 2:12; 3:1; Eph. 2:6) and perhaps the
theology of "eternal life" in John.

Somewhat strangely for what is presented as an apostolic "gospel," this text includes remarkably few explicit teachings of Jesus,
whether similar to the canonical gospels or not. What is more, virtually nothing he says is addressed directly to the disciples (see
Klauck 2003, 123, for references).

This puzzlingly "inaccessible, cumbersome text" (Schmid
2010, 293) stands at odds with emerging Christian orthodoxy
about Jesus in several other respects. One of these pertains to
its skepticism about the idea of the virgin birth. However, as is
the case for the bridal chamber imagery and for Jesus' complex
relationship with the compound figure of Mary his sister, spouse,
and mother (32 [=59.6–11]) as the most loved disciple, things are
rather less scurrilous or salacious on this front than they might at
first appear to journalistic scholarship. What is critiqued in passages like 17a–c [=55.23–36] is the misunderstanding of the virginal conception as a physical act by a spiritual power, let alone by
a (female, Sophia-like) Holy Spirit. Contrary to some interpreters,
this is not critique of Mary's virginity per se, but rather an insistence on that virginity as compatible with sexual continence and
with the spiritual fatherhood of God (cf. Foster 2008b, 77, citing
Thomassen 2006, 90–92).

The *Gospel of Philip* may represent the excerpted summary of
the teachings of a gnostic preacher or catechist whose precise setting is difficult to determine with confidence. In highly metaphorical language, an affirmation of ritual and sacrament is combined
with gnostic convictions about saving knowledge and the spiritualizing reconfiguration of material and bodily—especially sexual—
existence. For all its obscurity, this is clearly an imaginative and
captivating text.

The *Gospel of Philip* also appears at some level conversant with
several of the writings that became the New Testament, including
both the Gospels and the Letters of Paul. Using a term we have
repeatedly deployed in this book, we may say that it is in that sense
epiphenomenal upon the canonical gospels (and other canonical
texts). And yet it represents an expression of Christianity that has
moved a considerable distance from the religious context of their

189

composition or mainstream reception. Its apparent marginality in the early church is also highlighted by the fact that it survives in only a single manuscript, with no known distribution or commentary literature.

Other Dialogue "Gospels" or Gospel-Like Texts from Nag Hammadi

A significant number of other texts from Nag Hammadi are often identified as apocryphal gospels or seem at any rate to constitute gospel-like texts. Standard editions and translations of the noncanonical gospels differ in how many of these texts are included. A full discussion is beyond the scope of this volume, but we will here offer brief comments on another five of these texts. (The *Gospel of the Egyptians* [NHC III,2; IV,2] will be discussed under a separate heading below.) Texts and translations are found in Meyer 2007.

The Gospel of Truth

The third tractate of Nag Hammadi Codex I identifies itself by its opening words in Coptic, "The gospel of truth is joy to those who have received from the Father of truth the gift of knowing him." Although this is not self-evidently a title, scholars have frequently considered if this might be the work identified by Irenaeus as the Valentinian *Gospel of Truth* (*Against Heresies* 3.11.9). While its advocates treat it as additional to the mainstream apostolic gospels, Irenaeus concludes it has nothing to do with them—a judgment apparently reached without firsthand acquaintance.

No confident identification of this text with the one known to Irenaeus seems possible, even if some scholars understandably consider the existence of two such works of Valentinian origin and identification unlikely (e.g., Nagel 2014, 31; Klauck 2003, 135–36). The text in Codex I was subsequently supplemented by the discovery of six fragments of an additional copy in Codex XII. (Bizarrely, that same Codex I came at first to be known as Codex Jung when for a few years it was housed in Zurich's C. G. Jung Institute as a present for the great twentieth-century psychoanalyst.)

Unlike most of the Nag Hammadi documents, the *Gospel of Truth* was sometimes thought to have been originally composed

190

in either Coptic or Syriac, but the majority view remains that our Coptic text is a translation from a Greek original. Despite clear Valentinian tendencies, there can be little confidence about an original geographic location. The reference in Irenaeus and the apparent use of a gospel harmony resembling the *Diatessaron* means that many scholars favor a date around 180. Authorship by Valentinus himself (fl. 130–160) is sometimes proposed, but impossible to confirm. Most see in this work a development of Valentinian views, even if these predate the gnostic cosmologies and soteriologies found in third-century texts.

The *Gospel of Truth* is not in any obvious sense a gospel, as it offers little interest in any narrative or direct speech of Jesus, whether before or after the resurrection: there are no stories and no logia, although most interpreters accept that the text shows some familiarity with images, titles, and theological ideas in the New Testament writings—though this familiarity may again be indirect, possibly through the *Diatessaron* or another gospel harmony, whether formal or informal. Although not therefore straightforwardly a gospel, the *Gospel of Truth* is perhaps best understood as a poetically vibrant homily or "gospel meditation" (thus Markschies 2012f), for which "the gospel" is the proclamation *about* Jesus rather than the story of his life or the content of his teaching. The gospel is the revelation of hope that enables those who seek him to find, and which reveals the hidden mystery of Jesus Christ to those who are perfected by the mercy of the Father (17.3; 18.16).

The main subject of the text is the return of the aeons to the Father and his fullness (Pleroma): they are ignorant of their departure from him and long for the way back to their eternal rest, but cannot know it except by the Father's merciful disclosure of it by means of heavenly knowledge. That knowledge is communicated through the Logos, and redemption and "rest" are achieved by the conversion of ignorance into this knowledge. Interestingly, and unlike later gnostic texts, the *Gospel of Truth* regards the suffering of Jesus Christ the Son as instrumental in preparing the return of the aeons (e.g., 20.26–21.25).

The heavenly revelation exposes the "fog" of terror and deception as merely apparent rather than real, resulting only from ignorance—a mere dream from which one awakes as through Jesus one acquires knowledge and opens one's eyes (30.13–16). That said, deception personified (Planē) here operates as the evil adversary of the Father and the Son in much the way that the demiurge (who fashions matter into the created order) or fallen Wisdom does in other Valentinian texts. Jesus became a guide and a "person of rest," speaking as a teacher and refuting those wise in their own eyes. Instead he welcomed the "little children" who have knowledge of the Father; and as a result of knowing and being known they were glorified and in turn they glorified (19.17–34). He offers them perfection through the anointing and sealing with salvation (36.19–35). And they are called to offer spiritual works of mercy to others and to the Father's will (33.1–32).

In keeping with the homiletical, edifying style, the text proceeds quite freely without obvious structure or sequence (though this has not prevented scholars from attempting to discern one!). The text concludes by affirming that the aeons are returned to the rest and the Pleroma by the Father's mercy and by the revelation of the Son (who is himself the Name of the Father: 39.15–28; 40.25–29).

The gently poetic cadences of the *Gospel of Truth* have a captivating quality even where its logic and meaning often remain obscure or inaccessible. But central themes include the redemption from alienation and ignorance through seeking, finding, return to the Pleroma, and rest. It is in this sense that the newly discovered text's interest to Jungian psychoanalysis is perhaps less surprising, although it does of course inhabit a very different world of early Christian reflection on salvation. The author offers an unusual and often confusing mix of Valentinian dualistic conceptions of the restoration of the universe and a seemingly orthodox idea of the saving significance of Christ's death on the cross.

The Sophia of Jesus Christ
(or Wisdom of Jesus Christ)

We have three partial manuscripts of a post-resurrection dialogue known variously as the *Sophia* or *Wisdom of Jesus Christ*, two in Coptic translation and one in the original Greek. The more fragmentary of the two complete Coptic manuscripts appears as the fourth tractate in Codex III at Nag Hammadi, while a virtually complete version is attested in manuscript BG 1/BG 8502 in Berlin, a Coptic gnostic codex that came to light in Upper Egypt (possibly at Akhmim) in 1896 and that also contains the *Gospel of Mary*, the *Apocryphon of John*, and the Coptic *Act of Peter* (a narrative episode about Peter's daughter, apparently independent of the better-known *Acts of Peter*: see Molinari 2000). Finally, about fifty lines of this text on an early-fourth-century Greek papyrus also turned up at Oxyrhynchus (P.Oxy. 1081, on which see Blumell and Wayment 2015, No. 72). The standard edition remains that of Parrott 1991. The document therefore seems relatively well attested, despite being unknown under this title prior to the twentieth-century Nag Hammadi discoveries.

Following the resurrection, Jesus meets with the Twelve and with seven women followers on a mountain in Galilee, although the text appears confused about this in relation to the Mount of Olives. Appearing as an angel of light (and therefore presumably not raised bodily), Jesus teaches them about cosmology and soteriology, offering often lengthy discursive answers to general gnostic questions concerning matters like truth, the nature of the universe and of salvation, the origin of spiritual beings and the nature of perishability and imperishability, the number of aeons, and so forth. By the time the document concludes, the disciples find themselves encouraged to go out and proclaim God's gospel.

This text clearly represents an advanced form of gnostic revelation discourse, in which many standard topics are developed in familiar tropes. Scholars have long recognized that this dialogue represents the gnostic Christian reworking of another document known as *Eugnostos the Blessed*, an apparently pre-Christian (or at any rate non-Christian) tractate of Middle Platonic religious philosophy in the form of a letter rather than a dialogue, with which the *Wisdom* often overlaps verbatim. The importance of *Eugnostos* for the Nag Hammadi gnostics can be seen in the fact that it exists in two copies in this collection, one of which immediately precedes our text in Codex III (NHC III,3; cf. V,1). Scopello (2007b, 271–72) suggests that the name "Eugnostos" may well have carried symbolic significance for the true gnostic as "the one who knows well."

The revision of this text in the *Wisdom of Jesus Christ* is primarily a matter of reframing it into a revelatory discourse between Jesus and the disciples. Nevertheless the resultant document merits study on its own terms as a systematic account of cosmology and salvation from the perspective of Christian gnostics, reliant not only on *Eugnostos* but also on distinctively Christian themes found, for example, in the *Apocryphon of John* as well as in Matthew and other gospels, and possibly even in 1 Corinthians 15:45–47 (thus Barry

193

1993, 32–33, as cited in Scopello 2007d, 286). A third-century date seems plausible in view of the relatively mature gnostic ideas, but earlier estimates have also been offered.

The *Sophia of Jesus Christ* must be distinguished from the document known as *Pistis Sophia*. The sole Coptic fourth-century manuscript of *Pistis Sophia* (British Library Add. 5114, sometimes known as the Askew Codex after its first owner) was discovered in 1773. It presents a scene of Jesus teaching some of his disciples at the end of a twelve-year period following the resurrection. But despite its familiar narrative frame, the substance of the work is mostly concerned with a lengthy (346 pages) and elaborate disquisition about gnostic mythology, and it does not present itself as a gospel. A gnostic divine mother figure identified as Pistis Sophia (Faith Wisdom) is said to have been saved from imprisonment by a demon known as Self-Will. The Greek original of *Pistis Sophia* is thought to date from the third century. (See Schmidt and MacDermot 1978.)

The Dialogue of the Savior

The *Dialogue of the Savior* (not to be confused with the *Gospel of the Savior*, i.e., the *Unknown Berlin Gospel*: see p. 152 above) is also partially extant in Nag Hammadi Codex III. It represents another substantial gnostic dialogue—indeed it emphatically identifies itself in the first and last lines of the manuscript by the title *Dialogue of the Savior*. A major difference from other gnostic dialogues is, however, the absence of a narrative frame identifying (usually) a resurrection appearance. In this case the setting could be either pre- or post-Easter, although the former seems more likely in view of hints at the passion. Indeed despite the presence of such themes as the bridal chamber (138) and the androgynously restored destiny of the elect children of light (124–27, 144–45), the properly gnostic character of this text seems nevertheless partly tempered by the Father's creation of the world through the Logos, without requiring the involvement of an evil and inferior demiurge (129–30). (See, e.g., Scopello 2007a, 299; contrast Petersen and Bethge 2012, 1141.)

194

The risen Jesus (referred to as Savior and Lord, but not by name) appears to the male and female disciples and answers their generic questions with discourses or (esp. 133–34) wisdom sayings. Topics include the kingdom of light and saving knowledge; the migration of the soul through the celestial spheres; a myth of creation; the basic elements of darkness, light, fire, water, and wind. At one point (134–37) there is the unexpected insertion of an apocalyptic vision of the Son of Man and of heaven and hell granted to Matthew, Mary Magdalene, and Judas (Thomas, not Iscariot), who are consistently singled out among the disciples. The text concludes with the Lord's admonition (fragmentarily preserved) to guard against anger, envy, and error.

Scholarly discussion has sometimes supposed that the sudden transitions and changes of style in this text may result from its character as a pastiche of different texts, among which writers like Koester and Pagels (1984) have sought to identify a very early core analogous to the composition of dialogues and discourses in the Gospel of John. This is not, however, widely followed. Instead, a number of allusions to Synoptic Gospel texts have been noted, along with links to the so-called *Gospel according to the Egyptians* referenced in Clement of Alexandria, *Stromateis* 3.63.1 (see further Petersen and Bethge 2012, 1139–40).

The Apocryphon of James

The document known as the *Apocryphon of*, *Secret Book of*, or *Letter of James* is extant in a single copy as the second tractate of Nag Hammadi Codex I (NHC I,2). It is written pseudonymously in the name of James the apostle and calls itself explicitly an *apokryphon*, that is, a hidden or secret text (1.10). Its formal presentation is as a secret *letter* from "James" (apparently the brother of the Lord but also blended with the figure of James the apostle), written "in Hebrew" to an uncertain recipient. The text is defective in its first line, although an individual addressee seems to be intended. One recurring scholarly suggestion, especially among German scholars, has been that this addressee could be Cerinthus, a name that features polemically in the *Epistle of the Apostles*, a more proto-orthodox resurrection dialogue of which the *Apocryphon* may be aware (see Hartenstein 2000, 215–16 and n6, 224–29; cf. Hartenstein and Plisch 2012, 1094–95). The Coptic manuscript is assumed to represent the translation of a lost Greek original.

195

Even its self-understanding, therefore, is not as a gospel. Interestingly, however, the substance of this "letter" does follow the pattern of other dialogue gospels, including in particular the narrative framing of the risen Jesus' conversation with his eleven disciples to supplement his instruction with esoteric teaching. Unlike some other gnostic texts, the *Apocryphon of James* represents a setting that especially connects with the Easter narratives and also relates in a number of other ways to sayings paralleled in the canonical gospels, although without any obvious literary dependence. A similar post-resurrection dialogue cast in the form of a letter can be seen in the *Epistle of the Apostles* (see below, p. 215), a more deliberately mainstream and proto-orthodox document. Despite such generic as well as thematic connections, a direct dependence of one of these texts on the other seems unlikely, notwithstanding occasional claims to the contrary (so, e.g., Müller 2012, 1065; cf. Hartenstein and Plisch 2012, 1095).

As with many documents of this kind, the lack of linguistic and literary indicators means that neither the date nor the place of composition can be determined with any degree of confidence. It is further complicated by the scholarly debate about whether the content is properly identified as Valentinian and gnostic. Given its relatively uncomplicated relation to Jesus traditions compatible with the canonical gospels, including a realistic (i.e., nondocetic) interpretation of the Savior's passion, some would posit a date as early as the first half of the second century. Others consider a Valentinian (and therefore later) orientation more strongly indicated by the company the document keeps within Nag Hammadi's Codex I.

The opening polemic against memories of Jesus' teachings written by disciples other than Peter and James (2.7–3.38) suggests that several such literary gospels with apostolic attributions are known and established. (It is also worth comparing Justin Martyr's frequent reference to the gospels as "memoirs" of the apostles: esp. *Dialogue* 100.4; 101.3; 102.5; 103.6, 8; 104.1; 105.1, 5, 6; 106.1, 3, 4; 107.1; cf. *First Apology* 33.5; 66.3; 67.3.) A late-second- or early-third-century composition, perhaps in Egypt, seems plausible (cf., e.g., Scopello 2007c, 21; Hartenstein and Plisch 2012, 1097).

The narrative setting presupposes an encounter between Jesus and his disciples eighteen months (550 days) after the resurrection. While this time frame seems incompatible with the forty days envisaged in Acts 1:3, it was known to Irenaeus as a standard belief of the Valentinians and Sethians (*Against Heresies* 1.3.2; 30.14)—possibly

196

encouraged by Paul's claim in 1 Corinthians 15 that his encounter with the risen Lord was the last of the resurrection appearances.

Having taken aside James and Peter from the other disciples in order to "fill" them with true knowledge, soberness, and light, Jesus encourages them to see their suffering as emulating his own. They should remember the Savior's cross and death in order to live, since God's kingdom belongs only to those who believe in his cross. Prophecy ceased with John the Baptist (cf. Matt. 11:13), and now those who wish to follow Jesus should instead concentrate on his parables and teachings. Salvation is clearly for the few: believers are like foreigners in the world, and not many will find the kingdom of heaven. They must seek its harvest of life and not let it become a desert within. In response to this teaching, Peter declares himself confused and uncomprehending, but Jesus somewhat mysteriously offers faith and life before bidding farewell as he is about to ascend, in a quasi-apocalyptic "chariot of the Spirit" and with a trumpet blast, to his heavenly place of origin at the right hand of the Father and in the midst of the angelic worship. James and Peter share in this vision but are not allowed to see or hear any additional detail. James finally dispatches the disciples in different directions, apparently for the avoidance of conflict rather than the furtherance of the gospel. He himself goes up to Jerusalem, declaring that the Savior revealed nothing more.

The text develops a number of polemical themes that may be aimed against the emerging proto-orthodox church, although the language still remains relatively restrained. Clearly James is favored over Peter and the two of them over the other disciples, who are excluded from the Savior's direct revelation and whose writings are never quoted here. The majority are depicted as angry about later "children" of faith, whom they reject—and who perhaps embody the self-understanding of the author's group. But there is as yet no explicit animus against ecclesial or protocanonical authority, and little development of full-fledged gnostic cosmologies. Given its intellectual and literary context, however, it seems fair to conclude that the document originates in a Valentinian setting well on the way to separation from a catholic and apostolic understanding of Christianity toward a deliberately sectarian, restricted access to saving knowledge.

197

The *Apocryphon* is sometimes alleged to cite an earlier written work by James that may fit Nag Hammadi's *First Apocalypse of James* (so, e.g., Hartenstein 2000, 229–32, with reference to 1.28–32; 8.31–36; 13.38–14.1), but this is not widely supported. That said, the *First Apocalypse of James*, attested both at Nag Hammadi (NHC V,3) and as the second document in Codex Tchacos (best known for containing the *Gospel of Judas*), does feature similar but in some respects more clearly gnostic themes in a post-resurrection dialogue between Jesus and a rather fainthearted and fearful James, to whom the Savior again reveals things intended to be kept secret from the remainder of the Twelve (but to be passed on to Addai [= Thaddeus], apostle to the church in Syria). This document, which also references the martyrdom of James, is one of several examples of texts that appear to cross the blurred boundary between post-Easter gospel-like texts and pseudepigraphal apostolic acts. The same Nag Hammadi codex also contains a document titled *The Revelation of James* (NHC V,4). For ease of reference this is known as the *Second Apocalypse of James*, in which James faces death and reports on the risen Jesus' gnostic teaching about the conflict between the supreme deity (the true Father) and the evil demiurge.

Book of Thomas [the Contender]

Yet another post-resurrection dialogue turned up at the end of Nag Hammadi Codex II under the title *The Book of Thomas* (NHC II,7). In this case the conversation is between Jesus and the person here identified as his twin brother Jude or Judas, also called Thomas, that is, "Twin." (The scribe on this occasion is Matthias, whom other early Christian writers also identify as a disciple with whom secret gospel traditions were sometimes associated: e.g., Hippolytus, *Refutation* 7.20.1; Clement of Alexandria, *Stromateis* 3.4.26; cf. *Pistis Sophia* 1.42.) A later document in the same tradition, representing part of the reception history of the *Gospel of Thomas*, is the third-century *Acts of Thomas*, with stories about that apostle's mission to India.

Thomas is identified in the manuscript's concluding scribal colophon as the "Contender" or "Struggler" (*athlētēs*), writing to those who are perfect. (This stands in potential contrast to the pre-script's identification of Matthias as the "recorder.") Jesus singles out Thomas for privileged secret revelation, as already in the *Gospel of Thomas* where Jesus takes him aside to reveal to him three

198

secret teachings that cannot even be revealed to the other disciples (*Thomas* 13). Jesus at first engages his "brother" and trusted companion in a dialogue about nature and the greatness of perfection that is reserved for the few, which finds its completion in liberation from the body. Those who delight in the flesh, by contrast, are deprived of the kingdom and will suffer physical punishment in the fiery abyss.

Before long, however, Jesus moves from dialogue to a lengthy monologue about these themes of the coming judgment and woes on the godless (beginning at 142.26). The document closes with blessings on those who are oppressed by the wicked and resist temptation (145.1–18): their watchfulness and prayer will grant them rest and the reward of reigning with the King forever.

The *Book of Thomas the Contender*'s combination of a Thomasine attribution with starkly ascetical themes opposed to sexuality and the body has been thought to point to a late-second-century origin in eastern (Mesopotamian) Syria, east of Edessa—though once again this is difficult to assert with confidence.

The Gospel of Mary

Somewhat surprisingly, perhaps, the *Gospel of Mary* is a discourse gospel *not* found among the Nag Hammadi volumes (despite its inclusion in an influential collection titled *The Nag Hammadi Scriptures*: King 2007). It is, however, in the light of those later Egyptian discoveries that the *Gospel of Mary* came to prominent scholarly attention in the second half of the twentieth century. While it is partially preserved in the original Greek on two third-century papyrus roll fragments from Oxyrhynchus (P.Ryl. 463 and P.Oxy. 3525), a fuller but still fragmentary Coptic translation also exists in the important fifth-century Berlin Gnostic Codex (BG 1 = BG [or sometimes BP, for Berlin manuscript P] 8502). This latter papyrus manuscript is in some respects more comparable to Nag Hammadi in that it represents a collection of primarily gnostic writings translated from Greek to Coptic: here, the *Gospel of Mary* is the first text followed by the *Apocryphon of John*, the *Wisdom of Jesus Christ*, and a document called the Coptic *Act of Peter* (see p. 192 above). The Oxyrhynchus fragment, written in an informal and quasi-documentary (rather than literary) hand, seems more

199

likely to be intended as a private copy rather than as a literary text for public reading.

Despite its attestation in three manuscripts, which may already presuppose the existence of previous copies in Greek as well as in Coptic, no *Gospel according to Mary* is otherwise known from antiquity. (However, Epiphanius does know of an apparently unrelated text known as the *Greater Questions of Mary*, included in Ehrman and Pleše 2011, 322, based on the brief citation at *Refutation of All Heresies* 26.8. Our text must also be distinguished from the recently published "Gospel of the Lots of Mary," a fifth- or sixth-century Coptic fortune-telling ["sortilege"] book of oracles associated not with Mary Magdalene but with Mary the mother of Jesus: see Luijendijk 2014.) The *Gospel of Mary* is not mentioned by any of the church fathers, even those like Clement of Alexandria, Origen, and Epiphanius who show extensive awareness of alternative early Christian literature; nor does it surface in otherwise near-comprehensive catalogs like the Gelasian Decree, quoted earlier. In other words, without the manuscript discoveries around the turn of the twentieth century we would have no idea that this text had ever even existed. (The same is true, to be sure, for some theologically more mainstream second-century documents like the *Epistle to Diognetus*, although that document is rather differently poised in its authority claims vis-à-vis the protocanonical documents.)

Scholars widely agree on the *Gospel of Mary*'s second-century date. Some, like King (2003a, 170–85) have proposed its composition during the earlier part of that century, on the grounds that this fits better with the supposed state of flux around the teaching authority of women and around a relative independence from gnostic ideas.

Tuckett 2007 remains the definitive edition and commentary (see there 4n4 for other editions; cf. additionally Lüdemann 2006; Dietzfelbinger 1989). For text and translation see further Ehrman and Pleše 2011, 2014; Blumell and Wayment 2015, nos. 61–62.

Content

200 Following perhaps as many as six missing pages, the extant text begins with a dialogue between the (risen?) Christ and the apostles including Mary Magdalene (not "his female and male disciples," *pace* Hartenstein 2012b, 1209), who exercises a leading role in

this document as the Savior's most loved disciple (cf. the *Gospel of Philip*). Jesus discusses the evils of matter and the origin of sin in Platonic terms as the mixing of matter with spirit, and goes on to offer a number of teachings vaguely reminiscent of the canonical accounts before warning about the introduction of requirements beyond those given by Jesus himself. This could imply a resistance either to the development of church governance or to Jewish Christian affirmation of the law of Moses. Jesus then leaves the disciples for an unspecified destination. They are left to mourn his departure and to wonder how to preach the gospel to the Gentiles.

Mary Magdalene now speaks for the first time and rises to comfort the disciples. Peter acknowledges that Jesus loved her more than other women and asks her to disclose to the disciples the secret teachings she alone has heard from the Savior. Mary then first relates her vision of Christ. The first part of the report is missing from the Greek and Coptic manuscripts, but the vision goes on to include the ascent of the gnostic soul through the seven dangerous spheres occupied by the heavenly rulers, including Desire, Ignorance, and eventually the seven powers of Wrath.

This report of the vision is then followed by a debate in which the disciples, including Andrew and Peter, explicitly question the validity of what Mary has said, both because it appears to innovate on apostolic teaching and because she is a woman. This is usually seen as emblematic of a resistance to second-century ecclesial authorities that claimed the mantle of the apostles. Mary reacts to the challenge with offended pique. Another disciple, Levi, speaks up for Mary and accuses Peter of inadequate control of his temper; he attempts to make peace and to commend the task of preaching the gospel, which finally he proceeds to undertake (in the Coptic version, joined with all the apostles—cf. Tuckett 2007, 193–94, on this textual difference).

Interpretation

Most scholars accept this is a document linking post-resurrection discourses with an additional debate about Mary's quasi-gnostic vision about the ascent of the soul in the face of demonic opposition. The text repeatedly presupposes the canonical gospels, both in terms of general themes and also in specific phraseology reflecting the language especially of Luke, Matthew, and John. In addition

201

to more general shared traditions, Tuckett (2007, 57–67) demonstrates several cases of specific dependence on the redacted final form of Luke and Matthew. Yet no explicit quotations of Old or New Testament texts are deployed, and there is some indication of the influence of early textual variants (cf. further Foster 2013c, 304–7). Dependence on the protocanonical gospels, then, seems likely to be indirect—for example, through an oral harmony and perhaps by way of other protognostic traditions like those found in the *Gospel of Thomas* or later in the *Gospel of Philip*.

Since the extant Greek manuscript fragments date from the early third century, a second-century origin seems virtually certain; nothing more specific can be known, although the middle decades or the third quarter of that century appear plausible to most interpreters.

Unsurprisingly, there has been much debate about the intended message and interpretation of this text. Faced with the reality of Mary's dream report as an evident vehicle of the Lord's teaching, there is a note of apparent misogyny associated with Peter's reaction—as already in *Thomas* 114. The writer clearly comes down in favor of the value and authenticity of Mary's testimony. But contrary to some twenty-first-century interpretative rhetoric, there is no consistently feminist or gender-based agenda. The text does not develop a clear and simple polarity between the male apostles and the female Mary; instead, a defense of her and a mediating resolution is offered by Levi, who may or may not be one of the Twelve (a group not mentioned here), and to whom the narrative thus assigns a "privileged" position almost over and above Mary (see Tuckett 2007, 23–24, 195).

For the same reason, and despite interpreters' claims to the contrary, it is also not clear that Peter's resistance to Mary—let alone to women in general—is here symbolically identified with the catholic, apostolic church. It seems at least equally plausible that the bone of contention actually resides *within* the gnostic movement itself, so that the critique of "Peter's" opposition to the role of Mary here is first and foremost a reaction against the sort of radical asceticism or monasticism that sought to exclude women from true spiritual knowledge unless and until they abandoned marriage and childbirth and were transformed into men. This is a pattern previously encountered in *Thomas* 11, 22, and 114—but which also, and perhaps not coincidentally, surfaces in the so-called *gnōsis* that so concerns the author of 1 Timothy (e.g., 2:15; 5:14; 6:20).

This text does point to Mary Magdalene as a mediator of revelation from the Lord, and specifically as a woman (17.18–22). Peter's rejection of this possibility is clearly criticized by Levi. At the same time, Andrew's earlier critique of doctrinal innovation in her vision (17.10–15) is not addressed: should the heritage of the apostles be accepted as defining the understanding of the true gospel of Christ, or can new visionary experiences add to the substance of revelation? (In a somewhat different fashion, the same problem may have been raised as early as 2 Cor. 12 by Paul's opponents, as it was in the second century by Montanism.) Like the *Gospel of Philip*, the *Gospel of Mary* affirms Mary Magdalene as Jesus' favorite disciple. Levi in a sense emerges as the paradigmatic male disciple, and is moreover singled out in P.Ryl. 463 (22.15) as one who in the end takes up the challenge to go out and preach the gospel.

It is characteristic of the discourse gospels that Jesus here introduces additional authoritative beliefs or practices which were in danger of being excluded by the emergence of a catholic rule of faith and of ecclesial structures. Whether the *Gospel of Mary* is specifically and systematically oriented in this way is, however, difficult to ascertain. There seem to be certain internal tensions between the polemic against "new rules" in 9 (cf. 18–19) and the new vision presented by Mary in 10–17, and similarly, between the generous image of Peter in 10 who recognizes Mary's privileged place and asks her to teach what only she has learned from the Savior, and the seemingly reactionary figure in 17 who dismisses what she has said because it was supposedly disclosed separately and to a woman. Nevertheless Tuckett (2007, 25–30) seems right to side with those who accept the unity of a document that recombines and develops strands of resistance to a variety of ecclesial trends felt to be unwelcome—be they "progressivist" or antimystical, authoritarian or for that matter misogynistic. Importantly, at no point does the *Gospel of Mary* assert that Jesus' teachings are secret or for an elite few: they are intended for *all* the apostles, who are to preach them to *the world*.

In the end we may safely conclude that the *Gospel of Mary* tells us nothing about the closeted sexual life of Jesus or about a primitive radical feminist message suppressed by the later catholic church. Mary's gender is certainly one significant theme for this writer (as it was for other second-century groups, like the Montanists), but it is not in the end more important than the content and newness of her vision or its implications for the apostolic mission (cf. similarly Tuckett 2007, 200–201, citing Perkins 1980). Nor for that matter should this text be taken as evidence of a specifically "Marian community," as has been suggested by some who feel that just as John's Gospel is (or used to be) read as documenting a specifically Johannine Christianity, so also "in exactly the same way, [the *Gospel of Mary*] is a rediscovered testimony to an early Christian community which appealed to the authority of Mary Magdalene" (Klauck 2003, 168, quoting Hartenstein and Petersen 1998, 766; cf. Hartenstein and Petersen 2012). Instead, cosmological and mythological speculation is attributed to Mary more as a way to secure the legitimacy of a direct mystical access to new post-Easter revelation, even for figures who stand outside a restricted chain of apostolic succession—a significant second-century bone of contention for gnostics, Montanists, and others. At the same time, the polemic and hostility between the orthodox and gnostic positions, here represented perhaps by Andrew and Peter on the one hand and Mary and Levi on the other, still seems relatively measured and managed overall (Tuckett 2007, 201–2, notes the moderating effect of Peter's early positive image on the later critique of his anger, which in turn may function to excuse more than to condemn his skepticism).

Unlike for *Thomas* or *Philip*, the eponymous Mary of this gospel is not presented as the text's implied author but rather as its key protagonist and the guarantor of the new revelation, initiated to the closest proximity with the risen Lord (see Tuckett 2007, 205–6). As is the case for most of the other noncanonical gospels we have studied, what is presented here clearly makes no bid to *substitute* for the narrative of the fourfold gospel. Instead, the *Gospel of Mary* deploys *additional* teaching of the Lord in support of a distinctive agenda for that narrative's *reception*—in this case, to legitimate independent visionary access to Jesus.

The Gospel of Judas (Codex Tchacos)

204

The most recently published major document to be discussed here is the so-called *Gospel of Judas*. This text made headlines in 2006 when the original discovery of Codex Tchacos in Egypt around 1978 finally came to light as a result of an extraordinary cloak-and-dagger series of sales and purchases—involving the codex's damaging storage in poor atmospheric conditions (including a safe deposit box and briefly even a freezer!) for the better part of two decades. What was left of the codex was restored in the first decade of this century by its Swiss owners with the help of America's National Geographic Society. Sensational headlines ensued with the publication of an English translation of the *Gospel of Judas* in 2006 and a subsequent first critical edition of the codex a year later (Kasser, Meyer, and Wurst 2006; Kasser and Wurst 2007). The *New York Times* hailed a discovery that it found sure to be "deeply troubling for many believers" (Wilford and Goodstein 2006).

As was more recently the case for the fake "Gospel of Jesus' Wife" fragment (see p. 187 above), the necessarily painstaking and lengthy process of critical sifting, assessment, and reassessment was repeatedly short-circuited by the *Gospel of Judas*'s release into the giddy world of instant Internet punditry that leaves no fleeting thought unblogged. At the same time, within a decade of its first publication this text has also generated a tidal wave of scholarly books, conferences, and conflicting interpretations (leading points of reference include DeConick 2007b, 2009; Ehrman 2007; Gathercole 2007; Jenott 2011; Kasser and Wurst 2007; Pagels and King 2007; Popkes and Wurst 2012; Scopello 2008). The fog of sensationalist publicity was initially slow to clear. One early reviewer wryly noted that, with fully 85–90 percent of the text accessible, the gaps in the manuscript appeared less problematic than those in the scholarly theories about "this alluring but protean gift of the Nile" (M. Edwards 2008). Several initially popularized interpretations now appear questionable in the light of further study, as a result of which there also appears to be a certain tapering of interest.

The fourth-century Codex Tchacos contains several noncanonical texts, the first two of which also appear at Nag Hammadi: the *Letter of Peter to Philip* and the *First Apocalypse of James*. This is followed by the *Gospel of Judas* (identified by that title in a concluding scribal colophon), and an unnamed work concerned in part with a figure called Allogenes (but apparently not related to Nag Hammadi's *Book of Allogenes*: see Scopello 2013). The pagination of a subsequently published fragment, possibly linked to the Hermetic corpus of writings, suggests that no fewer than forty-two

205

pages of the codex are missing (although the *Gospel of Judas* itself is largely complete, thanks in part to the subsequent publication of additional fragments: Schenke Robinson 2011; Wurst, Krosney, and Meyer 2010). The content of the codex may be described as Sethian gnostic (i.e., properly gnostic in a distinctively mythological sense: cf. Brakke 2010a and see below), and the *Gospel of Judas* was evidently included by a compiler who also understood it in those terms. That said, it is potentially interesting that Codex Tchachos was discovered together with fragments of several other volumes containing Exodus in Greek, several of Paul's Letters in Sahidic Coptic, and substantial portions of a treatise on geometry (now divided and held by the Schøyen Collection and various other collections around the world).

Content

The substance of this text consists of a series of dialogues between Jesus and the disciples. These are styled in some sense as "appearances," yet they are narratively set not after Easter but in the context of Jesus' final week *before* the passion. Intriguingly but perhaps appropriately in view of its perspective, the *Gospel of Judas* comes to a climax not with the crucifixion or resurrection but with the betrayal by Judas.

The prologue presents the text as the record of Jesus' secret tutorial with Judas Iscariot over a period of eight days leading up to the Passover. It then offers a summary of Jesus' earthly ministry, including miracles and the election of twelve disciples: somewhat unusually for a gnostic document, this summary approximates the synoptic narrative outline.

The main part of *Judas* appears to be structured according to dialogues between Jesus and the disciples over the course of three days (33–44). The first of these describes Jesus scoffing at the disciples concerning their prayer of thanksgiving after breaking bread, and provoking them to anger. He finds them misunderstanding God and his own mission; only Judas recognizes Jesus' true celestial origin and is invited to separate from the other disciples to learn privately about the mysteries of the kingdom (cf. *Gospel of Thomas* 13).

206   The second discourse on the following morning deals with the irreducible contrast between mortal humanity and the holy, superior race (36–37). This is followed, although perhaps not

immediately, by a third day of instruction in which Jesus interprets the disciples' vision of the Temple (37–39) in terms of a radical critique of all sacrifice and Temple worship, and of all those who engage in it (39–41). People led astray by the disciples will go on to do all manner of immoral and evil acts in the name of Jesus. When the disciples ask Jesus to help and save them, he holds them in disdain and abandons them (42), taking only Judas with him in order to instruct him privately on the contrast between the bodily and the immortal race.

After these three days, Jesus hears Judas's report of his vision of the hostility of the disciples. Jesus warns him that as the thirteenth "demon" he will become the accursed eschatological ruler of the earthly race but will be refused ascent to the heavenly race (44–45). A further lengthy dialogue with Judas is introduced as an instruction about mysteries inaccessible to human beings. The focus here is on the Sethian cosmic myth of salvation, from the creation of the world and of humanity to final decay and judgment (47–52).

The pace suddenly changes and Judas interjects a question about baptism and sacrifice (55–56). Jesus' response on the subject of baptism is given in two fragmentary lines that cannot be reconstructed. He rejects sacrifice as homage to the evil demiurge (here known as Saklas), by mortals destined for destruction. Judas's own function is to surpass all mortal humans by sacrificing the human that "bears" the spiritual Jesus (56, clearly a docetic expression of Christology).

The concluding section of the text features a surprising resumption of narrative with the scribes and high priests plotting to seize Jesus in his prayer room to avoid publicity. Approaching Judas, they negotiate with him and he betrays Jesus in return for money.

Interpretation

Ancient sources as early as Irenaeus (*Against Heresies* 1.31.1; cf. later Epiphanius, *Refutation of All Heresies* 38.1.2–5; 38.3.1.5) knew of the existence of a so-called *Gospel of Judas* associated with Sethian gnostics, based on an elaborate cosmological salvation myth in which the true God is beyond any contact with the material world. The upshot of this distinctive myth, which is attested in Nag Hammadi (e.g., in the *Apocryphon of John*) but also explicitly referenced within our newly discovered *Gospel of Judas*, is that

207

this supreme God gives rise to his creative thought, a female deity called Barbelo, who by a long series of divine emanations produces the celestial figure called Seth (or Christ). This correlation suggests that the document Irenaeus mentions may well bear a recognizable relation to the one now before us, without necessarily being identical to it (*pace* Ehrman and Pleše 2011, 390; more cautiously Plisch 2010, 389–92; Nagel 2014, 269–70). Irenaeus's brief reference to that Sethian document permits no confidence that he had read it at first hand.

A second-century date of origin is widely thought to be plausible in view of the citation in Irenaeus, although the material has no known second-century antecedents and its developed form of Sethian gnostic ideas suggests a date after the middle of the century (Nagel [2014, 268–69] suspects 150–170, perhaps in Asia Minor). Similarly, however, most would agree that the document is in some sense familiar with both protocanonical and extracanonical Jesus tradition. But inasmuch as *Judas* distances itself substantially from that heritage, it also seems clear that these traditions are here independent components recycled for quite explicitly contrarian purposes: the *Gospel of Judas* holds on any account a conception of Jesus that is radically incompatible with proto-orthodox and New Testament Christian views. This text emphatically severs true Christianity from an apostolic church and creed.

The precise interpretation of the text remains a matter of considerable debate, reflected, for example, in the fact that one recent volume of introductions to the noncanonical gospels contained two rival chapters by different scholars on this text: one of them interpreted the text as gnostic and Judas as its hero fulfilling Jesus' will while opposed to the mainstream church; the other read him as a tragic figure caught up in a plot of the forces of cosmic evil gathered against Jesus (DeConick 2008a; Gathercole 2008b; cf. DeConick 2007b; Gathercole 2007). Similarly, even Ehrman and Pleše (2011, 390) appear to acknowledge disagreement between themselves on the proper understanding of *Judas*.

This tension continues to be debated. The original translators and other early scholars writing on the text presented Judas as a hero, a spiritual figure who has a special place among the gnostic initiates. On this reading, while Jesus laughs at the other disciples because they do not understand their error (33–34), Judas alone is singled out for praise and taken aside for private teaching, having been granted unique understanding of who Jesus is and that he has "come from the immortal aeon of Barbelo" (35). The climactic statement of this interpretation comes in 56: "You will surpass them all for you will sacrifice the man who clothes [or: bears] me." On this understanding, Judas's betrayal demonstrates his understanding of the true nature of Jesus, enabling him to complete his task by effecting the sacrifice of Jesus' material body.

By contrast, most recent specialist studies tend to accept the criticisms of those who have exposed a number of mistranslations and misinterpretations of the original edition within the context of the Sethian myth (e.g., DeConick 2007b; Pearson 2009, 2008; J. Turner 2008; also Jenott 2011 and several of the contributors to Popkes and Wurst 2012). In particular, it has been pointed out that Judas is really identified as the "thirteenth demon" rather than the "thirteenth spirit" (44), that he is separated from the apostolic generation rather than set apart above it (46), and that Jesus nowhere expresses to Judas a desire that he should shed his blood and "sacrifice" him (56). Far from being the favorite disciple and collaborator, Judas is the instrument not of Jesus but of the powers of evil ranged against Jesus. (This idea of Judas as a demonic agent is also echoed in later Coptic magical texts, including a tenth-century curse amulet on a knife-shaped parchment claiming, "I am that which raised Judas against . . . Jesus until he was crucified": Louvre E.14.250 [www.trismegistos.org/text/99997]; see text in Pernigotti 1995, 3725; English translation in Meyer and Smith 1994, 218–22.)

Judas's "sacrifice" is particularly problematic: the very notion is here opposed as an act of worshiping the demiurge, a false god. On the one hand Judas laughs at the disciples' "thanksgiving" (34, possibly noneucharistic) and tells them to stop sacrificing and venerating the demonic crucifixion of Jesus as if it were somehow an act of salvation (41). And yet to this writer Judas's own sacrifice of Jesus is the most evil of all, and tragically misunderstood by the disciples who suppose this work of a demon to bring about "salvation" through atonement (cf. DeConick 2008a, 108).

All in all, this book seems to be "good news" (gospel), even "of" or for Judas, only in a rather sarcastic sense. It is really, as Foster (2009, 123) puts it, "a bitter satire of apostolic Christianity."

Gospels of the Egyptians

Clement of Alexandria's Gospel according to the Egyptians

Clement of Alexandria, Hippolytus, Origen, Epiphanius, Jerome, and others knew of a so-called *Gospel according to the Egyptians*. This text is so widely attested in early Christian sources that one is initially led to wonder if it may have been a document of considerable import and popularity. In that respect it is bewildering to find that these ancient attestations are in fact so diverse and sometimes contradictory that we seem to be dealing with several documents identified by this name. And many of the writers who attest to its existence appear to have had no firsthand knowledge of it, including those like Clement and Origen who show a well-documented interest in extracanonical works. Knowledge of this text, therefore, appears to be at best secondhand: no *Gospel according to the Egyptians* was readily available to Alexandrian readers of the later second or third centuries.

Only Clement provides any quotations. He does so in the context of resisting the interpretations of opponents like Julius Cassianus and others who appeal to this text in support of their strictly ascetic hostility to sexuality, marriage, and childbirth. Clement insists (probably wrongly) that the ascetics pervert its meaning. The relevant sayings include Jesus telling Salome that death will continue as long as women bear children (*Stromateis* 3.45); this is subsequently linked with a saying that "I have come to destroy the works of the female," which is interpreted to mean the birth and corruption of desire (3.63–64). What is interesting about Clement's interaction with this radical text is that he attempts to defend it against his opponents' seemingly plausible use of it to deny marriage and childbirth, preferring instead to read it in a more spiritually wholesome, allegorizing sense (a point also stressed by Watson [2013, 425–27], who thinks Clement reads this document as scripture).

While the narrow focus and selection of Clement's citations suggests that perhaps he too had no direct access to the text, on at least one occasion he does appeal to a specific passage that he claims has been deliberately omitted by his opponents: in reply to Salome's conclusion that she would have done well to refrain from

210

giving birth, Jesus supposedly goes on to offer the (admittedly some-what cryptic) answer that one should eat every plant except for that which is bitter. But on this point Clement's somewhat spiritualizing and moralizing interpretation seems to do less than justice to the text's quasi-gnostic antipathy to sex and marriage, which it associates with "the entire complex of fall, gender duality, childbirth and death" (Klauck 2003, 57). This combination of themes and sayings does seem reminiscent of the *Gospel of Thomas*, as Watson rightly notes (2013, 235n62; cf. 256–59).

Given this fragmentary and potentially somewhat tendentious attestation in Clement, it seems difficult or impossible to establish the original shape of this gospel as a whole. This impression is confirmed by the existence of several isolated sayings traditions (beginning with *2 Clement* 12.1–2 and *Gospel of Thomas* 22, 37, 61) that reflect closely cognate dialogical exchanges between Jesus and Salome. Some modern editions include these traditions in their sequentially numbered fragments of the *Gospel of the Egyptians*.

Clement's awareness and use at least of excerpts of the text necessitates a date before the 190s, but it is difficult to be more specific. Because every one of Clement's eight quotations from this work expresses the theme of a distinctly ascetical hostility to sexuality and procreation, he himself may only have known this work in the form of a thematic (and possibly already antiheretical?) collection of such excerpts, rather than as now preserved. (Cf. similarly Markschies 2012d, 666, 672.)

Like other proposed connections, especially with the Nag Hammadi *Dialogue of the Savior* (Codex III,5), these texts help to confirm a certain contextual and ideological proximity between the *Gospel of the Egyptians* and the gnostic dialogue gospels, as well as with the *Gospel of Thomas* and its emphasis on the neutralization of the difference between male and female. The fact that the extant quotations highlight Jesus' instruction mainly of his female disciple Salome might seem to point to familiar (Sethian) gnostic themes (as, for example, in the *Gospel of Mary*, discussed above), but it is impossible to be certain about the specific origin or indeed to derive much useful insight from third- and fourth-century citations, for example, in Hippolytus or Epiphanius. Even the closest of these links remain speculative and are of little help in establishing the substance or integrity of the document known, however indirectly, to Clement and other early Christian writers. In particular, there would appear to be no good reason to identify or closely relate this text with better-known early Christian apocrypha (so rightly Markschies [2012d, 678–79], with reference to the *Gospel of Peter*, the Strasbourg Coptic Papyrus, and others).

The "Egyptian Gospel" at Nag Hammadi ("The Holy Book of the Great Invisible Spirit")

Confusingly, another *Gospel of the Egyptians* came to light at Nag Hammadi (NHC III,2/IV,2) in two differing, possibly indirect Coptic translations of an ultimately underlying Greek original. This form of the title is, however, a modern rather than an ancient designation. Its primary ancient title is "The Holy Book of the Great Invisible Spirit." It is true that the concluding colophon also identifies it as "the Egyptian gospel," but this may well be the addition of a translator or copyist. Other early Christian descriptions confirm that this is clearly a different work—a verdict with which all recent scholarship agrees. This text is a treatise of Sethian gnostic salvation mythology, thought by some critics to be a possible baptismal liturgy. It probably dates from the third century rather than the second. Although it is occasionally included in editions of the apocryphal gospels, its content and genre clearly have nothing to do with any "gospel," whether canonical or noncanonical (so rightly Plisch 2012a, 1263).

Gospel of Bartholomew

A cycle of visions and especially discourses about the passion and resurrection was transmitted in the name of the apostle Bartholomew. Significantly, a *Gospel according to Bartholomew* does not survive from antiquity, which is why it is often omitted from editions of the apocryphal gospels (e.g., Ehrman and Pleše 2011, 2014). Nevertheless, a text of that designation was indeed deemed sufficiently problematic to be condemned by the sixth-century Gelasian Decree, and may previously have been known to Jerome and possibly Pseudo-Dionysius. And we do have a substantial but highly divergent later manuscript tradition in Greek, Latin, Coptic, and Slavonic for two distinct cycles of Bartholomew narratives, one of them usually identified as "Questions of Bartholomew" and the

212

other as "The Book of the Resurrection of Jesus Christ" (see Markschies 2012e; Schenke 2012b; also Klauck 2003, 99–104; Elliott 1993, 652–72; more fully Kaestli and Cherix 1993). No direct literary relationship exists between the two traditions, but both appear to represent dialogue gospels incorporating visionary or apocalyptic aspects into their narrative frame. The fullest translation and account of the history and genealogy of the text is offered by Markschies (2012e, with the help of his seven research assistants, 702n1; see discussion, 703–8, and synopsis, 710–850).

As identified by his patronymic, the apostle Bartholomew (*Bartholomaios*, probably "son of Tolmai/Ptolemy": see, e.g., M. H. Williams 2013, 301) is not prominent in the canonical gospels. But in some early Christian circles he came to be identified with Nathanael in the Gospel of John, since Bartholomew is absent there and yet both names are closely affiliated with the disciple Philip. From the late second century Bartholomew was also associated with a mission to India, where he made known the Gospel of Matthew; but his eventual martyrdom was commonly located in Armenia.

The Bartholomew cycle capitalizes on the fact that in the New Testament Nathanael is praised as an "Israelite in whom there is no deceit" and promised visions of "greater things" like the angels descending and ascending on the Son of Man. He is also included in the small circle of named resurrection witnesses on the shore of the Sea of Galilee (John 1:47, 50–51; 21:2), while Bartholomew is a witness to the ascension (Acts 1:13). It is in a sense this promise to Nathanael that the Bartholomew material brings to fulfillment.

"Questions of Bartholomew"

While the subject matter of the Bartholomew cycle includes both passion and resurrection traditions, the general narrative setting clearly appears as a post-resurrection dialogue involving the risen Jesus and the disciples. Bartholomew begins in the first chapter with a question about his angelic visions during the passion, anticipated perhaps by the prophecy of John 1:51 about angels descending and ascending upon the Son of Man. He saw angels descending to worship the crucified Lord and heard loud lamenting voices from Hades. He further saw the angels escorting a superhuman Adam to Calvary when the dead came out of their tombs, until eventually the largest of all angels with a fiery sword tore in two the curtain in the Temple. Jesus himself accounts for these visions in terms of his descent to the dead for the traditional "harrowing of hell" and the vanquishing of its ruler before his departure for the sacrifice of the righteous in paradise.

Next, the apostles are joined in chapter 2 by Mary, the mother of Jesus. It is again Bartholomew who acts as the apostles' spokesman, addressing her as the "tabernacle" or the "unblemished Temple" (manuscripts differ; see Markschies 2012e, 729) and marveling at how it was possible for her to conceive and bear the Lord. Although hesitant about unveiling the unspeakable or indeed about leading the apostles in prayer, Mary eventually utters a prayer in (gibberish) Hebrew before narrating her experience of the annunciation as associated with a "cloud of dew" coming upon her face when she "lived in the Temple of God" and received (quasi-eucharistic) bread and wine from the hand of an angel (cf. *Infancy Gospel of James* 8.1).

After a brief vision of the underworld, unveiled when the earth is rolled up like a scroll (chap. 3), the disciples ascend with Jesus to the Mount of Olives (chap. 4). Here, in a dramatic encounter, Bartholomew is offered a terrifying vision of Satan (or the antichrist) and given power to step on the monster's neck and compel him to relate the story of his rebellion and evil deeds, revealing the names of his evil angels and their various portfolios of power. Having had to reveal his (usefully apotropaic) secret, Satan is sent back to hell and the text ends in an extended doxology.

"The Book of the Resurrection of Jesus Christ"

"The Book of the Resurrection of Jesus Christ" is mostly a collection of fragmentary narratives, extant in three distinct medieval manuscripts that were only in recent times recompiled out of a mass of individual leaves of parchment distributed among libraries in Paris, Vienna, London, and Cairo (Kaestli and Cherix 1993; cf. Schenke 2012b, 852–55).

In addition to an episode apparently surrounding the Last Supper, there are a number of nonsequential narrative vignettes relating to the tomb of Jesus, his descent to Hades, and various resurrection appearances on the Mount of Olives and in Galilee, as well as an expanded version of the appearance to Thomas. Jesus ascends to heaven, and after a common Eucharist the disciples

214

disperse to commence their global mission. In the course of these narratives, Bartholomew is granted a vision of the seventh heaven and its hymnic worship as Jesus returns from earth. The texts also feature a notably high Mariology.

Interestingly, this "Book of the Resurrection of Jesus Christ" seems to follow narrative features of the fourfold gospel more closely than other works we have discussed in this chapter. Klauck (2003, 104) also points out that it has in a sense moved on from the genre of gospel to that of apostolic acts, including the telltale perspectival shift to appropriating the experience of key disciples, often in support of particular practical or doctrinal emphases.

A similar observation about mixed or shifting genre could be made in relation to Nag Hammadi's influential *Apocryphon of John*, which survives in no fewer than four manuscripts (it is placed first in Codices II, III, and IV, and also appears in the Berlin Gnostic Codex BG 1/BG 8502.2): an evidently visionary post-resurrection encounter with Jesus introduces a new gnostic revelation after a narrative frame featuring John's experience of Pharisaic questioning in the Temple. Jesus addresses John with extensive discourses on Sethian ideas about the origin of the world and soteriology.

Like many other texts we have encountered, however, the Bartholomew gospel cycle itself is in no obvious sense subversive, sectarian, or anticatholic vis-à-vis the canonical gospels, which it engages intertextually. Instead, these texts reflect a piety that seems more at home in the diverse theological seedbed of the majority church. In its central affirmation of the sin-canceling power of the cross and of sacraments, the role of Mary, and the bodily expectation of the resurrection, the Bartholomew gospel material embodies strong and remarkably widespread themes of mainstream Christian faith (see Markschies 2013, 344–52).

The Epistle of the Apostles

Finally in this section, we must consider a post-resurrection text remarkably unlike others we have examined. The so-called *Epistle of the Apostles* (still sometimes identified in Latin as *Epistula Apostolorum*) is an intriguing document, probably from Egypt, that represents an orthodox rejoinder against the Valentinian appeal to alternative secret revelations supposedly given by the risen Jesus.

215

The text is fully preserved only in Ethiopic, attested in a series of fourteen early modern manuscripts (fifteenth to nineteenth centuries) that did not come to scholarly attention until the twentieth century. Nothing survives in what is generally agreed to be the original Greek, but partial translations from late antiquity survive in Coptic (and in a single page from a Latin palimpsest in Vienna). The document may also have had some influence on various other "apostolic church orders" (e.g., the list of apostles in the so-called Apostolic Church Ordinance, on which see Stewart-Sykes 2006).

It is widely assumed that the text reached Ethiopia only via an Arabic translation. Alternatively, an early Ethiopic translation from the Greek or Coptic is at least conceivable: *1 Enoch*, *Jubilees*, the *Ascension of Isaiah*, the *Apocalypse of Ezra*, and the *Paralipomena of Jeremiah* all appear to have been translated from Greek into Ethiopic (possibly via Coptic), perhaps during the heyday of the Christian Aksumite kingdom in the fourth through sixth centuries.

The *Epistle*'s relatively wide circulation is suggested by the existence of several translations, including not only Coptic and Ethiopic but even Latin, based presumably on a Greek original. Its relative popularity in the Ethiopian church is reflected in the influence on its liturgical and theological developments, including angel Christology, Christ's disguised descent from heaven, and even the creedal allegory of the five loaves of bread (see Abraha and Assefa 2010, 613, 616). English translations include Cameron 1982, 131–62; Hills 2009; Schneemelcher 1991–92, 1:252–84.

Content

In substance, the *Epistle of the Apostles* is a major work stretching over fifty-one chapters. It is formally "revealed" by Christ as a *letter* from the apostolic Twelve to all "catholic" churches of the world to encourage them in the true "word of the gospel that you have heard" (1). (Only eleven apostles are listed in a somewhat unexpected constellation of that group, including Nathanael alongside Bartholomew, and Judas the Zealot in place of Simon the Zealot and Judas son of James (cf. Acts 1:13), omitting James the son of Alphaeus, but listing Cephas in addition to Simon Peter.) The point seems to be that in contrast to gnostic texts reserving the true

216

revelation of the risen Christ for one favored apostle and the elite few, here the risen Lord speaks through all the apostles to all the churches they founded.

This apostolic witness to the "Lord and Savior Jesus Christ" and "Son of God" is explicitly intended to confound the false apostles Simon Magus and Cerinthus, the arch-heretics in second-century Christian imagination, who are here identified as "enemies of our Lord Jesus Christ" (1, 7). The epistolary setting is soon abandoned in favor of a précis of several chapters (3–12) covering the birth, ministry, death, and resurrection of Jesus, leading up to the main body of post-resurrection teaching (13–50). In light of this, it has sometimes been suggested that the Ethiopic term for "letter" should instead be rendered "book" (e.g., Klauck 2003, 153, citing Isaak Wajnberg's translation in Schmidt and Wajnberg 1919).

The Lord's incarnation by the Virgin Mary is followed by a single infancy episode about Jesus learning the alphabet (also attested in the *Infancy Gospel of Thomas*: see above p. 73). There then ensues in chapters 4–5 a remarkable catalog weaving together a dozen or more clearly Johannine and synoptic miracles, from the wedding at Cana to the hemorrhaging woman healed by touching Jesus, to exorcisms and the stilling of the storm, to the feeding of the five thousand—with five loaves interpreted creedally as symbolizing the Great Church's faith in God the Father, Jesus Christ the Savior, the Holy Spirit the Paraclete, the holy church, and the forgiveness of sins. (See on this passage Hills 2008, 37–66.)

Jesus is crucified under Pontius Pilate (and, confusingly, Archelaus, who in fact ruled Judea 4 BCE–7 CE), buried at Calvary, and his empty grave discovered by the otherwise unknown Sarah along with Martha and Mary Magdalene. When the apostles refuse to believe the women's witness to the resurrection, the Lord himself takes Mary and her sisters to the apostles in hiding. Thomas, Peter, and Andrew are all encouraged to observe the marks of the nails and the wound in his side as well as his feet actually touching and leaving a print on the ground.

Beginning with chapter 13, the narrative genre gives way to Jesus' post-resurrection instructions, punctuated periodically by didactic questions and answers. The revelation discourses that follow begin with Jesus rehearsing his incarnation as a descent from heaven disguised as an angel (cf. *Ascension of Isaiah* 10:8–11) who already appears personally to Mary at the annunciation as the angel Gabriel (14). The discourse then fast-forwards to the eucharistic remembrance of his death to be celebrated in an Agape meal as the true Passover.

In chapter 21 the writer's attention turns to eschatology. The first topic concerns the resurrection of the body—indeed of the flesh—together with the soul, on which subject Jesus criticizes the disciples' lack of faith, before adding a brief comment on his descent to Hades to preach the gospel to the patriarchs and offer them the baptism of life and forgiveness (27; cf. 1 Pet. 3:19).

After the apostles are commissioned to preach the gospel to the twelve tribes of Israel and the Gentiles in all the world (30), the *Epistle of the Apostles* next turns to the position of Paul, a topic understandably ignored in other apocryphal gospels. Intriguingly, it is none other than the risen Christ himself who provides the apostles with a remarkably detailed introduction (adapted largely from Acts 9) to their future associate Saul/Paul, who will be called after the ascension, having initially persecuted the apostolic foundation in Syria (31–33).

An extended passage on apocalyptic phenomena preceding the final judgment culminates in the contrast between the punishment of the wicked and the blessedness of those who keep Christ's commandments as children of light while nevertheless remaining concerned to intercede on behalf of sinners (34–40). The parable of the Five Wise and Five Foolish Virgins is extensively expounded as concerning the watchful and the indolent within the church (43–45). The five wise virgins are those who are saved and enabled to enter into the bridal chamber of the Lord. (This is an image similarly encountered in the *Gospel of Philip* and elsewhere. Klauck [2003, 158] suggests that this could be the "orthodox" author of the *Epistle of the Apostles* adapting a popular notion of his gnostic opponents for his own purposes, although the notion of the church as the bride of Christ also reflects a widespread allegorical interpretation of the Song of Songs in early Christian literature, beginning perhaps as early as Eph. 5:32.)

Finally, in chapter 51 Jesus bids his disciples farewell and is taken away to heaven by a cloud. This seems to take place "three days and three hours" after the crucifixion—and thus apparently on the very first day of the resurrection, as Luke 24 could also be taken to imply.

Interpretation

The *Epistle of the Apostles* is, like the *Infancy Gospel of James* and one or two other apocryphal documents, a rare example of a second-century gospel-like text that not only positioned itself in deliberate proximity to the protocanonical New Testament gospel narratives but went on to exercise a lasting influence on Christian conceptions of its subject matter. For both of the cases just mentioned, that influence extends in their respective ecclesial traditions to the present day—not in the use of these texts as holy scripture, but not as apocryphal or heretical either. Instead, they seem to function as works "useful for the soul" (to use a Byzantine term that François Bovon [2012] adopts in support of a widely recognized third category beyond the Gelasian Decree's binary categories of scriptural vs. apocryphal—though it is worth noting the only gospel-like text Bovon cites in this category is the much later *Gospel of Nicodemus*).

The text is richly if loosely interwoven with quotations and allusions to the Old and New Testaments. One feature of this dynamic intertextuality consists in intriguing prophetic quotations that are not otherwise attested in extant canonical or pseudepigraphical literature. Examples include supposed prophecies like, "The foot of a ghost or demon leaves no trace on the ground" (12); "Behold, out of the land of Syria I will begin to call a New Jerusalem, and I will subdue Zion and it will be captured; and the barren woman without children will bear many children and will be called the daughter of my Father and my bride for me" (33); and the five wise virgins of Matthew 25 being interpreted by recourse to "the prophet" who called them "daughters of God" (43). Of these, the last perhaps alludes to Psalm 82:6 ("You are . . . children of the Most High, all of you"), while the second could be a rather free development of Isaiah 54:1 following Galatians 4:26–27. The first, however, looks traditional: there is an intriguing conceptual parallel in the detection of humans by their footsteps in Bel and the Dragon 19–20 (Septuagint Additions to Daniel; Vulgate Daniel 14:18–19: *vestigia*), while the poet Commodian (fl. ca. 250) has the risen Jesus similarly insisting that "a shadow leaves no trace" (*Carmen Apologeticum* = *Apologetic Poem* 564: *vestigium*). There is clearly an apologetic, antidocetic counterpoint here against claims in accounts like the apocryphal *Acts of John* 93 that the risen Jesus sometimes did *not* leave a footprint (cf. further Luke 24:39).

219

A date around 140–150 CE seems plausible to many scholars. The place of composition has been variously sought in Egypt, Syria, and Asia Minor (the latter, with reference to its eschatology and paschal themes, relating to concerns in Polycarp and perhaps Polycrates; Hill [1999] argues specifically for Smyrna). Müller (2012, 1064–65) proposes a Jewish Christian teacher from the region of Alexandria for this work, while a Lower Egyptian origin seems to him most compatible with its characteristically free handling of scripture, involvement of the Father and Son in the final judgment, antidocetism, and emphasis on the resurrection of the flesh. This coincides with the document's desire to provide christological authorization for the apparently less familiar apostle Paul.

Given the number of (admittedly recent) Ethiopic manuscripts combined with the virtual absence of a continuing textual tradition elsewhere, it is clear that the *Epistle of the Apostles* was and remains of particular importance for the Ethiopian church, even if perhaps nowhere else. There is surprisingly little critical scholarship on this text, despite its remarkably early attestation of the fourfold gospel in a doctrinal framework deployed against gnostic alternatives (as noted in an important study by Hannah [2008], but ignored by Watson [2013]). In this connection it belongs with a small number of other mid-second-century texts like Tatian's *Diatessaron* and perhaps the secondary longer ending of Mark (16:9–20), of which the *Epistle of the Apostles* is sometimes thought to be aware.

Conclusion: Post-Resurrection Discourse Gospels

Just as the New Testament's infancy narratives left plenty of room for imaginative engagement with the "silent" years of Jesus' life in Nazareth when he "increased in wisdom and in years, and in divine and human favor" (Luke 2:51–52), so the canonical resurrection accounts remain strikingly general on his precise teaching and whereabouts in the period from Easter Sunday to his ascension, let alone his appearance to Paul on the road to Damascus. Luke suggests that Jesus repeatedly met with the disciples, appearing with "many convincing proofs" throughout the forty days to teach them about the kingdom of God (Acts 1:3)—that is, perhaps rather more than is explicitly narrated. John also appears to include the post-Easter period in his assurance that Jesus did "many other things" too numerous to recount in books (John 21:25).

It is therefore easy to see how the second-century Christian imagination might seize on Jesus' private post-resurrection teaching of the disciples as one of the open-ended topics within the received and by then largely standardized narrative outline of the gospel. The popularity of this trope especially in gnostic circles suggests the appeal of a narrative setting that invites the sublimation of historical narrative under the heading of direct access to revealed knowledge from the heavenly Lord. Irenaeus's sense that the Valentinians felt themselves superior in knowledge to the apostles (*Against Heresies,* 3.2–4) may or may not be fair to that movement's originators, but it does seem to comport with a theme we have repeatedly encountered in this chapter.

In some ways the dialogue situated outside earthly space and time supplied a setting that both appropriates and yet also—at least in some cases—transcends the more restrained pre-Easter versus post-Easter narratives of the protocanonical gospels. As we saw, this may already be the case for the *Gospel of Thomas*: there, existential and timeless knowledge of the secret sayings of Jesus has superseded the sequential and narrative constraints of an interest in the life and fate of Jesus of Nazareth, let alone his connection with the sick and the oppressed awaiting the kingdom of God in Jewish Palestine. Unlike the New Testament Gospel of John, which in its own way also favors an eternal Son descended to earth and ascended to heaven, *Thomas* and texts like *Philip* and *Judas* make no bid for a public ecclesial canon but present themselves as "secret" and at least in that sense quite deliberately apocryphal. A text like the *Gospel of Mary* in that respect stands out as advocating a message that is at least in principle intended for public proclamation.

Many of the discourse gospels have traveled quite a long way from narratives of a risen Jesus reunited a few days after his crucifixion with his eleven disciples in Jerusalem or Galilee. Instead, we encounter sketchily contextualized engagements with a timeless Savior who teaches a saving knowledge of the escape from earthly entrapments and the cosmological reunion of alienated opposites. Capitalizing on the gospel scenario of private post-Easter instruction with only a minimal narrative frame, several of the works in this chapter address concerns that were particularly favorable to gnostic

221

beliefs about the cosmos and about salvation. While Luke and John among the New Testament gospels may seem conducive to this influential scenario, it is particularly the *Gospel of Thomas* that lent itself to this mode of reading. This is exemplified most clearly by the nature of its reception at Nag Hammadi, where it is sandwiched between the *Apocryphon of John* and the *Gospel of Philip*.

In keeping with this focus, *Philip* and other later gnostic gospels appear less and less interested in teachings, let alone narratives, of the pre-Easter Jesus—to the point where a genre identification of gospels or gospel-like texts necessarily shades over into what Markschies and Schröter (2012) prefer to call "gospel meditations," in some cases bearing a greater resemblance to apostolic acts. That said, one does encounter occasional affirmations of the positive saving significance of the cross, both in gnostic sources (e.g., in the *Apocryphon of James* or the *Gospel of Truth*) and in others like the Bartholomew cycle.

One question that has accompanied us throughout this book is the apparently epiphenomenal nature of the apocryphal gospels in relation to the four that became canonical. A narrowly literary, *textual* dependence on or independence from the New Testament gospels was widely contested by scholars in the twentieth century, but can almost never be proved or disproved. In previous chapters we saw time and again that a more *mediated* consciousness of the protocanonical gospel narratives, whether orally or through a gospel harmony, often seems to account for the relationship between the gospels that became canonical and a great many of those that did not. This requires us to imagine a different sort of intertextuality, as Schröter (2013b, 264) also notes: although highly free and flexible in their handling of the tradition, "the writings that were emerging in the second century presuppose the already existing Jesus narratives, but do not feel bound to them in linguistic form or in the interpretation of the content."

For the post-resurrection and other discourse gospels, however, that relationship with the protocanonical Four is decidedly more tenuous—perhaps increasingly so the more the textual genre in question moves in the direction of a gnostic "gospel meditation" and minimizes verbal links or narrative themes. Nevertheless that epiphenomenal character of relationship is never entirely abandoned in the texts we have studied. References to such matters as the risen Jesus meeting with groups of named disciples in

222

Jerusalem or on a mountain still assume a rudimentary familiarity with elements of the gospel story, relationships, teaching, or identity of Jesus. These links are undeniably stronger for some texts than for others. And in cases like the *Apocryphon of James*, the *Gospel of Judas*, or the *Gospel of Mary* (and possibly already in the *Gospel of Thomas*), the relationship with at least some of the ecclesial gospels is in certain respects strained and polemical, if not explicitly contrarian.

The *Epistle of the Apostles*, however, concluded our discussion of post-resurrection gospels with a rather differently conceived exploration of this theme, in which the trope of the risen Jesus' extensive instruction of the disciples is developed in support of a vision that is emphatically ecclesial rather than individual, public and apostolic rather than secret and elitist, and founded on the authorized apostolic witness explicitly understood to reside in the four New Testament gospels (and by implication in Paul, whose ministry is anticipated). The footprint of this document in the history especially of the Ethiopian church is unlike that of any other discourse gospel. In the sheer scale of its ecclesial influence and intertextual connection to both Testaments, the only specific early apocryphal gospel to match it may be the *Infancy Gospel of James*. The *Epistle of the Apostles* is in that sense not merely proto-orthodox in orientation but it is already para-canonical in the sense of responding to the singular and unquestioned authority of the fourfold gospel in particular.

Suggested Further Reading

DeConick, April D. 2008a. "The *Gospel of Judas*: A Parody of Apostolic Christianity." In *The Non-Canonical Gospels*, edited by P. Foster, 96–109. London: T&T Clark.

Foster, Paul. 2008b. "The *Gospel of Philip*." In *The Non-Canonical Gospels*, edited by P. Foster, 68–83. London: T&T Clark.

Gathercole, Simon J. 2014a. *The Gospel of Thomas: Introduction and Commentary*. Texts and Editions for New Testament Study 11. Boston: Brill.

Goodacre, Mark. 2012. *Thomas and the Gospels: The Case for Thomas's Familiarity with the Synoptics*. Grand Rapids: Eerdmans.

Hannah, Darrell D. 2008. "The Four-Gospel 'Canon' in the *Epistula Apostolorum*." *Journal of Theological Studies* 59:598–633.

Pagels, Elaine H. 2003. *Beyond Belief: The Secret Gospel of Thomas*. New York: Random House.

Schröter, Jens. 2012. "B.IV.1. Das Evangelium nach Thomas." In *Antike christliche Apokryphen in deutscher Übersetzung*, 1.1–2, *Evangelien und Verwandtes*, edited by C. Markschies and J. Schröter, 483–526. Tübingen: Mohr-Siebeck.

Tuckett, Christopher. 2007. *The Gospel of Mary*. Oxford Early Christian Gospel Texts. Oxford: Oxford University Press.

Turner, Martha Lee. 1996. *The Gospel according to Philip: The Sources and Coherence of an Early Christian Collection*. Nag Hammadi and Manichaean Studies 38. Leiden: Brill.

Watson, Francis. 2013. *Gospel Writing: A Canonical Perspective*. Grand Rapids: Eerdmans.

CHAPTER 6

How to Read Apocryphal Gospels

The ancient apocryphal gospels open an invaluable window on early Christianity's remarkably diverse engagement with the story and teaching of Jesus of Nazareth during the turbulent second century. The canon of the present New Testament was only formally finalized in official decrees of the fourth and subsequent centuries. But both before and after that time, the Christian engagement with Jesus was neither wholly independent of, nor wholly circumscribed by, the fourfold witness of Matthew, Mark, Luke, and John.

At the same time, the eighty-odd known gospel-like texts from antiquity are so diverse in literary, geographic, and ideological terms that, as Tobias Nicklas (2014a, 222) puts it, "Any overall statement about apocryphal writings must be at least partly wrong." These apocryphal texts document the sheer social and cultural complexity of the early Christian diaspora across the Roman Empire, many of whose churches for a long time did not share the same forms of worship or ecclesial life—let alone enjoy access to the same complete canon or collection of authoritative books.

Needless to say, this diversity makes a concluding summary of results problematic! Any definitive conclusion will be in some measure only partially correct. It makes sense, therefore, to limit ourselves to a brief synthesis of a few recurrent themes that we encountered in the discussion of the previous chapters.

225

I offer the following five theses less as firm conclusions than as points of reference for further reflection and discussion. Several of them came as a significant surprise to me and were not what I expected when I set out on this project. No single one of them adequately characterizes these sources, and exceptions can (or could) be found for almost all. Yet to pick up on previously introduced imagery (p. 9 above), perhaps this analysis resembles both a cartoon and a pointillist painting: for all its distorting, confusing, or incompatible close-up detail, our conclusions can provide a meaningful and viable overall account when taken together and viewed as a big picture.

1. The canonical gospels appear to be unique and distinctive.

The narrative outline of the gospels that became canonical appears to have been formative and at least indirectly defining for virtually all early Christian reflection about the person and teaching of Jesus. As narrative accounts of the public ministry of Jesus from his baptism by John to his crucifixion and resurrection, Matthew, Mark, Luke, and John are without peer among extant early Christian writings, in both their form and their reception. In other words: Mark wins. It may have generated very few manuscript copies in the earliest Christian centuries, but the influence of this gospel's narrative outline, associated with Peter in the New Testament (Acts 10:37–41) and in persistent patristic tradition, meant that Mark's biographical frame became the reference point for all successful gospel writing.

And yet, strikingly, no extant ancient apocryphal gospels replicate this biographical narrative from baptism to cross and resurrection. Possible exceptions are either late non-Christian antigospels (like the *Toledot Yeshu* or the *Gospel of Barnabas*), overtly derivative from one or more New Testament gospels (like Marcion's gospel or Tatian's *Diatessaron*)—or else partial and conjectural at best (like the hypothetical larger narratives of which some have supposed the fragmentary *Gospel of Peter* or Papyrus Egerton 2 to form a part, but none of which survive).

To be sure, even at the end of this book it would be unwise to rush to extrapolations from such an observation. The lack of any clear alternative narrative gospels could in theory be due merely to historical accident: after all, not just the *Gospel of Peter* and P.Eger. 2 but *any* of the ministry or passion gospel fragments discussed above might in principle have been part of such a larger narrative (as is often claimed or assumed), just as this is theoretically possible for the dozen or more "gospels" known to us exclusively from patristic reports. Among the latter are *Gospels of the Four Heavenly Realms, of Perfection, of the Twelve, of the Seventy, of Judas, of Cerinthus, of Basilides, of Marcion, of Apelles, of Bardesanes* (Bardaisan)*; The Memoir of the Apostles* and the *Gospel of the Twelve, of the Manicheans,* and *of the Quqites*; and others. How much can we know about what they contained?

Nevertheless, on balance the sheer number and diversity of what does survive among ancient noncanonical gospel-like texts makes the absence of any rival narrative frames significant. It thus remains the case that *no extant or attested ancient apocryphal gospels are known to offer a consecutive narrative of the life of Jesus from his baptism by John to his death and resurrection.*

At the same time, it seems that all the surviving texts nevertheless implicitly *presuppose* at least a vague outline of some such narrative. Without it, references to named disciples or miscellaneous Jewish opponents, let alone to the minimally identified "Jesus" who is their subject, would remain virtually meaningless or inconsequential. Ancient apocryphal gospels either supplement or otherwise presuppose the biographical narrative outline associated with the Gospel of Mark and its protocanonical successors.

We can only speculate on the reasons for this. Given how many ancient authors produced writings they called gospels, why is it that so few—if indeed any!—of them chose to imitate or revise the overall outline and genre of that story of Jesus which their texts about his infancy, ministry, passion, or post-resurrection discourses at least at some level plainly presuppose? Answers vary quite widely, and might reflect either acceptance or indeed rejection of the fourfold narrative that became canonical. We have found in this book that a text called gospel is not necessarily a *bios*, despite occasional scholarly assertions to that effect. Instead, however, even noncanonical gospels at least tacitly presuppose the biographical narrative associated with the Gospel of Mark and its canonical companions.

In other words, the written accounts of Jesus that found the earliest and most enduring appeal are quite clearly the four gospels contained in the Christian Bible. It was their early identification as gospels in the name of an apostle that established this genre of presentation as authoritative—and which moreover seems to have exerted a powerful magnetism on subsequent choices of

227

title, attribution, and subject matter (see Hengel 2008b, 110–11, 182–83; also Bird 2014, 289–90).

For several centuries, many or even most early Christians would not have heard all four New Testament gospels read as discrete books in their churches. More commonly they encountered these books through the public reading of Matthew, John, or a gospel synthesis like the *Diatessaron*), as well as through more informal vehicles of secondary orality.

While it is clear that numerous other texts were popularly read despite periodic expressions of ecclesial disapproval, in fact *no other gospel-like text was ever remotely a contender for formal inclusion alongside these four*. And conversely, even though Mark was at first rarely copied and a few late-second-century Roman Christians apparently had short-lived misgivings about John, *no serious or widespread doubt was ever cast on any of the canonical Four*. In other words, the gospels that became canonical are those that enjoyed widespread ecclesial use and acceptance in worship and interpretation—and even in secondary gospel writing!

2. Noncanonical gospels did not "become apocryphal" and were not "suppressed" from the canon.

It is theoretically conceivable that some noncanonical gospels were at first serious alternatives to supersede or replace the canonical Four before being relegated to the margins. But the attested evidence overwhelmingly suggests that this was not the case.

Among the canonical gospels, Matthew and Luke retained and in a sense improved on the Markan outline. Like them, John too may be written for readers of Mark (so, e.g., Bauckham 1998). But while Matthew and John eclipsed Mark's circulation for centuries, this was never a threat to the latter's perceived authority or eventual canonicity, which ancient sources do not question. The reason for Mark's secure position among the Four has a lot to do with the early and apparently uncontested attribution of these texts to the living memory of specific named apostolic figures (Matthew, John) or authorized students of such figures (Mark, Luke). While arguments from silence are necessarily precarious, neither friend nor foe in antiquity appears to have questioned these attributions for the New Testament Four—rather unlike for gospels in the names of Thomas, Peter, and Judas.

228

Of course we have encountered a multitude of noncanonical gospels claiming an apostolic association, whether wholly fictitious or deriving from prior tradition or hearsay. But all or virtually all of these texts date from a later period than the canonical Four, which most of them presuppose at least in outline.

Importantly, *none of these epiphenomenal texts ever generated commentaries*, whereas for Matthew, John, and probably Luke we have commentaries or scholia beginning in the first half of the second century. Even Valentinian or gnostic Christians, it seems, composed commentaries only on the protocanonical gospels, rather than on their own or other secondary compositions. A Valentinian commentator like Heracleon wrote on the protocanonical gospel of John and probably on Luke (see Löhr 2003), while Ptolemy's *Letter to Flora* about scriptural interpretation discusses only canonical sources like Matthew, John, and the Pentateuch as Scripture. Earlier in the second century, the Alexandrian philosophical theologian Basilides (sometimes incongruously considered a gnostic) seems to have produced scholia on a gospel text closely resembling Luke (Löhr 1996, 34).

Some gospels, including *Thomas* and several others read at Nag Hammadi, deliberately *set out* to be apocryphal and plainly never contended for the status of public canonical gospels. But their limited acceptance and minimal circulation meant not that they "became apocryphal" but more accurately that they "did not became canonical"—and never had any purpose or prospect of doing so. In that sense it is historically misleading to speak of noncanonical gospels as texts that "did not make it" (e.g., Ehrman 2003). Indeed, aside from Marcion's singular (and largely unsuccessful) efforts in relation to Luke, *no alternative process of gospel canon formation was ever in evidence*. Noncanonical gospels, whether they subsequently came to be seen as heretical or (like the *Diatessaron*) as orthodox, rely on the outline of the protocanonical Four in a way that is not true in reverse. With only a tiny handful of late exceptions that did not circulate widely, these texts are therefore in no meaningful sense "countercanonical" (a term usefully discussed in relation to their "afterlives" by Reed [2015, esp. 407–17]).

A few other texts, including the infancy gospels of *James* and (to a lesser extent) *Thomas*, the "Jewish Christian" gospels, the *Epistle of the Apostles*, and the later Pilate, Nicodemus, and Bartholomew traditions, *did* attain considerably greater and sometimes lasting public influence. Indeed a small number of mainly Marian texts were both prevalent and read liturgically for certain festivals (as were some martyrs' acts and even bishops' letters: cf. Markschies 2015, 216 and n110 with reference to Eusebius, *Ecclesiastical History* 4.23.11). But all of these were clearly designed as partial and occasional *supplements rather than substitutes* for the fourfold gospel.

Somewhat exceptionally, the unitary gospel of Marcion and the synthesis or harmony of Tatian did retain the full (originally Markan) narrative gospel form. And these texts may have been designed to displace their protocanonical predecessors, although in quite different ways. Even such functional replacement, of course, implicitly presumes existing gospel testimony and accepts its authority—selectively so in Marcion's case (Luke), but in Tatian's more comprehensively. Whether intended or not, both projects did for a time and in certain places eclipse the four discrete New Testament gospels for public liturgical reading in the churches that followed them. Marcion's soon proved a marginal and increasingly sectarian initiative. But the Syrian church's widespread adoption of Tatian's synthesis never entailed any definitive rejection of the original Four. In the fifth century, this in turn facilitated the acceptance of the wider church's usage and thus the *Diatessaron*'s replacement with the fourfold gospel.

In the early centuries there is surprisingly little evidence of any official clampdown or authoritarian censorship that might have caused other gospels to "become" apocryphal. From the second century onward there were approved books, sometimes identified in lists like the much-debated Muratorian Canon. One also recalls the apparently not very successful efforts of Bishop Serapion of Antioch in rejecting the *Gospel of Peter,* or Irenaeus's more sustained critique of miscellaneous writings of the Valentinians. (We may wonder why, since to the best of our knowledge the Valentinian gospels were never widely read or copied, Irenaeus is quite so exercised about these texts; but it could have something to do with the fact that he was Valentinus's contemporary in Rome and became deeply troubled by observing at first hand the corrosive effect of that teaching on believers like his fellow priest and childhood friend Florinus: cf. Eusebius, *Ecclesiastical History* 5.15, 20.)

By the fourth century, Eusebius's critical survey of Christian writings famously attempted a more precise distinction between agreed (*homologoumena*), debated (*antilegomena*), and spurious (*notha*) works under consideration in relation to what was now called the New Testament (*Ecclesiastical History* 3.25.1–7). His inventory includes in the first category, prominently and without contest, the "holy tetrad" of the gospels. Of the apocryphal gospels, Eusebius includes only the Jewish Christian *Gospel according to the Hebrews* among the disputed or spurious works that are nevertheless cited by some orthodox writers, along with the *Acts of Paul, Shepherd of Hermas, Apocalypse of Peter, Letter of Barnabas*—and the book of Revelation. All other apocryphal gospels clearly fall outside that threefold inventory, even if some (like *Peter, Thomas,* and *Matthias*) are mentioned in passing. This is on the grounds that they are created by heretics, remote from the apostolic style and content, and above all "not one of them has ever been considered worth citing in the writings of anyone in the succession of the church." For Eusebius the upshot of his survey is that, far from *becoming* apocryphal, these other gospels never managed to attract significant support for their apostolicity. Such an argument might of course seem rhetorically convenient for someone of his persuasion. Nevertheless, it is important to note that his claimed inventory of the range of mainstream opinion does accommodate considerable diversity, rather than representing any sort of narrowly authoritarian clampdown on primitive Christian witness to Jesus.

We saw that the best-known ancient example of a formal anathema against the apocryphal gospels is the Gelasian Decree, once associated with Popes Damasus I (366–384) and Gelasius I (492–496) but apparently an anonymous document from the sixth century. In addition to lists of Old and New Testament books and approved patristic writings, this text includes an extensive list of more than 120 named apocryphal writings and a large number of other authors deemed to be rejected. This notably late effort at censorship admittedly suggests an attempt to exclude and at least sideline noncanonical gospels—while at the same time, ironically, attesting both the abiding popularity of some of these documents and the powerlessness of haphazard official opposition to achieve anything like the suppression that Dan Brown and other popular or scholarly conspiracy theorists like to imagine. The *Gospel of Peter* evidently continued to be read in some circles for several centuries after Serapion tried to discourage it. The *Infancy Gospel of James*, having been ostensibly banned by the Gelasian Decree in the West, went instead from strength to strength as it was reintroduced to Latin readers through an even more popular document known as

Pseudo-Matthew. Where the apocryphal gospels disappeared, in other words, this had much more to do with their use, circulation, and popularity than with authoritarian churchmen who allegedly "resolved to hack down the forest of 'apocryphal and illegitimate' writings" (Pagels 2003, 111; cf. the critique in Bird 2014, 290–98, 312; Hill 2010b, 57–62). Advocates of such scenarios forget that polemic does not equal power, least of all in the Middle East.

The noncanonical gospels, in other words, did not *become* apocryphal but *remained* so.

3. The apocryphal gospels are epiphenomenal to the gospel tradition that became canonical.

Most of the texts discussed here relate in some fashion to the central narrative of one or more of the canonical Four. Many attempt to fill in a perceived gap, whether this is chronological (as in the case of the infancy gospels building on implicit openings in Luke 1–2), thematic (as in the Jewish Christian gospels' sporadic glossing of Jesus' ministry and teaching with traditions relevant to their particular communities' concerns), or more comprehensive (as in the more expansive approach taken by some of the resurrection or discourse gospels). Even Mark's Gospel, with its abrupt beginning and uncertain conclusion, might already seem to invite a certain scope for prequels and sequels to its authoritative narrative from John's baptism to Easter Sunday.

Many of the sources in question may not have been conceived as fresh gospel compositions at all, but rather as creative expositions—perhaps homiletically intended "rewritten gospel" material (so possibly even the *Gospel of Peter*). The same could account for many of the isolated traditions and agrapha that appear in various papyri and early Christian citations. A derivative or epiphenomenal relationship to the narrative tradition that became canonical seems discernible in singular episodes as well as in more extensive or theologically substantive rereadings of the tradition.

In that sense, virtually all of the surviving noncanonical gospels can be understood as part of the protocanonical tradition's history of effects and interpretation. Whether in direct textual or only quite indirect awareness of it, whether sympathetic or contrarian in their own approach, they are part of the organic reception of that apostolic tradition. (In some ways, of course, this is not fundamentally different from the relationship between the canonical Four themselves—or between them and the earlier oral teaching, as is argued in relation to Acts 10:34–43 by Guelich [1991, 198–99], following Stuhlmacher 1968 and Stanton 1974. Comparable (even if not directly analogous) Jewish processes of traditioning have also been repeatedly highlighted by Hindy Najman (e.g., 2003, 2010, 2012).

This difficult question of the relationship between the apocryphal and the canonical gospels was in the past often reduced to the issue of *literary* dependence, viewed from one particular angle. As a result, if a text contained synoptic or Johannine wording it was clearly secondary, directly dependent on the canonical gospels— and therefore often (it was thought) of no interest for the understanding of Christian origins. On the other hand, where such a text showed no verbatim *literary* dependence, some scholars readily leapt to the conclusion that it ("probably") constitutes independent and early testimony to the original Jesus tradition, predating and superior to the gospels in the New Testament.

In this book we have discovered a more complex picture of intertextual relations that proved far more intricate. Contact often seems mediated by an encounter not so much with the written text of the discrete four gospels but equally, or perhaps more commonly, with a secondary oral, hybrid, or harmonized form of tradition. Such texts remained epiphenomenal (and sometimes para-canonical) in relation to the gospel tradition that became canonized, but that relationship was both more informal and more intricate than has often been assumed in the past.

This sort of secondary gospel writing need not signify disapproval and intentional subversion of what goes before. Rather, it inevitably discloses a desire to reappropriate and to reread—perhaps to read better, or at least freshly or differently. Within the fourfold gospel itself, the effect of this kind of "metatext" is at least as much to endow the evangelical predecessor with an implied authority as it is to improve and perhaps to replace. The same is also true for many or most of the apocryphal rewritten gospel narratives and agrapha whose production and transmission continued during the second century, even at a time when apocalypses and other traditional literary forms seem to have declined.

4. Only a minority of the apocryphal gospels seem to intend explicit subversion or displacement of the fourfold gospel.

To say that the apocryphal gospels are in significant respects *epiphenomenal* upon the shape of the tradition that became canonical does not yet answer the question of whether they seek to support

233

or to subvert it. We have certainly come across texts that are decidedly uninterested in the Four, whether as a narrative account of Jesus' ministry or as public, authoritative liturgical documents.

Some texts set out deliberately to present an alternative and indeed a *rival* account to the church's public proclamation. Gospels that understand themselves as "secret" or addressing only an elite of true gnostics include *Thomas, Philip*, and *Judas*, as well as Nag Hammadi's *Book of Thomas, Apocryphon of John*, and *Apocryphon of James.* Far from contending for canonicity, these writings understand themselves as an explicitly secret and apocryphal alternative to an ecclesial gospel that they deem inadequate or in some cases false and damaging. Partly for that reason, they appear to have enjoyed only very limited circulation. An implicit critique of the apostolic ecclesial tradition is also present in some other texts like the *Gospel of Mary*, which is not intrinsically secret but affirms a continuing dialogue with the apostolic tradition and its global mission.

The *Gospel of Judas* in particular seems patently antagonistic to the tradition that became canonical, even while ironically articulating its subversion in ways that depend rhetorically on the existence of something very like the canonical outline, which is here supplemented so as to demand a radical reinterpretation. This document's degree of explicit distance from the emerging canonical gospel tradition is greater than for most other texts we have seen, and perhaps illustrates the tendency on the part of some gnostic groups to develop not merely as a schismatically deviant Christian "sect" but a radically alternative, repristinating or innovating "cult" (terminology usefully deployed by Logan [2006, 58–59]).

5. The apocryphal gospels illustrate the diversity of early Christianity's cultural and religious engagement with the memory of Jesus.

The apocryphal gospels, written in virtually every case to supplement the tradition of the canonical Four, shed interestingly diverse light on how these New Testament texts were understood. They may foreground subjects and areas that readers instructed only in the ecclesial interpretation might well miss. Sometimes they attempt to supply narrative or theological details that are explicitly or implicitly missing from the traditional accounts (patently so in the case of the infancy narratives). Or they may more broadly retell the gospel story in such a way as to make it freshly applicable to a new audience—whether relating to the gnostic intellectual engagement with Hellenism, fourth-century disputes about baptism, or the personified message of the cross.

For the second-century compositions in particular, criteria of creedal orthodoxy are almost invariably an anachronistic and blunt measuring instrument to apply to a period in Christianity's early life that has been aptly termed its theological "laboratory" (see p. 9 above). To think of these gospels as the false cuckoo threatening the survival of the native canonical chicks is to mistake them as both more subversive and more of a threat to emerging creedal Christianity than they ever were. Some of these texts may later have been deemed orthodox, others heretical; but most are less straightforwardly identifiable. In fact we have seen that a wide range of Christian apocrypha across chapters 2–4 above express a remarkably mainstream Christian piety (so also Markschies 2013, with particular reference to the *Gospel of Bartholomew*).

Most of these texts were never widely read, while those that were remain largely sympathetic rather than antagonistic to the mainstream gospel tradition—as informal expressions of a devout but unsophisticated faith. (C. H. Turner [1920, 12] was perhaps not totally wide of the mark when he called the Christian pseudepigrapha "the Sunday afternoon literature of the ancient Church.")

The sense of puzzlement or alienation experienced by modern Christians reading some of the more exotic ideas in these texts may be put to constructive use in engaging the early popular reception history of the New Testament gospels. The strangeness of these texts is perhaps in the first instance a mark not of their heretical otherness, but rather of the breadth and diversity of Christians who encountered and appropriated the gospel narrative in the cultural maelstrom of antiquity, to which that story spoke of salvation in many different registers. The ancient apocryphal gospels do indeed reflect the "many faces of Jesus" in early Christian experience (so Jenkins 2015, on their role in late antiquity and the Middle Ages). And we have seen that some writers appreciated the extent to which believers might encounter Christ in the appearance of an old man and others as a boy or a youth; indeed to Irenaeus this was the mark of Christ's incarnate recapitulation of all human experience (*Against Heresies* 2.22.4; cf. 3.21.9; cf. p. 142 above).

And yet it seems that in order to thrive and prosper in more than just a single manuscript or geographic location, such pluriformity evidently needed to be balanced by an element of consensus,

235

some point of reference in the narrative outline of the Markan or Petrine type that is represented in all four New Testament gospels. The image of Jesus had "many faces" and a surprising degree of diversity that to later Christian eyes sometimes displays an unfamiliar strangeness. Yet even in popular, mainstream Christianity that diversity was always to an extent bounded by the precedent of gospel narrative, and rarely if ever wholly cast adrift from traditional outlines. The evidence of texts and manuscripts suggests that, perhaps unlike some of their contemporary heirs and successors, only the tiniest minority of the ancient authors or readers of apocryphal gospels favored gratuitously "weird" portraits of Jesus or truly believed that "the 'more strange' Jesus becomes . . . , the closer we get to the 'innermost nature' of Jesus" (Robbins 2013, 10).

Many of the ancient apocryphal gospels predate the period of the great orthodox councils, creeds, and canonical definitions. And it is therefore unsurprising that their accounts of Christ exemplify ways that were later taken alongside other ways that came to be rejected. Like the New Testament itself, they are engaged, sometimes controversially, in the process of claiming Jesus for Christology and for what it means to be "Christian." They do so with a host of diverse emphases—whether on the story of Jesus or on his sayings, on his incarnation or on his timeless teaching after the resurrection. In studying them we discover something of why the New Testament is as it is, and what we can learn from the ancient history of its reception about early Christianity's gradual and often challenged articulation of faith in Jesus Christ as fully man and fully God.

To read the apocryphal gospels in this way alongside the New Testament is at the same time to open one's eyes to the uniqueness and remarkably fine-grained particularity of the four canonical accounts of Jesus. The New Testament gospels give us an insistence on his incarnation and on the historical embeddedness of his birth, life, and death. They present a Word of God whose true significance lies not only in his divinity but equally in his humanity; not only in his resurrection and subsequent heavenly life but also in his death on a cross; not just in disembodied words but crucially in their setting among deeds of redemptive power and of compassion. And they insist on the salient significance of his life, of a consecutive public ministry narrated from the baptism by John to his public crucifixion followed by his resurrection on the third

236

day. This outline, which uniquely characterizes all four New Testament gospels, clearly carries enormous theological implications for a serviceable account of Christian faith—then or now. "The church has four gospels; the heretics have many," said Origen (*Homilies on Luke* 1.2; cf. Ambrose, *Commentary on Luke* 1.2). And yet, perhaps both the Four and the many that so diversely reflect them express a desire above all to encounter and embrace through their words the compelling person of Jesus Christ.

GLOSSARY OF TECHNICAL TERMS

agrapha. A collective term (singular: agraphon) conventionally used for sayings that are attributed to Jesus but not attested in the New Testament gospels. For further discussion, see p. 45.

amulet. An object like an ornament or piece of jewelry, worn to ward off evil, danger, witchcraft, or disease. In this context, ancient Christian amulets are of interest because they sometimes included short gospel extracts (see p. 33).

book roll or scroll. Ancient books were commonly produced by sewing or gluing individual sheets of suitable writing material (parchment or papyrus: see below) into a long roll, which would generally have writing on one side only. The main alternative book form was the codex (see below).

codex. During the early Christian centuries, the codex was the main alternative book format to the scroll, and eventually displaced it almost entirely. The codex is what readers today are most familiar with as a traditional paper book: folded sheets (usually of parchment or papyrus in antiquity) are stacked and bound together at one edge (the spine). Written text generally appears on both sides of the page.

colophon. In ancient and medieval manuscripts, a colophon is a brief concluding comment or annotation by a scribe to give information about the manuscript and the circumstances of its production.

genizah. An enclosed storeroom found in many historic synagogues, used to hold discarded manuscripts that are no longer in use (see p. 28).

logion. An individual saying (plural: logia) or a unit in a collection of sayings, used typically of the teachings of Jesus.

Mishnah. The normative rabbinic collection of Jewish legal traditions and rulings compiled by Rabbi Yehudah Ha-Nasi in the early third century, and around which subsequent collections of the Babylonian and Jerusalem Talmuds are based.

nomina sacra. Special abbreviations used by ancient scribes for common sacred Christian words and names (singular: *nomen sacrum*). These abbreviations are most frequently used in Greek manuscripts, where they are commonly represented by contractions of the word's first and last letter marked with a horizontal line above. Typical examples include words like God, Lord, Jesus, Christ, Son, Spirit, Mother, Father, and Savior.

ostracon. A fragment of pottery (plural: ostraca) reused as a writing surface.

palimpsest. A manuscript from which the original writing has been (often partially) rubbed or scraped off in order to be overwritten with another text.

papyrus. Writing material made from the papyrus plant, a tall reed or sedge typically found in the valley of the Nile. In Egypt and elsewhere it was manufactured into paper-like sheets for writing and painting. The term is also used for a manuscript (plural: papyri) written on such sheets.

parchment. A durable writing material made of processed animal skin (typically calf, sheep, or goat). The word also denotes a manuscript written on such material. Fine calfskin parchment is called vellum.

Platonism. Here used as a collective term denoting various ancient philosophical ideas or schools in the tradition of Plato (ca. 428–347 BCE). For our purposes the most important is Middle Platonism, which influentially revived and developed the reception of Plato's philosophy from around the middle of the first century BCE to the end of the second century CE. One of its characteristics was to incorporate elements of other contemporary schools of thought, including Pythagorean and Stoic ideas. It was followed by Neoplatonism.

Q. The hypothetical source of the sayings tradition shared by the Gospels of Matthew and Luke. Its existence and importance were widely taken for granted in twentieth-century gospels scholarship, but they have in recent years once again become the subject of lively debate (see further p. 89).

recto. The front of a manuscript page, or in the case of a codex with facing pages, the right-hand page. The other side is the verso. In the case of papyrus rolls, the recto denotes the side on which the plant fibers run horizontally.

240

scholia. Marginal notes or explanatory glosses (singular: scholion) made by ancient teachers or grammarians on classical texts, often for pedagogical purposes. Scholia may represent original notes that could later be compiled into a commentary, or they may already be extracted from existing commentaries.

Septuagint. The most influential Greek translation of the Pentateuch, and later the whole of the Old Testament. It is named after the seventy-two (lit., seventy) Jews who, according to ancient tradition, produced it, in seclusion on the island of Pharos, at the request of the Ptolemy II Philadelphus (ca. 309–246 BCE), the king of Egypt. (The term is often abbreviated as LXX.)

Sethianism. A prominent gnostic group during the second, third, and perhaps fourth Christian centuries, known above all for an elaborate mythology of spiritual creation by a series of emanations from a wholly unknown God, disrupted by the evil Demiurge's creation of matter and of Adam. Themes from the early chapters of Genesis are fused with a strong influence of Platonism. The most important writings thought to belong to this orientation include the Gospel of Judas and the Nag Hammadi texts known as the *Apocryphon of John*, the *Holy Book of the Great Invisible Spirit*, and the *Trimorphic Protennoia.*

synoptic. A term used to denote comparative study of texts; of Greek origin, the word literally means "seeing together." Here it is used especially of the Gospels of Matthew, Mark, and Luke (hence the Synoptic Gospels or Synoptics), and of the literary relationships between them.

Talmud. Normative commentary on the Jewish legal traditions, developed in terms of an explanatory or illustrative complement to the Mishnah (see above). The Talmud exists in a slightly earlier Jerusalem (or Palestinian) Talmud and a fuller and more definitive Babylonian Talmud. These collections are also known by their Hebrew names, respectively, Talmud Yerushalmi and Talmud Bavli.

Tosefta. A corpus of early rabbinic legal traditions, compiled in the mid-third century as a supplement (lit., addition) to the Mishnah.

Valentinianism. A leading second-century gnostic sect founded by Valentinus (ca. 100–180), a Christian teacher who came to Rome from Egypt. Although the spiritual world emanated from

241

the supreme God in a complicated system of heavenly aeons, the material world derives from the Old Testament's Creator god, who is here merely ignorant rather than (as in Sethianism) positively evil. A divine spark is imprisoned in all human beings, which in the "spiritual" or "pneumatic" elite (i.e., Valentinian gnostics) is redeemed and liberated through the saving gnosis realized in Jesus Christ. Some scholars credit Valentinus with the *Gospel of Truth* preserved at Nag Hammadi. Famous Valentinians include Theodotus in the East and Heracleon, Ptolemy, and Marcus in the West.

verso. The "reverse" side of a manuscript page or, in the case of a codex, the left-hand page (opposite of recto).

BIBLIOGRAPHY

Aasgaard, Reidar. 2009. *The Childhood of Jesus: Decoding the Apocryphal Infancy Gospel of Thomas.* Eugene, OR: Cascade Books.

Abraha, Tedros, and Daniel Assefa. 2010. "Apocryphal Gospels in the Ethiopic Tradition." In *Jesus in apokryphen Evangelienüberlieferungen: Beiträge zu außerkanonischen Jesusüberlieferungen aus verschiedenen Sprach- und Kulturtraditionen*, edited by J. Frey and J. Schröter, 611–53. Wissenschaftliche Untersuchungen zum Neuen Testament 254. Tübingen: Mohr Siebeck.

Alexander, Philip S. 2011. "Jesus and His Mother in the Jewish Anti-Gospel (the *Toledot Yeshu*)." In *Infancy Gospels: Stories and Identities*, edited by C. Clivaz et al., 588–616. Wissenschaftliche Untersuchungen zum Neuen Testament 281. Tübingen: Mohr Siebeck.

Anderson, Gary A. 2009. "Towards a Theology of the Tabernacle and Its Furniture." In *Text, Thought, and Practice in Qumran and Early Christianity: Proceedings of the Ninth International Symposium of the Orion Center for the Study of the Dead Sea Scrolls and Associated Literature*, edited by R. A. Clements and D. R. Schwartz, 161–94. Studies in the Texts of the Desert of Judah 84. Leiden: Brill.

Askeland, Christian. 2014. "A Fake Coptic John and Its Implications for the 'Gospel of Jesus's Wife.'" *Tyndale Bulletin* 65:1–10.

Augustin, Philipp. 2015. *Die Juden im Petrusevangelium: Narratologische Analyse und theologiegeschichtliche Kontextualisierung.* Beihefte zur Zeitschrift für die Neutestamentliche Wissenschaft 214. Berlin: de Gruyter.

Barker, Don. 2009. "How Long and Old Is the Codex of Which P.Oxy. 1353 Is a Leaf?" In *Jewish and Christian Scripture as Artifact and Canon*, edited by C. A. Evans and H. D. Zacharias, 192–202. London: T&T Clark.

Barry, Catherine. 1993. *La Sagesse de Jésus-Christ (BG, 3; NH III,4).* Bibliothèque copte de Nag Hammadi Section "Textes" 20. Quebec: Presses de l'Université Laval.

Barton, John. 1998. *Holy Writings, Sacred Text: The Canon in Early Christianity*. Louisville, KY: Westminster John Knox Press.

Bauckham, Richard. 1990. *Jude and the Relatives of Jesus in the Early Church*. Edinburgh: T&T Clark.

———. 1994. "The Brothers and Sisters of Jesus: An Epiphanian Response to John P. Meier." *Catholic Biblical Quarterly* 56:687–700.

———. 1998. "John for Readers of Mark." In *The Gospels for All Christians*, edited by R. J. Bauckham, 147–71. Grand Rapids: Eerdmans.

———. 2014. "Gospels before Normativization: A Critique of Francis Watson's *Gospel Writing*." *Journal for the Study of the New Testament* 37:185–200.

Bauer, Walter. 1967. "Jesus der Galiläer." In *Aufsätze und kleine Schriften*, edited by G. Strecker, 91–108. Tübingen: Mohr (Siebeck).

———. 1971. *Orthodoxy and Heresy in Earliest Christianity*. Translated by R. A. Kraft and G. Krodel. Philadelphia: Fortress.

Becker, Adam H., and Annette Yoshiko Reed, eds. 2003. *The Ways That Never Parted: Jews and Christians in Late Antiquity and the Early Middle Ages*. Tübingen: Mohr Siebeck.

BeDuhn, Jason. 2013. *The First New Testament: Marcion's Scriptural Canon*. Salem, OR: Polebridge Press.

Bernhard, Andrew. 2006. *Other Early Christian Gospels: A Critical Edition of the Surviving Greek Manuscripts*. Library of Biblical Studies. London: T&T Clark.

———. 2015. "The *Gospel of Jesus's Wife*: Textual Evidence of a Modern Forgery." *New Testament Studies* 61:335–55.

Bird, Michael F. 2014. *The Gospel of the Lord: How the Early Church Wrote the Story of Jesus*. Grand Rapids: Eerdmans.

Black, David Alan, ed. 2008. *Perspectives on the Ending of Mark: 4 Views*. Nashville: B&H Academic.

Blumell, Lincoln H. 2012. *Lettered Christians: Christians, Letters, and Late Antique Oxyrhynchus*. New Testament Tools, Studies, and Documents 39. Leiden: Brill.

Blumell, Lincoln H., and Thomas A. Wayment. 2015. *Christian Oxyrhynchus: Texts, Documents, and Sources*. Waco, TX: Baylor University Press.

Bock, Darrell L. 2006. *The Missing Gospels: Unearthing the Truth behind Alternative Christianities*. Nashville: Nelson Books.

Bockmuehl, Markus. 1990. *Revelation and Mystery in Ancient Judaism and Pauline Christianity*. Wissenschaftliche Untersuchungen zum Neuen Testament 2:36. Tübingen: Mohr Siebeck.

———. 2005. "The Making of Gospel Commentaries." In *The Written Gospel*, edited by M. Bockmuehl and D. A. Hagner, 274–95. Cambridge: Cambridge University Press.

———. 2009. "The Dead Sea Scrolls and the Origins of Biblical Commentary." In *Text, Thought, and Practice in Qumran and Early Christianity: Proceedings of the Ninth International Symposium of the Orion Center for the Study of the Dead Sea Scrolls and Associated Literature*, edited by R. A. Clements and D. R. Schwartz, 3–29. Leiden: Brill.

———. 2010. *The Remembered Peter in Ancient Reception and Modern Debate*. Wissenschaftliche Untersuchungen zum Neuen Testament 262. Tübingen: Mohr Siebeck.

———. 2011. "The Son of David and His Mother." *Journal of Theological Studies* 62:476–93.

———. 2012a. "Origins of *Creatio ex Nihilo* in Palestinian Judaism and Early Christianity." *Scottish Journal of Theology* 65:253–70.

———. 2012b. *Simon Peter in Scripture and Memory: The New Testament Apostle in the Early Church*. Grand Rapids: Baker Academic.

———. 2014. Review of *Gospel Writing*, by Francis Watson. *Journal of Theological Studies* 65:195–211.

Bovon, François. 1988. "The Synoptic Gospels and the Noncanonical Acts of the Apostles." *Harvard Theological Review* 81:19–34.

———. 1991. "The Suspension of Time in Chapter 18 of Protevangelium Jacobi." In *The Future of Early Christianity: Essays in Honor of Helmut Koester*, edited by B. A. Pearson, 393–405. Minneapolis: Fortress.

———. 2000. "Fragment Oxyrhynchus 840, Fragment of a Lost Gospel, Witness of an Early Christian Controversy over Purity." *Journal of Biblical Literature* 119:705–28.

———. 2012. "Beyond the Canonical and the Apocryphal Books, the Presence of a Third Category: The Books Useful for the Soul." *Harvard Theological Review* 105(2):125–37.

Boyarin, Daniel. 2004. *Border Lines: The Partition of Judaeo-Christianity*. Divinations. Philadelphia: University of Pennsylvania Press.

———. 2009. "Rethinking Jewish Christianity: An Argument for Dismantling a Dubious Category (to Which Is Appended a Correction of My *Border Lines*)." *Jewish Quarterly Review* 99:7–36.

Brakke, David. 2010a. *The Gnostics: Myth, Ritual, and Diversity in Early Christianity*. Cambridge. MA: Harvard University Press.

———. 2010b. "A New Fragment of Athanasius's Thirty-Ninth Festal Letter: Heresy, Apocrypha, and the Canon." *Harvard Theological Review* 103:47–66.

Broadhead, Edwin K. 1994. "What Are the Gospels? Questioning Martin Kähler." *Pacifica* 7:145–59.

———. 2010. *Jewish Ways of Following Jesus: Redrawing the Religious Map of Antiquity*. Wissenschaftliche Untersuchungen zum Neuen Testament 266. Tübingen: Mohr Siebeck.

Broek, Roelof van den. 2013. *Gnostic Religion in Antiquity*. Cambridge: Cambridge University Press.

Brown, Dan. 2003. *The Da Vinci Code: A Novel*. New York: Doubleday.

Brown, Raymond E. 1987. "The Gospel of Peter and Canonical Gospel Priority." *New Testament Studies* 33:321–43.

Brown, Scott G. 2005. *Mark's Other Gospel: Rethinking Morton Smith's Controversial Discovery*. Waterloo, ON: Wilfrid Laurier University Press.

Brown, Scott G., and Allan Pantuck. 2013. "Craig Evans and the *Secret Gospel of Mark*: Exploring the Grounds for Doubt." In *Ancient Gospel or Modern Forgery? The Secret Gospel of Mark in Debate: Proceedings from the 2011 York University Christian Apocrypha Symposium*, edited by T. Burke, 101–34. Eugene, OR: Cascade Books.

Bruyn, Theodore S. de. 2010. "Papyri, Parchments, Ostraca, and Tablets Written with Biblical Texts in Greek and Used as Amulets: A Preliminary List." In *Early Christian Manuscripts*, edited by T. J. Kraus and T. Nicklas, 145–90. Leiden: Brill.

———. 2015. "Christian Apocryphal and Canonical Narratives in Greek Amulets and Formularies in Late Antiquity." In *Rediscovering the Apocryphal Continent: New Perspectives on Early Christian and Late Antique Apocryphal Texts and Traditions,* edited by P. Piovanelli and T. Burke, 153–74. Wissenschaftliche Untersuchungen zum Neuen Testament 349. Tübingen: Mohr Siebeck.

Bruyn, Theodore S. de., and Jitse H. F. Dijkstra. 2011. "Greek Amulets and Formularies from Egypt Containing Christian Elements: A Checklist of Papyri, Parchments, Ostraka, and Tablets." *Bulletin of the American Society of Papyrologists* 48:163–216.

Buchinger, Harald, and Elisabeth Hernitscheck. 2014. "P. Oxy. 840 and the Rites of Christian Initiation: Dating a Piece of Alleged Anti-Sacramentalistic Polemics." *Early Christianity* 5:117–24.

Burke, Tony. 2004. "The Greek Manuscript Tradition of the *Infancy Gospel of Thomas*." *Apocrypha* 14:129–51.

———. 2008. "The *Infancy Gospel of Thomas*." In *The Non-Canonical Gospels*, edited by P. Foster, 126–38. London: T&T Clark.

———. 2010. *De infantia Iesu Evangelium Thomae Graecae*. Corpus Christianorum Series Apocryphorum 17. Turnhout: Brepols.

———. 2013a. *Secret Scriptures Revealed: A New Introduction to the Christian Apocrypha*. London: SPCK.

———, ed. 2013b. *Ancient Gospel or Modern Forgery? The Secret Gospel of Mark in Debate: Proceedings from the 2011 York University Christian Apocrypha Symposium*. Eugene, OR: Cascade Books.

Burridge, Richard A. 2004. *What Are the Gospels? A Comparison with Graeco-Roman Biography*. 2nd ed. Grand Rapids: Eerdmans.

———. 2013. "Gospel: Genre." In *Dictionary of Jesus and the Gospels*, edited by Joel B. Green, 335–42. 2nd ed. Downers Grove, IL: IVP Academic.

———. 2015. "The Art of Biography in Antiquity: A Review." *Journal for the Study of the New Testament* 37:474–79.

Burtea, Bogdan. 2012. "B.VII.6.3 Die äthiopische Fassung des Gamalielevangeliums." In *Antike christliche Apokryphen in deutscher Übersetzung*, 1.1–2, *Evangelien und Verwandtes*, edited by C. Markschies and J. Schröter, 1336–47. Tübingen: Mohr Siebeck.

Byrskog, Samuel. 2000. *Story as History—History as Story: The Gospel Tradition in the Context of Ancient Oral History*.

Wissenschaftliche Untersuchungen zum Neuen Testament 123. Tübingen: Mohr (Siebeck).

Cahill, Michael. 1998. *The First Commentary on Mark: An Annotated Translation*. Oxford: Oxford University Press.

Cameron, Ron. 1982. *The Other Gospels: Non-Canonical Gospel Texts*. Philadelphia: Westminster.

Campenhausen, Hans von. 1972. *The Formation of the Christian Bible*. Philadelphia: Fortress Press.

Carleton Paget, James. 2010a. "The Ebionites in Recent Research." In *Jews, Christians and Jewish Christians in Antiquity*, 325–79. Wissenschaftliche Untersuchungen zum Neuen Testament 251. Tübingen: Mohr Siebeck.

———. 2010b. *Jews, Christians and Jewish Christians in Antiquity*. Wissenschaftliche Untersuchungen zum Neuen Testament 251. Tübingen: Mohr Siebeck.

Carlson, Stephen C. 2005. *The Gospel Hoax: Morton Smith's Invention of Secret Mark*. Waco, TX: Baylor University Press.

Carp, Teresa C. 1980. "*Puer Senex* in Roman and Medieval Thought." *Latomus* 39:736–39.

Cartlidge, David R., and J. K. Elliott. 2001. *Art and the Christian Apocrypha*. London: Routledge.

Chapa, Juan. 2011. "5072. Uncanonical Gospel?" In *The Oxyrhynchus Papyri* 76, edited by J. Chapa and D. Colomo, 1–19. London: Egypt Exploration Society.

———. 2012. "A Newly Published 'Gospel Fragment.'" *Early Christianity* 3:381–89.

Combs, Jason Robert. 2014. "A Walking, Talking Cross: The Polymorphic Christology of the Gospel of Peter." *Early Christianity* 5:198–219.

Crawford, Matthew R. 2013. "Diatessaron, a Misnomer? The Evidence from Ephrem's Commentary." *Early Christianity* 3:362–85.

———. 2015a. "Reading the Diatessaron with Ephrem: The Word and the Light, the Voice and the Star." *Vigiliae Christianae* 69:70–95.

———. 2015b. "Ammonius of Alexandria, Eusebius of Caesarea and the Origins of Gospels Scholarship." *New Testament Studies* 61:1–29.

Crossan, John Dominic. 1988. *The Cross That Spoke: The Origins of the Passion Narrative*. San Francisco: Harper & Row.

———. 1991. *The Historical Jesus: The Life of a Mediterranean Jewish Peasant*. San Francisco: HarperSanFrancisco.

———. 2007. "The *Gospel of Peter* and the Canonical Gospels." In *Das Evangelium nach Petrus: Text, Kontexte, Intertexte*, edited by T. J. Kraus and T. Nicklas, 117–34. Texte und Untersuchungen 158. Berlin: de Gruyter.

Danker, Frederick W., Walter Bauer, William F. Arndt, and F. Wilbur Gingrich. 2000. *A Greek-English Lexicon of the New Testament and Other Early Christian Literature*. 3rd ed. Chicago: University of Chicago Press.

Davis, Stephen J. 2014. *Christ Child: Cultural Memories of a Young Jesus*. Synkrisis. New Haven, CT: Yale University Press.

DeConick, April D. 1996. *Seek to See Him: Ascent and Vision Mysticism in the Gospel of Thomas*. Supplements to Vigiliae Christianae 33. Leiden: Brill.

———. 2001. *Voices of the Mystics: Early Christian Discourse in the Gospels of John and Thomas and Other Ancient Christian Literature*. Journal for the Study of the New Testament Supplement Series 157. Sheffield: Sheffield Academic Press.

———. 2005. *Recovering the Original Gospel of Thomas: A History of the Gospel and Its Growth*. London: T & T Clark.

———. 2007a. *The Original Gospel of Thomas in Translation: With a Commentary and New English Translation of the Complete Gospel*. London: T&T Clark.

———. 2007b. *The Thirteenth Apostle: What the Gospel of Judas Really Says*. London: Continuum.

———. 2008a. "The *Gospel of Judas*: A Parody of Apostolic Christianity." In *The Non-Canonical Gospels*, edited by P. Foster, 96–109. London: T&T Clark.

———. 2008b. "The *Gospel of Thomas*." In *The Non-Canonical Gospels*, edited by P. Foster, 13–29. London: T&T Clark.

———, ed. 2009. *The Codex Judas Papers: Proceedings of the International Congress on the Tchacos Codex Held at Rice University, Houston, Texas, March 13–16, 2008*. Nag Hammadi and Manichaean Studies 71. Leiden: Brill.

Deissmann, Adolf. 1904. "Das angebliche Evangelium-Fragment von Kairo." *Archiv für Religionswissenschaft* 7:387–92.

———. 1927. *Light from the Ancient East: The New Testament Illustrated by Recently Discovered Texts of the Graeco-Roman World*. Translated by L. R. M. Strachan. Rev. ed. New York: Doran.

249

Denzey Lewis, Nicola. 2014. "A New Gnosticism: Why Simon Gathercole and Mark Goodacre on the *Gospel of Thomas* Change the Field." *Journal for the Study of the New Testament* 36:240–50.

Denzey Lewis, Nicola, and Justine Ariel Blount. 2014. "Rethinking the Origins of the Nag Hammadi Codices." *Journal of Biblical Literature* 133:399–419.

Dietzfelbinger, Konrad. 1989. *Apokryphe Evangelien aus Nag Hammadi: Evangelium der Wahrheit, Evangelium nach Philippus, Brief an Reginus über die Auferstehung, Über die Seele, Evangelium nach Thomas, Das Buch Thomas des Wettkämpfers, Evangelium nach Maria: Vollständige Texte, neu formuliert und kommentiert.* 2nd ed. Andechs: Dingfelder Verlag.

Dignas, Beate, R. R. R. Smith, and S. R. F. Price. 2012. *Historical and Religious Memory in the Ancient World.* Oxford: Oxford University Press.

Dodd, C. H. 1936. *The Present Task in New Testament Studies: An Inaugural Lecture Delivered in the Divinity School on Tuesday 2 June 1936.* Cambridge: University Press.

Drecoll, Volker Henning. 2013. "Martin Hengel and the Origins of Gnosticism." In *Gnosticism, Platonism and the Late Ancient World: Essays in Honour of John D. Turner,* edited by K. Corrigan and T. Rasimus, 139–66. Nag Hammadi and Manichaean Studies 82. Leiden: Brill.

Dunderberg, Ismo. 2006. *The Beloved Disciple in Conflict? Revisiting the Gospels of John and Thomas.* Oxford: Oxford University Press.

———. 2013. "Johannine Traditions and Apocryphal Gospels." In *The Apocryphal Gospels within the Context of Early Christian Theology,* edited by J. Schröter, 67–93. Bibliotheca Ephemeridum Theologicarum Lovaniensium 260. Leuven: Peeters.

———. 2015. *Gnostic Morality Revisited.* Wissenschaftliche Untersuchungen zum Neuen Testament 347. Tübingen: Mohr Siebeck.

Dungan, David L. 1999. *A History of the Synoptic Problem: The Canon, the Text, the Composition, and the Interpretation of the Gospels.* Anchor Bible Reference Library. New York: Doubleday.

Dunn, James D. G. 1991. *The Partings of the Ways between Christianity and Judaism and Their Significance for the Character of*

Christianity. London: SCM Press; Philadelphia: Trinity Press International.

———, ed. 1992. *Jews and Christians: The Parting of the Ways, A.D. 70 to 135*. Tübingen: Mohr.

———. 2006. *The Partings of the Ways between Christianity and Judaism and Their Significance for the Character of Christianity*. 2nd ed. London: SCM.

———. 2007. "Social Memory and the Oral Jesus Tradition." In *Memory and Remembrance in the Bible and Antiquity: The Fifth Durham-Tübingen Research Symposium (Durham, September 2004)*, edited by S. C. Barton et al., 179–94. Wissenschaftliche Untersuchungen zum Neuen Testament 212. Tübingen: Mohr Siebeck.

Dzon, Mary. 2005. "Joseph and the Amazing Christ-Child of Late-Medieval Legend." In *Childhood in the Middle Ages and the Renaissance: The Results of a Paradigm Shift in the History of Mentality*, edited by A. Classen, 135–58. Berlin: de Gruyter.

Eastman, Daniel. 2015. "Cursing in the Infancy Gospel of Thomas." *Vigiliae Christianae* 69:186–208.

Edwards, James R. 2009. *The Hebrew Gospel and the Development of the Synoptic Tradition*. Grand Rapids: Eerdmans.

Edwards, Mark J. 1989. "Gnostics and Valentinians in the Church Fathers." *Journal of Theological Studies* 40:26–47.

———. 1990. "Neglected Texts in the Study of Gnosticism." *Journal of Theological Studies* 41:26–50.

———. 2008. Review of *The Gospel of Judas: Rewriting Early Christianity*, by Simon Gathercole. *Journal of Ecclesiastical History* 59:515.

Ego, Beate, Armin Lange, and Peter Pilhofer, eds. 1999. *Gemeinde ohne Tempel = Community without Temple: Zur Substituierung und Transformation des Jerusalemer Tempels und seines Kults im Alten Testament, antiken Judentum und frühen Christentum*. Wissenschaftliche Untersuchungen zum Neuen Testament 118. Tübingen: Mohr Siebeck.

Ehlen, Oliver. 2012a. "B.V.5.5 Das Pseudo-Matthäusevangelium." In *Antike christliche Apokryphen in deutscher Übersetzung, 1.1–2, Evangelien und Verwandtes*, edited by C. Markschies and J. Schröter, 983–1002. Tübingen: Mohr Siebeck.

———. 2012b. "B.V.5.6 Das Evangelium der Arundel-Handschrift (London, British Library, Arundel 404)." In *Antike christliche*

Apokryphen in deutscher Übersetzung, 1.1–2, *Evangelien und Verwandtes*, edited by C. Markschies and J. Schröter, 1003–12. Tübingen: Mohr Siebeck.

Ehrman, Bart D., ed. 2003. *Lost Scriptures: Books That Did Not Make It into the New Testament*. Oxford: Oxford University Press.

———. 2007. *The Lost Gospel of Judas Iscariot: A New Look at Betrayer and Betrayed*. Oxford: Oxford University Press.

———. 2013. *Forgery and Counterforgery: The Use of Literary Deceit in Early Christian Polemics*. Oxford: Oxford University Press.

Ehrman, Bart D., and Zlatko Pleše, eds. 2011. *The Apocryphal Gospels: Texts and Translations*. New York: Oxford University Press.

———, eds. 2014. *The Other Gospels: Accounts of Jesus from outside the New Testament*. New York: Oxford University Press.

Eisele, Wilfried. 2010. *Welcher Thomas? Studien zur Text- und Überlieferungsgeschichte des Thomasevangeliums*. Wissenschaftliche Untersuchungen zum Neuen Testament 259. Tübingen: Mohr Siebeck.

Eissler, Friedmann. 2012. "A.I.3. Jesuslogien aus arabisch-islamischer Literatur." In *Antike christliche Apokryphen in deutscher Übersetzung*, 1.1–2, *Evangelien und Verwandtes*, edited by C. Markschies and J. Schröter, 193–208. Tübingen: Mohr Siebeck.

Elliott, J. K. 1993. *The Apocryphal New Testament: A Collection of Apocryphal Christian Literature in an English Translation*. Oxford: Clarendon.

———. 2006. *A Synopsis of the Apocryphal Nativity and Infancy Narratives*. New Testament Tools and Studies 34. Leiden: Brill.

Emmel, Stephen. 2002. "Unbekanntes Berliner Evangelium = The Strasbourg Coptic Gospel: Prolegomena to a New Edition of the Strasbourg Fragments." In *For the Children, Perfect Instruction: Studies in Honor of Hans-Martin Schenke on the Occasion of the Berliner Arbeitskreis für koptisch-gnostische Schriften's Thirtieth Year*, edited by H.-G. Bethge, 353–74. Nag Hammadi and Manichaean Studies 54. Leiden: Brill.

———. 2003. "Preliminary Reedition and Translation of the Gospel of the Savior: New Light from the Strasbourg Coptic Gospel and the Stauros-Text from Nubia." *Apocrypha* 14:9–53.

———. 2005. "Ein altes Evangelium der Apostel taucht in Fragmenten aus Agypten und Nubien auf." *Zeitschrift für Antikes Christentum* 9:85–99.

———. 2015. *The Codicology of the New Coptic (Lycopolitan) Gospel of John Fragment (and Its Relevance for Assessing the Genuineness of the Recently Published Coptic "Gospel of Jesus' Wife" Fragment)*. http://www.uni-muenster.de/imperia/md/content/iaek/_v/emmel-codicologyharvardjohn-2015-03-26.pdf.

Ericksen, Robert P. 1985. *Theologians under Hitler: Gerhard Kittel, Paul Althaus, and Emanuel Hirsch*. New Haven, CT: Yale University Press.

Erlemann, Kurt. 1996. "Papyrus Egerton 2: 'Missing Link' zwischen synoptischer und johanneischer Tradition." *New Testament Studies* 42:12–34.

Evans, Craig A. 2007. "The Jewish Christian Gospel Tradition." In *Jewish Believers in Jesus: The Early Centuries*, edited by O. Skarsaune and R. Hvalvik, 241–77. Peabody, MA: Hendrickson Publishers.

———. 2015. "How Long Were Late Antique Books in Use? Possible Implications for New Testament Textual Criticism." *Bulletin for Biblical Research* 25:23–37.

Farmer, William R. 1993. "The Minor Agreements of Matthew and Luke against Mark and the Two Gospel Hypothesis." In *Minor Agreements: Symposium Göttingen 1991*, edited by G. Strecker, 163–208. Göttinger theologische Arbeiten 50. Göttingen: Vandenhoeck & Ruprecht.

Farrer, Austin M. 1955. "On Dispensing with Q." In *Studies in the Gospels: Essays in Memory of R. H. Lightfoot*, edited by D. E. Nineham, 55–88. Oxford: Blackwell.

Fentress, James, and Chris Wickham. 1992. *Social Memory*. Oxford: Blackwell.

Fieger, Michael. 1991. *Das Thomasevangelium: Einleitung, Kommentar und Systematik*. Neutestamentliche Abhandlungen NS 22. Münster: Aschendorff.

Fine, Steven. 2007. "'When I Went to Rome . . . There I Saw the Menorah . . .': The Jerusalem Temple Implements during the Second Century C.E." In *The Archaeology of Difference: Gender, Ethnicity, Class and the "Other" in Antiquity; Studies in Honor of Eric M. Meyers*, edited by D. R. Edwards and C. T. McCullough, 171–82. Annual of the American Schools of

Oriental Research 60–61. Boston: American Schools of Oriental Research.

Fishbane, Michael A. 1985. *Biblical Interpretation in Ancient Israel*. Oxford: Clarendon.

Förster, Hans. 2013. "Geheime Schriften und geheime Lehren? Zur Selbstbezeichnung von Texten aus dem Umfeld der frühchristlichen Gnosis under Verwendung des Begriffs ἀπόκρυφος (bzw. *hep*)." *Zeitschrift für die neutestamentliche Wissenschaft* 114:118–45.

Förster, Niclas. 1999. *Marcus Magus: Kult, Lehre und Gemeindeleben einer valentinianischen Gnostikergruppe. Sammlung der Quellen und Kommentar*. Wissenschaftliche Untersuchungen zum Neuen Testament 114. Tübingen: Mohr Siebeck.

Foster, Paul. 2005. "The Epistles of Ignatius of Antioch and the Writings That Later Formed the New Testament." In *Trajectories through the New Testament and the Apostolic Fathers*, edited by A. F. Gregory and C. M. Tuckett, 159–86. Oxford: Oxford University Press.

———. 2006. "Are There Any Early Fragments of the So-Called *Gospel of Peter*?" *New Testament Studies* 52:1–28.

———. 2007a. "The Disputed Early Fragments of the So-Called Gospel of Peter—Once Again." *Novum Testamentum* 49:402–5.

———. 2007b. "The Gospel of Peter." *Expository Times* 118:318–25.

———. 2008a. "The *Gospel of Peter*." In *The Non-Canonical Gospels*, edited by P. Foster, 30–42. London: T&T Clark.

———. 2008b. "The *Gospel of Philip*." In *The Non-Canonical Gospels*, edited by P. Foster, 68–83. London: T&T Clark.

———. 2008c. "Secret Mark." In *The Non-Canonical Gospels*, edited by P. Foster, 171–82. London: T&T Clark.

———. 2009. *The Apocryphal Gospels: A Very Short Introduction*. Oxford: Oxford University Press.

———. 2010a. *The Gospel of Peter: Introduction, Critical Edition and Commentary*. Texts and Editions for New Testament Study 4. Leiden: Brill.

———. 2010b. "P.Oxy. 2949—Its Transcription and Significance: A Response to Thomas Wayment." *Journal of Biblical Literature* 129:173–76.

———. 2010c. "Papyrus Oxyrhynchus X 1224." In *Early Christian Manuscripts: Examples of Applied Method and Approach*,

254

edited by T. J. Kraus and T. Nicklas, 59–96. Texts and Editions for New Testament Study 5. Leiden: Brill.

———. 2011. "The Gospel of Peter: Directions and Issues in Contemporary Research." *Currents in Biblical Research* 9:310–38.

———. 2013a. "Do Crosses Walk and Talk? A Reconsideration of Gospel of Peter 10.39–42." *Journal of Theological Studies* 64:89–104.

———. 2013b. Foreword to *Ancient Gospel or Modern Forgery? The Secret Gospel of Mark in Debate: Proceedings from the 2011 York University Christian Apocrypha Symposium*, edited by T. Burke, xii–xxi. Eugene, OR: Cascade Books.

———. 2013c. "The Reception of the Canonical Gospels in the Non-Canonical Gospels." *Early Christianity* 4:281–309.

Foster, Paul, A. Gregory, J. S. Kloppenborg, and J. Verheyden, eds. 2011. *New Studies in the Synoptic Problem: Oxford Conference, April 2008: Essays in Honour of Christopher M. Tuckett.* Bibliotheca Ephemeridum Theologicarum Lovaniensium 239. Leuven: Peeters.

Fraade, Steven D. 2009. "The Temple as a Marker of Jewish Identity before and after 70 C.E.: The Role of the Holy Vessels in Rabbinic Memory and Imagination." In *Jewish Identities in Antiquity: Studies in Memory of Menahem Stern*, edited by L. I. Levine and D. R. Schwartz, 235–63. Texte und Studien zum antiken Judentum 130. Tübingen: Mohr Siebeck.

Frey, Jörg. 2010. "Zur Vielgestaltigkeit judenchristlicher Evangelienüberlieferungen." In *Jesus in apokryphen Evangelienüberlieferungen: Beiträge zu außerkanonischen Jesusüberlieferungen aus verschiedenen Sprach- und Kulturtraditionen*, edited by J. Frey and J. Schröter, 93–137. Wissenschaftliche Untersuchungen zum Neuen Testament 254. Tübingen: Mohr Siebeck.

———. 2011. "How Could Mark and John Do without Infancy Stories?" In *Infancy Gospels: Stories and Identities*, edited by C. Clivaz et al., 189–215. Wissenschaftliche Untersuchungen zum Neuen Testament 281. Tübingen: Mohr Siebeck.

———. 2012a. "B.V.1.1 Die Fragmente judenchristlicher Evangelien." In *Antike christliche Apokryphen in deutscher Übersetzung*, 1.1–2, *Evangelien und Verwandtes*, edited by C. Markschies and J. Schröter, 560–92. Tübingen: Mohr Siebeck.

———. 2012b. "B.V.1.2 Die Fragmente des Hebräerevangeliums." In *Antike christliche Apokryphen in deutscher Übersetzung*,

1.1–2, *Evangelien und Verwandtes*, edited by C. Markschies and J. Schröter, 593–606. Tübingen: Mohr Siebeck.

———. 2012c. "B.V.1.4 Die Fragmente des Nazoräerevangeliums." In *Antike christliche Apokryphen in deutscher Übersetzung*, 1.1–2, *Evangelien und Verwandtes*, edited by C. Markschies and J. Schröter, 623–54. Tübingen: Mohr Siebeck.

———. 2012d. "B.V.1.5 Die Textvarianten nach dem 'Jüdischen Evangelium.'" In *Antike christliche Apokryphen in deutscher Übersetzung*, 1.1–2, *Evangelien und Verwandtes*, edited by C. Markschies and J. Schröter, 655–60. Tübingen: Mohr Siebeck.

———. 2012e. "B.VI.1 Das Freer-Logion." In *Antike christliche Apokryphen in deutscher Übersetzung*, 1.1–2, *Evangelien und Verwandtes*, edited by C. Markschies and J. Schröter, 1059–61. Tübingen: Mohr Siebeck.

Gallagher, Edmon L. 2014. "Writings Labeled 'Apocrypha' in Latin Patristic Sources." In *Sacra Scriptura: How "Non-Canonical" Texts Functioned in Early Judaism and Early Christianity*, edited by J. H. Charlesworth et al., 1–14. Jewish and Christian Texts in Contexts and Related Studies 20. London: Bloomsbury T&T Clark.

Gamble, Harry A. 2006. "Marcion and the 'Canon.'" In *Origins to Constantine*, edited by M. M. Mitchell and F. M. Young, 195–213. Cambridge History of Christianity 1. Cambridge: Cambridge University Press.

Gathercole, Simon. 2007. *The Gospel of Judas: Rewriting Early Christianity*. Oxford: Oxford University Press.

———. 2008a. "The Influence of Paul on the Gospel of Thomas (53.3 and 17)." In *Das Thomasevangelium: Entstehung, Rezeption, Theologie*, edited by J. Frey et al., 72–94. Beihefte zur Zeitschrift für die neutestamentliche Wissenschaft und die Kunde der älteren Kirche 157. Berlin: Walter de Gruyter.

———. 2008b. "The *Gospel of Judas*: An Unlikely Hero." In *The Non-Canonical Gospels*, edited by P. Foster, 84–95. London: T&T Clark.

———. 2011. "'The Heavens and the Earth Will Be Rolled Up': The Eschatology of the *Gospel of Thomas*." In *Eschatologie-Eschatology. The Sixth Durham-Tübingen Research Symposium: Eschatology in Old Testament, Ancient Judaism and Early Christianity (Tübingen, September, 2009)*, edited by H.-J. Eckstein et al., 280–302. Tübingen: Mohr Siebeck.

———. 2012a. *The Composition of the Gospel of Thomas: Original Language and Influences.* Society for New Testament Studies Monograph Series 151. Cambridge: Cambridge University Press.

———. 2012b. "The Earliest Manuscript Title of Matthew's Gospel (BnF Suppl. gr. 1120 ii 3 / $\mathfrak{P}^4$)." *Novum Testamentum* 54:209–35.

———. 2013. "The Titles of the Gospels in the Earliest New Testament Manuscripts." *Zeitschrift für die neutestamentliche Wissenschaft* 104:33–76.

———. 2014a. *The Gospel of Thomas: Introduction and Commentary.* Texts and Editions for New Testament Study 11. Boston: Brill.

———. 2014b. "Thomas Revisited: A Rejoinder to Denzey Lewis, Kloppenborg and Patterson." *Journal for the Study of the New Testament* 36:262–81.

———. 2015. "The Gospel of Jesus' Wife: Constructing a Context." *New Testament Studies* 61:292–313.

Gnilka, Joachim. 2007. *Die Nazarener und der Koran: Eine Spurensuche.* Freiburg: Herder.

Gonis, Nikolaos, et al., eds. 2016. *The Oxyrhynchus Papyri: Volume LXXXII.* Graeco-Roman Memoirs 103. London: The Egypt Exploration Society.

Goodacre, Mark. 2002. *The Case against Q: Studies in Markan Priority and the Synoptic Problem.* Harrisburg, PA: Trinity Press International.

———. 2012. *Thomas and the Gospels: The Case for Thomas's Familiarity with the Synoptics.* Grand Rapids: Eerdmans.

———. 2013. "How Reliable Is the Story of the Nag Hammadi Discovery?" *Journal for the Study of the New Testament* 35:303–22.

———. 2014. "Did Thomas Know the Synoptic Gospels? A Response to Denzey Lewis, Kloppenborg and Patterson." *Journal for the Study of the New Testament* 36:282–93.

Goodacre, Mark, and Nicholas Perrin, eds. 2004. *Questioning Q.* Downers Grove, IL: InterVarsity Press.

Goodstein, Laurie. 2012. "A Faded Piece of Papyrus Refers to Jesus' Wife." *New York Times*, September 18, 2012. http://www.nytimes.com/2012/09/19/us/historian-says-piece-of-papyrus-refers-to-jesus-wife.html.

Goulder, Michael D. 1996. "Is Q a Juggernaut?" *Journal of Biblical Literature* 115:667–81.

———. 1999. "Self-Contradiction in the IQP." *Journal of Biblical Literature* 118:506–17.

Gregory, Andrew. 2008. "Jewish-Christian Gospels." In *The Non-Canonical Gospels*, edited by P. Foster, 54–67. London: T&T Clark.

———. 2014. "Jewish-Christian Gospel Traditions and the New Testament." In *Christian Apocrypha: Receptions of the New Testament in Ancient Christian Apocrypha*, edited by T. Nicklas and J.-M. Rössli, 41–59. Novum Testamentum Patristicum 26. Göttingen: Vandenhoeck & Ruprecht.

Greschat, Katharina. 2007. "Justins 'Denkwürdigkeiten der Apostel' und das Petrusevangelium." In *Das Evangelium nach Petrus: Text, Kontexte, Intertexte*, edited by T. J. Kraus and T. Nicklas, 197–214. Texte und Untersuchungen zur Geschichte der altchristlichen Literatur 158. Berlin: Walter de Gruyter.

Grosheide, Frederik Willem. 1948. *Some Early Lists of the Books of the New Testament*. Textus minores 1. Leiden: Brill.

Grosso, Matteo. 2011. *Vangelo secondo Tommaso*. Rome: Carocci.

———. 2012. *Detti segreti: Il Vangelo di Tommaso nell'antichità*. Multa Paucis 13. Acireale/Rome: Bonanno.

Grundmann, Walter. 1940. *Jesus der Galiläer und das Judentum*. Leipzig: Georg Wigand.

Guelich, Robert A. 1991. "The Gospel Genre." In *The Gospel and the Gospels*, edited by P. Stuhlmacher, 173–208. Grand Rapids: Eerdmans.

Hägg, Tomas. 2012. *The Art of Biography in Antiquity*. Cambridge: Cambridge University Press.

Hannah, Darrell D. 2008. "The Four-Gospel 'Canon' in the *Epistula Apostolorum*." *Journal of Theological Studies* 59:598–633.

Harnack, Adolf von. 1924. *Marcion: Das Evangelium vom fremden Gott*. Texte und Untersuchungen 45. 2nd ed. Leipzig: J. C. Hinrichs.

———. 2003. *Marcion, der moderne Gläubige des 2. Jahrhunderts, der erste Reformator: Die Dorpater Preisschrift (1870); Kritische Edition des handschriftlichen Exemplars mit einem Anhang*. Edited by F. Steck. Texte und Untersuchungen zur Geschichte der altchristlichen Literatur 149. Berlin: W. de Gruyter.

Hartenstein, Judith. 2000. *Die zweite Lehre: Erscheinungen des Auferstandenen als Rahmenerzählungen frühchristlicher Dialoge.* Texte und Untersuchungen zur Geschichte der altchristlichen Literatur 146. Berlin: Akademie.

―――. 2007. *Charakterisierung im Dialog: Die Darstellung von Maria Magdalena, Petrus, Thomas und der Mutter Jesu im Kontext anderer frühchristlicher Traditionen.* Novum Testamentum et Orbus Antiquus/Studien zur Umwelt des Neuen Testaments 64. Göttingen: Vandenhoeck & Ruprecht.

―――. 2012a. "B.VI Dialogische Evangelien." In *Antike christliche Apokryphen in deutscher Übersetzung*, 1.1–2, *Evangelien und Verwandtes*, edited by C. Markschies and J. Schröter, 1051–58. Tübingen: Mohr Siebeck.

―――. 2012b. "B.VI.10. Das Evangelium nach Maria (BG1/P.Oxy. L 3525/P.Ryl. III 463)." In *Antike christliche Apokryphen in deutscher Übersetzung*, 1.1–2, *Evangelien und Verwandtes*, edited by C. Markschies and J. Schröter, 1208–16. Tübingen: Mohr Siebeck.

Hartenstein, Judith, and Silke Petersen. 1998. "Das Evangelium nach Maria: Maria Magdalena als Lieblingsjüngerin und Stellvertreterin Jesu." In *Kompendium Feministische Bibelauslegung*, edited by L. Schottroff and M.-T. Wacker, 757–67. Gütersloh: Mohn.

―――. 2012. "Gospel of Mary: Mary Magdalene as Beloved Disciple and Representative of Jesus." In *Feminist Biblical Interpretation: A Compendium of Critical Commentary on the Books of the Bible and Related Literature*, edited by L. Schottroff and M.-T. Wacker, 943–56. Translated by L. E. Dahill et al. Grand Rapids: Eerdmans.

Hartenstein, Judith, and Uwe-Karsten Plisch. 2012. "B.VI.3 Der Brief des Jakobus (NHC I,2)." In *Antike christliche Apokryphen in deutscher Übersetzung*, 1.1–2, *Evangelien und Verwandtes*, edited by C. Markschies and J. Schröter, 1093–106. Tübingen: Mohr Siebeck.

Hays, Christopher M. 2008. "Marcion vs. Luke: A Response to the *Plädoyer* of Matthias Klinghardt." *Zeitschrift für die neutestamentliche Wissenschaft* 99:213–32.

Hays, Richard B. 2014. *Reading Backwards: Figural Christology and the Fourfold Gospel Witness.* Waco, TX: Baylor University Press.

Hays, Richard B. 2016. *Echoes of Scripture in the Gospels*. Waco: Baylor University Press.

Head, Peter M. 1992a. "On the Christology of the Gospel of Peter." *Vigiliae Christianae* 46:209–24.

————. 1992b. "Tatian's Christology and Its Influence on the Composition of the Diatessaron." *Tyndale Bulletin* 43:121–37.

————. 2004. "The Nazi Quest for an Aryan Jesus." *Journal for the Study of the Historical Jesus* 2:55–89.

————. 2012. "The Early Text of Mark." In *The Early Text of the New Testament*, edited by C. E. Hill and M. J. Kruger, 108–20. Oxford: Oxford University Press.

————. 2013. "Additional Greek Witnesses to the New Testament (Ostraca, Amulets, Inscriptions and Other Sources)." In *The Text of the New Testament in Contemporary Research: Essays on the Status Quaestionis*, edited by B. D. Ehrman and M. W. Holmes, 429–60. New Testament Tools, Studies, and Documents 42. 2nd ed. Leiden: Brill.

Heckel, Theo K. 1999. *Vom Evangelium des Markus zum viergestaltigen Evangelium*. Wissenschaftliche Untersuchungen zum Neuen Testament 120. Tübingen: Mohr Siebeck.

Hedrick, Charles W. 2010. *Unlocking the Secrets of the* Gospel according to Thomas*: A Radical Faith for a New Age*. Eugene, OR: Cascade Books.

Hedrick, Charles W., and Paul Allan Mirecki. 1999. *Gospel of the Savior: A New Ancient Gospel*. California Classical Library. Santa Rosa, CA: Polebridge Press.

Heimola, Minna. 2015. "Christians and Jews in the *Gospel of Philip*." In *Rediscovering the Apocryphal Continent: New Perspectives on Early Christian and Late Antique Apocryphal Texts and Traditions*, edited by P. Piovanelli and T. Burke, 137–51. Wissenschaftliche Untersuchungen zum Neuen Testament 349. Tübingen: Mohr Siebeck.

Henderson, Timothy P. 2011. *The Gospel of Peter and Early Christian Apologetics: Rewriting the Story of Jesus' Death, Burial, and Resurrection*. Wissenschaftliche Untersuchungen zum Neuen Testament 2:301. Tübingen: Mohr Siebeck.

Hengel, Martin. 1984. *Die Evangelienüberschriften*. Sitzungsberichte der Heidelberger Akademie der Wissenschaften, Philosophisch-Historische Klasse Jahrg. 1984, Bericht 3. Heidelberg: C. Winter.

———. 2000. *The Four Gospels and the One Gospel of Jesus Christ: An Investigation of the Collection and Origin of the Canonical Gospels*. Translated by J. Bowden. London: SCM Press.

———. 2008a. "Die Ursprünge der Gnosis und das Urchristentum." In *Studien zum Urchristentum: Kleine Schriften VI*, edited by M. Hengel and C.-J. Thornton, 549–93. Wissenschaftliche Untersuchungen zum Neuen Testament 234. Tübingen: Mohr Siebeck.

———. 2008b. *Die vier Evangelien und das eine Evangelium von Jesus Christus: Studien zu ihrer Sammlung und Entstehung*. Wissenschaftliche Untersuchungen zum Neuen Testament 224. Tübingen: Mohr Siebeck.

Hennecke, Edgar, Wilhelm Schneemelcher, and R. McL. Wilson. 1963. *New Testament Apocrypha* 2. Philadelphia: Westminster Press.

Heschel, Susannah. 2008. *The Aryan Jesus: Christian Theologians and the Bible in Nazi Germany*. Princeton, NJ: Princeton University Press.

Hezser, Catherine. 1996. "Die Verwendung der hellenistischen Gattung Chrie im frühen Christentum und Judentum." *Journal for the Study of Judaism* 27:371–439.

Hill, Charles E. 1999. "The Epistula Apostolorum: An Asian Tract from the Time of Polycarp." *Journal of Early Christian Studies* 7:1–54.

———. 2004. *The Johannine Corpus in the Early Church*. Oxford: Oxford University Press.

———. 2006. *From the Lost Teaching of Polycarp: Identifying Irenaeus' Apostolic Presbyter and the Author of* Ad Diognetum. Wissenschaftliche Untersuchungen zum Neuen Testament 186. Tübingen: Mohr Siebeck.

———. 2010a. "'The Orthodox Gospel': The Reception of John in the Great Church Prior to Irenaeus." In *The Legacy of John: Second-Century Reception of the Fourth Gospel*, edited by T. Rasimus, 233–300. Supplements to Novum Testamentum 132. Leiden: Brill.

———. 2010b. *Who Chose the Gospels? Probing the Great Gospel Conspiracy*. Oxford: Oxford University Press.

Hills, Julian V. 2008. *Tradition and Composition in the Epistula Apostolorum*. Harvard Theological Studies 57. Expanded ed. Cambridge, MA: Harvard University Press.

261

————. 2009. *The Epistle of the Apostles*. Early Christian Apocrypha 2. Santa Rosa, CA: Polebridge Press.

Hock, Ronald F. 1995. *The Infancy Gospels of James and Thomas: With Introduction, Notes, and Original Text Featuring the New Scholars Version Translation*. Scholars Bible 2. Santa Rosa, CA: Polebridge Press.

Hofius, Otfried. 1991. "Isolated Sayings of the Lord." In *New Testament Apocrypha*, edited by W. Schneemelcher and R. M. Wilson, 1:88–91. Translated by R. M. Wilson. Rev. ed. Louisville, KY: Westminster/John Knox Press.

————. 2012. "A.I.1. Außerkanonische Herrenworte." In *Antike christliche Apokryphen in deutscher Übersetzung*, 1.1–2, *Evangelien und Verwandtes*, edited by C. Markschies and J. Schröter, 184–89. Tübingen: Mohr Siebeck.

Holtzmann, H. J. 1863. *Die synoptischen Evangelien: Ihr Ursprung und geschichtlicher Charakter*. Leipzig: Engelmann.

Horbury, William. 1970. "A Critical Examination of the Toledoth Jeshu." PhD dissertation, University of Cambridge.

————. 1997. "Appendix: The Hebrew Text of Matthew in Shem Tob Ibn Shaprut's *Eben Bohan*." In *A Critical and Exegetical Commentary on the Gospel according to Saint Matthew*, by W. D. Davies and D. C. Allison, 3:729–38. International Critical Commentary. Edinburgh: T&T Clark.

————. 2005. "'Gospel' in Herodian Judaea." In *The Written Gospel*, edited by M. Bockmuehl and D. A. Hagner, 7–30. Cambridge: Cambridge University Press.

————. 2006. *Herodian Judaism and New Testament Study*. Wissenschaftliche Untersuchungen zum Neuen Testament 193. Tübingen: Mohr Siebeck.

Horn, Cornelia B., and Robert R. Phenix, eds. 2009. *Children in Late Ancient Christianity*. Studien und Texte zu Antike und Christentum 58. Tübingen: Mohr Siebeck.

Horner, Timothy J. 2004. "Jewish Aspects of the Protoevangelium of James." *Journal of Early Christian Studies* 12:313–35.

Houston, George W. 2014. *Inside Roman Libraries: Book Collections and Their Management in Antiquity*. Studies in the History of Greece and Rome. Chapel Hill: University of North Carolina Press.

Howard, George. 1981. *The Teaching of Addai*. Chico, CA: Scholars Press.

———. 1995. *Hebrew Gospel of Matthew*. 2nd ed. Macon, GA: Mercer University Press.

Hunter, J. H. 1940. *The Mystery of Mar Saba*. New York: Evangelical Publishers.

Hurtado, Larry W. 2006. *The Earliest Christian Artifacts: Manuscripts and Christian Origins*. Grand Rapids: Eerdmans.

———. 2008. "The Greek Fragments of the *Gospel of Thomas* as Artefacts: Papyrological Observations on Papyrus Oxyrhynchus 1, Papyrus Oxyrhynchus 654 and Papyrus Oxyrhynchus 655." In *Das Thomasevangelium: Entstehung, Rezeption, Theologie*, edited by J. Frey et al., 19–32. Beihefte zur Zeitschrift für die neutestamentliche Wissenschaft 157. Berlin: Walter de Gruyter.

———. 2013. "Christian Literary Texts in Manuscripts of Second & Third Centuries." http://larryhurtado.files.wordpress.com/2010/07/second-third-century-christian-texts1.pdf.

———. 2015. "Who Read Early Christian Apocrypha?" In *The Oxford Handbook of Early Christian Apocrypha*, edited by A. Gregory and C. Tuckett, 153–66. Oxford: Oxford University Press.

Ilan, Tal. 1997. *Mine and Yours Are Hers: Retrieving Women's History from Rabbinic Literature*. Arbeiten zur Geschichte des antiken Judentums und des Urchristentums 41. Leiden: Brill.

Jacobovici, Simcha, and Barrie A. Wilson. 2014. *The Lost Gospel: Decoding the Ancient Text That Reveals Jesus' Marriage to Mary the Magdalene*. Translated by T. Burke. New York: Pegasus Books.

James, M. R. 1924. *The Apocryphal New Testament: Being the Apocryphal Gospels, Acts, Epistles, and Apocalypses with Other Narratives and Fragments*. Oxford: Clarendon.

Jeffery, Peter. 2007. *The Secret Gospel of Mark Unveiled: Imagined Rituals of Sex, Death, and Madness in a Biblical Forgery*. New Haven, CT: Yale University Press.

Jenkins, Philip. 2001. *Hidden Gospels: How the Search for Jesus Lost Its Way*. Oxford: Oxford University Press.

———. 2015. *The Many Faces of Christ: The Thousand-Year Story of the Survival and Influence of the Lost Gospels*. New York: Basic Books.

Jenott, Lance. 2011. *The Gospel of Judas: Coptic Text, Translation, and Historical Interpretation of "the Betrayer's Gospel."*

Studien und Texte zu Antike und Christentum 64. Tübingen: Mohr Siebeck.

Jensen, Robin M. 2015. "The Apocryphal Mary in Early Christian Art." In *The Oxford Handbook of Early Christian Apocrypha*, edited by A. Gregory and C. Tuckett, 289–305. Oxford: Oxford University Press.

Jenson, Robert W. 2008. "Identity, Jesus, and Exegesis." In *Seeking the Identity of Jesus: A Pilgrimage*, edited by B. R. Gaventa and R. B. Hays, 43–59. Grand Rapids: Eerdmans.

Jeremias, Joachim. 1947. "Der Zusammenstoß Jesu mit dem pharisäischen Oberpriester auf dem Tempelplatz." *Coniectanea Neotestamentica* 2:97–108.

———. 1964. *Unknown Sayings of Jesus*. 2nd English ed. London: SPCK.

Jeremias, Joachim, and Wilhelm Schneemelcher. 1991. "Papyrus Egerton 2." In *New Testament Apocrypha*, edited by W. Schneemelcher, 1:96–99. Louisville, KY: Westminster/John Knox Press.

Johnson, Luke Timothy. 2008. "John and *Thomas* in Context: An Exercise in Canonical Criticism." In *The Word Leaps the Gap: Essays on Scripture and Theology in Honor of Richard B. Hays*, edited by J. R. Wagner et al., 284–309. Grand Rapids: Eerdmans.

Johnston, Jeremiah. 2016. *The Resurrection of Jesus in the Gospel of Peter: A Tradition-Historical Study of the Akhmîm Gospel Fragment*. Jewish and Christian Texts in Contexts and Related Studies. New York: T&T Clark Bloomsbury.

Jones, F. Stanley. 2007. "The Gospel of Peter in Pseudo-Clementine Recognitions 1,27–71." In *Das Evangelium nach Petrus: Text, Kontexte, Intertexte*, edited by T. J. Kraus and T. Nicklas, 237–44. Texte und Untersuchungen zur Geschichte der altchristlichen Literatur 158. Berlin: Walter de Gruyter.

Jones, Kenneth R. 2011. *Jewish Reactions to the Destruction of Jerusalem in A.D. 70: Apocalypses and Related Pseudepigrapha*. Supplements to the Journal for the Study of Judaism 151. Leiden: Brill.

Joosten, Jan. 2010. "The Date and Provenance of the Gospel of Barnabas." *Journal of Theological Studies* 61:200–215.

Josua, Maria, and Friedmann Eissler. 2012a. "B.V.5.4 Das arabische Kindheitsevangelium." In *Antike christliche Apokryphen in deutscher Übersetzung*, 1.1–2, *Evangelien und Verwandtes*, edited by C. Markschies and J. Schröter, 963–82. Tübingen: Mohr Siebeck.

———. 2012b. "B.V.5.7 Der Auszug aus dem Leben Johannes des Täufers." In *Antike christliche Apokryphen in deutscher Übersetzung*, 1.1–2, *Evangelien und Verwandtes*, edited by C. Markschies and J. Schröter, 1013–29. Tübingen: Mohr Siebeck.

———. 2012c. "B.VII.6.2 Die arabische Fassung des Gamaliel-evangeliums." In *Antike christliche Apokryphen in deutscher Übersetzung*, 1.1–2, *Evangelien und Verwandtes*, edited by C. Markschies and J. Schröter, 1314–35. Tübingen: Mohr Siebeck.

Kaestli, Jean-Daniel, and Pierre Cherix. 1993. *L'Evangile de Barthélemy d'après deux écrits apocryphes: I. Questions de Barthélemy*. Apocryphes 1. Paris: Brepols.

Kähler, Martin. 1964. *The So-Called Historical Jesus and the Historic, Biblical Christ*. Translated by C. E. Braaten. Philadelphia: Fortress.

Kaiser, Ursula Ulrike. 2010. "Neuere Forschungen zur Jesusüberlieferung in den apokryphen 'Kindheitsevangelien.'" In *Jesus in apokryphen Evangelienüberlieferungen: Beiträge zu außerkanonischen Jesusüberlieferungen aus verschiedenen Sprach- und Kulturtraditionen*, edited by J. Frey and J. Schröter, 253–69. Wissenschaftliche Untersuchungen zum Neuen Testament 254. Tübingen: Mohr Siebeck.

———. 2012a. "B.V.5.2 Die Kindheitserzählung des Thomas." In *Antike christliche Apokryphen in deutscher Übersetzung*, 1.1–2, *Evangelien und Verwandtes*, edited by C. Markschies and J. Schröter, 930–59. Tübingen: Mohr Siebeck.

———. 2012b. "B.V.5.3 Die Erzählung des Justin (Hipp., haer. V 26, 29–32)." In *Antike christliche Apokryphen in deutscher Übersetzung*, 1.1–2, *Evangelien und Verwandtes*, edited by C. Markschies and J. Schröter, 960–62. Tübingen: Mohr Siebeck.

Karmann, Thomas R. 2007. "Die Paschahomilie des Melito von Sardes und das Petrusevangelium." In *Das Evangelium nach Petrus: Text, Kontexte, Intertexte*, edited by T. J. Kraus and T. Nicklas, 215–36. Texte und Untersuchungen zur Geschichte der altchristlichen Literatur 158. Berlin: Walter de Gruyter.

Kasser, Rodolphe, Marvin Meyer, and Gregor Wurst. 2006. *The Gospel of Judas from Codex Tchacos*. Washington, DC: National Geographic.

Kasser, Rodolphe, and Gregor Wurst. 2007. *The Gospel of Judas together with the Letter of Peter to Philip, James, and a Book of Allogenes from Codex Tchacos. Critical Edition*. Washington, DC: National Geographic Society.

Kee, Howard Clark. 1977. *Community of the New Age: Studies in Mark's Gospel*. Philadelphia: Westminster.

Keith, Chris. 2009. *The Pericope Adulterae, the Gospel of John, and the Literacy of Jesus*. Leiden: Brill.

Kelber, Werner H. 2002. "The Case of the Gospels: Memory's Desire and the Limits of Historical Criticism." *Oral Tradition* 17:55–86.

Kelhoffer, James A. 2000. *Miracle and Mission: The Authentication of Missionaries and Their Message in the Longer Ending of Mark*. Wissenschaftliche Untersuchungen zum Neuen Testament 2:112. Tübingen: Mohr Siebeck.

———. 2004. *The Diet of John the Baptist: "Locusts and Wild Honey" in Synoptic and Patristic Interpretation*. Wissenschaftliche Untersuchungen zum Neuen Testament 176. Tübingen: Mohr Siebeck.

———. 2014. *Conceptions of "Gospel" and Legitimacy in Early Christianity*. Wissenschaftliche Untersuchungen zum Neuen Testament 324. Tübingen: Mohr Siebeck.

King, Karen L. 2003a. *The Gospel of Mary of Magdala: Jesus and the First Woman Apostle*. Santa Rosa, CA: Polebridge Press.

———. 2003b. *What Is Gnosticism?* Cambridge, MA: Belknap Press of Harvard University Press.

———. 2007. "The Gospel of Mary with the Greek Gospel of Mary: BG 8502,1; P.Oxy. 3525; P.Ryl. 463." In *The Nag Hammadi Scriptures: The International Edition*, edited by M. Meyer, 737–47. New York: HarperCollins.

———. 2014. "'Jesus Said to Them, "My Wife . . ."': A New Coptic Papyrus Fragment." *Harvard Theological Review* 107:131–59.

———. 2015. *The Gospel of Jesus' Wife: May 2015 Update*. http://gospelofjesuswife.hds.harvard.edu/.

Kinzig, Wolfram. 1994. "*Kaine Diatheke*: The Title of the New Testament in the Second and Third Centuries." *Journal of Theological Studies* 45:519–44.

Kirk, Alan. 2007. "Tradition and Memory in the *Gospel of Peter*." In *Das Evangelium nach Petrus: Text, Kontexte, Intertexte*, edited by T. J. Kraus and T. Nicklas, 135–58. Texte und Untersuchungen zur Geschichte der altchristlichen Literatur 158. Berlin: Walter de Gruyter.

Kirk, Alan, and Tom Thatcher, eds. 2005. *Memory, Tradition, and Text: Uses of the Past in Early Christianity*. Semeia Studies 52. Atlanta: Society of Biblical Literature.

Klauck, Hans-Josef. 1992. "Die dreifache Maria: Zur Rezeption von Joh 19,25 in EvPhil 32." In *The Four Gospels 1992: Festschrift Frans Neirynck*, edited by F. v. Segbroeck, 3:2343–58. Bibliotheca Ephemeridum Theologicarum Lovaniensium 100. Leuven: Peeters.

———. 2002. *Apokryphe Evangelien: Eine Einführung*. Stuttgart: Katholisches Bibelwerk.

———. 2003. *Apocryphal Gospels: An Introduction*. Translated by B. McNeil. London: T&T Clark International.

Klinghardt, Matthias. 2006. "Markion vs. Lukas: Plädoyer für die Wiederaufnahme eines alten Falles." *New Testament Studies* 52:484–513.

———. 2008. "The Marcionite Gospel and the Synoptic Problem: A New Suggestion." *Novum Testamentum* 50:1–27.

———. 2015. *Das älteste Evangelium und die Entstehung der kanonischen Evangelien*. Texte und Arbeiten zum neutestamentlichen Zeitalter 60:1–2. Tübingen: Francke Verlag.

Knox, John. 1942. *Marcion and the New Testament: An Essay in the Early History of the Canon*. Chicago: University of Chicago Press.

Koester, Helmut. 1965. "ΓΝΩΜΑΙ ΔΙΑΦΟΡΟΙ: The Origin and Nature of Diversification in the History of Early Christianity." *Harvard Theological Review* 58(3):279–318.

———. 1980. "Apocryphal and Canonical Gospels." *Harvard Theological Review* 73:105–30.

———. 1990. *Ancient Christian Gospels: Their History and Development*. London: SCM Press.

Koester, Helmut, and Elaine H. Pagels. 1984. "Introduction." In *Nag Hammadi Codex III,5, The Dialogue of the Savior*, edited by S. Emmel et al., 1–17. Nag Hammadi Studies 26. Leiden: Brill.

Koester, Helmut, and James M. Robinson. 1971. *Trajectories through Early Christianity*. Philadelphia: Fortress Press.

Kok, Michael J. 2015. *Gospel on the Margins: The Reception of Mark in the Second Century.* Minneapolis: Fortress Press.

Kraus, Thomas J. 2001. "P.Vindob.G 2325: Das sogenannte Fayum-Evangelium—Neuedition und kritische Rückschlüsse." *Journal of Ancient Christianity* 5:197–212.

———. 2003. "Petrus und das Ostrakon van Haelst 741—einige klärende Anmerkungen." *Journal of Ancient Christianity* 7:203–11.

———. 2004. "P.Oxy. V 840—Amulett oder Miniaturkodex? Grundsätzliche und ergänzende Anmerkungen zu zwei Termini." *Journal of Ancient Christianity* 8:485–97.

———. 2007. "Amulette als wichtige Zeugnisse für das frühe Christentum: Einige grundsätzliche Anmerkungen." *Annali di Storia dell'Esegesi* 24:423–35.

———. 2009. "Other Gospel Fragments." In *Gospel Fragments*, edited by T. J. Kraus et al., 219–80. Oxford Early Christian Gospel Texts. Oxford: Oxford University Press.

———. 2012a. "B.I.5. Das sogenannte Faijumfragment (P.Vindob. G. 2325)." In *Antike christliche Apokryphen in deutscher Übersetzung*, 1.1–2, *Evangelien und Verwandtes*, edited by C. Markschies and J. Schröter, 375–76. Tübingen: Mohr Siebeck.

———. 2012b. "B.I.9. Der Papyrus Merton II 51 (P.Mert. II 51)." In *Antike christliche Apokryphen in deutscher Übersetzung*, 1.1–2, *Evangelien und Verwandtes*, edited by C. Markschies and J. Schröter, 385–86. Tübingen: Mohr Siebeck.

Kraus, Thomas J., Michael J. Kruger, and Tobias Nicklas, eds. 2009. *Gospel Fragments*. Oxford Early Christian Gospel Texts. Oxford: Oxford University Press.

Kraus, Thomas J., and Tobias Nicklas, eds. 2004. *Das Petrusevangelium und die Petrusapokalypse: Die griechischen Fragmente mit deutscher und englischer Übersetzung.* Neutestamentliche Apokryphen 1. Berlin: Walter de Gruyter.

———, eds. 2007. *Das Evangelium nach Petrus: Text, Kontexte, Intertexte.* Texte und Untersuchungen zur Geschichte der altchristlichen Literatur 158. Berlin: Walter de Gruyter.

Kraus, Thomas J., and Stanley E. Porter. 2012. "B.I. Fragmente unbekannter Evangelien auf Papyrus." In *Antike christliche Apokryphen in deutscher Übersetzung*, 1.1–2, *Evangelien und Verwandtes*, edited by C. Markschies and J. Schröter, 353–56. Tübingen: Mohr Siebeck.

Kruger, Michael J. 2005. *The Gospel of the Savior: An Analysis of P. Oxy. 840 and Its Place in the Gospel Traditions of Early Christianity*. Texts and Editions for New Testament Study 1. Leiden: Brill.

———. 2008. "Papyrus Oxyrhynchus 840." In *The Non-Canonical Gospels*, edited by P. Foster, 157–70. London: T&T Clark.

———. 2009. "Papyrus Oxyrhynchus 840." In *Gospel Fragments*, edited by T. J. Kraus et al., 123–215. Oxford Early Christian Gospel Texts. Oxford: Oxford University Press.

Labahn, Michael. 2000. *Offenbarung in Zeichen und Wort: Untersuchungen zur Vorgeschichte von Joh 6,1–25a und seiner Rezeption in der Brotrede*. Wissenschaftliche Untersuchungen zum Neuen Testament 2:117. Tübingen: Mohr Siebeck.

Lahe, Jaan. 2012. *Gnosis und Judentum: Alttestamentliche und jüdische Motive in der gnostischen Literatur und das Ursprungsproblem der Gnosis*. Nag Hammadi and Manichaean Studies 75. Leiden: Brill.

Lambers-Petry, Doris. 2003. "Verwandte Jesu als Referenzpersonen für das Judenchristentum." In *The Image of the Judaeo-Christians in Ancient Jewish and Christian Literature*, edited by P. J. Tomson and D. Lambers-Petry, 32–52. Wissenschaftliche Untersuchungen zum Neuen Testament 158. Tübingen: Mohr Siebeck.

Lapham, Fred. 2003. *An Introduction to the New Testament Apocrypha*. London: T&T Clark International.

Layton, Bentley. 1987. *The Gnostic Scriptures: A New Translation*. London: SCM.

———. 1995. "Prolegomena to the Study of Ancient Gnosticism." In *The Social World of the First Christians: Essays in Honor of Wayne A. Meeks*, edited by L. M. White and O. L. Yarbrough, 334–50. Minneapolis: Fortress.

Leach, Bridget, and John Tait. 2000. "Papyrus." In *Ancient Egyptian Materials and Technology*, edited by P. T. Nicholson and I. Shaw, 227–53. Cambridge: Cambridge University Press.

Le Donne, Anthony. 2009. *The Historiographical Jesus: Memory, Typology and the Son of David*. Waco, TX: Baylor University Press.

Leloir, Louis, ed. 1966. *Ephraem: Commentaire de l'Évangile concordant ou Diatessaron*. Sources Chrétiennes 121. Paris: Éditions du Cerf.

Lemcio, Eugene E. 1991. *The Past of Jesus in the Gospels*. Cambridge: Cambridge University Press.

Leonard, James M. 2014. *Codex Schøyen 2650: A Middle Egyptian Coptic Witness to the Early Greek Text of Matthew's Gospel; A Study in Translation Theory, Indigenous Coptic, and New Testament Textual Criticism*. New Testament Tools, Studies, and Documents 46. Boston: Brill.

Levin, Yigal. 2006. "Jesus, 'Son of God' and 'Son of David': The 'Adoption' of Jesus into the Davidic Line." *Journal for the Study of the New Testament* 28(4):415–42.

Lieu, Judith M. 2015. *Marcion and the Making of a Heretic: God and Scripture in the Second Century*. New York: Cambridge University Press.

Lindemann, Andreas. 2011. "Zur frühchristlichen Taufpraxis: Die Taufe in der Didache, bei Justin und in der Didaskalia." In *Ablution, Initiation, and Baptism: Late Antiquity, Early Judaism, and Early Christianity = Waschungen, Initiation und Taufe: Spätantike, frühes Judentum und frühes Christentum*, edited by D. Hellholm, 767–815. Beihefte zur Zeitschrift für die neutestamentliche Wissenschaft 176. Berlin: de Gruyter.

Logan, Alastair H. B. 2006. *The Gnostics: Identifying an Early Christian Cult*. London: T&T Clark.

Löhr, Winrich A. 1996. *Basilides und seine Schule: Eine Studie zur Theologie und Kirchengeschichte des zweiten Jahrhunderts*. Wissenschaftliche Untersuchungen zum Neuen Testament 83. Tübingen: Mohr Siebeck.

———. 2003. "Valentinian Variations on Lk 12,8–9/Mt 10,32." *Vigiliae Christianae* 57:437–55.

Lüdemann, Gerd. 2006. *Das Judas-Evangelium und das Evangelium nach Maria: Zwei gnostische Schriften aus der Frühzeit des Christentums*. Stuttgart: Radius.

Lührmann, Dieter. 1981. "POx 2949: EvPt 3–5 in einer Handschrift des 2./3. Jahrhunderts." *Zeitschrift für die neutestamentliche Wissenschaft* 72:216–26.

———. 1993. "POx 4009: Ein neues Fragment des Petrusevangeliums?" *Novum Testamentum* 35:390–410.

———. 2004. *Die apokryph gewordenen Evangelien: Studien zu neuen Texten und zu neuen Fragen*. Supplements to Novum Testamentum 112. Leiden: Brill.

———. 2005. "Das Petrusbildnis van Haelst 741: Eine Replik." *Zeitschrift für antikes Christentum* 9:424–34.

———. 2006. "Kann es wirklich keine frühe Handschrift des Petrusevangeliums geben? Corrigenda zu einem Aufsatz von Paul Foster." *Novum Testamentum* 48:379–83.

———. 2007. "Die Überlieferung des apokryph gewordenen Petrusevangeliums." In *Das Evangelium nach Petrus: Text, Kontexte, Intertexte*, edited by T. J. Kraus and T. Nicklas, 31–51. Texte und Untersuchungen 158. Berlin: Walter de Gruyter.

Lührmann, Dieter, and P. J. Parsons. 1994. "4009. Gospel of Peter?" In *The Oxyrhynchus Papyri* 60, edited by R. A. Coles et al., 1–5. London: British Academy/Egypt Exploration Society.

Lührmann, Dieter, and Egbert Schlarb, eds. 2000. *Fragmente apokryph gewordener Evangelien in griechischer und lateinischer Sprache*. Marburger theologische Studien 59. Marburg: Elwert.

Luijendijk, AnneMarie. 2010. "Sacred Scriptures as Trash: Biblical Papyri from Oxyrhynchus." *Vigiliae Christianae* 64:217–54.

———. 2011. "Reading the Gospel of Thomas in the Third Century: Three Oxyrhynchus Papyri and Origen's Homilies." In *Reading New Testament Papyri in Context: Lire les papyrus du Nouveau Testament dans leur contexte*, edited by C. Clivaz and J. Zumstein, 241–67. Leuven: Peeters.

———. 2014. *Forbidden Oracles? The Gospel of the Lots of Mary*. Studien und Texte zu Antike und Christentum 89. Tübingen: Mohr Siebeck.

Luomanen, Petri. 2012. *Recovering Jewish-Christian Sects and Gospels*. Vigiliae Christianae Supplements 110. Leiden: Brill.

Luther, Martin. 1883–2009. *D. Martin Luthers Werke: Kritische Gesamtausgabe*. 120 vols. Weimar: H. Böhlau.

———. 1955–86. *Luther's Works*. Edited by J. Pelikan et al. 55 vols. American ed. St. Louis: Concordia.

Luttikhuizen, Gerard P. 1985. *The Revelation of Elchasai: Investigations into the Evidence for a Mesopotamian Jewish Apocalypse of the Second Century and Its Reception by Judeo-Christian Propagandists*. Texte and Studien zum antiken Judentum 8. Tübingen: Mohr Siebeck.

———. 2006. *Gnostic Revisions of Genesis Stories and Early Jesus Traditions*. Nag Hammadi and Manichaean Studies 58. Leiden: Brill.

————. 2008. "Elchasaites and Their Book." In *A Companion to Second-Century Christian "Heretics,"* edited by A. Marjanen and P. Luomanen, 335–64. Supplements to Vigiliae Christianae 76. Leiden: Brill.

Marjanen, Antti. 1998. "Is Thomas a Gnostic Gospel?" In *Thomas at the Crossroads: Essays on the Gospel of Thomas,* edited by R. Uro, 107–39. Studies of the New Testament and Its World. Edinburgh: T&T Clark.

————, ed. 2005. *Was There a Gnostic Religion?* Helsinki: Finnish Exegetical Society.

————. 2008. "Gnosticism." In *The Oxford Handbook of Early Christian Studies,* edited by S. A. Harvey and D. G. Hunter, 203–20. Oxford: Oxford University Press.

Markschies, Christoph. 1992. *Valentinus Gnosticus? Untersuchungen zur valentinianischen Gnosis mit einem Kommentar zu den Fragmenten Valentins.* Wissenschaftliche Untersuchungen zum Neuen Testament 65. Tübingen: Mohr Siebeck.

————. 1998. "'Neutestamentliche Apokryphen': Bemerkungen zu Geschichte und Zukunft einer von Edgar Hennecke im Jahr 1904 begründeten Quellensammlung." *Apocrypha* 9:97–132.

————. 2002. "Lehrer, Schüler, Schule: Zur Bedeutung einer Institution für das frühe Christentum." In *Religiöse Vereine in der römischen Antike: Untersuchungen zu Organisation, Ritual und Raumordnung,* edited by U. Egelhaaf-Gaiser et al., 97–120. Studien und Texte zu Antike und Christentum 13. Tübingen: Mohr Siebeck.

————. 2003. *Gnosis: An Introduction.* London: T&T Clark.

————. 2012a. "B.V. Erzählende Evangelien." In *Antike christliche Apokryphen in deutscher Übersetzung,* 1.1–2, *Evangelien und Verwandtes,* edited by C. Markschies and J. Schröter, 558–59. Tübingen: Mohr Siebeck.

————. 2012b. "B.II.3 Die 'Geburt Mariens.'" In *Antike christliche Apokryphen in deutscher Übersetzung,* 1.1–2, *Evangelien und Verwandtes,* edited by C. Markschies and J. Schröter, 416–19. Tübingen: Mohr Siebeck.

————. 2012c. "B.III. Nachrichten über außerkanonische Evangelien." In *Antike christliche Apokryphen in deutscher Übersetzung,* 1.1–2, *Evangelien und Verwandtes,* edited by C. Markschies and J. Schröter, 429–79. Tübingen: Mohr Siebeck.

———. 2012d. "B.V.2 Das Evangelium nach den Ägyptern." In *Antike christliche Apokryphen in deutscher Übersetzung*, 1.1–2, *Evangelien und Verwandtes*, edited by C. Markschies and J. Schröter, 661–82. Tübingen: Mohr Siebeck.

———. 2012e. "B.V.4.1 Die Fragen des Bartholomaeus." In *Antike christliche Apokryphen in deutscher Übersetzung*, 1.1–2, *Evangelien und Verwandtes*, edited by C. Markschies and J. Schröter, 702–850. Tübingen: Mohr Siebeck.

———. 2012f. "B.VII. Evangelienmeditationen." In *Antike christliche Apokryphen in deutscher Übersetzung*, 1.1–2, *Evangelien und Verwandtes*, edited by C. Markschies and J. Schröter, 1239–41. Tübingen: Mohr Siebeck.

———. 2012g. "Haupteinleitung." In *Antike christliche Apokryphen in deutscher Übersetzung*, 1.1–2, *Evangelien und Verwandtes*, edited by C. Markschies and J. Schröter, 1–183. Tübingen: Mohr Siebeck.

———. 2013. "Apokryphen als Zeugnisse mehrheitskirchlicher Frömmigkeit: Das Beispiel des Bartholomaeus-Evangeliums." In *The Apocryphal Gospels within the Context of Early Christian Theology*, edited by J. Schröter, 333–55. Bibliotheca Ephemeridum theologicarum Lovaniensium 260. Leuven: Peeters.

———. 2015. *Christian Theology and Its Institutions in the Early Roman Empire: Prolegomena to a History of Early Christian Theology*. Translated by W. Coppins. Baylor-Mohr Siebeck Studies in Early Christianity. Waco, TX: Baylor University Press.

Markschies, Christoph, and Jens Schröter, eds. 2012. *Antike christliche Apokryphen in deutscher Übersetzung*. With the assistance of Andreas Heiser. 2 vols. Vol. 1.1–2, *Evangelien und Verwandtes*. Tübingen: Mohr Siebeck.

McCarthy, Carmel, ed. 1993. *Saint Ephrem's Commentary on Tatian's Diatessaron: An English translation of Chester Beatty Syriac MS 709*. Journal of Semitic Studies Supplement 2. Oxford: Oxford University Press.

McFarland, Ian A. 2005. "'Naturally and by Grace': Maximus the Confessor on the Operation of the Will." *Scottish Journal of Theology* 58:410–33.

McGuire, Anne. 2010. "Gnosis and Nag Hammadi." In *The Routledge Companion to Early Christian Thought*, edited by D. J. Bingham, 204–26. London: Routledge.

Meiser, Martin. 2007. "Das Petrusevangelium und die spätere grosskirchliche Literatur." In *Das Evangelium nach Petrus: Text, Kontexte, Intertexte*, edited by T. J. Kraus and T. Nicklas, 183–96. Texte und Untersuchungen zur Geschichte der altchristlichen Literatur 158. Berlin: Walter de Gruyter.

Merkel, Helmut. 2012. "B.I.11 Das geheime Markusevangelium." In *Antike christliche Apokryphen in deutscher Übersetzung*, 1.1–2, *Evangelien und Verwandtes*, edited by C. Markschies and J. Schröter, 390–99. Tübingen: Mohr Siebeck.

Metzger, Bruce Manning. 1997. *The Canon of the New Testament: Its Origin, Development, and Significance*. Oxford: Clarendon Press.

Meyer, Marvin W. 1992. *The Gospel of Thomas: The Hidden Sayings of Jesus*. San Francisco: HarperSanFrancisco.

———, ed. 2007. *The Nag Hammadi Scriptures: The International Edition*. New York: HarperOne.

———. 2013. "The Young Streaker in Secret and Canonical Mark." In *Ancient Gospel or Modern Forgery? The Secret Gospel of Mark in Debate: Proceedings from the 2011 York University Christian Apocrypha Symposium*, edited by T. Burke, 145–56. Eugene, OR: Cascade Books.

Meyer, Marvin W., and Richard Smith. 1994. *Ancient Christian Magic: Coptic Texts of Ritual Power*. San Francisco: HarperSanFrancisco.

Migne, J.-P., ed. 1857–86. *Patrologiae Cursus Completus: Series Graeca*. 162 vols. Paris: Migne.

Miller, Robert J., ed. 1994. *The Complete Gospels: Annotated Scholars Version*. Rev. and expanded ed. San Francisco: HarperSanFrancisco.

Miller, Ron. 2003. *Wisdom of the Carpenter: 365 Prayers & Meditations of Jesus from the Gospel of Thomas, Lost Gospel Q, Secret Book of James, and the New Testament*. Berkeley, CA: Seastone.

———. 2004. *The Gospel of Thomas: A Guidebook for Spiritual Practice*. Woodstock, VT: SkyLight Paths Publishing.

Mirkovic, Alexander. 2004. *Prelude to Constantine: The Abgar Tradition in Early Christianity*. Arbeiten zur Religion und Geschichte des Urchristentums 15. Frankfurt: Lang.

Molinari, Andrea Lorenzo. 2000. *I Never Knew the Man: The Coptic Act of Peter (Papyrus Berolinensis 8502.4); Its Independence from the Apocryphal Acts of Peter, Genre and Legendary Origins*. Bibliothèque copte de Nag Hammadi. Section "Etudes" 5. Quebec: Presses de l'Université Laval.

Moll, Sebastian. 2010. *The Arch-Heretic Marcion*. Wissenschaftliche Untersuchungen zum Neuen Testament 250. Tübingen: Mohr Siebeck.

Morrice, William G. 1997. *Hidden Sayings of Jesus: Words Attributed to Jesus outside the Four Gospels*. London: SPCK.

Müller, C. Detlef G. 2012. "B.VI.2. *Die Epistula Apostolorum.*" In *Antike christliche Apokryphen in deutscher Übersetzung*, 1.1–2, *Evangelien und Verwandtes*, edited by C. Markschies and J. Schröter, 1062–92. Tübingen: Mohr Siebeck.

Murcia, Thierry. 2014. *Jésus dans le Talmud et la littérature rabbinique ancienne*. Turnhout: Brepols.

Myllykoski, Matti. 2008. "Cerinthus." In *A Companion to Second-Century Christian "Heretics,"* edited by A. Marjanen and P. Luomanen, 213–46. Supplements to Vigiliae Christianae 76. Leiden: Brill.

———. 2009a. "The Sinful Woman in the Gospel of Peter: Reconstructing the Other Side of P.Oxy. 4009." *New Testament Studies* 55:104–15.

———. 2009b. "Tears of Repentance or Tears of Gratitude? P.Oxy. 4009, the Gospel of Peter and the Western Text of Luke 7.45–49." *New Testament Studies* 55:380–89.

Nagel, Peter. 2003. "'Gespräche Jesu mit seinen Jüngern vor der Auferstehung': Zur Herkunft und Datierung des 'Unbekannten Berliner Evangeliums.'" *Zeitschrift für die neutestamentliche Wissenschaft* 94:215–57.

———. 2014. *Codex apocryphus gnosticus Novi Testamenti*. Vol. 1, *Evangelien und Apostelgeschichten aus den Schriften von Nag Hammadi und verwandten Kodizes. Koptisch und deutsch*. Wissenschaftliche Untersuchungen zum Neuen Testament 326. Tübingen: Mohr Siebeck.

Najman, Hindy. 2003. *Seconding Sinai: The Development of Mosaic Discourse in Second Temple Judaism*. Supplements to the Journal for the Study of Judaism 77. Leiden: Brill.

———. 2010. *Past Renewals: Interpretative Authority, Renewed Revelation, and the Quest for Perfection in Jewish Antiquity*. Supplements to the Journal for the Study of Judaism 53. Leiden: Brill.

————. 2012. "The Vitality of Scripture within and beyond the 'Canon.'" *Journal for the Study of Judaism* 43:497–518.

Neirynck, Frans. 2001. *Q-Parallels: Q-Synopsis and IQP/CritEd Parallels*. Leuven: Peeters.

Nestle, Eberhard, Erwin Nestle, Barbara Aland, Kurt Aland, et al., eds. 2012. *Novum Testamentum Graece*. 28th ed. Stuttgart: Deutsche Bibelgesellschaft.

Nicklas, Tobias. 2001. "Die 'Juden' im Petrusevangelium (PCair 10759): Ein Testfall." *New Testament Studies* 47:206–21.

————. 2005. "Zwei petrinische Apokryphen im Akhmim-Codex oder eines? Kritische Anmerkungen und Gedanken." *Apocrypha* 16:75–96.

————. 2009. "The 'Unknown Gospel' on *Papyrus Egerton 2* (+*Papyrus Cologne* 255)." In *Gospel Fragments*, edited by T. J. Kraus et al., 9–120. Oxford Early Christian Gospel Texts. Oxford: Oxford University Press.

————. 2010. "Das Petrusevangelium in Rahmen antiker Jesustraditionen." In *Jesus in apokryphen Evangelienüberlieferungen: Beiträge zu außerkanonischen Jesusüberlieferungen aus verschiedenen Sprach- und Kulturtraditionen*, edited by J. Frey and J. Schröter, 223–52. Wissenschaftliche Untersuchungen zum Neuen Testament 254. Tübingen: Mohr Siebeck.

————. 2011. "'Apokryph Gewordene Schriften'? Gedanken zum Apokryphenbegriff bei Grosskirchlichen Autoren und in einigen 'Gnostischen' Texten." In *"In Search of Truth": Augustine, Manichaeism and Other Gnosticism; Studies for Johannes van Oort at Sixty*, edited by J. A. van der Berg et al., 547–65. Leiden: Brill.

————. 2012a. "B.I.7 PSI XI 1200bis." In *Antike christliche Apokryphen in deutscher Übersetzung*, 1.1–2, *Evangelien und Verwandtes*, edited by C. Markschies and J. Schröter, 379. Tübingen: Mohr Siebeck.

————. 2012b. "The Development of the Christian Bible." In *What Is Bible?*, edited by K. Finsterbusch and A. Lange, 393–426. Contributions to Biblical Exegesis and Theology 67. Leuven: Peeters.

————. 2012c. "Eine neue alte Erzählung im Rahmen antiker Jesustraditionen: Reste eines Exorzismus auf P.Oxy. lxxvi 5072." *Annali di Storia dell'Esegesi* 29:13–27.

———. 2013. "'Werde rein . . . und sündige nicht mehr!' Die Heilung eines Aussätzigen (P.Egerton 2 + P. Köln 255)." In *Kompendium der frühchristlichen Wundererzählungen*, edited by R. Zimmermann, 1:869–72. Gütersloh: Gütersloher Verlagshaus.

———. 2014a. "Christian Apocrypha and the Development of the Christian Canon." *Early Christianity* 5:220–40.

———. 2014b. "Das 'Unbekannte Evangelium' auf P. Egerton 2 und die 'Schrift.'" In *Christian Apocrypha: Receptions of the New Testament in Ancient Christian Apocrypha*, edited by J.-M. Roessli and T. Nicklas, 7–26. Novum Testamentum Patristicum 26. Göttingen: Vandenhoeck & Ruprecht.

———. 2014c. *Jews and Christians? Second-Century "Christian" Perspectives on the "Parting of the Ways" (Annual Deichmann Lectures 2013)*. Tübingen: Mohr Siebeck.

———. Forthcoming. *Das Evangelium nach Petrus*. Kommentare zur Apokryphen Literatur. Göttingen: Vandenhoeck & Ruprecht.

Niessen, Friedrich. 2009. "New Testament Translations from the Cairo Genizah." *Collectanea Christiana Orientalia* 6:201–22.

Noy, David. 1998. "Letters out of Judaea: Echoes of Israel in Jewish Inscriptions from Europe." In *Jewish Local Patriotism and Self-Identification in the Graeco-Roman Period*, edited by S. Jones and S. Pearce, 106–17. Journal for the Study of the Pseudepigrapha Supplements 31. Sheffield: Sheffield Academic Press.

Nutzman, Megan. 2013. "Mary in the *Protevangelium of James*: A Jewish Woman in the Temple?" *Greek, Roman, and Byzantine Studies* 53:551–78.

Omerzu, Heike. 2007. "Die Pilatusgestalt im Petrusevangelium: Eine erzählanalytische Annäherung." In *Das Evangelium nach Petrus: Text, Kontexte, Intertexte*, edited by T. J. Kraus and T. Nicklas, 327–47. Texte und Untersuchungen zur Geschichte der altchristlichen Literatur 158. Berlin: Walter de Gruyter.

Ong, Walter J. 1982. *Orality and Literacy: The Technologizing of the Word*. London: Routledge.

Pagels, Elaine H. 1979. *The Gnostic Gospels*. New York: Random House.

———. 2003. *Beyond Belief: The Secret Gospel of Thomas*. New York: Random House.

Pagels, Elaine H., and Karen L. King. 2007. *Reading Judas:* The Gospel of Judas *and the Shaping of Christianity*. London: Allen Lane.

Parker, David C., David G. K. Taylor, and Mark Goodacre. 1999. "The Dura-Europos Gospel Harmony." In *Studies in the Early Text of the Gospels and Acts: The Papers of the First Birmingham Colloquium on the Textual Criticism of the New Testament*, edited by D. G. K. Taylor, 192–228. Atlanta: Society of Biblical Literature.

Parrott, Douglas M. 1991. *Nag Hammadi Codices III,3–4 and V,1 with Papyrus Berolinensis 8502,3 and Oxyrhynchus Papyrus 1081: Eugnostos and the Sophia of Jesus Christ*. Nag Hammadi Studies 27. Leiden: Brill.

Patterson, Stephen J. 1993. *The Gospel of Thomas and Jesus: Thomas Christianity, Social Radicalism, and the Quest of the Historical Jesus*. Sonoma, CA: Polebridge Press.

———. 2013. "The Gospel of Thomas and Christian Beginnings." In *The Gospel of Thomas and Christian Origins: Essays on the Fifth Gospel*, 261–76. Nag Hammadi and Manichaean Studies 84. Leiden: Brill.

Patterson, Stephen J., and James M. Robinson. 1998. *The Fifth Gospel: The Gospel of Thomas Comes of Age*. Harrisburg, PA: Trinity Press International.

Pearson, Birger A. 2007. *Ancient Gnosticism: Traditions and Literature*. Minneapolis: Fortress Press.

———. 2008. "Judas Iscariot among the Gnostics: What the Gospel of Judas Really Says." *Biblical Archaeology Review* 34(3):52–57.

———. 2009. "Judas Iscariot in the *Gospel of Judas*." In *The Codex Judas Papers: Proceedings of the International Congress on the Tchacos Codex Held at Rice University, Houston, Texas, March 13–16, 2008*, edited by A. D. DeConick, 137–52. Nag Hammadi and Manichaean Studies 71. Leiden: Brill.

Pellegrini, Silvia. 2012. "B.V.5.1 Das Protevangelium des Jakobus." In *Antike christliche Apokryphen in deutscher Übersetzung*, 1.1–2, *Evangelien und Verwandtes*, edited by C. Markschies and J. Schröter, 903–29. Tübingen: Mohr Siebeck.

Peppard, Michael. 2012. "Illuminating the Dura-Europos Baptistery: Comparanda for the Female Figures." *Journal of Early Christian Studies* 20:543–74.

278

Perkins, Pheme. 1980. *The Gnostic Dialogue: The Early Church and the Crisis of Gnosticism.* Theological Inquiries. New York: Paulist Press.

Pernigotti, Sergio. 1995. "La Magia Copta: I Testi." *Aufstieg und Niedergang der römischen Welt* II.18.5:3685–730.

Perrin, Nicholas. 2002. *Thomas and Tatian: The Relationship between the Gospel of Thomas and the Diatessaron.* Academia Biblica 5. Atlanta: Society of Biblical Literature.

———. 2007. *Thomas: The Other Gospel.* London: SPCK.

Petersen, Silke, and Hans-Gebhard Bethge. 2012. "B.VI.6. Der Dialog des Erlösers (NHC III,5)." In *Antike christliche Apokryphen in deutscher Übersetzung,* 1.1–2, *Evangelien und Verwandtes,* edited by C. Markschies and J. Schröter, 1137–51. Tübingen: Mohr Siebeck.

Petersen, William L. 1994. *Tatian's Diatessaron: Its Creation, Dissemination, Significance, and History in Scholarship.* Vigiliae Christianae Supplements 25. Leiden: Brill.

Pilhofer, Peter. 1990. "Justin und das Petrusevangelium." *Zeitschrift für die neutestamentliche Wissenschaft* 81:60–78.

Piovanelli, Pierluigi. 2011. "The Toledot Yeshu and Christian Apocryphal Literature: The Formative Years." In *Toledot Yeshu ("The Life Story of Jesus") Revisited,* edited by P. Schäfer et al., 89–100. Texts and Studies in Ancient Judaism 143. Tübingen: Mohr Siebeck.

———. 2012. "Thursday Night Fever: Dancing and Singing with Jesus in the Gospel of the Savior and the Dance of the Savior around the Cross." *Early Christianity* 3:229–48.

———. 2013. "Halfway between Sabbatai Tzevi and Aleister Crowley: Morton Smith's 'Own Concept of What Jesus "Must" Have Been' and, Once Again, the Question of Evidence and Motive." In *Ancient Gospel or Modern Forgery? The Secret Gospel of Mark in Debate: Proceedings from the 2011 York University Christian Apocrypha Symposium,* edited by T. Burke, 157–83. Eugene, OR: Cascade Books.

Plisch, Uwe-Karsten. 2005. "Zu einigen Einleitungsfragen des Unbekannten Berliner Evangeliums (UBE)." *Zeitschrift für antikes Christentum* 9:64–84.

———. 2008. *The Gospel of Thomas: Original Text with Commentary.* Freiburg: Deutsche Bibelgesellschaft.

———. 2010. "Judasevangelium und Judasgedicht." In *Jesus in apokryphen Evangelienüberlieferungen: Beiträge zu außerkanonischen Jesusüberlieferungen aus verschiedenen Sprach- und Kulturtraditionen*, edited by J. Frey and J. Schröter, 387–96. Wissenschaftliche Untersuchungen zum Neuen Testament 254. Tübingen: Mohr Siebeck.

———. 2012a. "B.VII.2 Das heilige Buch des großen unsichtbaren Geistes (das ägyptische Evangelium) (NHC III,2/IV,2)." In *Antike christliche Apokryphen in deutscher Übersetzung*, 1.1–2, *Evangelien und Verwandtes*, edited by C. Markschies and J. Schröter, 1261–76. Tübingen: Mohr Siebeck.

———. 2012b. "A.I.2. Herrenworte aus Nag Hammadi." In *Antike christliche Apokryphen in deutscher Übersetzung*, 1.1–2, *Evangelien und Verwandtes*, edited by C. Markschies and J. Schröter, 190–92. Tübingen: Mohr Siebeck.

Pokorny, Petr. 2009. *A Commentary on the Gospel of Thomas: From Interpretations to the Interpreted*. Jewish and Christian Texts in Contexts and Related Studies 5. New York: T&T Clark.

Ponder, Ross. 2016. "Papyrus Oxyrhynchus 5072: A New Translation and Introduction." In *New Testament Apocrypha*. Vol. 1, *More Noncanonical Scriptures*, edited by T. Burke and B. Landau. Grand Rapids: Eerdmans.

Popkes, Enno Edzard. 2010. "Das Thomasevangelium als crux interpretum: Die methodischen Ursachen einer diffusen Diskussionslage." In *Jesus in apokryphen Evangelienüberlieferungen: Beiträge zu ausserkanonischen Jesusüberlieferungen aus verschiedenen Sprach- und Kulturtraditionen*, edited by J. Frey and J. Schröter, 271–92. Wissenschaftliche Untersuchungen zum Neuen Testament 254. Tübingen: Mohr Siebeck.

Popkes, Enno Edzard, and Gregor Wurst, eds. 2012. *Judasevangelium und Codex Tchacos: Studien zur religionsgeschichtlichen Verortung einer gnostischen Schriftensammlung*. Wissenschaftliche Untersuchungen zum Neuen Testament 297. Tübingen: Mohr Siebeck.

Porter, Stanley E. 2012. "B.I.2.2 Der Papyrus Berolinensis 11710 (P.Berl. 11710)." In *Antike christliche Apokryphen in deutscher Übersetzung*, 1.1–2, *Evangelien und Verwandtes*, edited by C. Markschies and J. Schröter, 368–69. Tübingen: Mohr Siebeck.

———. 2013. "What Do We Know and How Do We Know It? Reconstructing Early Christianity from Its Manuscripts." In *Christian Origins and Greco-Roman Culture: Social and Literary Contexts for the New Testament*, edited by S. E. Porter and A. W. Pitts, 41–70. Text and Editions for New Testament Study 9. Leiden: Brill.

Porter, Stanley E., and Wendy Porter, eds. 2008. *New Testament Greek Papyri and Parchments: New Editions; Texts*. Mitteilungen aus der Papyrussammlung der Nationalbibliothek in Wien (Papyrus Erzherzog Rainer) NS 29. Berlin: Walter de Gruyter.

Quasten, Johannes. 1950. *Patrology.* 4 vols. Westminster: Newman Press.

Ragg, Lonsdale, et al. 1907. *The Gospel of Barnabas.* Oxford: Clarendon Press.

Ramelli, Ilaria. 2015. "The Addai-Abgar Narrative: Its Development through Literary Genres and Religious Agendas." In *Early Christian and Jewish Narrative: The Role of Religion in Shaping Narrative Forms*, edited by I. Ramelli and J. Perkins, 205–45. Wissenschaftliche Untersuchungen zum Neuen Testament 348. Tübingen: Mohr Siebeck.

Rasimus, Tuomas. 2009. *Paradise Reconsidered in Gnostic Mythmaking: Rethinking Sethianism in Light of the Ophite Evidence.* Nag Hammadi and Manichaean Studies 68. Leiden: Brill.

———, ed. 2010. *The Legacy of John: Second-Century Reception of the Fourth Gospel.* Supplements to Novum Testamentum 132. Leiden: Brill.

Rau, Eckhard. 2010a. "Das Geheimnis des Reiches Gottes: Die esoterische Rezeption der Lehre Jesu im geheimen Markusevangelium." In *Jesus in apokryphen Evangelienüberlieferungen: Beiträge zu außerkanonischen Jesusüberlieferungen aus verschiedenen Sprach- und Kulturtraditionen*, edited by J. Frey and J. Schröter, 187–221. Wissenschaftliche Untersuchungen zum Neuen Testament 254. Tübingen: Mohr Siebeck.

———. 2010b. "Weder gefälscht noch authentisch? Überlegungen zum Status des geheimen Markusevangeliums als Quelle des antiken Christentums." In *Jesus in apokryphen Evangelienüberlieferungen: Beiträge zu außerkanonischen Jesusüberlieferungen aus verschiedenen Sprach- und Kulturtraditionen*, edited by J. Frey and J. Schröter, 139–86. Wissenschaftliche

Untersuchungen zum Neuen Testament 254. Tübingen: Mohr Siebeck.

Reed, Annette Yoshiko. 2015. "The Afterlives of New Testament Apocrypha." *Journal of Biblical Literature* 134:401–25.

Reeves, John C. 1999. "Exploring the Afterlife of Jewish Pseude-pigrapha in Medieval Near Eastern Religious Traditions: Some Initial Soundings." *Journal for the Study of Judaism in the Persian, Hellenistic and Roman Period* 30:148–77.

Ritter, Adolf Martin. 2012. Review of *The Arch-Heretic Marcion*, by Sebastian Moll. *Theologische Literaturzeitung* 137:309–11.

Robbins, Vernon K. 2013. *Who Do People Say I Am? Rewriting Gospel in Emerging Christianity*. Grand Rapids: Eerdmans.

Robinson, James M., ed. 2000. *The Coptic Gnostic Library: A Complete Edition of the Nag Hammadi Codices*. 5 vols. Leiden: Brill.

———. 2006. *The International Q Project*. http://iac.cgu.edu /research/qproject.html.

Robinson, James M., Paul Hoffmann, and John S. Kloppenborg, eds. 2000. *The Critical Edition of Q*. The International Q Project/Hermeneia. Minneapolis: Fortress.

Roche, Paul, ed. 2005. *Aristophanes: The Complete Plays*. New York: New American Library.

Ross, Hugh McGregor. 1998. *Jesus Untouched by the Church: His Teaching in the Gospel of Thomas*. York: Sessions.

———. 2010. *Spirituality in the Gospel of Thomas*. N.p.: Authors Online Ltd.

Roth, Dieter T. 2008. "Marcion's Gospel and Luke: The History of Research in Current Debate." *Journal of Biblical Literature* 127:513–27.

———. 2010. "Marcion's Gospel: Relevance, Contested Issues, and Reconstruction." *Expository Times* 121:287–94.

———. 2015. *The Text of Marcion's Gospel*. New Testament Tools, Studies, and Documents 49. Leiden: Brill.

Rowland, Christopher, and Christopher R. A. Morray-Jones. 2009. *The Mystery of God: Early Jewish Mysticism and the New Testament*. Compendia Rerum Iudaicarum ad Novum Testamentum 3:12. Leiden: Brill.

Sabar, Ariel. 2016a. "The Unbelievable Tale of Jesus's Wife." *The Atlantic*, July/August edition. http://www.theatlantic.com /magazine/archive/2016/07/the-unbelievable-tale-of-jesus-wife /485573/.

Sabar, Ariel 2016b. "Karen King Responds to 'The Unbelievable Tale of Jesus's Wife.'" http://www.theatlantic.com/politics/archive/2016/06/karen-king-responds-to-the-unbelievable-tale-of-jesus-wife/487484/.

Sandnes, Karl Olav. 2011. *The Gospel "According to Homer and Virgil": Cento and Canon.* Supplements to Novum Testamentum 138. Leiden: Brill.

Sanzo, Joseph Emanuel. 2014. *Scriptural Incipits on Amulets from Late Antique Egypt: Text, Typology, and Theory.* Studien und Texte zu Antike und Christentum 84. Tübingen: Mohr Siebeck.

Schäfer, Peter. 2007. *Jesus in the Talmud.* Princeton, NJ: Princeton University Press.

———. 2011. *Toledot Yeshu ("The Life Story of Jesus") Revisited: A Princeton Conference.* Texts and Studies in Ancient Judaism 143. Tübingen: Mohr Siebeck.

———. 2012. *The Jewish Jesus: How Judaism and Christianity Shaped Each Other.* Princeton, NJ: Princeton University Press.

Schärl, Monika. 2012a. "A.III.2.1 Die sonstige Pilatusliteratur." In *Antike christliche Apokryphen in deutscher Übersetzung,* 1.1–2, *Evangelien und Verwandtes,* edited by C. Markschies and J. Schröter, 262–79. Tübingen: Mohr Siebeck.

———. 2012b. "A.III.2. Das Nikodemusevangelium, die Pilatusakten und die 'Höllenfahrt Christi.'" In *Antike christliche Apokryphen in deutscher Übersetzung,* 1.1–2, *Evangelien und Verwandtes,* edited by C. Markschies and J. Schröter, 231–61. Tübingen: Mohr Siebeck.

Scheck, Thomas P., ed. 2008. *St. Jerome: Commentary on Matthew.* Fathers of the Church 117. Washington, DC: Catholic University of America Press.

Schenke, Hans-Martin, ed. 2001. *Coptic Papyri.* Vol. 1, *Das Matthäus-Evangelium im mittelägyptischen Dialekt des Koptischen (Codex Schøyen).* Manuscripts in the Schøyen Collection. Oslo: Hermes.

———. 2012a. "B.IV.2 Das Philippusevangelium (NHC II,3)." In *Antike christliche Apokryphen in deutscher Übersetzung,* 1.1–2, *Evangelien und Verwandtes,* edited by C. Markschies and J. Schröter, 527–57. Tübingen: Mohr Siebeck.

———. 2012b. "B.V.4.2 Die koptischen Bartholomaeustexte: 'Das Buch der Auferstehung Jesu Christi, unseres Herrn.'" In *Antike christliche Apokryphen in deutscher Übersetzung,*

1.1–2, *Evangelien und Verwandtes*, edited by C. Markschies and J. Schröter, 851–85. Tübingen: Mohr Siebeck.

———. 2012c. "B.VII.3 Das Unbekannte Berliner Evangelium, auch 'Evangelium des Erlösers' genannt." In *Antike christliche Apokryphen in deutscher Übersetzung*, 1.1–2, *Evangelien und Verwandtes*, edited by C. Markschies and J. Schröter, 1277–89. Tübingen: Mohr Siebeck.

———. 2012d. "B.VII.6 Das Gamalielevangelium." In *Antike christliche Apokryphen in deutscher Übersetzung*, 1.1–2, *Evangelien und Verwandtes*, edited by C. Markschies and J. Schröter, 1307–9. Tübingen: Mohr Siebeck.

———. 2012e. "B.VII.6.1 Die koptischen Fragmente des Gamalielevangeliums." In *Antike christliche Apokryphen in deutscher Übersetzung*, 1.1–2, *Evangelien und Verwandtes*, edited by C. Markschies and J. Schröter, 1310–13. Tübingen: Mohr Siebeck.

Schenke Robinson, Gesine. 2011. "An Update on the *Gospel of Judas* (after Additional Fragments Resurfaced)." *Zeitschrift für die neutestamentliche Wissenschaft* 102:110–29.

———. 2015. "How a Papyrus Fragment Became a Sensation." *New Testament Studies* 61:379–94.

Schirrmacher, Christine. 1992. *Mit den Waffen des Gegners: Christlich-muslimische Kontroversen im 19. und 20. Jahrhundert, dargestellt am Beispiel der Auseinandersetzung um Karl Gottlieb Pfanders 'Mîzân al-ḥaqq' und Raḥmatullâh ibn H̲alîl al-'Utmânî al-Kairânawîs 'Izhâr al-ḥaqq' und der Diskussion über das Barnabasevangelium*. Islamkundliche Untersuchungen 162. Berlin: Schwarz Verlag.

Schlichting, Günter. 1982. *Ein jüdisches Leben Jesu: Die verschollene Toledot-Jeschu-Fassung Tam û-mû'âd*. Wissenschaftliche Untersuchungen zum Neuen Testament 24. Tübingen: Mohr (Siebeck).

Schmid, Herbert. 2010. "Zur Funktion der Jesusüberlieferung im so genannten Philippusevangelium." In *Jesus in apokryphen Evangelienüberlieferungen: Beiträge zu außerkanonischen Jesusüberlieferungen aus verschiedenen Sprach- und Kulturtraditionen*, edited by J. Frey and J. Schröter, 293–314. Wissenschaftliche Untersuchungen zum Neuen Testament 254. Tübingen: Mohr Siebeck.

Schmidt, Carl, and Violet MacDermot. 1978. *Pistis Sophia*. Nag Hammadi Studies 9. Leiden: Brill.

Schmidt, Carl, and Isaak Wajnberg. 1919. *Gespräche Jesu mit seinen Jüngern nach der Auferstehung: Ein katholisch-apostolisches Sendschreiben des 2. Jahrhunderts*. Texte und Untersuchungen zur Geschichte der altchristlichen Literatur 42 (3:13). Leipzig: J. C. Hinrichs.

Schneemelcher, Wilhelm, ed. 1991–92. *New Testament Apocrypha*. Translated by R. M. Wilson. 2 vols. Rev. ed. Louisville, KY: Westminster/John Knox Press.

Schröter, Jens. 2012. "B.IV.1. Das Evangelium nach Thomas." In *Antike christliche Apokryphen in deutscher Übersetzung*, 1.1–2, *Evangelien und Verwandtes*, edited by C. Markschies and J. Schröter, 483–526. Tübingen: Mohr Siebeck.

———. 2013a. "Die apokryphen Evangelien im Kontext der frühchristlichen Theologiegeschichte." In *The Apocryphal Gospels within the Context of Early Christian Theology*, edited by J. Schröter, 19–66. Bibliotheca Ephemeridum theologicarum Lovaniensium 260. Leuven: Peeters.

———. 2013b. *From Jesus to the New Testament: Early Christian Theology and the Origin of the New Testament Canon*. Translated by W. Coppins. Baylor-Mohr Siebeck Studies in Early Christianity. Waco, TX: Baylor University Press.

Schwartz, Daniel R. 1986. "Viewing the Holy Utensils (= P. Ox. V, 840)." *New Testament Studies* 32:153–59.

Scopello, Madeleine. 2007a. "The Dialogue of the Savior: NHC III,5." In *The Nag Hammadi Scriptures: The International Edition*, edited by M. Meyer, 297–311. New York: HarperCollins.

———. 2007b. "Eugnostos the Blessed: NHC III,3; V,1." In *The Nag Hammadi Scriptures: The International Edition*, edited by M. Meyer, 271–82. New York: HarperCollins.

———. 2007c. "The Secret Book of James: NHC I,2." In *The Nag Hammadi Scriptures: The International Edition*, edited by M. Meyer, 19–30. New York: HarperCollins.

———. 2007d. "The Wisdom of Jesus Christ: NHC III,4; BG 8502,3; P. Oxy. 1081." In *The Nag Hammadi Scriptures: The International Edition*, edited by M. Meyer, 283–96. New York: HarperCollins.

———, ed. 2008. *The Gospel of Judas in Context: Proceedings of the First International Conference on the Gospel of Judas, Paris, Sorbonne, October 27–28, 2006*. Nag Hammadi and Manichaean Studies 62. Leiden: Brill.

———. 2013. "The Temptation of Allogenes (Codex Tchacos, Tractate IV)." In *Gnosticism, Platonism and the Late Ancient World: Essays in Honour of John D. Turner*, edited by K. Corrigan and T. Rasimus, 117–37. Nag Hammadi and Manichaean Studies 82. Leiden: Brill.

Shoemaker, Stephen J. 1999. " 'Let Us Go and Burn Her Body': The Image of the Jews in the Early Dormition Traditions." *Church History* 68:775–823.

———. 2010. "Apocrypha and Liturgy in the Fourth Century: The Case of the 'Six Books' Dormition Apocryphon." In *Jewish and Christian Scriptures: The Function of "Canonical" and "Non-Canonical" Religious Texts*, edited by J. H. Charlesworth and L. M. McDonald, 153–63. New York: Continuum.

———. 2015. "Mary in Early Christian Apocrypha: Virgin Territory." In *Rediscovering the Apocryphal Continent: New Perspectives on Early Christian and Late Antique Apocryphal Texts and Traditions*, edited by P. Piovanelli and T. Burke, 175–90. Wissenschaftliche Untersuchungen zum Neuen Testament 349. Tübingen: Mohr Siebeck.

Skarsaune, Oskar, and Reidar Hvalvik, eds. 2007. *Jewish Believers in Jesus: The Early Centuries*. Peabody, MA: Hendrickson Publishers.

Skeat, T. C. 1997. "The Oldest Manuscript of the Four Gospels?" *New Testament Studies* 43:1–34.

Skinner, Christopher W. 2012. *What Are They Saying about the Gospel of Thomas?* New York: Paulist Press.

Smith, Morton. 1973a. *Clement of Alexandria and a Secret Gospel of Mark*. Cambridge, MA: Harvard University Press.

———. 1973b. *The Secret Gospel: The Discovery and Interpretation of the Secret Gospel according to Mark*. New York: Harper & Row.

Stanton, Graham N. 1974. *Jesus of Nazareth in New Testament Preaching*. Society for New Testament Studies Monograph Series 27. London: Cambridge University Press.

———. 2004. "The Fourfold Gospel." In *Jesus and Gospel*, 63–91. Cambridge: Cambridge University Press.

————. 2013. *Studies in Matthew and Early Christianity*. Edited by M. Bockmuehl and D. Lincicum. Wissenschaftliche Untersuchungen zum Neuen Testament 309. Tübingen: Mohr Siebeck.

Stewart-Sykes, Alistair. 2006. *The Apostolic Church Order: The Greek Text with Introduction, Translation and Annotation*. Early Christian Studies 10. Strathfield, NSW: St. Pauls Publications.

————. 2009. "Bathed in Living Waters: Papyrus Oxyrhynchus 840 and Christian Baptism Reconsidered." *Zeitschrift für die neutestamentliche Wissenschaft* 100:278–86.

Streeter, B. H. 1924. *The Four Gospels: A Study of Origins, Treating of the Manuscript Tradition, Sources, Authorship, & Dates*. London: Macmillan.

Stroker, William D. 1989. *Extracanonical Sayings of Jesus*. Resources for Biblical Study 18. Atlanta: Scholars Press.

Stroumsa, Guy G. 2009. *The End of Sacrifice: Religious Transformations in Late Antiquity*. Chicago: University of Chicago Press.

Strycker, Émile de. 1961. *La forme la plus ancienne du Protévangile de Jacques*. Subsidia Hagiographica 33. Brussels: Société des Bollandistes.

————. 1980. "Die griechischen Handschriften des Protevangeliums Iacobi." In *Griechische Kodikologie und Textüberlieferung*, edited by D. Harlfinger, 577–612. Darmstadt: Wissenschaftliche Buchgesellschaft.

Stuhlmacher, Peter. 1968. *Das paulinische Evangelium. I. Vorgeschichte*. Forschungen zur Religion und Literatur des Alten und Neuen Testaments 95. Göttingen: Vandenhoeck & Ruprecht.

Swartz, Michael D. 2006. "Mystical Texts." In *The Literature of the Sages, Second Part: Midrash and Targum, Liturgy, Poetry, Mysticism, Contracts, Inscriptions, Ancient Science and the Languages of Rabbinic Literature*, edited by S. Safrai et al., 393–420. Compendia Rerum Iudaicarum ad Novum Testamentum 2:3b. Assen: Van Gorcum.

Taussig, Hal. 2013. *A New New Testament: A Bible for the Twenty-First Century, Combining Traditional and Newly Discovered Texts*. Boston: Houghton Mifflin Harcourt.

Terian, Abraham. 2008. *The Armenian Gospel of the Infancy: With Three Early Versions of the Protevangelium of James*. Oxford: Oxford University Press.

287

Thomassen, Einar. 1997. "How Valentinian Is the *Gospel of Philip?*" In *The Nag Hammadi Library after 50 Years: Proceedings of the 1995 Society of Biblical Literature Commemoration*, edited by J. D. Turner and A. McGuire, 251–79. Nag Hammadi and Manichaean Studies 44. Leiden: Brill.

———. 2006. *The Spiritual Seed: The Church of the "Valentinians."* Nag Hammadi and Manichaean Studies 60. Leiden: Brill.

Tite, Philip L. 2009. *Valentinian Ethics and Paraenetic Discourse: Determining the Social Function of Moral Exhortation in Valentinian Christianity*. Nag Hammadi and Manichaean Studies 67. Leiden/Boston: Brill.

Tomson, Peter J. 2001. "'Jews' in the Gospel of John as Compared with the Palestinian Talmud, the Synoptics, and Some New Testament Apocrypha." In *Anti-Judaism and the Fourth Gospel*, edited by R. Bieringer et al., 176–212. Louisville, KY: Westminster John Knox Press.

Torallas Tovar, Sofía, and Klaas A. Worp, eds. 2014. *Greek Papyri from Montserrat (P.Monts.Roca IV)*. Scripta Orientalia 1. Barcelona: Publicacions de l'Abadia de Montserrat.

Tov, Emanuel. 2003. "The Corpus of the Qumran Papyri." In *Semitic Papyri in Context: A Climate of Creativity; Papers from a New York University Conference Marking the Retirement of Baruch A. Levine*, edited by L. H. Schiffman, 85–103. Culture and History of the Ancient Near East 14. Leiden: Brill.

Tuckett, Christopher. 1988. "Thomas and the Synoptics." *Novum Testamentum* 30:132–57.

———. 2002. "Q and the Historical Jesus." In *Der historische Jesus: Tendenzen und Perspektiven der gegenwärtigen Forschung*, edited by J. Schröter and R. Brucker, 213–41. Berlin: Walter de Gruyter.

———. 2005. "Forty Other Gospels." In *The Written Gospel*, edited by M. Bockmuehl and D. A. Hagner, 238–53. Cambridge: Cambridge University Press.

———. 2007. *The Gospel of Mary*. Oxford Early Christian Gospel Texts. Oxford: Oxford University Press.

———. 2014. "Thomas and the Synoptics." In *From the Sayings to the Gospels*, 359–82. Wissenschaftliche Untersuchungen zum Neuen Testament 328. Tübingen: Mohr Siebeck.

Turner, C. H. 1913. "The Gospel of Peter." *Journal of Theological Studies* 14:161–87.

———. 1920. *The Study of the New Testament, 1883 and 1920: An Inaugural Lecture Delivered before the University of Oxford on October 22 and 29, 1920*. Oxford: Clarendon Press.

Turner, John D. 2008. "The Place of the *Gospel of Judas* in Sethian Tradition." In The Gospel of Judas *in Context: Proceedings of the First International Conference on the* Gospel of Judas, edited by M. Scopello, 187–237. Nag Hammadi and Manichaean Studies 62. Leiden: Brill.

Turner, Martha Lee. 1996. *The Gospel according to Philip: The Sources and Coherence of an Early Christian Collection*. Nag Hammadi and Manichaean Studies 38. Leiden: Brill.

Tyson, Joseph B. 2006. *Marcion and Luke-Acts: A Defining Struggle*. Columbia: University of South Carolina Press.

Vinzent, Markus. 2014. *Marcion and the Dating of the Synoptic Gospels*. Studia Patristica Supplements 2. Leuven: Peeters.

Vinzent, Markus, and Tobias Nicklas. 2012. "B.V.3 Das Petrusevangelium." In *Antike christliche Apokryphen in deutscher Übersetzung*, 1.1–2, *Evangelien und Verwandtes*, edited by C. Markschies and J. Schröter, 683–95. Tübingen: Mohr Siebeck.

Viviano, Benedict T. 2013. *What Are They Saying about Q?* Mahwah, NJ: Paulist Press.

Voicu, Sever J. 2011. "Ways to Survival for the Infancy Apocrypha." In *Infancy Gospels: Stories and Identities*, edited by C. Clivaz et al., 401–17. Wissenschaftliche Untersuchungen zum Neuen Testament 281. Tübingen: Mohr Siebeck.

Vuong, Lily C. 2013. *Gender and Purity in the Protevangelium of James*. Wissenschaftliche Untersuchungen zum Neuen Testament 2:358. Tübingen: Mohr Siebeck.

Wasmuth, Jennifer. 2012. "A.III.1. Die Abgarlegende." In *Antike christliche Apokryphen in deutscher Übersetzung*, 1.1–2, *Evangelien und Verwandtes*, edited by C. Markschies and J. Schröter, 222–30. Tübingen: Mohr Siebeck.

Watson, Francis. 2010. "Beyond Suspicion: On the Authorship of the Mar Saba Letter and the Secret Gospel of Mark." *Journal of Theological Studies* 61:128–70.

———. 2012. "The Gospel of Jesus' Wife: How a Fake Gospel-Fragment Was Composed." http://markgoodacre.org/Watson.pdf.

———. 2013. *Gospel Writing: A Canonical Perspective*. Grand Rapids: Eerdmans.

————. 2016. *The Fourfold Gospel: A Theological Reading of the New Testament Portraits of Jesus*. Grand Rapids: Baker Academic.

Weisse, Christian Hermann. 1838. *Die evangelische Geschichte, kritisch und philosophisch bearbeitet*. 2 vols. Leipzig: Breitkopf & Härtel.

Wiedemann, Thomas E. J. 1989. *Adults and Children in the Roman Empire*. New Haven, CT: Yale University Press.

Wilford, John Noble, and Laurie Goodstein. 2006. "'Gospel of Judas' Surfaces after 1,700 Years." *New York Times*, April 6, 2006. http://www.nytimes.com/2006/04/06/science/06cnd-judas.html.

Williams, Margaret H. 2013. *Jews in a Graeco-Roman Environment*. Wissenschaftliche Untersuchungen zum Neuen Testament 312. Tübingen: Mohr Siebeck.

Williams, Michael A. 1996. *Rethinking "Gnosticism": An Argument for Dismantling a Dubious Category*. Princeton, NJ: Princeton University Press.

Wright, N. T. 2013. *Pauline Perspectives: Essays on Paul, 1978–2013*. London: SPCK.

Wucherpfennig, Ansgar. 2002. *Heracleon Philologus: Gnostische Johannesexegese im zweiten Jahrhundert*. Wissenschaftliche Untersuchungen zum Neuen Testament 142. Tübingen: Mohr Siebeck.

————. 2012. "B.I.8 Der Straßburger koptische Papyrus (P.Argent. Copt. 5, 6 und 7)." In *Antike christliche Apokryphen in deutscher Übersetzung*, 1.1–2, *Evangelien und Verwandtes*, edited by C. Markschies and J. Schröter, 380–84. Tübingen: Mohr Siebeck.

Wurst, Gregor, Herbert Krosney, and Marvin Meyer. 2010. "Preliminary Report on New Fragments of Codex Tchacos." *Early Christianity* 1:282–94.

Wüstenfeld, Ferdinand. 1861. *Geschichte der Stadt Mekka: Nach den arabischen Chroniken bearbeitet*. Leipzig: Brockhaus.

Zelyck, Lorne R. 2013. *John among the Other Gospels: The Reception of the Fourth Gospel in the Extra-Canonical Gospels*. Wissenschaftliche Untersuchungen zum Neuen Testament 2:347. Tübingen: Mohr Siebeck.

————. 2014. "Recontextualizing Papyrus Oxyrhynchus 840." *Early Christianity* 5:179–98.

INDEX OF SCRIPTURE AND OTHER ANCIENT SOURCES

OLD TESTAMENT

Pentateuch 229

Genesis 19
1:1 73
2:22 167

Exodus
23:17 112

Numbers
5:11–28 64

Deuteronomy
29:28 (29:29 in Vulgate and English) 38

1 Samuel
1 59

Job
12:22 38

Psalms
82:6 219
118:22–23 179

Proverbs 99
1:7 38
2:6 38
20:27 38

Song of Songs 218

Isaiah 3
29:13 108
52:7 5
54:1 219
61:1 5
64:3 180

Jeremiah
9:11–16 176
50:3 176

Daniel
7:9–14 142

Amos
3:7 38

NEW TESTAMENT

Synoptic Gospels
7, 47, 90, 102–3, 109, 125, 146, 148, 151, 163, 171–73, 176–77, 180, 195, 241

Matthew 1–2, 5–13, 23, 25–26, 28, 41, 47, 56–58, 60–62, 67, 71, 75, 80, 83–85, 88, 91, 95, 98–101, 107, 111–17, 132, 134, 139, 144, 159, 167, 171–74, 193, 201–2, 225–26, 228–29, 240–41
1:21 60
2:13 80
2:16 57
2:19–21 57
3:13 57
3:15 6
4:23 1
5–28 103–4
5:17 25
5:19 25
5:44 116
6 166
6:9–13 6
7–8 111
7:6 111
7:16–20 115
8:28–34 118
8:29 119
9:35 1
10 101
10:27 40
10:32–33 119
11:13 197
11:25 119
12:6 179
12:33–35 115
15 111
15:7–9 108
15:26–27 111
16:17–19 147
17:1–9 99
17:14–21 119
17:18 119
18:20 167
19:21–23 119
23:16–28 113
23:25–28 111
23:34 119
23:35 81
23:37 119
24:14 1–2, 5
25 219
25:1–14 168
26:13 2, 5
26:30–34 151
26:31 154
26:32 151
26:38 155
26:41 155
26:45 155
27:24 139
27:26–35 145
27:52–53 158
27:55–61 127
27:62–66 139
28 162
28:4 139
28:11–15 139
28:16 99
28:17 142

Mark 1–3, 9, 11–13, 23–26, 30,

Mark (*continued*)		16:12	142	16:10–11	6
40–42, 48, 56, 58,		16:15	5, 40	21:38	44
84, 89, 91, 117,				22:28–30	89
120–21, 128, 139,		**Luke**	1–3, 5–13,	23:13	145
142, 144, 146, 159,			24–26, 41–42,	23:25–26	145
162, 167, 177,			45, 47, 56–58, 60–62,	23:48	146
220, 225–28, 232,			67, 74–75, 80, 83–85,	24	133, 162, 218
235, 241			91, 97, 123–26,	24:16	142
1:1	2, 5		132–34, 144, 171–74,	24:31	142
1:1–2	34		201–2, 218, 225–26,	24:34	146
1:9	56		229, 240–41	24:35	142
1:14	2	1–2	232	24:37–40	142
1:23–28	119	1:1	91	24:39	219
1:25	119	1:3–4	25		
1:27	116	1:26–38	60	**John**	7, 9–11, 13,
1:14–15	1	1:27	64		23–25, 28–29,
1:40–44	107	1:31–35	67		41–42, 56, 58, 84,
2:15–17	116	1:36	80		88, 95, 97, 101,
3	102	1:42	74		107–9, 111, 132–34,
3:27	168	1:46–55	57		155, 177, 189, 195,
4:9	165	1:48–49	67		202, 204, 213, 221,
4:11	121	2:7	70		225–26, 228–29, 233
4:12	40	2:19	57, 133	1:3	95
5:1–20	118	2:25–35	158	1:8	25
5:4	119	2:34–35	78	1:29	115
6:5	12	2:40	57	1:46	56
7:6–7	108	2:41–52	74, 75	1:47	213
8:33	119	2:51	57, 133	1:49	115
8:35	1	2:51–52	57, 220	1:50–51	213
9:2–9	142	2:52	57	2:20–21	176
9:9	40	4:30	107	3:13	181
9:14–29	119	4:33–37	119	3:14	139
9:25	119	4:35	119	4:14	111
9:40	116	6–7	117	4:20–24	176
9:49	45	6:4	45	5:14	107
10:10	14	6:28	116	5:39	107, 179
10:18	12	6:45–46	117	5:45–46	107
10:29	1	7:29–30	117	6:42	56
10:34	120	7:36	117	6:66	25
12:10–11	179	7:36–50	149	7:15	44
12:13–17	108	8:26–39	118	7:30	107
13:10	1–2	8:29	119	7:36	44
14:9	2, 5, 40	9:37–42	119	7:38	111
14:26–30	151	9:42	119	7:42	56
14:28	151	10:7	14	7:44	44
15:15–24	145	10:21	119	7:53–8:11	44, 89,
16:1–8	162	12:8–9	119		97, 100
16:9–20	12, 89, 128,	14:27	165	8:11	107
	162, 220	14:31–32	168	8:19	56

8:41	56	13:12–14	112	**Philemon**
9:29	107	16:25	5	13	5
10:11	154			
10:39	107	**1 Corinthians**		**Hebrews**	42
12:32–33	139	2:9	180		
15:20	155	9:14	5	**James**	42, 96
16:33	155	11:23	56	**1 Peter**	28, 42, 101
17:1	155	11:23–25	2	2:21–25	144
17:11	181	13:11	78	3:19	140, 147,
19:15–18	145	15	6, 188, 197		158, 218
20	162	15:1–6	2	5:1	144, 147
20:30	133	15:5	146		
21	140, 162	15:7	100	**2 Peter**	42, 144
21:2	213	15:3	56	1:16–18	144
21:4	142	15:14–18	25	**1 John**	
21:7	142	15:45–47	193	4:2–3	25
21:12	142				
21:23–24	25	**2 Corinthians**		**2 John**	161
21:25	133, 221	12	203	**3 John**	161
		12:8–9	46		
Acts	2, 5, 9, 26, 28,			**Revelation**	41, 231
	89, 101, 133	**Galatians**	124	1:14	142
1	162	1:18	144	5:8	153
1:3	142, 196, 220	2	124	10:7	6
1:3–11	133	3:27	112	14:6	6
1:13	213, 216	4:26–27	219		
1:23–26	131			**APOCRYPHA**	
1:51	213	**Ephesians**			
4:36	131	2:6	189	**Bel and the Dragon**	
8:39–40	99	4:8	140	**(Septuagint Additions**	
9	218	4:22–24	112	**to Daniel)**	
10:34–43	233	5:32	218	19–20 (Vulgate Daniel	
10:36	2			14:18–19)	219
10:37–41	3, 226	**Colossians**		**Sirach**	28
12:1–23	60	2:12	189	3:22	39
13:1	131	3:1	189	20:30	39
13:32–33	5	3:9–14	112		
10:34–42	6			**Tobit**	
10:38	163	**1 Thessalonians**		12:7	39
14:14	131	2:14–15	145		
15:7	2, 5			**Wisdom**	42
15:22	131	**1 Timothy**			
20:24	2, 5	1:4	18	**PSEUDEPIGRAPHA**	
20:35	45	2:15	203		
		5:14	203	*Apocalypse*	
Letters of Paul	2–3,	5:18	14	*of Ezra*	216
	5–6, 9, 124, 189	6:20	18, 203		
				Aramaic Levi	28
Romans	172, 174	**2 Timothy**		*Ascension*	
10:15–16	5	1:10	2	*of Isaiah*	216
		2:8	2, 5	10:8–11	217
		2:18	188		

2 Baruch
10:18–19   65

Damascus Document
    28

1 Enoch   216
1–27   138

**Joseph and
Asenath**   21

Jubilees   216

**Paralipomena
of Jeremiah**   216

Psalms of Solomon
11:1   5

Sibylline Oracles
4.4–11   176
4.27–30   176

Testament of Levi   28

**JOSEPHUS
AND PHILO**

PHILO

Posterity
134   70

Preliminary Studies
7   70

JOSEPHUS

Antiquities
3.127–28   112

**NONCANONICAL
GOSPEL
LITERATURE**

Abgar Legend   33–34,
    121–23, 132

Acts of Pilate   34,
    156–58, 229

**Anonymous
Apocryphal Gospel**
    37, 105

**First Apocalypse of
James**   36, 162,
    197–98, 205

**Second Apocalypse
of James (=Revelation
of James)**   36, 62, 162

**Apocryphon [Letter]
of James**   18, 29,
    36, 62, 162,
    178–79, 182,
    195–98, 222–23,
234
1.10   195
1.28–32   198
2.7–3.38   196
8.31–36   198
13.38–14.1   198

Apocryphon of John
    29, 182, 184,
    192–93, 199, 207,
    215, 222, 234, 241

Arabic Infancy Gospel
    36, 55, 68, 79,
    81–82, 85
1   72
36   72

Birth of Mary   35, 81

Book of Allogenes
    37, 205

Books of Jeû   37

**Book of the
Resurrection of Jesus
Christ**   36, 214–15

**Book of Thomas [the
Contender]**   18, 36,
    182, 198–99, 234
142.26   199
145.1–18   199

**Christ's Descent to
Hell**   34, 157

Dialogue of the Savior
    18, 36,
    194–95, 211
124–127   194
129–130   194
133–134   194
134–137   195

138   194
144–145   194

Discourse on the Cross
    52, 155–56, 160

**Dormition and
Assumption of Mary**
    35

Epistle of the Apostles
    12–13, 36, 41,
    43, 89, 128, 144,
    153, 162–63, 89,
    195–96, 215–20,
    223, 229
1   216–17
3–12   217
4   73
4–5   217
7   217
12   219
13   217
13–50   217
14   218
21   218
27   218
30   218
31–33   218
33   219
34–40   218
43   219
43–45   218
51   218

**Epistle of James to
Peter** (Nag Hammadi)
    62

**Extract from the Life
of John the Baptist**
    36, 83–84
20   83

**Gospel of the
Arundel Manuscript
(British Library MS
Arundel 404)**   36, 55,
    68, 82

Gospel of Barnabas
    30, 130–31, 134, 226
41   132

44 132

***Gospel of
Bartholomew*** 33, 36,
158, 212–13,
222, 229, 235

***Gospel of the
Ebionites***
36, 92, 96–97,
100–3
frag. 5 102
frag. 6 102

***Gospel according
to the Egyptians***
18, 28, 36, 190,
195, 210–12

The Gospel of Eve 35

Gospel(s) of Gamaliel
37, 105, 158–59

***Gospel according to
the Hebrews*** 28, 92,
95–97, 99–100,
102, 231
frag. 4a/b 99
frag. 7 99

Gospel of Judas
20–21, 26–27,
29, 36–37, 40,
52, 58, 73, 177,
182, 198, 204–9,
221, 223, 227–28,
234, 241
33–34 208
33–44 206
34 209
35 209
36–37 206
37–39 207
39–41 207
41 209
42 207
44 209
44–45 207
46 209
47–52 207
55–56 207

56 207, 209

***Gospel of the Lots
of Mary*** 200

Gospel of Mani 36

Gospel of Mary 10–11,
24, 26–27, 40,
162, 177, 192,
199–204, 221,
223, 234
9 8, 203
10 203
10–17 203
17 39, 203
17.10–15 203
17.18–22 203
18 8
18–19 203
19.4 177
22.15 203

***Gospel [Traditions]
of Matthias*** 35, 231

***Gospel of the
Nazoreans*** 36, 96–98,
100–1

Gospel of Nicodemus
34, 157–58, 229
B 14.1 8

Gospel of Peter
7, 10–11, 17, 27,
30–31, 36, 44, 48,
71, 128–29, 137–51,
153–54, 159,
176–77, 212,
226, 231
1 145
3–5 148
5–6 145
6 146
9 146
9–10 139
10 139
14 145
19 139
23 139, 145
25 146

26–27 147
28 146
29 146
41 140
41–42 147
45–48 146
58–60 140
59–60 147

Gospel of Philip
18, 27, 36, 44,
163–64, 177–78,
183–90, 202–3,
218, 221–22,
234
6 (52.21–24) 188
8 (52.34) 188
16.2 (55.27–33) 188
17a–c (55.23–36) 189
21 (56.17–20) 188
30b–32
(58.34–59.11) 185
32 (59.6–11) 189
53 (63.22) 187
55b (63.33–34) 184,
187
76a (69.15–21] 188
76a (69.15-25) 188
81–82 (70.35–71.14)
188
90a (73.1–9) 188
91 (73.9) 183
91 (73.9–15) 186
112 (78.13–25) 188
113 (78.26–79.13) 188
115 (79.20–25) 188
122 (82.5–10) 188
123a (82.26–29) 188
125a (84.24–31) 188

***Gospel of Pseudo-
Matthew*** 36, 55, 68,
82, 85, 232

***Gospel of the Savior
(Unknown Berlin
Gospel)*** 37, 52,
104, 152–56,
160, 194
13–21 154

Gospel of Thomas

	6–7, 10–11,	
	16–18, 23–24,	
	26–27, 29, 36,	
	40, 44, 48, 58,	
	89–91, 96, 163–85,	
	187, 198–99, 202,	
	221–23, 228–29,	
	231, 234	
prologue	39, 42, 99,	
	164–65, 182	
1–5	178	
1–7	169	
1	39, 182	
2	164–65	
3	165	
4	168	
6	166	
7	166	
8	165	
9	168	
10	164	
11	164, 166,	
	178, 202	
12	167	
13	164, 167, 180,	
	199, 206	
14	166	
16	178	
17	172, 180	
18	178	
21	165	
21.6	166	
22	46, 164, 166–68,	
	180, 202, 211	
22.6	167	
24	165, 169	
26–33	169	
27	166	
28	178	
29	178	
30	167	
36–39	169	
37	211	
38–39	178	
42	166	
45	117	
46	178	
49	178	

49–50	178
51	165
52	179
53.3	172
55	164–65
56	164, 176, 178
58	165
60	164
60–61	180
61	211
63	165
65	165
65–66	179
67	178
71	175
77	167, 169, 180
80	164
81	164
82	164
83–84	166
85	153, 178
86	174
90	165
92	164
94	164
96	165
97	168
98	168
108	164
111	164
113	165
114	166–67, 202

Gospel of Truth

	8, 18, 37,
	105, 190–92,
	222, 242
17.1–4	8
17.3	191
18.11	8
18.16	191
19.17–34	192
20.26–21.25	191
30.13–16	191
33.1–32	192
34.34–35	8
36.19–35	192
39.15–28	192
40.25–29	192

Handing Over of Pilate   157, 229

History of Joseph the Carpenter

	8, 35, 55, 83
prologue	83
1	83
1.2	8
1.9	83
12–29	83
30	83
30–32	83
30.3	8

Holy Book of the Great Invisible Spirit

	37, 212, 241
64.1–3	164

Infancy Gospel [Protevangelium] of James

	13, 17,
	26–27, 36, 44,
	55, 58–71,
	75–76, 80–84,
	143, 182, 219,
	223, 229, 231
8–16	59
8.1	214
9.2	70–71
10	64
10.1	66, 69
11.1–2	69
16.1–8	70
17–24	60
17.2	69
18	60, 62
18.1	69–70
18.2	66
18–19	63
19–20	60
19.1	70
19.2	70
19.3	70
19.8	70
19.19–20.12	70
21.2	71
22.2	70
23	60

23–24	81
25	61–62
25.4	66

Infancy Gospel of Thomas 36, 55, 72–80, 82, 84–85, 130, 217, 229

1.1	72
2–9	75
2.1–5	72
3	72
4.1–5.2	72
5.3	73
6	73
7.2	73
7.4	73
8.2	73
9–13	73
11–16	75
14–15	73
15	73
16.1–2	71
16–18	74
17.2	73
17.4	73
18.3	74
19	74–75
20–22	74
22	74

Interpretation of Knowledge 47

Letter of Peter to Philip 36, 162

Memory [Memoir] of the Apostles 227

Narrative of Joseph of Arimathea 158, 229

Pistis Sophia 37, 194
| 1.42 | 198 |

Questions of Bartholomew 36, 212–14, 222, 229
| 2 | 214 |

3	214
4	214

[Greater] Questions of Mary 35, 200

Report of Pontius Pilate 157, 229

Revelation of Peter
| 81.3–82.3 | 164 |

Second Treatise of the Great Seth 180

Secret Gospel of Mark 35, 120–21

Sophia of Jesus Christ 18, 27, 36, 162, 192–94, 199
| 1.42–44 | 186 |
| 104.1 | 8 |

Testimony of Truth 47

Toledot Yeshu 28, 30, 101, 129–31, 134, 226

Trimorphic Protennoia 241

NONCANONICAL ACTS AND APOCALYPSES

Act of Peter 192–93, 199

Acts of Andrew
| 18 | 143 |

Acts of Barnabas 131

Acts of John
89	142
91	143
93	219

Acts of Paul 231

Acts of Peter 74, 130, 193
| 20–21 | 143 |

Acts of Thaddeus 122

Acts of Thomas 182, 198
| 43 | 143 |

Apocalypse of Peter 42, 138, 147, 149, 231

PSEUDO-CLEMENT

Contestatio
| 1.2 | 113 |

Homilies
| 19.19–20 | 46 |

Kerygma Petrou (=*Preaching of Peter*)
| frag. 6 | 147 |

Recognitions 180
| 1.60 | 131 |

APOSTOLIC FATHERS

2 Clement
4.5	46
5.2–4	46, 148–50
8.5	6
12.2–6	46
12.1–2	211
12.2	168–69

Didache 6, 62, 114
7:1–3	113
8:2	6
13:2	14

Epistle of Barnabas 114, 131, 231
| 6.13 | 118 |

Epistle to Diognetus 200

IGNATIUS

Ephesians
| 8.2 | 67 |
| 19.1 | 67 |

Smyrnaeans
| 7.2 | 6 |

Shepherd of Hermas
42, 231

**OTHER EARLY
CHRISTIAN
WRITINGS**

AMBROSE

Commentary on Luke
1.2   12, 237

ANONYMOUS

Apostolic Tradition
21.2   113

**Dialogue of
Adamantius**   124

Gelasian Decree
27, 32, 39, 48,
68, 122, 131, 200,
212, 219, 231

Muratorian Canon
41–42, 230

Teaching of Addai
122–23

ATHANASIUS

**Thirty-Ninth Festal
Letter**   10

AUGUSTINE

Letter
112.13   94

CLEMENT OF
ALEXANDRIA

Stromateis
1.24.158   46
2.45.5   99
3.4.26   198
3.10.68–70   167
3.45   210
3.63.1   195
5.10.63   46
5.96.3   99
6.15.128   147

COMMODIAN

**Carmen Apologeticum
(=Apologetic Poem)**
564   219

DIDYMUS
THE BLIND

**Commentary on
the Psalms**
184.8–10   100

EGERIA

Itinerary
17.1   122

EPHREM

**Commentary on
the Gospel**   127

EPIPHANIUS

**Refutation of All
Heresies (=Panarion)**
26.8   81
26.13.2–3   183, 186
30.13.2–3   102
36   81
38.1.2–5   207
38.3.1.5   207
46.1   96
50.1   156
51.100   14

EUSEBIUS OF
CAESAREA

Ecclesiastical History
1.9.4   122
1.13   122
3.3.2   141
3.25.1–7   231
3.25.5   95
3.25.6   141
3.27.4   100
3.39.17   100
4.22.8   39
4.23.11   230
5.15   230
5.20   230
6.12.3–6   141

9.5.1   157
9.7.1   157

Gospel Canons
12, 128

Letter to Carpianus
4–5   12

FALTONIA BETITIA
PROBA

**Cento Vergilianus de
Laudibus Christi**   33

HIPPOLYTUS

**Refutation of All
Heresies**
1, preface   40
5.7.20   168
5.26   81
5.29–32   81
6.1   40
6.4   40
6.36   40
6.37   40
7.20.1   198
9.10   40
10.8   40
10.9   142
13.2–3   142
15.1   142

INNOCENT I

Letter to Exsuperius
7   68

IRENAEUS OF LYON

Against Heresies
1, preface   40
1.20   75
1.26.2   102
1.27.2   125
1.3.2   196
1.30.14   196
1.31.1   207
2.22.4   235
3.11.8   9
3.11.9   190
3.2–4   40, 221

3.2.9   14
3.21.9   235

JEROME

Against the Pelagians
2.15   162

Commentary on Matthew
Preface 4   11
23.35   101

Commentary on the Psalms
85   103

Epistle
46.11   70
58.3   70
108.10   70
112   96
121.6   12

De viris illustribus
2   99
25   12

JUSTIN MARTYR

Dialogue with Trypho
78   13, 69
88   13
100.4   196
101.3   196
102.5   196
103.6   196
103.8   12, 196
104.1   196
105.1   196
105.5–6   196
106.1   196
106.3–4   196
107.1   196

First Apology   13
33.5   196
35.9   156
48.3   156
66.3   6, 196
67   12
67.3   196

ORIGEN

Against Celsus
1.28   63, 67
1.32   63, 67
1.51   69–70
2.1   102

Commentary on John
2.12   95, 99
2.31.188   39
19.7.2   46

Commentary on Matthew
10.17   71, 143
10.18   39
15.14   95

Epistle to Africanus   39

First Principles
4.2   102

Hexapla   28

Homilies on Jeremiah
15.4   95, 99

Homilies on Luke
1.2   10, 237

PTOLEMY

Letter to Flora   13, 20,
    114, 180, 229

TATIAN

Diatessaron
    10–12, 26–27,
    30, 41, 71, 96,
    118, 123, 125–29,
    132, 171, 174, 191,
    220, 226, 228, 230

TERTULLIAN

Apology
5   156
21   156
21.24   156

Prescription
30   123

GRECO-ROMAN LITERATURE

ANONYMOUS

Eugnostos the Blessed   193

Sentences of Sextus   185

ARISTOPHANES

Knights
642–45   4

CICERO

Letters to Atticus
2.3.1   4

HOMER

Odyssey
14.152   4
14.166   4

PLATO

Gorgias   118

SUETONIUS

Augustus
94   76

Vergil
3–5   66
4   76

VIRGIL

Fourth Eclogue   3

RABBINIC LITERATURE

MIDRASH

Genesis Rabbah
10:7   112

Sifre Numbers
16   95

MISHNAH

Avot
3:2   113

299

Mikwa'ot
4:4 112
5:5 112

Sheqalim
8:5 65

Yoma
3:3 112

TOSEFTA

Shabbat
13:5 95

Sheqalim
2:6 65

Yoma
2:16 112

BABYLONIAN TALMUD

Hullin
90b 65

Shabbat
116a–b 95

Tamid
29b 65

PALESTINIAN TALMUD

Yoma
4:1 (41c) 112

TARGUM

Fragment Targum 98

ISLAMIC LITERATURE

AL-AZRAQI

Kitab Akhbar Makka 68

QUR'AN
3:46 72
3:49 72, 79
4:157 131
5:110 72, 79
19:28 72

PAPYRI, PARCHMENTS, AND OSTRACA

PAPYRI AND PARCHMENTS

Aland 0171 118

Louvre E.14.250 209
$\mathfrak{P}^4$ 7, 26, 118
$\mathfrak{P}^5$ 118
$\mathfrak{P}^{45}$ 11, 25–26
$\mathfrak{P}^{52}$ 118
$\mathfrak{P}^{64}$ 26, 118
$\mathfrak{P}^{66}$ 118
$\mathfrak{P}^{67}$ 26, 118
$\mathfrak{P}^{75}$ 118
$\mathfrak{P}^{77}$ 118
$\mathfrak{P}^{88}$ 11, 25–26
$\mathfrak{P}^{90}$ 25, 118
$\mathfrak{P}^{95}$ 25
$\mathfrak{P}^{101}$ 25
$\mathfrak{P}^{102}$ 25
$\mathfrak{P}^{103}$ 25, 118
$\mathfrak{P}^{104}$ 25, 118
$\mathfrak{P}^{106}$ 25
$\mathfrak{P}^{107}$ 25
$\mathfrak{P}^{108}$ 25
$\mathfrak{P}^{109}$ 25
$\mathfrak{P}^{110}$ 25
$\mathfrak{P}^{111}$ 26
$\mathfrak{P}^{119}$ 25
$\mathfrak{P}^{121}$ 25

P.Aberdeen 3 152

P. Argentoratenses Copt. 5–7 (Strasbourg Coptic Papyrus) 35, 152, 154–55, 212

P.Berolinenses 11710 35, 115

P.Berolinenses 22220 152–54

P.Cairensis 10735 35, 80–81

P.Dura 10 (Dura Parchment 24) 10–11, 118, 127–28

P.Egerton 2 (+ P.Köln 255) 30, 35, 37, 105–10, 118, 120, 122, 133, 226
frag. 1 107
frag. 1, line 8 106
frag. 2 108

P.Merton 51 35, 115, 117

P.Montserratenses Roca IV 59 (inv. no. 996) 46

P.Oxyrhynchus 1 11, 163, 167, 169

P.Oxyrhynchus 210 35, 115–16

P.Oxyrhynchus 654 11, 36, 169

P.Oxyrhynchus 655 11, 36, 169

P.Oxyrhynchus 840 35, 105, 110–13, 133–34, 151
10 110
25–26 113
32–34 113
35–41 113

P.Oxyrhynchus 1081 193

P.Oxyrhynchus 1224 35, 116–17, 120

P.Oxyrhynchus 1384 104–5

P.Oxyrhynchus 2949 11, 118, 147–50

P.Oxyrhynchus 3525 11, 37, 199

P.Oxyrhynchus 4009
11, 46, 118, 147–50

P.Oxyrhynchus 5072
118–20

P.Oxyrhynchus 5073
11, 25–26, 34

P.Rylands 463   11, 37,
199, 203

**P.Rylands 464
(Rylands Gospel)**   35

**P.Vindobonensis G.
2325 (Fayûm Gospel)**
35, 150–51, 160

PSI XI 1200bis   35,
117–18

Ostraca

*"Peter" Ostracon
(van Haelst 741)*   152

**OTHER LATE
ANCIENT CODICES**
Akhmim Codex
(P.Cair. 10759)   138,
147, 149
Berlin Gnostic Codex
(BG 1/BG 8502)   18,
27, 36–37, 162,
186, 192–94,
199, 215

British Library MS Add.
5114 (Askew Codex)
194
British Library MS
Arundel 404   36, 55,
68, 82
Codex Bezae   45
Codex Brucianus
(Bruce Codex)   37
Codex Bodmer V   60
Codex Schøyen 2650
103–4
Codex Tchachos
36–37, 39, 162,
197–98, 204–6
Codex Washingtonianus
162

INDEX OF SUBJECTS

abbreviations, 7
See also nomina sacra
Abgar legend, 33–34, 121–23, 132
Abgar Ukkama, 122
Abgar V, 122
Abraham, 188
abstinence, 166
abyss, 199
Acts of the Apostles
in Cairo genizah, 28, 101
early Christian access to, 9
and long ending of Mark, 89
manuscripts of, 28
on Paul's definition of gospel, 5
on Peter's preaching to Cornelius,
2–3, 6
papyri of, 26
sayings of Jesus in, 45
Adam, 132, 167, 178, 213, 241
Adamantius, Dialogue of, 124
Addai (Thaddeus), 122, 198
Addai, Teaching (Doctrina) of, 122–23
adoption, 66–67
adultery
Mary suspected of, 64–65
See also pericope adulterae
aeon(s), 168, 191–93, 209, 242
Agape meal, 218
agrapha (unwritten sayings of Jesus),
13, 45–47, 50, 88, 99, 118, 132,
148, 185, 232–33, 239
about bankers, 46
about male and female, 46, 210–11
about man working on Sabbath, 45
about sheep and wolves, 46, 148–49
agriculture, 188
Akhmim (city in Upper Egypt), 138,
141, 148, 192
Akhmim Codex, 138, 147, 149, 150
See also Peter, Gospel of
Aksumite kingdom (Ethiopia), 216

Al-Bahnasa. See Oxyrhynchus
Alcibiades of Apamea, 142
Alexander Jannaeus (Hasmonean
king), 130
Alexandria, 9, 84, 95, 98–99, 120, 144,
175, 210, 220, 229
See also Ammonius of Alexandria;
Clement of Alexandria; Didymus
the Blind
allegory and allegorical interpretation,
33, 124, 179, 210, 216, 218
Allogenes, the Book of, 37, 205
almsgiving, 166
Alogi, 14
alpha (Greek letter)
child Jesus explains mystical
meaning, 73, 75, 79, 217
Ambrose of Milan, 12, 237
Ammonius of Alexandria, 12, 128, 132
amulet, 33–34, 104–5, 110, 115, 122,
209, 239
Ananias (servant of Abgar), 122
Andrew (apostle)
in Epistle of the Apostles, 217
in Gospel of Mary, 201, 203–4
in Gospel of Peter, 140
gospels attributed to, 33
Andrew, Acts of, 143
androgynous state, 166–67, 187–88,
194
angel(s), 33, 59–60, 79, 81, 115, 140,
142, 153, 197, 213–14, 216–17
anger, 73, 166, 195, 204, 206
Anglicans, 43, 69
Anna (mother of Mary), 59, 66, 69
Annas, 72
annunciation
of Jesus' birth, 57, 59–60, 69, 214,
218
of John's birth, 80
of Mary's birth, 59

anointing, 3, 187–88, 192
Anonymous Apocryphal Gospel, 37, 105
anthology, 45, 112, 116, 185
anthropology, 167
antichrist, 214
antigospel, 50, 209, 226
    Jewish, 129–30
anti-Judaism, 74, 111, 141, 145–47, 159
antilegomena (debated texts), 230
Antioch, 94, 124
    See also Ignatius of Antioch; Sera-
      pion of Antioch; Theophilus of
      Antioch
Antonine era, 175
Apamea. *See* Alcibiades of Apamea
Apelles, Gospel of, 35, 227
apocalypse of the mind, 171
apocalypses. *See specific named*
    apocalypses
apocalyptic and eschatological thought,
    3, 20, 90, 142, 147, 164, 171, 173,
    178, 195, 213, 218, 220, 233
    eschatological teaching of Jesus, 90,
      118, 171
    See also specific named apocrypha
apocrypha, 16, 18, 28, 32, 212
    as "hidden" texts, 38–39, 120
    as self-designation, 38–40, 120
    meaning of term, 38–39, 42
    See also gospels, noncanonical
apocryphon, 43
Apollo at Delphi, 165
apologist(s), 41, 126, 156–57
apostles (the Twelve), 1, 5, 8–9, 12–13,
    31, 35, 124, 131, 152–55, 186, 193,
    197, 200–3, 214–21
    memoirs of, 12, 196
    See also Acts of the Apostles; dis-
      ciples; *and specific apostles.*
Apostles, Epistle of the, 12–13, 36, 41,
    43, 89, 128, 144, 153, 162–63, 89,
    195–96, 215–20, 223, 229
    allusions to Old and New Testa-
      ments, 219
    as discourse gospel, 163, 215–20
    and footprint of Jesus, 219
    and gnostic motifs, 218
    and *Gospel of Peter*, 144
    and *Gospel of the Savior*, 153

    and *Infancy Gospel of Thomas*, 217
    as Jewish Christian text, 220
    and John, 217
    and long ending of Mark, 89, 128,
      220
    and Mark, 12
    and Paul, 218
    post-resurrection setting of, 162–63
    prophetic quotations in, 219
    proximity to protocanonical gospels,
      219
    and Synoptics, 217
Apostles, Memoir [Memory] of the,
    35, 227
apostolic acts, 122, 132, 158, 163, 215,
    218, 222
    See also specific named apostolic acts
apostolic church orders, 216
Apostolic Fathers, 41
apostolic generation, 64, 122, 209
apostolic succession, 204, 231
apostolic teaching, 201
appropriation (and reappropriation), 5,
    105, 133, 144, 146, 176, 188, 215,
    221, 233, 235
Aquila, revision of Old Greek, 28, 98
Arabian peninsula, 68, 93
Arabic, 15, 28
    and *Dormition of the Virgin Mary*,
      83
    and *Epistle of the Apostles*, 216
    and *Gospel of Gamaliel,* 37, 159
    and pre-Islamic Jesus traditions, 34,
      68, 81–82, 131
    and pre-Islamic Jewish Christianity,
      68
    and sayings of Jesus, 47
    translations of *Diatessaron*, 127
Arabic Infancy Gospel, 36, 55, 68, 72,
    79, 81–82
    and *Infancy Gospel of James*, 82
    and *Infancy Gospel of Thomas*, 82
Aramaic, 99–100, 102, 171, 173
    See also Jewish Palestinian Aramaic
arch-heretic, 102, 217
Archelaus, 217
archiereus (high priest). *See* high
    priest
archon(s) (heavenly rulers), 186–87,
    201

Aristophanes (Greek playwright), 4
ark (of the covenant), 65
Armenia, 213
Armenian (language), 67, 127
art, 68, 70–71, 77, 79, 85
Arundel manuscript, 36, 55, 68, 82
ascent
    heavenly, 154, 207
    of the soul, 163, 184–86, 201
asceticism
    in *Book of Thomas*, 199
    in *Gospel according to the Egyptians*, 210–11
    in *Gospel of Mary*, 202
    in *Gospel of Philip*, 184, 187
    in *Gospel of Thomas*, 166
ascetics, 76
Asia Minor, 3, 9, 93, 208, 220
assimilation, secondary, 171
Athanasius, 10
athlētēs, 198
atonement, 163, 209
Augustine
    on childlessness, 59
    and Jewish Christians, 93
    on perpetual virginity, 70
Augustus, Emperor, 3, 76
Austrian National Library, 150
autographs (of New Testament), 8

baptism, 111–14, 116, 134, 187–89, 207, 212, 218, 226, 235
    See also: Jesus, baptism
baptistery, Dura Europos, 69
Barbelo, 208–9
Barbelo gnostics, 19, 208
    See also gnostics
Bardaisan, Gospel of, 35, 227
Bar Kokhba, Simon, 93
bar mitzvah, 75
Barnabas (apostle), 131
Barnabas, Acts of, 131
Barnabas, Epistle of, 114, 118, 131, 231
Barnabas, Gospel of
    in Gelasian Decree, 33, 131
    Muslim text, 30, 130–32, 134, 226
Bartholomew (*Bartholomaios*), 213–16
Bartholomew, Gospel of, 33, 36, 158, 212–13, 222, 229, 235

Bartholomew, Questions of, 36, 212–14, 222, 229
Baruch, Book of, 80
basileia, 120
Basilides, 12, 20, 175, 229
Basilides, Gospel of, 12, 35, 227
bath. *See* ritual purity
Bauckham, Richard, 57, 71, 109, 128, 228
Bauer thesis (Walter Bauer), 22–25, 27
Behnesa. *See* Oxyrhynchus
Beloved Disciple
    and Gospel of John, 56
    as Mary. *See* Mary Magdalene
Belloc, Hilaire, 79
Ben Ezra (Old) Synagogue (Cairo), 28, 101
Berlin, Egyptian Museum, 152, 192
Berlin Gnostic Codex, 18, 27, 36–37, 162, 177, 186, 192–94, 199, 215
Bethlehem, 60, 62, 64, 69–70, 84
Bible, 1, 179, 227
    See also rewritten Bible
Biblia Hebraica Stuttgartensia, 38
bios (ancient biography), 76, 78, 83, 177, 227
birds made from clay, 72, 79–80, 85, 130
Black Sea, 123
blessings, 164, 199
blindness, 72, 111, 178
body
    of boy which Jesus causes to wither, 72
    of Jesus, 81, 124, 139, 148, 193, 209
    of John the Baptist, 83–84
    liberation from, 185–86, 189, 199, 207
    resurrection of, 215, 218
Bogomils, 19
book roll (or scroll), 15, 45, 95, 106, 117, 129, 148, 150, 199, 214, 239
"books of the dead," 17
book technology, 15
Bovon, François, 7, 66, 113, 219
bread
    breaking of, 99, 206
    five loaves, 216
    in Lord's Prayer, 103
    quasi-eucharistic, 214

bridal chamber, 184–85, 187–89, 194, 218
bride (of Christ) 218–19
British Library, 36, 82, 194
British Museum, 106
Brown, Dan, 21, 23, 58, 184, 231
burial, 17, 93, 99
Byzantine period, 79–80, 97, 158, 183, 186, 219

Caesar, 108
   See also specific emperors
Caesarea, 100, 143–44
Caiaphas, 122, 146
Cairo, 15–17, 28, 101, 138, 214
calendar, 93
Calvary, 213, 217
Cana, wedding at, 217
canon and canonization. *See* New Testament
Capernaum, 102, 119, 124
Cappadocian fathers, 70
Carinus, 158
Carpocratians, 120
catechesis, 185
catechist, 189
Cathars, 19
cave
   as site for birth of Jesus, 13, 60, 64, 69–70, 84
   world as cave of darkness, poverty, and death, 178
celestial spheres, 195, 201
celibacy, 166
Celsus (pagan scholar), 63, 67, 69, 102, 130
censorship, 27, 231–32
cento, 33
centurion, 139
Cephas, 2, 216
   See also Peter
Cerinthus, 139, 195, 217
Cerinthus, Gospel of, 35, 227
Chalcedon, 8
chariot of the Spirit, 197
Chenoboskion. *See* Nag Hammadi
childbirth, 202, 210–11
childlessness, 59
children, 5, 21, 38, 46, 59, 74, 76–77, 143, 168, 188, 192, 210, 219

of light, 194, 218
of faith, 197
   See also Israel, children of; massacre of innocents
Christ, 2, 8, 33, 37–38, 79, 94, 140, 142, 145, 147, 156–58, 186–87, 192, 200–1, 203, 208, 216–18, 235–36
   as *nomen sacrum*, 107, 240
   See also Jesus (Christ)
Christianity, 21, 56, 68, 99, 131–32, 170, 175, 181, 189, 197, 208, 236
   catholic and apostolic, 9, 107, 197, 202, 209, 235
   creedal, 235
   critics, 67
   early, 1–2, 4, 9–11, 15, 17, 23–24, 26, 58, 88, 90, 92, 94, 96, 137, 143, 159, 173, 190, 225, 228, 235–36
   mainstream, 14, 19, 23, 25, 41, 71, 79, 161, 170, 188, 190, 196, 200, 208, 215, 231, 235–36
   Marcionite, 124
   origins, 9, 20–22, 62–63, 90, 233
   See also Jewish Christians; Johannine Christianity
Christians, 1, 4, 9–10, 12, 15, 26–27, 57–60, 70, 88, 93–96, 157, 159, 186, 188–89, 228–29, 235
   Christian as powerful name, 187
   catholic, 96, 125
   See also Christianity; Jewish Christians
Christmas, 59, 68–69, 77
Christology, 56, 58, 61, 65–67, 78, 108, 117, 139, 142, 184, 236
   adoptionist, 66
   angel, 216–17
   docetic, 131, 139–41, 196, 207, 219
   and Marian theology, 61, 66–67
Chromatius, bishop, 82
church, 10, 13, 22, 31, 59, 84, 94–95
   in Alexandria. *See* Alexandria
   apostolic origins, 41, 217
   in Asia. *See* Asia Minor
   as bride of Christ, 218
   church order, 163, 201, 203
   diversity, 25
   Eastern, 69, 122
   Ethiopian, 220, 223

305

church (*continued*)
  in *Gospel of Thomas*, 178
  meetings, 2, 12
  public teaching, 42, 223, 234
  in Rome. *See* Rome
  Scriptures, 42
  and synagogue, 113
  in Syria. *See* Syria
  use of term "apocryphal," 38
  Western, 68, 82, 122
  See also Christianity; suppression of
    gospels
circumcision, 131, 188
cistern, 112
citations, ancient Christian, 30–32,
    43–44, 63, 87, 92, 95–97, 99,
    101, 104, 127, 132–33, 138, 143,
    168–69, 183n1, 186, 200, 208,
    210–11, 232
Claudius, Emperor, 157
2 Clement, 6, 211
  agrapha in, 46
  and *Gospel of Thomas*, 168–69
  and P.Oxy. 4009, 148–50
Clement of Alexandria, 19, 46, 92, 95,
    147, 167
  and agrapha, 46
  and *Gospel according to the Egyp-
    tians*, 195, 210–11
  and *Gospel according to the
    Hebrews*, 99
  and *Gospel of Mary*, 200
  and *Gospel of Thomas*, 167
  and *Secret Gospel of Mark*, 120–21
clothes, 110, 112, 119
cloud, 60, 218
  of dew, 214
codex (plural: codices), 7, 11, 15, 17,
    26, 106, 110, 115–16, 118, 138,
    148–49, 152, 154, 173, 183, 199,
    205–6, 239–40, 242
  of the four gospels, 11, 13, 26
  See also specific codices
Codex Bezae, 45
Codex Fuldensis, 127
Codex Jung, 190
Codex Schøyen 2650, 103–4
Codex Tchachos. *See* Gospel of Judas
Codex Washingtonianus, 162
Cologne, 106

colophon, 8, 61, 115, 176, 183, 198,
    205, 212, 239
commentary (ancient), 11, 20, 24, 105,
    127, 129, 138, 182, 190, 229, 241
  See also specific commentaries
Commodian, poet, 219
conception by a kiss, 185
consonants, 106
Constantine, Emperor, 23, 123
Constantinople, Council of, 70
contradiction, 17, 126, 167, 210
Coptic (language), 15, 18, 34–37, 52,
    69, 83, 103–4, 115, 152–54, 158,
    167, 169, 171, 174–77, 183, 185,
    187, 190–92, 194–95, 199–201,
    206, 209, 212–13, 216
  alternate version of Matthew, 103–4
Cornelius, 2
cosmology, 191, 193, 197, 204, 207,
    221–22
  dualistic, 166, 185–86, 192
councils, 70, 236
creation, 65, 84, 166, 178, 194–95, 207,
    241
creator, 19, 84, 124, 132, 178, 242
  See also demiurge
creeds, 94, 208, 236
  and allegory of five loaves of bread,
    216–17
  and harrowing of hell, 140
  and perpetual virginity, 70
  Trinitarian, 8
cross
  as sacrifice, 132
  made from tree planted by Joseph
    the carpenter, 186
  mentioned in *Gospel of Thomas*,
    164, 167
  personified, 153, 155
  saving significance, 153–55, 191–92,
    197, 215, 222, 236
  that walks and talks, 140, 142, 159,
    235
  See also Jesus, crucifixion
Cross, Discourse on the, 52, 154–56,
    160
Cross Gospel, 48, 144
cry of dereliction, 139, 141
cult, 234
  See also hero cult

curtain. *See* Temple, curtain
Cyriacus of Behnesa, bishop, 158

Damascus, 220
Damascus Document, 28
Damasus I (pope), 32, 231
darkness, 178, 188, 195
daughters of God, 219
David
    pool of, 110
    See also Jesus, descent from David
Da Vinci Code (Dan Brown), 21, 23,
    58, 184, 231
Dead Sea Scrolls. *See* Qumran and
    Dead Sea Scrolls
death, 39, 60, 74, 83, 120, 165, 178,
    188, 210–11
    See also Jesus, death
deception, 21, 191
DeConick, April D., 166, 170–72, 181,
    205, 208–9
Deissmann, Adolf, 81
demiurge (also workman), 19, 178,
    192, 194, 198, 207, 209, 241
demon(s), 33, 118–19, 194, 201, 207,
    209, 219
demoniac, 118–19
Demotic Egyptian (language), 15
denarius, 123
Dennis the Menace, 77
dependence, 140, 174, 202
    literary, 30–31, 61, 107–9, 114, 117,
        120, 133, 141, 144, 159, 169, 171,
        181, 196, 222, 233
    oral, hybrid and informal, 31, 61, 88,
        103, 109, 117, 120, 133, 144, 151,
        159, 174, 181, 202, 222, 232–33.
        See also orality, secondary
Derveni, 10
devil, 3, 163
dialogue(s), 7, 46, 50, 119, 152–53,
    164, 181, 193–95, 206–7, 211, 213
dialogue gospels. *See post-resurrection*
    discourse gospels
Diatessaron, 10–12, 30, 41, 71, 96,
    118, 123, 125–29, 132, 220, 226,
    228–29
    and *Gospel of Thomas*, 171, 174
    and *Gospel of Truth*, 191
    manuscripts, 26, 118, 127

omits gospel genealogies, 126
    translations, 26, 127
    use, 27, 71, 125–27, 230
    use of Mark, 12, 127
    use of Matthew, Luke, and John,
        127
    See also Tatian
Didache, 6, 14, 62, 113–14
Didymus the Blind, 98, 100
    and *Gospel of Peter*, 143
diet, 93, 102
Diognetus, Epistle to, 200
disciple(s), 1–2, 111–12, 119, 140, 142,
    161, 164, 167, 183–84, 189, 193,
    196, 199–201, 206–7, 209, 214,
    220, 223, 227
    call, 102, 206
    commissioning, 155, 215, 218, 234
    flight, 151, 154
    suffering, 197
    See also apostles
discipleship, 166
discourse collections. *See* post-resur-
    rection discourse gospels
discourse gospels. *See* post-resurrec-
    tion discourse gospels
disease, 122, 239
dissemination and circulation of early
    Christian texts, 9, 11, 27, 80, 108,
    182, 231
diversity, ecclesial, 9, 203, 225, 234
divine emanations, 208, 241–42
divine mother figure, 194
divine name, 101, 130
    Son as Name of Father, 192
divine spark, 19, 184, 242
docetism. *See* Christology, docetic
dogs, 111
dominical discourses. *See* post-resur-
    rection discourse gospels
donkey, 60, 69, 81, 84
doxology, 74, 214
dream report, 202
drunkenness, 178
Dura Europos, 10–11, 69, 127

Easter, 88, 115, 146, 156, 159, 162–63,
    180, 194, 196, 198, 204, 206,
    220–21, 232
Ebion, 102

Ebionites, 100–3
and observance of Jewish law, 102
and Origen, 102
Ebionites, Gospel of the, 36, 92, 96–97,
100–3
and Epiphanius, 102–3
and *Gospel according to the
Hebrews*, 100, 102
and *Gospel according to the
Nazoreans*, 101
and John the Baptist, 102
and Matthew, 102–3
ebyon ("poor"), 102
ecclesial and episcopal authority, 25,
93, 95, 197, 201, 203, 228, 231
See also suppression
ecclesial order. *See* church order
echoes, 73, 114, 122, 144, 167, 209
of gospels, 34, 46, 75, 99, 105, 119,
153
eclipse, 156
Edessa, 122–23, 129, 132, 199
royal dynasty of, 122–23
editorial distance, 30
Egeria, 122
Egypt, 220, 241
and early Christianity, 24, 83, 88,
106, 143, 173, 175, 196
and *Gospel of Thomas*, 176
Holy Family in, 57, 60, 74–75,
80, 82
and *Infancy Gospel of James*, 63
manuscripts from, 9–10, 15–18,
23–25, 83, 93, 138, 155, 175, 182,
192, 199, 205
Egyptians, Gospel according to [or
of], 7, 18, 28, 36–37, 50, 190, 195,
210–12
and Clement of Alexandria, 210–11
and *Gospel of Mary*, 211
and *Gospel of Thomas*, 211
as scripture, 210
*See also Holy Book of the Great
Invisible Spirit*
Ehrman, Bart, 7, 32, 42, 45, 47, 50–52,
55, 58, 60, 63, 68, 72, 81, 83, 92,
97–100, 103, 107, 110, 115–17,
122, 128, 138, 144, 148–50,
152–53, 156–58, 164–65, 183n1,
200, 205, 208, 212, 229

Elchasai, Book of, 142
elders
Jewish, 139, 145
twenty-four, 153
elect, 94, 167, 178–79, 194, 206
Elijah, 101
elite(s), 19, 40, 120, 129, 161, 165–66,
178, 203, 217, 234, 242
Elizabeth (mother of John), 60, 74
emotions, control of, 20
Empire, Roman, 3, 4, 123, 225
encomium, 63
enemies
of Christians, 58, 157
instruction to pray for, 116
See also Jesus, enemies
enlightenment, 188
1 Enoch, 138, 216
Ephrem, 127, 129
Commentary on the Gospel, 127
Epicurus, 166
Epiphanius, 14, 124
and family of Jesus, 57
and file submitted by Pilate to
Tiberius, 156
and *Gospel according to the Egyptians*, 210–11
and *Gospel of Judas*, 207
and *Gospel of Mary*, 200
and *Gospel of Philip*, 183, 186
and Jewish Christian Gospels, 92,
95–97, 102–3
eschatology. *See* apocalyptic and eschatological thought
ethics, Valentinian, 20
Ethiopia, 216
Ethiopic (language), 37, 75, 79, 159,
216–17, 220
ethnicity, Jewish, 93–94
euangelion (gospel), 1–5, 12
euangelisasthai (to proclaim good
news), 2, 4–5
Eucharist, 187, 209, 214, 218
Eugnostos the Blessed, 193
eunuch, Ethiopian, 99
Europe, 21, 98, 157, 158
Eusebius of Caesarea, 12, 92, 141,
230–31
and Abgar legend, 122
and *Acts of Pilate*, 157

and family of Jesus, 57
gospel canons, 12, 128
and *Gospel according to the
    Hebrews*, 100
and *Gospel of Peter*, 143
evangelists. *See* Matthew; Mark; Luke;
    John
Eve, Gospel of, 35
excerpts and excerpting, 10, 34, 45,
    106, 151, 171, 185, 189, 211, 239
and ancient notebooks, 185, 211
Exodus, Greek codex of, 206
exorcism, 82, 93, 118–19, 164, 217
Exsuperius, Letter to, 68
eyewitnesses, 3, 57, 146, 175, 180

faith, 1, 8–9, 22, 28, 40, 64, 93, 122–23,
    161, 188, 197, 203, 215, 217–18,
    235–37
    See also rule of faith
fall, 211
Faltonia Betitia Proba, 33
fasting, 59, 166
Father as *nomen sacrum*, 240
Father Elohim, 81
Fayûm, 16
Fayûm Gospel (P.Vindob. G. 2325), 35,
    150–51
    significance of Peter, 150–51, 160
    use of Matthew and Mark, 151
feeding of five thousand, 217
female, 46, 65, 99, 166–67, 186, 189,
    194, 200, 202, 208, 210–11
feminism, 202–3
fishing, 140
flesh, 19, 187–88, 199, 218, 220
    Word made flesh, 56
Flora, Letter to (Ptolemy), 13, 20, 114,
    180, 229, 241
Florinus, 230
flute girl, 111
flyleaf, of manuscript, 7
fog, of terror and deception, 191
food, impurity of, 131
footprint, 217, 219
forgery, 7, 33, 121, 157, 187
forgiveness of sins, 217–18
Fortschreibung, 133, 157
fortune-telling. *See* sortilege
foundation legend, 132

Four Heavenly Realms, Gospel of,
    227
*Four Zones of the World, Gospel
    of*, 37
fragments. *See* gospel fragments
Fragment Targum, 98
Freer Logion, 36
    and long ending of Mark, 162
    and Jewish Christian gospels, 162
Fustat. *See* Cairo

Gabriel, 59, 218
Galatians, Epistle to, 124, 219
Galilee, 3, 60, 140, 151, 170, 181, 193,
    214, 221
    See also Sea of Galilee
Gamaliel, Gospel of, 37, 105, 158–59
Gathercole, Simon, 6–7, 26, 164–69,
    172–76, 178, 180–83, 187, 208
Gelasian Decree, 27, 32, 39, 48, 68,
    122, 131, 200, 212, 219, 231
Gelasius I (pope), 32, 231
gender and gender distinctions, 20, 78,
    99, 166, 188, 202–4, 210–11
genealogy, 18, 65–67, 69, 126
Genesis, 19, 73, 241
genizah, 28, 101, 239
    absence of apocryphal gospels, 28
    and Greek New Testament manu-
        scripts, 101
genre, 48–50, 105, 115, 130, 155, 161,
    163, 176–77, 183, 196, 212, 215,
    217, 222, 227
Gentiles, 2, 111, 186, 201
    Gentile Christians, 114, 174
    and Jewish Christianity, 92, 94, 101,
        114
    Paul as apostle to, 132
    preaching to, 2, 22, 201, 218
geometry, treatise on, 206
Georgian (language), 75, 79
German Christians, 22
Gethsemane, 153–55
ghost, 219
gilyonim, 95
Giotto, 69
glory, 155, 162
gloss(es), 97–98, 232, 241
gnōsis, 18–19, 174, 203
gnosticism, definitions, 17–20

gnostics and gnostic literature, 17–20,
40, 43, 81, 88, 105, 113, 137, 139,
141–42, 154, 161, 164, 166–68,
171, 175, 184–86, 188–89, 191–94,
196–98, 201–4, 206–8, 211–12,
215–16, 218, 220–22, 229, 234,
241–42
  and *Gospel of Thomas*, 171, 175,
    177–79, 181
God, 38, 57, 59, 102, 108, 112, 132,
142, 153, 180, 207–8, 240
  as Father, 153, 163, 166, 186,
    188–89, 190–92, 194, 197–98, 217,
    219–20
  as Father of truth, 190
  as God of Israel, 38, 124
  as God of Law, 124, 126
  as Good God (opp. Father Elohim),
    81
  as Jewish God, 126
  as Lord (God) of grace and love, 124
  as unknown God, 241
Golgotha, 145
Goodacre, Mark, 17, 91, 128, 172–73,
179, 181
Gorgias, 118
gospel, 5, 8, 33, 95, 124, 177, 193, 203
  apostolic, 125, 203
  fourfold (four gospels), 1, 8–9,
    12–14, 23, 25, 27, 29–31, 40–42,
    49–50, 56, 85, 108–9, 120, 125–26,
    128–29, 131–32, 134, 141, 154,
    157, 177, 204, 215, 220, 222–23,
    225, 229–34, 236–37
  as message about Jesus, 2, 5, 191
  as message of judgment, 6
  as written source, 6, 8, 9
  pluriform, 125, 127
  See also individual gospels
gospel fragments, 31, 35, 37, 43–45,
49–51, 80, 87–89, 104–20, 122,
128, 132, 133–34, 137–38, 147–48,
150, 169, 171, 182, 187, 193, 205,
226, 232
  See also manuscripts; papyri
gospel harmony, 10, 12, 41, 44, 61,
80–81, 86, 96, 101, 103–4, 109,
115, 126–28, 131–33, 171, 174,
181, 191, 202, 222, 230, 233

created by Theophilus of Antioch,
12, 128
informal, 10, 31, 61, 103, 128, 133,
174, 181, 191, 202, 233
  See also Diatessaron
gospel meditations, 37, 105, 191, 222
gospel narrative (Markan) outline, 2–3,
6, 12, 30, 44, 46, 49, 85, 87–89,
97, 100, 104–6, 115–16, 119, 126,
130–31, 146, 159, 173, 176–77,
182, 191, 194, 214–15, 221,
225–28, 232, 234–36
  as scaffold for new gospel writings,
    45, 85, 119, 225, 227
gospels, 1–2, 7–8, 10–11, 13, 22–23, 26,
37–42, 44, 51, 88, 91, 96–97, 109,
117, 172, 189, 200–4, 212, 227
  attributed to apostles, 6–7, 31, 177,
    196, 227–29
  becoming apocryphal, 41, 228,
    231–32
  canonical (New Testament), 6–7,
    10–11, 13, 22–23, 25, 40–42, 44,
    55–56, 61, 85, 88, 90, 97, 102,
    108–9, 111, 123, 144–45, 159, 171,
    173, 180, 183, 189, 201, 213, 222,
    227, 233
  and canonization. *See* New Testament, canon
  and canons created by Eusebius of
    Caesarea, 12, 128
  and commentaries. *See*
    commentaries
  and cross-referencing, 14
  excerpts, 10, 151
  four gospels. *See* gospel, fourfold
  fragmentary. *See* gospel fragments
  gnostic. *See* gnostics
  Islamic, 104
  Jewish. *See* Jewish Christian
    Gospels; *Toledot Yeshu*
  and Justin Martyr, 13, 128
  lost, 47–48, 50, 90–91
  manuscripts. *See* manuscripts
  and Muratorian canon, 42
  noncanonical (also apocryphal),
    6–8, 10–11, 13–14, 17, 19, 23–25,
    28–32, 38–43, 45–47, 50–51, 58,
    61, 80, 95, 104, 106, 117, 123,

129, 133, 139, 181, 183, 189, 210, 221–22, 233. *See also specific named gospels*
and orality. *See* dependence, oral
protocanonical, 30, 60, 89, 111, 114, 132–33, 144, 200, 202, 221–22, 227, 229, 232
and public reading, 1, 7, 11–13, 27, 85, 115, 118, 169, 182, 200, 222, 228–30
and scholia, 11, 229
and supplementary gospel traditions. *See* supplementation
and synopsis created by Ammonius of Alexandria, 12, 132
and textual variants. *See* textual variants
titles, 6–8, 62, 227–28
unknown, 26, 80, 104, 106, 114–15
See also infancy gospels; ministry gospels; passion gospels; post-resurrection discourse gospels
gospel tradition, 25, 29, 31, 43, 48, 91, 96, 98–99, 103, 106, 108, 123, 141, 144, 157, 168, 170, 175–76, 202, 222
authoritative, 126
canonical (New Testament), 29, 41, 47, 88–89, 97, 103, 108–9, 123, 144, 162, 172, 196, 233–34
early, 46, 82, 89, 97, 101–3, 171, 173, 176, 222
familiar, 133–34
fragmentary. *See* gospel fragments
gnostic, 43
harmonized. *See* gospel harmony
Jewish Christian. *See* Jewish Christian Gospels and gospel tradition
Johannine. *See* Johannine tradition
late, 176
mainstream and public, 39, 235
manuscript (or textual), 3, 11, 13, 28, 41, 43–45, 59, 61, 67, 71, 74–75, 79, 82, 97, 101, 113, 125, 157, 162, 182, 212, 220
noncanonical (or apocryphal), 47, 75, 78–79, 108, 117, 160, 183, 229, 232
orthodox, 94

post-synoptic, 96, 176
protocanonical, 61, 132, 144, 208, 232
protognostic, 202
secret, 198
supplementary. *See* supplementation
synoptic. *See* synoptic tradition
written, 95–96, 144,
Goulder, Michael D., 91
grace, 74, 185
and law, 124, 126
grammateis (scribes), 119
grammatikoi (scribes), 119
grave goods, 17, 173
Greek (language), 11, 15, 18, 34, 42, 52, 61–62, 70, 73–74, 83, 99–100, 104, 110, 115, 117, 121, 126–27, 150–51, 153, 162, 169, 171, 173, 175–76, 183, 191–95, 199–202, 206, 212, 216, 241
Greek(s), 187
Grenfell, Bernard, 15, 80
Griesbach Hypothesis, 91
guards at tomb, 139–40

Hades, 140, 147, 158, 213–14, 218
hadith, 68
hagiography, 63
halakah. *See* ritual practice
handkerchief
of Veronica, 158
with image of Jesus' face, 122
Hanina (deputy high priest), 113
Harnack, Adolf von, 24, 126
harrowing of hell, 34, 140, 147, 153, 158, 214, 218
and 1 Peter, 140, 147, 158
in creeds, 140
heart, 57, 108, 133
heaven, 73–74, 140, 142, 147, 153–55, 164–65, 167, 186, 188, 191, 195, 197, 201, 207, 214–18, 221, 236
See also kingdom of heaven
to hebraikon (the Hebrew version), 92
Hebrew (language), 61, 73, 92, 96, 99–102, 195, 214
Hebrews (as opposed to Christians), 186, 188
Hebrews, Epistle to, 42

Hebrews, Gospel according to, 28, 95–96, 99–100, 231
  citations of, 99
  and Ebionites, 100
  and other Jewish Christian gospels, 99
  and *pericope adulterae,* 100
Hebrews, Gospel of, 36, 92, 96
Hegel, Georg F. W., 24
Hegesippus, 39, 62
Heliodorus, bishop, 82
hell, 34, 157, 195, 214
  See also harrowing of hell
Hellenism, 3–4, 166, 175, 235
hemorrhaging woman, healing of, 217
Henderson, Timothy P., 129, 138, 141, 146
Hengel, Martin, 6–7, 13, 20, 91, 126–27, 129, 228
Heracleon, 20, 229, 242
Herculaneum papyri, 10
heresy, 71, 81, 94, 183
  heretic(s), 8, 10, 39–40, 102, 120, 123, 142, 217, 231, 236
  heretical beliefs, 22, 25, 120, 127, 142, 183
  heretical texts, 25, 71, 95, 142, 219, 229, 235
  of Minim, 94
Hermas, Shepherd of, 42, 231
Hermetic corpus, 205
hero cult, 4
Herod Agrippa I, 60
Herod Antipas, 139, 148, 157
Herod the Great, 60, 64, 70
Hesychius, 33
heterodoxy, 24
high priest (or chief priest), 60, 113, 145, 188, 207
Hill, Charles E., 6, 11, 13–14, 108–9, 127, 220, 232
Hippolytus, 11, 36, 40, 81, 142, 168
  and *Gospel according to the Egyptians,* 210–11
  and *Gospel of Thomas,* 168
history of effects, 81, 232
Hofius, Otfried, 47
Hollywood, 21, 69
Holtzmann, H. J., 90

Holy Book of the Great Invisible Spirit (Egyptian Gospel), 37, 164, 212, 241
Holy Family, 60, 63, 69, 73, 75, 80, 82–83
Holy Grail, 158
holy of holies
  as "bridal chamber," 188
  in Temple, 65
Holy Spirit, 3, 73–74, 99, 139, 186–87, 189, 197, 217
Homer, 4
homily, 46, 80, 83, 105–6, 115–18, 154, 158–59, 189, 191–92, 232
homologoumena (agreed texts), 230
honey cakes, 102
hope, 188, 191
Hopkins, Gerard Manley, 77
Horbury, William, 5, 101, 130
human(s), 38, 57, 81, 180, 187, 207, 213, 219–20, 235
humanity, 19, 188, 206–7, 242
Hunt, Arthur, 15, 80
Hurtado, Larry W., 9–11, 15, 26, 107, 169

Iakōb, 61
icons of infancy stories, 68–71
Ignatius of Antioch, 6, 31, 67, 120
ignorance, 56, 112, 191–92, 201
image, Platonic, 166
immersion, 93, 110–13
  See also baptism; ritual purity
implements
  eucharistic, 113–14
  See also Temple implements
incarnation, 47, 56, 58, 65, 67, 70, 161, 167, 217, 235, 236
incipit, 34, 42, 152
India, 198, 213
infancy gospels, 36, 41, 43–44, 49–52, 55–85, 88, 227, 229, 232
infancy narrative of Justin the Gnostic, 81
initiation, 188
Injil Barnaba. See Gospel of Barnabas
ink, 116, 150–51
inn at Bethlehem, 70
inner-trinitarian dynamism, 154
Innocent I, 68

inscriptio, 7
insertions, 97, 130, 162, 195
International Q Project, 90
    See also Q
Interpretation of Knowledge, 47
intertextuality, 30, 180, 215, 219,
    222–23, 233
to ioudaikon (the Jewish text), 98
Irenaeus of Lyon, 9, 14, 27, 31, 40–41,
    75, 102, 114, 125, 127–28, 196,
    221, 230, 235
    and *Gospel of Judas*, 207, 208
    and *Gospel of Truth*, 190–91
    and long ending of Mark, 89
    and Marcion, 125
Irish (language), 79
Isaiah, 3, 5, 107–8, 219
Islam, 104, 131, 132
Islamic literature, 47, 85, 104, 130–31,
    134
Israel, 38, 65–66, 92, 94, 107, 112, 124,
    154, 163, 179, 218
Israelites, 2, 59, 213
Italian (language), 131

James, Apocryphon [Letter] of, 18, 36,
    62, 162, 182, 195–98, 222–23, 234
    as deliberately apocryphal, 195
    and *First Apocalypse of James*,
        197–98
    and *Gospel of Thomas*, 178
    in Hebrew, 195
    and Peter, 196
    post-resurrection setting, 162
James, Epistle of, 42, 62, 96
James, Epistle to Peter, 62
James, First Apocalypse of, 36, 162,
    197–98, 205
*James, Infancy Gospel of (Protevan-
    gelium)*, 13, 17, 36, 44, 55, 58–71,
    75, 182, 219, 223, 229, 231
    citation by Origen, 63
    dependence on canonical infancy
        narratives, 60–61, 85
    emphasis on Mary, 84
    in Gelasian Decree, 33
    link to historical figure, 61
    manuscript transmission of, 27, 67,
        71
    nonapocryphal, 71, 182

papyri of, 26, 27, 63
    translations into other languages,
        67–68
James, ossuary of, 21
*James, Second Apocalypse of (Revela-
    tion of James)*, 36, 62, 162, 198
James son of Alphaeus, 216
James son of Zebedee, 33, 195, 197–98
James the Just
    and *Apocryphon of James*, 195
    death, 61
    and *Gospel of Thomas*, 167
    and *Infancy Gospel of James*, 60–62,
        65, 69
    and *Infancy Gospel of Thomas*, 74
    in New Testament, 62
    prominent apostolic figure, 100
    and Pseudo-Clementine literature, 62
    and resurrected Jesus, 99–100
    unique access to childhood of Jesus,
        62
Jenkins, Philip, 58, 235
Jeremias, Joachim, 47, 109, 113
Jericho, 28
Jerome, 11, 12, 92, 94
    and birth of Jesus in cave, 64, 69–70
    and childlessness, 59
    and Freer Logion, 162
    and *Gospel of Bartholomew*, 212
    and *Gospel according to the Ebion-
        ites*, 101, 103
    and *Gospel according to the Egyp-
        tians*, 210
    and *Gospel according to the
        Hebrews*, 99–100
    and *Gospel according to the
        Nazoreans*, 100–1
    and *Gospel of Peter*, 143
    and *Gospel of Pseudo-Matthew*, 82
    and Jewish Christians, 93–94, 96
    and Jewish Christian gospels, 97–99,
        101
Jerusalem, 3, 5, 21, 57, 62, 69, 75, 96,
    103, 112, 119, 145, 170, 181, 197,
    219, 221, 223
Jesus (Christ)
    abandons disciples, 207
    accusations of illegitimacy, 56, 67
    adulterous woman. *See pericope
        adulterae*

Jesus (Christ) (*continued*)
as angel of light, 193
anointed by God, 3
ascension, 133, 153–55, 214, 218, 220
baptism, 30, 45, 56–58, 83, 88, 96, 100, 116, 123, 227, 232, 236
betrayal, 2, 206–9
biographical account, 51, 87, 129
birth and childhood of, 30, 49, 55–85, 89, 92, 115, 123–24, 129–30, 133, 139, 158, 161, 193, 209, 217, 220, 236
body, 139, 193, 209
as bringer of saving knowledge, 178, 197
as brother of James, 61
childhood miracles, 72–74, 76, 82
children, 21
correspondence with Abgar. *See* Abgar legend
dances around cross, 156
denied by disciples, 119
descent from David, 59, 64, 66, 69, 84
descent from heaven to earth, 216–17, 221
descent into hell. *See* harrowing of hell
as divine, 1, 58, 67, 236
as earthly, 7
encounter with Nathanael, 115
as enfant terrible, 78
enemies, 56, 146, 217
as Eucharist, 187
exaltation or lifting up, 139
as false prophet, 130
family, 56–58, 102
family tomb, 21
farewell discourse, 152–55
as fountain of water, 153
as Gabriel, 218
genealogies, 66, 126
given gall and vinegar to drink, 153
as god of Rome, 156
as guide, 192
half-siblings, 70
healing, 122, 163, 177, 217
heals boy, 119
heals builder with withered hand, 101
heals leper, 107
heals Salome, 60
heavenly enthronement and intercession, 155
as human, 1, 8, 58, 66, 73, 78, 84, 139, 161, 207, 236
illegitimate birth, 130
and James the Just, 99–100
"Jesus Christ, God," 115
and Jewish opponents, 107, 227
and John the Baptist, 57, 227, 232, 236
as King, 153
as King of Israel, 154
kneels before God in seventh heaven, 153
laughs at disciples, 208
laughs at frustration of human teachers, 73
as light, 167
as Lord, 154, 187, 194, 217
marriage, 21
as martyr, 163
and Mary Magdalene. *See* Mary Magdalene
as Messiah (of Israel), 58, 66, 93–94, 101, 124, 130, 163, 179, 187
ministry, 2–3, 5–6, 30, 34, 44, 50–51, 87–134, 159, 170, 173, 177, 180, 206, 217, 226, 232, 234, 236
miracles, 84, 88, 107–8, 130, 164, 206, 217, 236
as mischievous child, 72–80
mission, 206
mockery, 145
murdered by Jews, 145, 147. *See also* anti-Judaism
name Jesus as *nomen sacrum*, 240
as Nazarene, 187
painless passion, 139, 141–42
passion and death, 2–3, 6, 30, 34, 44–45, 50–51, 81, 89, 92, 100–1, 122–24, 130, 127–30, 133, 137–41, 137–61, 164–65, 173, 177, 181, 188–89, 194, 196–97, 206, 209, 212–13, 217–18, 226–27, 236
and Pharisees. *See* Pharisees
pierced by lance, 153
post-incarnate, 46
pre-incarnate, 46

predicts flight of disciples, 151
as Prophet, 131–32, 163
as Protestant, 22
and rabbinic literature, 96
replaced on cross by Judas, 131
resurrection and resurrection
  appearances, 2–3, 6, 30, 40,
  44–45, 49–51, 88–89, 92, 99–100,
  121, 129, 137, 139–41, 146, 151,
  155, 158–59, 164, 173, 177,
  180–81, 188–89, 193–97, 206,
  212–14, 217, 220, 226–27, 236
risen, 140, 142, 186, 194, 196–98,
  200, 204, 213, 217–19, 221–23,
  235
sacrificed by Judas, 209
as sage teacher, 163
secret teaching, 40, 161, 179, 186,
  203, 206, 221. *See also* knowledge,
  secret
as Seth, 208
as Shepherd, 154
as Son of God, 58, 67, 94, 130–31,
  139, 146, 163, 186, 188, 191–92,
  217, 220
as Son of King, 153
as Son of Man, 8, 174, 195, 213
as son of Mary, 67, 77
as sorcerer, 130
speaks as infant, 72
suffering, 191, 197
as syncretistic, 22
teaches Law as a child, 73–74
teaching, 1–3, 5–7, 23, 51, 87–88,
  105, 107, 116–17, 119, 124,
  129, 162–63, 170, 177, 189, 191,
  193–94, 196–97, 199, 201, 217,
  223, 232
in Temple, 57, 74, 77, 84
temptation, 100
trial, 138
unwritten sayings. *See* agrapha
virgin birth. *See* virgin birth
Jesus Seminar, 22, 90
Jesus tradition, 12, 34–35, 51, 75–76,
  88, 111, 114, 140–41, 147, 159,
  173, 181–82, 196, 211, 229, 233
apostolic and ecclesial, 232, 234
early, 1–3, 23, 40, 46, 57, 64, 67,
  69–70, 82, 168, 174

hidden and secret, 39
independent, 97, 111, 140, 169, 173,
  208, 232
noncanonical (or extracanonical), 13,
  47, 68–69, 106, 108, 117, 150, 208
non-Christian, 34, 46–47
orthodox, 94
protocanonical, 208
public and nonapocryphal, 40
transmission, 56
unattested, 159
See also Jesus, birth and infancy;
  Jesus, passion and death; Jesus,
  resurrection
Jesus' Wife, Gospel of, 21, 187, 205
Jewish Christian Gospels, 41, 44, 50,
  87, 92–104, 132, 134, 229, 232
early citations, 36, 44, 92, 95–97, 99,
  132
and gospel harmony, 101
and Gospel of Matthew, 36, 98–104,
  134, 162
and gospel tradition, 43, 70, 92,
  96–97, 103, 114, 162, 232
and synoptic outline, 97, 100–2, 232
titles of, 95
Jewish leaders (or authorities), 60, 93,
  96, 108–10, 145–46
Jewish Christians, 92–95, 103, 114,
  134, 142, 179, 188, 201
and Christology, 66
definition, 92–94
and *Epistle of the Apostles*, 220
and Jesus' family origins, 57
and perpetual virginity, 70
and ritual purity, 111–14, 134
and translational usage, 101
See also Jesus, descent from David
Jewish Palestinian Aramaic, 98
Jewish teachers, 72–73
Jewish War
first (66–73 AD), 20, 93
second (132–35 AD), 93, 175
Jews, 5, 22, 59, 62, 92–97, 112, 187,
  241
and Gospel of John, 145
and plots against Jesus' life, 122
and trial and crucifixion of Jesus,
  139, 145–46, 153
Joachim (father of Mary), 59, 66, 69, 82

Johannine Christianity, 170, 204
Johannine epistles, 161
Johannine language, 139, 145, 233
Johannine miracles, 217
Johannine tradition, 108–9, 132–33, 153–55, 175
Johannine writings, 5–6, 18
John, Acts of, 142–43, 219
John, Apocryphon of, 29, 179, 182, 184, 192–93, 199, 207, 215, 222, 234, 241
John the Baptist, 3, 36, 80–81, 83–84, 132, 197
    diet, 102
    extract from the *Life of John,* 36, 83
    and *Gospel of the Ebionites,* 102–3
    and Jesus, 56–58, 227, 232, 236
    and massacre of innocents, 60, 64
John Chrysostom, 70, 94
John, Gospel of, 7, 9–10, 24–25, 107, 111, 155, 189, 204, 213, 215, 221, 225–26, 233
    atemporality, 181
    avoidance of term *gnōsis,* 174
    and Beloved Disciple, 56
    and Cairo genizah, 28, 101
    canonical setting, 29
    commentaries on, 11, 30, 229
    and *Dialogue of the Savior,* 195
    and disciples, 174
    and "Doubting" Thomas, 175, 214
    early manuscripts, 11, 24–26, 28, 108
    farewell discourses, 152–54, 174–75
    and Gospel of Mark, 228
    and *Gospel of Peter,* 140
    and *Gospel of Thomas,* 174–75, 177
    Heracleon's commentary, 20, 229
    and incarnate Logos, 167
    and Jesus on cross, 139
    and Jesus' paternity, 56
    and the "Jews," 110, 145
    John 21 as separate tradition, 140, 162
    and Justin Martyr, 13, 127
    lack of infancy narrative, 56, 84
    and Muratorian canon, 42
    opposition to, 14, 228
    and origin of Jesus, 56
    and P.Eger. 2, 108–9
    and Ptolemy's *Letter to Flora,* 22
    reading, 24, 228
    rejection by Marcion, 125
    and resurrection appearances, 140, 194, 220–21
    and school of Valentinus, 20, 127, 229
    and story of woman caught in adultery. *See pericope adulterae*
    and Synoptics, 108–9, 127
    and Tatian, 127, 132, 134
    use and influence, 11, 25, 88, 108–9
Jordan (modern country), 120
Jordan River, 13, 108
Joseph of Arimathea, 139, 148, 156–58
Joseph and Asenath, 21
Joseph Barsabbas, 131
Joseph the Carpenter, 56–57, 69–70, 72–73, 78, 82–83
    bios, 83
    engaged to Mary, 59–60
    first-person in *Infancy Gospel of James,* 62
    plants tree from which cross is made, 186
    previous marriage, 59, 70, 143
    and vision of time standing still, 59–60, 65–66, 84
    See also Jesus, descent from David
Joseph the Carpenter, History of, 8, 35, 55, 83
Joseph (the patriarch), 21
Josephus, Flavius, 4, 62, 112
joy, 59, 190
Judaism, 4, 65–66, 75, 84, 93–95, 101, 108, 112, 114, 123, 125–26, 132
    See also anti-Judaism
Judaizing, 93, 114, 124, 126
Judas, Gospel of, 21, 29, 36–37, 52, 73, 177, 198, 204–9, 221, 223, 227–28, 241
    apocryphal intent, 39–40, 182, 234
    as discourse gospel, 163
    discovery, 37, 204–6
    and *Gospel of Jesus' Wife,* 205
    and *Gospel of Thomas,* 206
    and Irenaeus, 207–8
    and mainstream Christianity, 208, 221, 234
    manuscript of (Codex Tchachos), 26–27, 39, 198

popular attention, 58, 204–5
and Sethianism, 241
and synoptic outline, 206
and texts from Nag Hammadi, 205
and *Toledot Yeshu*, 28
Judas (Iscariot), 100, 130–31, 177, 206–7
See also Judas, Gospel of
Judas son of James, 216
Judas Thomas, 195, 198–99, 207–9, 214
as brother of Jesus, 199
charged by risen Jesus to write discourses, 186
Didymus Judas Thomas, 164
Judas the Zealot, 216
Jude (brother of Jesus), 57
Judeo-Arabic, 28
judgment, final, 6, 146, 199, 207, 218, 220
Julian the Apostate, 84
Julian, Saint, 138
Julius Cassianus, 210
Jung, C. G., 190, 192
Justin the Gnostic, infancy narrative (in Hippolytus), 36, 81
Justin Martyr, 6, 12–13, 31, 36, 41, 126, 157
and extracanonical traditions, 13, 64, 69
and file submitted by Pilate to Tiberius, 156
and Gospel of John, 13
and *Gospel of Peter*, 144
and memoirs of apostles, 12, 196
and pluriform gospel, 127–28

Kaaba, 68
katalyma (guest room), 70
Kerygma Petrou (*Preaching of Peter*), 147
King, Karen L., 21, 187
kingdom
of God, 1, 120–21, 146, 165–67, 171, 174 ,197–99, 206, 220–21
gospel of, 2,
of heaven, 197
of light, 178, 195
parables about, 168
kiss, 184–85, 187

Klauck, Hans-Josef, 32, 48, 50, 96, 98, 101, 109, 113, 130, 132, 158, 167, 179–80, 183n1, 185–86, 189, 190, 204, 211, 213, 215, 217–18
knowledge, 18, 165, 188, 192, 197, 202, 221
secret, 18–19, 31, 38–40, 42, 120–21, 161, 163, 165, 171, 178, 186, 221, 233
saving, 40, 161, 174, 178, 182, 184, 188–89, 195, 197, 221, 242
self-knowledge, 163, 165, 184
apotropaic, 214
Koester, Helmut, 22–23, 25, 121, 170, 195
Kraus, Thomas J., 34, 81, 115–17, 138, 149, 151–52
Kruger, Michael J., 110–12, 116, 151

lament, 59, 105, 158–59, 213
Last Supper, 100, 102, 137, 153, 214
late antiquity, 17, 19, 79, 96, 114, 127, 149, 151, 153, 216, 235
Latin, 4, 11, 15, 32, 42–43, 52, 65, 68, 74–75, 79, 82–83, 85, 99, 127, 158, 212, 215–16, 231
law, 22, 46, 94, 101–2, 107, 109, 114, 124–26, 201
God of, 124, 126
in *Gospel of Thomas*, 164
and grace, 124, 126
Layton, Bentley, 20, 183n1
Lazarus, 120
lectionary, 28, 34, 126
Leonard, James M., 104
leper, 107
letters, 10, 12–13, 20, 28, 36, 67–68, 114, 120, 122–23, 157, 162, 180, 182, 193, 195–96, 205, 216–17, 230–31, 234
See also Paul, Letters of; and *specific named letters*
Leucius, 158
Leucius Charinus, 158
Levi
in *Gospel of Mary*, 201–3
in *Gospel of Peter*, 140
and Matthias, 100
as paradigmatic male disciple, 203
in P.Oxy. 840, 110, 113

317

Lieu, Judith M., 124
life, eternal, 111, 153, 189, 197
light, 70, 167, 178, 188, 193–95, 197, 218
lion, proverb about, 166
litany, 153, 155–56
liturgy, 1, 8, 13, 27–28, 40, 43, 71, 85, 103, 114, 128, 134, 153, 160, 169, 182, 184, 188, 212, 216, 229–30, 234
locusts, 102
logion (plural: logia), 36, 47, 91, 119, 164, 182–83, 191, 239
logos, 2
Logos (Word) of God, 56, 167, 191, 194, 236
Lord (God). *See* God
Lord (Jesus). *See* Jesus
Lord, as *nomen sacrum*, 240
Lord's Prayer, 34, 103, 162
lots. *See* sortilege
Lots of Mary, Gospel of, 200
love, 124, 188
Lucian, 33
Lührmann, Dieter, 10, 22, 40, 118, 128, 147–49, 151–52
Luke, as author of Acts, 45, 125
Luke, Gospel of, 1–3, 5–6, 8–10, 24–25, 45, 57–58, 162, 225–26, 240–41
  and agrapha, 45
  and annunciation in, 60
  and ascension narrative, 3, 133, 218
  and birth and infancy narratives, 3, 56–58, 60, 62, 74–75, 77–78, 80, 83–84, 232
  commentaries, 11, 20, 229
  expansion of Markan ending, 162
  and *Gospel of Mary*, 201–2
  and *Gospel of Peter*, 144
  and *Gospel of Thomas*, 171–74, 181
  and Jesus on cross, 139
  and Jesus' Davidic ancestry, 56
  and Jesus' father, 56
  and John, 91
  lack of association with apostolic figure, 57
  Lukan priority, 125
  and Marcion. *See* Marcion, edition of Luke

  and Mark, 91, 228
  and Mary (mother of Jesus), 57
  and Matthew, 91
  and Muratorian canon, 42
  papyri, 26
  and P.Oxy. 5072, 119
  Proto-Luke, 48, 125
  public dimension of infancy narratives, 58
  and Q, 47, 90, 240
  relationship of Luke 24 and Acts 1, 162
  and risen Jesus, 219
  and scholia composed by Basilides, 229
  and Tatian, 127, 134
  title of, 7
  use and influence, 11, 13, 24–25, 124–25
  use of written narrative sources, 90–91
Luther, Martin, 24, 70
lynch mob, 139

magi, 58, 60, 70
magic, 33, 82, 93, 104, 130, 209
  See also amulets
Magnificat, 57, 67
male, 46, 166–67, 194, 211
manger, 70
Mani, Gospel of, 36
Manicheans, 19, 33, 35, 113, 123, 124
  and *Gospel of Philip*, 183, 186
  and *Gospel of Thomas*, 168
manuscripts, 7–8, 10–11, 15–18, 21, 24–26, 28, 43, 45, 75, 83, 85, 88, 98–99, 101, 106, 115, 121, 138, 143, 157, 176, 183, 190, 239
  noncontinuous, 33–34
  See also pericope adulterae
Marcion, 24, 114
  edition of Luke, 6, 35, 123–26, 132, 226–27, 229–30
  enmity against Judaism, 124–26
  and New Testament canon, 124–25, 129, 134, 229
  rejection of Matthew, Mark, and John, 125
  relationship between Old and New Testament, 123, 179

and Tatian, 125–26, 129, 132, 134, 226, 230
as textual critic, 124
twin emphasis on gospel and apostle, 125–26
Marcosians, 20
Marcus (founder of Marcosians), 20, 242
marginalia, 98
Mariology, 61, 66–67, 215
Mark Antony, 4
Mark the evangelist, 120, 144, 146
Mark, Gospel of, 1, 9, 24–25, 40, 107, 162, 225–28, 232, 241
  and apostle Peter, 144, 167, 226
  commentaries on, 11
  and *Fayûm Gospel*, 151
  and *Gospel of Mary*, 201
  and *Gospel of Peter*, 139
  and *Gospel of Thomas*, 171, 179, 181
  in Hebrew, 101
  on Jesus and John the Baptist, 56, 58
  lack of infancy narrative, 56, 84
  long ending, 12, 89, 128, 142, 162, 220
  modern scholarly preoccupation, 11–12
  and Muratorian canon, 42
  narrative outline. *See* gospel narrative
  papyri, 25–26
  and P.Oxy. 5072, 119
  Proto-Mark, 48
  rejection by Marcion, 125
  scarcity of manuscript witnesses, 11–12, 24, 226, 228
  secret edition, 120–21
  and Tatian, 12, 127, 129
  use by Matthew and Luke, 12, 90, 228
  use in early Christianity, 11–13, 25, 228
  See also Freer Logion
Mark, Secret Gospel of, 35, 120–21
Markschies, Christoph, 9, 13–14, 20, 32, 42, 47–50, 52, 55, 81, 100, 104–5, 107, 153, 159, 191, 211, 214, 215, 222, 230, 235
marriage
  of defilement, 187–88

rejection of, 202, 210–11
sacramental and ascetic, 187–88
See also Jesus, marriage; Joseph, previous marriage
Mar Saba (monastery), 120–21
Martha, 217
martyrdom, 4, 117, 138, 198, 213, 230
Mary, three-Marys-in-one, 185–86, 189
Mary, Birth of,
  alternate title for *Infancy Gospel of James*, 61
  mentioned by Epiphanius, 35, 81
Mary, Dormition and Assumption of, 35, 83
Mary, Gospel of, 8, 10–11, 17, 24, 27, 37, 39–40, 167, 177, 192, 199–204, 221, 234
  and canonical gospel tradition, 201, 204
  as discourse gospel, 163
  and *Gospel according to the Egyptians*, 211
  and *Gospel of Philip*, 203–4
  and *Gospel of Thomas*, 204
  and Nag Hammadi, 199
  manuscripts, 26, 199–200, 202
  post-resurrection setting, 162–63
Mary, Lament of, 158
Mary Magdalene, 21, 39, 140, 167, 195, 217
  as most loved disciple, 189, 200–1
  in *Gospel of Mary*, 200–4
  in *Gospel of Philip*, 184–87
  in *Gospel of Thomas*, 167
  male, 167, 202–3
  and Marian community, 204
  and secret teachings of Jesus, 195, 201–4
Mary (mother of Jesus), 33, 57–71, 73–74, 77–78, 84, 94, 113, 143, 185–86, 189, 214–15, 217–18, 229–30
  accused of sexual immorality, 65
  birth and family of, 55, 59, 63, 71
  childhood in Temple, 64–65, 214
  conception of Jesus, 186, 214
  death of, 50
  as descendant of David, 64–66, 69, 84
  and *Gospel of Gamaliel*, 105, 158

Mary (mother of Jesus) (*continued*)
  and Gospel of Luke, 57
  immaculate conception, 69
  Jewish attacks, 65
  postpartum virginity, 60, 65, 82
  pregnancy, 60, 189
  and *Questions of Bartholomew*, 214
  and Qur'an and hadith, 68
  raped by Roman soldier, 130
  as tabernacle, 214
  theotokos, 67
  See also annunciation; Lots of Mary,
    Gospel of; virgin birth
Mary, [*Greater*] *Questions of*, 35, 200
Mary, sister of Jesus, 185–86
Masoretic manuscripts, 38
massacre of innocents, 60, 64, 70
materiality, 19–20, 178, 189, 192, 201,
  207, 209, 241
Matthew, Gospel of, 1–2, 6, 8–10, 12,
  24–25, 57–58, 107, 111, 139, 162,
  195, 213, 225–26, 240–41
  alternate version in Coptic, 103–4
  and anti-Judaism, 159
  in Cairo genizah, 28, 101
  and collection of logia reported by
    Papias, 91
  commentaries, 11, 229
  and *Fayûm Gospel*, 151
  and *Gospel of the Ebionites*, 101–3
  and *Gospel of Mary*, 201–2
  and *Gospel of the Nazoreans*, 100–1
  and *Gospel of Peter*, 139, 144
  and *Gospel of Thomas*, 171–74, 181
  and identity of Jesus' father, 56
  and *Infancy Gospel of James*, 60, 62,
    67
  infancy narrative, 56–58, 67, 75, 80,
    83–84
  and Jewish Christian gospels, 98–99,
    101–4, 162
  manuscripts, 11, 24, 28
  and Mark, 91,146, 159, 228
  and Markan ending, 162
  original Hebrew version, 92, 101–2
  papyri of, 25–26, 103
  paratexts of, 98, 102–3
  and Peter, 147, 167
  popularity and use, 11, 88, 228
  and P.Oxy. 5072, 119

  and Ptolemy's *Letter to Flora*, 229
  public dimension of infancy narra-
    tives, 58
  and Q, 47, 90, 240
  rejection by Marcion, 125
  and *Sophia of Jesus Christ*, 193
  and star of Bethlehem, 71
  and synopsis of Ammonius, 132
  and Tatian, 127, 134
  title, 7
  and *Toledot Yeshu*, 130
Matthias, 186, 198
  and Levi, 100
  and Barnabas, 131
  gospel attributed to, 12, 33, 35, 231
Maximinus Daia, Emperor, 157
Maximus the Confessor, 154
Mecca, 68
Melito of Sardis, 144
memory, 1, 7, 31, 46, 64, 119, 147, 228,
  234
  living memory, 228
  social memory, 31
mercy, 191–92
Mesopotamia, 93, 199
Messiah. *See* Jesus (Messiah)
Messianic Judaism. *See* Jewish
  Christians
metaphors, 111, 184–85, 187–89
metatext, 106, 157, 182, 233
Meyer, Marvin W., 52, 121, 164, 166,
  183n1, 190, 205–6, 209
Middle Ages, 19, 43, 74, 76, 78, 96,
  101, 127, 129–30, 154, 158, 235
Middle East, 232
Middle Platonism, 18, 20, 193, 240
midrashic reformulation, 180
midwife, 60, 70, 82
mind, apocalypse of, 171
Minim, 93
ministry gospels, 50–51, 87–134, 137,
  226–27, 232
  See also Jesus, ministry
minor epistles (New Testament), 41
Minucius Felix, 142
miqvah, 111
miracles, 89
  See also Jesus, miracles
Mishnah, 112–13, 239, 241
misogyny, 167, 202–3

monachoi, 178
monasticism, 126, 138, 167, 202
monster (antichrist), 214
Montanism, 14, 203–4
Moreton, Lord, 121
Moses, 107, 110, 201
Mother, as *nomen sacrum*, 240
mountain, 223
    See also Mount of Olives
Muhammad, 68, 132
Muratorian Canon, 41, 230
mystery, 191, 206, 214
    of bridal chamber, 187–88
    plays, 158
    religions, 114
mysticism, 18, 142, 203–4
myths, 18, 195, 207, 209
mythology, 18, 178, 184–85, 194, 204,
    206, 212, 240

Naassenes, 168
Nag Hammadi texts, 7, 15, 17–18,
    22–24, 34, 39, 47, 49–52, 62, 87,
    105, 162–64, 167, 171, 173, 176,
    178, 182–83, 185, 190, 192–94,
    196–99, 205, 207, 211–12, 215,
    222, 229, 241–42
    discovery of manuscripts, 17, 166,
      169, 186
    and monasticism, 166
Nagel, Peter, 51, 105, 153, 176, 183n1,
    190, 208
nails, marks of, 217
narrative. See gospel narrative
Nathanael, 115, 216
    and Bartholomew, 213
    and Philip, 213
National Geographic, 21, 205
Nativity Story (movie), 69
Nazarenes, 94, 96
Nazareth, 57, 69, 81
    See also Jesus of Nazareth
Nazoreans, 100–102
    and Ebionites, 101–2
Nazoreans, Gospel of the, 36, 92, 96, 98
    and Jerome, 100–101
    and Matthew, 100–101
Neoplatonism, 240
Nessana papyri, 10
Nestorian controversy, 67

New Testament, 3, 4, 8, 10, 13, 16, 18,
    25, 29–30, 41, 45, 60, 62, 98–99,
    101, 105, 174, 177, 202, 208, 219,
    222–23, 231, 236
    canon and canonization, 7, 9–10,
      13–14, 17, 22, 24, 26, 29, 38–43,
      124–25, 128–29, 143, 184, 225,
      229, 236
    and Jewish Christianity, 95, 98–99
    and Old Testament, 114, 123
    See also gospels, canonical
New Testament Studies, 187
New York Times, 205
Nicaea, 8
Nicklas, Tobias, 12, 22, 94, 106–7,
    109, 116, 118, 120, 138, 141, 144,
    146–47, 149–50, 181–82, 225
Nicodemus, Gospel of, 8, 44, 145,
    156–58, 219, 229–30
Nile, 205
nomina sacra, 107, 110, 118, 120, 240
North America, 21–22, 152
notha (spurious works), 230
novel, 62, 121, 153
Nubian Stauros Text. *See* Discourse on
    the Cross

Octavia (wife of Mark Antony), 4
Old Greek. *See* Septuagint
Old Testament, 5, 14, 20, 38, 42–43,
    59, 61, 75, 114, 175, 202, 223, 231,
    240, 242
    and *Gospel of Peter*, 141
    and *Gospel of Thomas*, 179–80
    and New Testament, 114, 123–25
    See also Septuagint
Olives, Mount of, 153, 155, 193, 214
Ong, Walter J., 61
Ophites, 19
opposites, union of, 166, 184, 221
oracles, 200
orality, secondary, 61, 85, 117, 141,
    144, 151, 159, 171, 228
    See also dependence, oral
Origen, 9–11, 39, 81, 92, 95, 98, 128,
    237
    and agrapha, 46
    and birth of Jesus in a cave, 69–70
    on childlessness, 59
    and Ebionites, 102

321

Origen (*continued*)
and gnosticism, 19
and *Gospel according to the Egyptians*, 210
and *Gospel according to the Hebrews*, 99
and *Gospel of Mary*, 200
and *Gospel of Peter*, 143
and *Infancy Gospel of James*, 63
and Jewish Christian gospels, 97
ornamentation, 138
Orthodox Churches, Eastern, 43, 69–71
orthodoxy, 22, 24–25, 61, 94, 113, 124, 139, 142, 166, 171, 177, 189, 192, 195–96, 204, 215, 218, 223, 229, 231, 235–36
See also proto-orthodox
ostracon, 152, 240
Oxyrhynchus (city in Egypt), 24, 26, 158, 173, 175
book collections, 16, 173
excavations, 8, 15–17, 116
papyri, 11, 15–17, 22–24, 31, 44, 80, 105, 114–18, 163, 169, 173, 182, 199
See also individual Oxyrhynchus papyri

𝔓⁴⁵, 11, 26
Pachomian monastery, 166
Pachomius, Saint, 17
Padua, 69
page numbers, 116, 205
Pagels, Elaine H., 23, 29, 164, 170, 195, 205, 232
paidika, 75
paleography, 120
Palestine, 3–4, 62, 65, 67, 84, 88, 93–94, 101, 107, 109–10, 112, 221
palimpsest, 28, 101, 216, 240
Pandera, 130
Panopolis. *See* Akhmim
Papias of Hierapolis, 41, 91–92, 100
papyri, 10–12, 15, 21, 23, 25, 106
See also gospel fragments
papyrus, as writing material, 15, 187, 239–40
Papyrus Berlin 11710, 115
Papyrus Cairo 10735, 80–81

Papyrus Egerton 2 (P.Eger. 2 + P.Köln 255), 30, 35, 37, 105–10, 118, 120, 133, 226
and Gospel of John, 107–8
and Judaism, 108–10
Papyrus Merton 51, 115, 117
and Gospel of Luke, 117
and *Gospel of Thomas*, 117
Papyrus Oxyrhynchus 210, 115–16
and P.Merton 51, 115
Papyrus Oxyrhynchus 840, 35, 105, 110–13, 133–34, 151
as amulet, 110
and red ink, 151
and Synoptics, 111
Papyrus Oxyrhynchus 1224, 116–17, 120
as reception of Matthew and Mark, 117
Papyrus Oxyrhynchus 2949, 11, 118, 147–50
and *Gospel of Peter*, 147–50
Papyrus Oxyrhynchus 4009, 11, 46, 118, 147–50
and *2 Clement*, 148–49
and *Gospel of Peter*, 147–49
Papyrus Oxyrhynchus 5072, 118–20
and Gospel of Mark, 120
and Synoptics, 119
parables, 51, 164, 167–68, 171, 173, 179, 197
of the Five Wise and Five Foolish Virgins, 218
of the Sower, 168
of the Vineyard, 179
para-canonical texts, 27, 29, 85, 223, 233
Paraclete. *See* Holy Spirit
Paradise, 132, 214
paradox, 142
paragraph marker, 118
paraphrase of gospels, 46, 80–81, 98, 105, 115–17, 151
paratext, 98, 102–3
parchment, 11–12, 15, 110, 127–28, 138, 143, 147, 152, 158, 214, 239, 240
Paris, 21, 214
Parker, David C., 128
parochet (Temple curtain), 65

parody, 130
parting of the ways, 93–94,
passersby, 166
passion gospels, 48, 50–51, 89, 127–28,
  137–60, 181, 226–27
  See also Jesus, passion and death
passion play, 159
Passover, 57, 74–75, 102, 156, 206, 218
patriarchs, 218
Paul, 78, 125, 180, 197, 203, 220
  in Acts of the Apostles, 5, 45
  altercation with Peter at Antioch,
    124
  and Barnabas, 131
  and *Epistle of the Apostles*, 218, 220
  and *Gospel of Barnabas*, 131–32
  and *Gospel of Philip*, 188, 189
  and *Gospel of Thomas*, 172, 174
  and Jesus tradition, 3, 45–46, 56
  Letters of, 2–3, 5–6, 9, 124, 189, 206
  and Marcion, 124–26
  and visionary experience, 203
Paul, Acts of, 231
peace, 2–3, 201
Pentateuch, 229, 241
perfection, 188, 192, 199
Perfection, Gospel of, 35, 227
pericope adulterae, 44, 89, 97, 100
peripheral attraction, 89
perpetual virginity, 70
Perrin, Nicholas, 91, 171, 174
persecution of Christians, 60, 157, 218
Peshitta, 127
Peter (Simon Peter), 2–3, 6, 31, 120,
    138, 140, 146–47, 149, 152, 216
  absence in canonical passion and
    resurrection narratives, 146
  agraphon in *2 Clement*, 46
  altercation with Paul at Antioch, 124
  and *Apocryphon of James*, 196–97
  daughter, 193
  denies Jesus, 151
  and *Epistle of the Apostles*, 217
  and Fâyum Gospel, 150–51
  and Gospel of Mark, 56, 144, 167,
    226
  and *Gospel of Mary*, 39, 201–3
  and *Gospel of the Ebionites*, 102
  as guarantor of the passion narrative,
    144, 146–47, 160, 226, 236

as *nomen sacrum*, 150–51
  reception and memory, 147, 149, 151
  and Simon Magus, 130
1 Peter, 42
  in Cairo genizah, 28, 101
  and harrowing of hell, 140, 147
2 Peter, 42, 144
Peter, Act of (Coptic), 192–93, 199
Peter, Acts of, 74, 130, 143, 193
Peter, Apocalypse of, 149
  in Akhmim Codex, 138, 147
  and Eusebius, 231
  in Muratorian canon, 42
Peter, Gospel of, 7, 10, 17, 27, 30–31,
    36, 44, 48, 129, 137–51, 159, 176,
    212, 226, 228, 230, 232
  and Akhmim Codex, 138, 147,
    149–50
  and Eusebius, 141–43, 230–31
  and Gospel of John, 139–40
  and Gospel of Matthew, 139
  and *Gospel of the Savior*, 153
  and "the Jews," 139, 145–46
  and Old Testament, 141
  and Peter as witness, 146–47
  and P.Oxy. 2949, 147–49
  and P.Oxy. 4009, 147–49
  at Rhossus, 141–43, 230
  and Synoptics, 140–41, 144, 159
  use and circulation of, 138, 143–44
Peter, Letter to Philip, 36, 162, 205
Peter ostracon (van Haelst 741), 152
Peter, Revelation of, 164
Petersen, William L., 128, 195
Petra, 10
Petronius, 139
Pharisees, 44, 94, 110–11, 113, 116,
    145, 215
Pharos, island of, 241
Philip
  and Ethiopian eunuch, 99
  and Nathanael or Bartholomew, 213
  writer of secret teachings of Jesus,
    186
Philip, Gospel of, 18, 27, 36, 44, 163,
    167, 176, 178, 183–90, 201–2, 204,
    218, 221–22, 234
  and *Apocryphon of John*, 184
  and *Gospel of Mary*, 203–4
  and *Gospel of Thomas*, 178, 183, 184

323

Philip, Gospel of (continued)
  and *Gospel of Truth*, 184
  and Manicheans, 183
  and Mary Magdalene, 203
  in Nag Hammadi Codex II, 183–84
  and New Testament texts, 189
  and Pauline theology, 188
  reception, 189–90
  and sexual imagery, 184–85, 187
  and sexual libertinism, 183, 186
  and Valentinian gnostic ideas, 184
Philo, 4, 70
philosophers, ancient, 165
phōnēsai, 151
piety, 62–63, 69, 71, 79, 83–84, 158,
  166, 215
pigs, 74, 111, 119
Pilate, Acts of, 34, 156–58
  fourth-century anti-Christian text, 157
  Latin apocryphon, 158
Pilate, Pontius, 27, 34, 94, 122, 139,
  145, 148, 156–60, 217, 229
  and file submitted to Tiberius,
  156–57
pilgrim, 122
Piovanelli, Pierluigi, 28, 121, 130, 153,
  156
Pistis Sophia, 37, 194
Planē (deception personified), 191–92
Plato, 118, 240
Platonism, 126, 166, 178, 201, 240–41
Pleroma, 191–92
Plisch, Uwe-Karsten, 47, 153, 170,
  195–96, 208, 212
Plotinus, 19
poison and apostolic immunity, 89
polemic, 196–97, 223, 232
  anti-Christian polemic, 129–30
  anti-Gentile, 111
  anti-Jewish polemic. *See*
  anti-Judaism
Polycarp, 220
Polycrates, 220
Pontus (Roman province), 123
pope, 24, 32, 68, 231
Porter, Stanley E., 108, 115–16,
  151–52
post-resurrection discourse gospels, 36,
  44, 49–51, 83, 87–89, 105, 133,
  154, 161–223, 227, 232

and apostolic acts, 163
  See also Jesus, resurrection
post-resurrection incidents, 140, 151,
  161–62, 221
  See also Jesus, resurrection
praxis, 1, 34, 62, 93–94, 114, 188, 203
  See also ritual practice
prayer, 1, 46, 93, 153–54, 166, 199,
  206–7, 214
  See also Lord's Prayer
Priene inscription, 3
priests, 60, 99, 107, 116, 139, 145,
  207
  in P.Oxy. 840, 110–13
  See also high priest
private study, 148
procreation. *See* childbirth
prophecy, 89, 108, 153–54, 175, 197,
  219
prophets, 66, 130–32, 179
proselytes, 186
prostitute, 111
Protestants, 22, 24, 42–43, 69, 126
proto-orthodox, 123, 177, 195, 197,
  208, 223
proverbs, 77, 164
Proverbs, book of, 38, 99
Psalms, book of, 179, 219
pseudepigraphy, 143, 198, 219, 235
Pseudo-Clementine literature, 46, 62,
  113, 131, 144, 180
Pseudo-Dionysius
  and *Gospel of Bartholomew*, 212
Pseudo-Matthew, Gospel of, 36, 55, 68,
  82, 232
pseudonymity, 41
psychoanalysis, 191–92
Ptolemy (Valentinian author). *See*
  Flora, Letter to
Ptolemy II Philadelphus, 241
public office, 93
puer senex, 77
punctuation, 11, 118, 169
punishment of wicked, 218
purity
  inner and outer, 111, 113
  and Jewish Christians, 111, 114
  levitical, 22
  of Mary, 66
  menstrual, 66

sexual, 66
and Temple, 66, 110–14
Pythagoreanism, 240

Q (Synoptic Sayings Source), 6, 23, 41,
44, 47, 89–92, 96, 240
and apocalyptic thought, 173
as apocryphal gospel, 91
and *Gospel of Thomas*, 170, 173, 181
lack of interest in passion and death
of Jesus, 137, 181
narrative frame, 89
scholarly doubts about, 90–91
as source for Matthew and Luke, 47,
90, 240
as written gospel source, 90
Qasr El-Wizz. *See Discourse on the
Cross*
Quartodecimans, 156
questions and answers, 217
Qumran, 10, 129
and Dead Sea Scrolls, 45, 128–29
and ritual immersion, 112–13
quotations, 34, 106, 120
Qur'an, 47, 68, 72, 79, 85, 131

rabbinic literature, 95–96, 112, 120,
142, 239
rabbis, 93, 96, 112–13, 130, 239
race
bodily, 207
superior, 206–7
reader, implied, 85, 180
recapitulation, 235
reception history, 62, 98, 117, 204,
235
recto, 15, 80, 115–16, 240, 242
redaction, literary, 161, 51, 171–72,
181, 202
redemption, 191
relecture (rereading), 81, 119, 133,
144, 182, 233
relic, 158
religion, Greco-Roman philosophy
of, 20
reoralization. *See* orality, secondary
repentance, 117
rescript, 157
resolve, 168
rest, 191–92, 199

resurrection, 215, 218, 220
as stage of initiation, 188
See also Jesus, resurrection
resurrection discourse gospels. *See*
post-resurrection discourse
gospels
Resurrection of Jesus Christ Our Lord,
36
revelation, 7, 39, 49, 60–61, 66, 164,
191–92, 197–98, 204, 215, 217
Revelation, book of, 6, 41, 142, 153,
231
rewriting, 129, 133, 157
rewritten Bible (or rewritten Scripture), 45, 81, 129
See also relecture
rewritten gospel, 45, 106, 128–29, 132,
232–33
Rhossus, 26, 141
righteousness, 162
ritual practice, 31, 62, 64, 84, 93–94,
101, 112–13, 134, 189
Robinson, James M., 17, 22–23, 52, 90,
182, 187
Romans, 145, 187
Roman Catholics, 42, 69
Romans, Epistle to, 172, 174
romanticism, Protestant, 24
Rome, 9, 14, 93, 123–26, 129, 156–57,
168, 228, 230, 241
rooster, 151
Rosslyn Chapel, 21
ruach (spirit or wind), 99
rule of faith, apostolic, 8, 203
Rylands Gospel (P.Ryl. 464), 35

Sabbath, 166
clay sparrows that Jesus makes on,
72, 79–80, 130
in *Gospel of Philip*, 188
story of man working on, 45
sacrament(s), 185–89, 215
sacramentality, 114
sacrifice, 45, 81, 132, 214
abolition of, 102–3, 186
critique of, 207–9
See also Jesus, sacrifice of
Sadducees, 113
Saint-Sulpice, 21
Saklas (evil demiurge), 207

Salome, 60, 70, 210–11
salvation, 3, 165, 178, 184, 187–88, 192–93, 197, 207, 209, 212, 222, 235
same-sex love, 120–21
Samuel, 59, 64
Sarah (in *Epistle of the Apostles*), 217
Sarah (wife of Abraham), 70
Satan, 143, 162, 214
Saul. *See* Paul
Savior, 3, 60, 111, 142, 154, 194, 197–98, 201, 203, 217, 221
    as *nomen sacrum*, 240
    See also Jesus (Christ)
Savior, Dialogue of, 18, 36, 52, 194–95, 211
Savior, Gospel of (P.Berl. 22220/ Unknown Berlin Gospel), 37, 104, 152–56, 160, 194
    and *Gospel of Peter*, 153
    and *Gospel of Thomas*, 153
    and *Strasbourg Coptic Papyrus*, 155
sayings attributed to Jesus
    about assassin, 168
    based on Isaiah, 64:3, 180
    about birds, 165
    about bitter plant, 211
    in canonical gospels, 45, 88–89
    about cornerstone, 179
    about destruction of Temple, 175
    about fish, 165
    about flour spilled on road, 168
    about good tree and bad fruit, 115
    in *Gospel of Thomas*, 164–65, 174, 180
    about infants, 167
    in Islamic literature, 47
    about salt, 45
    about seeds and harvest, 108
    about seeking and finding, 165
    about wood and stone, 167
    See also Q
sayings, secret, 38–41, 173, 182, 221
sayings collection (or gospel), 44–49, 88–89, 92, 105, 173, 176, 178, 182
    See also Thomas, *Gospel of*; Q; Watson, Francis
Schenke, Martin, 104, 153, 155, 159, 183, 183n1, 185–87, 213–14
scholia, 11, 229, 241

schools, philosophical, 19
Schøyen Collection, 206
Schröter, Jens, 32, 34, 46–47, 49–50, 55, 104, 107, 153, 159, 168–69, 172–74, 176, 179, 181, 222
scorpion, 111
screens, in Eucharist, 113–14
scribal apostrophe, 106
scribal conventions, 151, 160, 169
    See also nomina sacra
scribal dots, 38
scribal hand, 138, 199
scribes, 30, 72, 74, 106, 116, 119, 126, 138, 143, 207, 239–40
scriptural features, 169
Scripture, 5, 8, 15, 19, 28, 40, 42–43, 45, 62, 65, 107, 123, 126, 179, 182, 210, 219–20, 229
    See also rewritten Scripture
scroll. *See* book roll
Scrovegni Chapel (Padua, Italy), 69
Sea of Galilee, 140, 213
Second Treatise of the Great Seth, 180
secret. *See* knowledge, secret; and wisdom, secret
Semitic languages, 99
Senate, Roman, 112
Sentences of Sextus, 185
Septuagint (Old Greek or Greek Old Testament), 5, 27, 42–43, 61–62, 98, 241
Serapion of Antioch, 27, 41, 141–43, 160, 230–31
Serapion, Egyptian bishop, 84
sermon. *See* homily
sesterce, 123
Seth, 180, 208
Sethianism, 19, 184, 196, 206–9, 211–12, 215, 241–42
Seventy, Gospel of the, 35, 227
sexuality, 20, 65, 120–21, 184–87, 189, 199, 203, 210–11
    asexuality, 166–67
shadow, 219
shahadah, 132
Shem Tob ben Isaac (ibn Shaprut), 101
shepherds, 58, 70
    Good Shepherd, 154
Shiloh, Israelite shrine, 59, 64
shi'ur qoma, 142

side, wound in, 217
signs and wonders, as marker of divine birth, 66
Simon ben Shetach, 130
Simeon, high priest, 60
Simon Magus, 130, 217
Simeon, in Temple, 78, 158
Simon the Zealot, 216
sin, 107, 146, 163, 184, 201, 215, 217
sinners, 116, 162, 218
Sinope, 123
Slavonic (language), 74, 79, 212
Smith, Morton, 120–21
Smyrna, 6, 220
soberness, 197
soldiers, 60, 67, 130, 140, 145
Son (Jesus), as *nomen sacrum*, 240
    See also Jesus as Son
Son of Man. *See* Jesus as Son of Man
Sophia, 8, 189
    See also Wisdom
Sophia of Jesus Christ, 8, 18, 27, 36, 162, 186, 192–94, 199
    and *Eugnostos the Blessed*, 193
sorcerer, 130
sortilege, 200
soteriology, 191, 193, 215
soul, 80, 140, 147, 184, 186, 195, 201, 218–19
source criticism, 179, 181
sparrows. *See* birds made from clay
speculation, 38, 57, 125, 204
Spirit, as *nomen sacrum*, 240
    See also Holy Spirit
spirituality, 46, 71, 164, 166
St. Martin, church of (Zillis, Switzerland), 79
stairs, 110
star of Bethlehem, 71
stations of the cross, 158
Stauros Text from Qasr El-Wizz. *See* Discourse on the Cross
Stoicism, 240
stone in front of tomb, 139–40
storm, stilling of, 217
Strasbourg Coptic Papyrus (P.Argent. Copt. 5–7), 35, 152, 154–55, 212
subversion, 29, 39, 42, 61, 95, 174, 215, 233–35
subscriptio, 7

Suetonius, 66, 76
Superman, 77
supplementation, 29, 33, 39, 44–45, 85, 88, 91, 97–98, 108, 123, 133–34, 140–41, 148, 157, 162, 182, 186, 190, 196, 204, 227, 230, 234, 241
suppression of gospels, 14, 21–28, 203, 228, 230–32
Streeter, B. H., 90
Symmachus, revision of Old Greek, 98
synagogue, 28, 94, 101, 113, 119
Synoptics (Synoptic Gospels), 7, 47, 90, 102–3, 109, 146, 148, 151, 163, 172, 195, 241
    and *Gospel of Thomas*, 171–73, 176–77, 180
    and John, 109, 127
    synoptic language, 120
    synoptic material, 100–3, 109, 111, 119–20, 132, 140, 144, 151, 153, 155, 159, 165, 170, 173–74, 179, 181, 232
    synoptic outline, 97, 117, 133, 144, 159, 206, 221
    Synoptic Problem, 90, 125, 163, 171–72
    synoptic tradition, 61, 117, 133, 144, 159, 162–63, 171–72, 177, 181
synopsis of gospels, 12, 132
synthesis of gospels, 12, 125–27, 174, 228, 230
    See also harmony
Syria, 69, 93, 96, 106, 122, 125–26, 129, 134, 168, 170, 198–99, 218–20, 230
    church in, 129, 134, 170, 199, 230
    and *Gospel of Thomas*, 170, 176
    and *Infancy Gospel of James*, 63
Syriac (language), 28, 75, 79, 81, 83, 99, 122, 126–28, 171, 173–74, 191

tabernacle, 214
Tabernacles, Feast of, 112
Tabor, Mount, 99
Talmud
    Babylonian, 239, 241
    Palestinian, 239, 241
Tatian, 10, 12–13, 96, 125–29, 132, 134, 142, 174, 220, 226, 230
    and Gospel of John, 127

Tatian (*continued*)
  and Gospel of Mark, 12, 127, 129, 230
  heretical views, 127
  and Justin Martyr, 13, 128
  and Marcion, 125–26, 129, 132, 134, 226, 230
  See also Diatessaron
taxes, 108
Temple, 22, 57–59, 64, 69, 71, 78, 80, 103, 110, 113–14, 175, 188, 214–15
  curtain, 59, 64–65, 213–14
  disciples' vision of, 207
  holy implements, 110, 112–13
  Jesus teaches in, 74, 77
  lintel smashed, 101
  in Mishnah, 113
  physical, 176
  saying about destruction, 175
  See also purity, Temple
Tertullian, 123–24
  and file submitted by Pilate to Tiberius, 156
testament, 83
textual criticism, 34, 45, 98, 124
textual variants, 36, 45, 55, 74, 97–100, 202
Thaddeus. *See* Addai
Thaddeus, Acts of, 122
thanksgiving (prayer), 206, 209
Theodoret of Cyrrhus, bishop
  and *Diatessaron*, 127
  and *Gospel of Peter*, 143
Theodosius the Great, 84
Theodotion, revision of Old Greek, 98
Theodotus (famous Valentinian), 242
theological laboratory, 9, 235
theology
  docetic. *See* Christology, docetic
  of *Gospel of Thomas*, 177
  Marian, 61, 66, 67
  Pauline, 188
Theophilus of Antioch, 11–12, 41, 128
theotokos, 67
thieves, crucified, 139
Thomas
  "doubting," 175
  in *Epistle of the Apostles*, 217
  See also Judas Thomas

Thomas, Acts of, 143, 182, 198
Thomas, Gospel of, 6, 7, 11–12, 16–18, 23–24, 29, 36, 39–40, 44–46, 88–91, 163–85, 198–99, 221–23, 228–29, 232–33
  absence of allegorical interpretation, 179
  ancient attestation, 168, 182
  anti-apocalyptic flavor, 164
  and *Apocryphon of John*, 184
  ascetic consciousness, 166
  and *2 Clement*, 168–69
  composed in Aramaic, 170–71
  date and original setting, 170–72, 175–78, 181
  as deliberately apocryphal, 39–40, 42, 164, 182, 221, 234
  dependence on Matthew and Luke, 171–74, 181
  dependence on Paul, 172, 174
  and *Diatessaron*, 171
  differences between Greek and Coptic, 169, 171, 174, 176
  as discourse gospel, 163
  and early Jesus tradition, 40, 46, 170–71, 173
  and early Syrian Christianity, 170
  and Eusebius, 231
  and *Gospel of the Egyptians*, 211
  and *Gospel of Jesus' Wife*, 187
  and *Gospel of Judas*, 206
  and *Gospel of Mary*, 204
  and *Gospel of the Savior*, 153
  as gnostic text, 177–78, 181, 184, 234
  groupings of logia, 164
  importance of understanding Jesus' sayings, 165, 168, 179
  and James the Just, 167
  and Jewish Christian gospels, 96, 99
  and Johannine literature, 170, 174–75, 177
  lack of commentary tradition, 182
  lack of interest in passion and death of Jesus, 137, 164, 181
  lack of narrative, 164, 180–81
  and mainstream Jesus tradition, 170
  manuscripts, 26–27, 36, 163, 169, 182
  modern rediscovery, 168–69
  and Naassenes, 168

in Nag Hammadi Codex II, 178
popular attention, 58, 163–64
post-Easter setting, 163, 180–81, 194
as protognostic, 202
and Q, 89, 170, 181
reception of, 168, 182
reconfiguration of Jesus tradition, 174
scribal features, 169
and Scripture, 179–80
and Synoptics, 170–73, 176–77, 179–81
and Syrian writers, 168
Thomas in, 167, 180
title of, 7, 176–77
title of text used by Manicheans, 33, 168
use of, 173
Thomas [the Contender], Book of, 18, 36, 182, 198–99, 234
Thomas, Infancy Gospel of, 36, 55, 72–80, 82, 84–85, 130, 217, 229
and *Arabic Infancy Gospel*, 82, 85
attribution to Thomas, 76
episodic character, 75
and *Gospel of Thomas*, 76
Greek and Latin variants, 74
historical influence, 72
and Jewish teachers, 72–73
and New Testament infancy narratives, 75, 85
original milieu, 75–76, 78–79
purpose, 77–78
recensions and manuscripts, 74–75, 79
reception, 78–79, 85
Slavonic additions, 74
and *Toledot Yeshu*, 130
See also alpha
Thomassen, Einar, 20, 184, 189
thread, 64, 115
three-gospel hypothesis, 96
Tiberius, Emperor, 122, 156–57
timelessness, 18, 21, 161, 163, 171, 173–75, 180–81, 221, 236
Timothy I, Patriarch, 28
Toledot Yeshu, 28, 30, 101, 129–31, 134, 226
tomb, 21, 138–40, 142, 146, 167, 213–14

Torah, 98
Tosefta, 65, 95, 112, 121, 241
tradition, Christian, 43, 59, 69, 144, 219
catholic and apostolic, 41, 163, 234
early, 1–3
later, 2
mainstream, 161
Western, 68
See also gospel tradition; Jesus tradition
transfiguration, 99, 119, 142
Transitus Mariae, 33
translator, 212
Trimorphic Protennoia, 241
trumpet, 197
truth, 178, 190, 193
knowledge of, 188
of resurrection, 146
secret, 31
Truth (personified), 186
Truth, Gospel of, 8, 18, 37, 105, 190–92, 222, 242
familiarity with New Testament material, 191
and *Gospel of Philip*, 183–84
as homily or gospel meditation, 191–92
and Irenaeus of Lyon, 190–91
title, 190
use of gospel harmony, 191
and Valentinians, 190–92
Tuckett, Christopher, 32, 39, 48–50, 90–91, 172, 180, 200–204
Turkey (modern nation), 123
Turner, C. H., 141, 235
Twelve, gospels attributed to, 12, 227
Gospel of the Twelve Apostles, The Gospel of the, 35, 227
The Manichean Gospel of the Twelve, 35, 227
The Ququite Twelve Gospels/Gospel of the Twelve, 35, 227
Tyre, 157

unbelief, 162
union (or reunion), 20, 151, 166, 186–88, 221
universe, 192–93

329

Unknown Berlin Gospel. See Gospel of the Savior
Unleavened Bread, Feast of, 140
unrighteousness, 111

Valentinianism, 13, 19–20, 40, 127, 184–85, 221, 229–30, 241
  and *Apocryphon of James*, 196–97
  and *Epistle of the Apostles*, 215
  and Gospel of John, 127
  and *Gospel of Truth*, 190–92
  and sexual libertinism, 184
  Valentinian texts, 192
  See also gnostics; Gnosticism
Valentinus, 20, 114, 127, 191, 241
vegetarianism, 102
vellum, 240
Veronica, 158
verso, 15, 80, 107, 110, 116–17, 119–20, 149, 155, 240, 242
Vienna, 150, 214, 216
Vinzent, Markus, 125, 138, 141, 144, 150
Virgil, 3, 33, 76
virgin birth, 58, 60, 64–66, 70, 82, 189
  See also perpetual virginity
vision(s), 81, 102, 116–17, 153, 155, 163, 166, 195, 197, 201, 203–4, 206–7, 212–15, 223
  See also Joseph and vision of time standing still
vows, 59, 93
Vulgate, 38, 43, 219

water
  as element, 195
  of eternal life, 111
  living, 112
  of refutation, 64
  stale, 111–12

Watson, Francis, 13, 14, 22, 38, 40, 48, 91, 107–8, 110, 121, 128, 171, 181, 187, 210–11
Wayment, Thomas A., 17, 110, 116–18, 148, 150, 164, 193, 200
Weisse, Christian Hermann, 90
well (site of annunciation), 59, 69
West Bank, 120
widower, Joseph as, 59
wind, 9, 99, 195
wine, 214
wisdom, 38, 57, 74, 163–67, 220
  genre, 185
  Hellenistic, 166
  personified as female figure, 99, 189, 192, 194. *See also* Sophia
  wisdom literature, 39, 185
  wisdom sayings, 194
Wisdom, Book of, 42
the wise, 119
woes, 111, 164, 199
women and teaching authority, 200–3
word of God, 2, 122,
  See also Logos (Word) of God
Wordsworth, William, 77
world, 197, 203, 207
  contempt for, 126, 178
  escape from, 178, 185
  guard against, 166
  origin of, 215
worship, 1, 8, 22, 65, 93, 161, 176, 197, 207, 209, 213, 215, 225, 228
wrath, 102, 201

Yehudah Ha-Nasi, Rabbi, 239

Zacchaeus (Jewish scribe in *Infancy Gospel of Thomas*), 73
Zacharias (=Zechariah, father of John), 60, 64, 81
Zion, 219